Middle School 2-2

중간고사 완벽대비

KB087225

적중 100

영어 기출 문제집

중2

미래 | 최연희

Best Collection

구성과 특징

교과서의 주요 학습 내용을 중심으로 학습 영역별 특성에 맞춰 단계별로 다양한 학습 기회를 제공하여 단원별 학습능력 평가는 물론 중간 및 기말고사 시험 등에 완벽하게 대비할 수 있도록 내용을 구성

Words & Expressions

Step1 Key Words 단원별 핵심 단어 설명 및 풀이
Key Expression 단원별 핵심 숙어 및 관용어 설명
Word Power 반대 또는 비슷한 뜻 단어 배우기
English Dictionary 영어로 배우는 영어 단어

Step2 실력평가 단원별 수시평가 대비 주관식, 객관식 문제풀이

Step3 서술형 대비 학업성취도 및 수행능력평가 대비 서술형 문제풀이

Conversation

Step1 핵심 의사소통 의사소통에 필요한 주요 표현 방법 요약
핵심 Check 기본적인 표현 방법 및 활용능력 확인

Step2 대화문 익히기 상황에 따른 대화문 활용 및 연습

Step3 기본평가 시험대비 기초 학습 능력 평가

Step4 실력평가 단원별 수시평가 대비 주관식, 객관식 문제풀이

Step5 서술형 대비 학업성취도 및 수행능력평가 대비 서술형 문제풀이

Grammar

Step1 주요 문법 단원별 주요 문법 사항과 예문을 알기 쉽게 설명
핵심 Check 기본 문법사항에 대한 이해 여부 확인

Step2 기본평가 시험대비 기초 학습 능력 평가

Step3 실력평가 단원별 수시평가 대비 주관식, 객관식 문제풀이

Step4 서술형 대비 학업성취도 및 수행능력평가 대비 서술형 문제풀이

Reading

Step1 구문 분석 단원별로 제시된 문장에 대한 구문별 분석과 내용 설명
확인문제 문장에 대한 기본적인 이해와 인지능력 확인

Step2 확인학습A 빈칸 채우기를 통한 문장 완성 능력 확인

Step3 확인학습B 제시된 우리말을 영어로 완성하여 작문 능력 키우기

Step4 실력평가 단원별 수시평가 대비 주관식, 객관식 문제풀이

Step5 서술형 대비 학업성취도 및 수행능력평가 대비 서술형 문제풀이
교과서 구석구석 교과서에 나오는 기타 문장까지 완벽 학습

Composition

|영역별 핵심문제|

단어 및 어휘, 대화문, 문법, 독해 등 각 영역별 기출문제의 출제 유형을 분석하여 실전에 대비하고 연습할 수 있도록 문제를 배열

|서술형 실전 및 창의사고력 문제|

학교 시험에서 점차 늘어나는 서술형 시험에 집중 대비하고 고득점을 취득하는데 만전을 기하기 위한 학습 코너

|단원별 예상문제|

기출문제를 분석한 후 새로운 시험 출제 경향을 더하여 새롭게 출제될 수 있는 문제를 포함하여 시험에 완벽하게 대비할 수 있도록 준비

|단원별 모의고사|

영역별, 단계별 학습을 모두 마친 후 실전 연습을 위한 모의고사

on the textbook ·· 교과서 파헤치기

- **단어Test1~2** 영어 단어 우리말 쓰기와 우리말을 영어 단어로 쓰기
- **대화문Test1~2** 대화문 빈칸 완성 및 전체 대화문 쓰기
- **본문Test1~5** 빈칸 완성, 우리말 쓰기, 문장 배열연습, 영어 작문하기 복습 등 단계별 반복 학습을 통해 교과서 지문에 대한 완벽한 습득
- **구석구석지문Test1~2** 지문 빈칸 완성 및 전문 영어로 쓰기

이책의 차례 Contents

Lesson 5

Bravo! Brava!

🎤 의사소통 기능

- 제안하기
  Why don't we see a magic show?

- 약속 정하기
  A: What time shall we meet?
  B: How about 10 o'clock on Saturday?

🎤 언어 형식

- 접속사 if
  You will appreciate it better **if** you know the story.

- as + 형용사/부사의 원급 + as
  Turandot is **as cold as** ice.

Words & Expressions

Key Words

- **actually** [ǽktʃuəli] 부 실은, 사실은, 실제로
- **add** [æd] 동 (말을) 덧붙이다, 더하다
- **agree** [əgríː] 동 동의하다
- **already** [ɔːlrédi] 부 이미, 벌써
- **amazing** [əméiziŋ] 형 놀라운
- **anniversary** [æ̀nəvə́ːrsəri] 명 기념일
- **answer** [ǽnsər] 동 대답하다(= reply)
- **appreciate** [əpríːʃièit] 동 감상하다, 감사하다, 진가를 알아보다
- **aria** [ɛ́əriə] 명 아리아, 영창
- **beauty** [bjúːti] 명 아름다움, 미
- **brave** [breiv] 형 용감한
- **celebrate** [séləbrèit] 동 기념하다
- **century** [séntʃəri] 명 세기
- **Chinese** [tʃàiníːz] 형 중국의 명 중국인
- **correctly** [kəréktli] 부 정확하게, 바르게
- **dawn** [dɔːn] 명 새벽
- **difficult** [dífikʌlt] 형 어려운
- **discount** [dískaunt] 명 할인
- **fail** [feil] 동 실패하다
- **famous** [féiməs] 형 유명한
- **find** [faind] 동 찾다, 알아내다, 발견하다
- **guess** [ɡes] 동 추측하다
- **incorrectly** [ìnkəréktli] 부 정확하지 않게, 틀리게
- **Italian** [itǽljən] 명 이탈리아어, 이탈리아인 형 이탈리아의
- **like** [laik] 전 ~처럼
- **marry** [mǽri] 동 ~와 결혼하다
- **mean** [miːn] 동 의미하다
- **moving** [múːviŋ] 형 감동적인
- **ostrich** [ɔ́ːstritʃ] 명 타조
- **part** [paːrt] 명 역할, 배역, 부분
- **perform** [pərfɔ́ːrm] 동 공연하다, 수행하다
- **performance** [pərfɔ́ːrməns] 명 공연
- **place** [pleis] 명 장소
- **play** [plei] 명 연극, 극, 희곡
- **practice** [prǽktis] 동 연습하다
- **princess** [prínsis] 명 공주
- **riddle** [rídl] 명 수수께끼
- **right** [rait] 부 즉시, 곧바로
- **safe** [seif] 형 안전한
- **secret** [síːkrit] 명 비밀
- **stranger** [stréindʒər] 명 낯선 사람, 이방인
- **storyline** [stɔ́ːrilain] 명 줄거리
- **subway** [sʌ́bwèi] 명 지하철
- **suggestion** [səgdʒéstʃən] 명 제안
- **theater** [θíːətər] 명 극장
- **tonight** [tənáit] 부 오늘밤에
- **until** [əntíl] 접 ~할 때까지
- **whole** [houl] 형 전체, 모든, 전부의

Key Expressions

- **as+형용사+as** ~ …만큼 ~한
- **at first sight** 첫눈에
- **be able to+동사원형** ~할 수 있다
- **be going to+동사원형** ~할 예정이다
- **be late for** ~ ~에 늦다, 지각하다
- **fall in love with** ~ ~와 사랑에 빠지다
- **find out** 알아내다, 발견하다
- **Guess what!** 있잖아.
- **have to+동사원형** ~해야 한다
- **How about+명사** ~? ~은 어때?
- **hurry up** 서두르다
- **in time** 제시간에, 늦지 않게
- **Let's+동사원형** ~. ~하자.
- **nothing more than** ~ ~에 지나지 않는
- **of beauty** 아름다운
- **one day** 어느 날
- **take off** (일을) 쉬다
- **take the subway** 지하철을 타다
- **Why don't you+동사원형** ~? ~하는 게 어때?
- **would like to+동사원형** ~하고 싶다

Word Power

※ 서로 반대되는 뜻을 가진 단어

- □ **brave**(용감한) ↔ **cowardly**(겁이 많은)
- □ **correctly**(정확하게) ↔ **incorrectly**(정확하지 않게)
- □ **difficult**(어려운) ↔ **easy**(쉬운)

- □ **safe**(안전한) ↔ **dangerous**(위험한)
- □ **fail**(실패하다) ↔ **succeed**(성공하다)
- □ **famous**(유명한) ↔ **unknown**(알려지지 않은)

※ 서로 비슷한 뜻을 가진 단어

- □ **answer** : **reply to** (~에 대답하다)
- □ **moving** : **touching** (감동적인)
- □ **suggestion** : **proposal** (제안)

- □ **amazing** : **surprising** (놀라운)
- □ **famous** : **well-known** (유명한)
- □ **agree** : **assent** (동의하다)

English Dictionary

- □ **already** 이미
  → earlier than the time expected
  예상된 시간보다 더 이르게

- □ **amazing** 놀라운
  → very surprising
  매우 놀라운

- □ **anniversary** 기념일
  → a day on which you remember or celebrate something that happened on that day in the past
  과거의 그 날에 일어난 일을 기억하거나 축하하는 날

- □ **appreciate** 진가를 알아보다
  → to understand how good something or someone is
  어떤 것이나 어떤 사람이 얼마나 좋은지 이해하다

- □ **aria** 아리아, 영창
  → a piece of music in an opera sung by one person
  한 사람이 부른 오페라의 음악

- □ **brave** 용감한
  → showing no fear of dangerous or difficult things
  위험하거나 어려운 일에 두려움을 보이지 않는

- □ **celebrate** 축하하다, 기념하다
  → to do something enjoyable on a special occasion
  특별한 경우에 즐거운 어떤 것을 하다

- □ **century** 세기
  → a period of 100 years
  100년

- □ **discount** 할인
  → a reduction in the normal price
  정상 가격에서의 감소

- □ **guess** 추측하다
  → to give an answer to a particular question when you do not have all the facts and so cannot be certain if you are correct
  모든 사실을 가지고 있지 않아서 당신이 옳은지 확신할 수 없을 때 특정한 질문에 답을 하다

- □ **marry** 결혼하다
  → to become the legally accepted husband or wife of someone in an official or religious ceremony
  공식적 또는 종교적 의식에서 합법적으로 인정된 남편이나 아내가 되다

- □ **moving** 감동적인
  → causing strong feelings of sadness or sympathy
  슬픔이나 공감의 강한 감정을 불러일으키는

- □ **perform** 수행하다, 공연하다
  → to do an action or piece of work
  행동이나 작품을 하다

- □ **riddle** 수수께끼
  → a type of question that describes something in a difficult and confusing way and has a clever or funny answer
  어렵고 혼란스러운 방식으로 무언가를 묘사하고 교묘하거나 재미있는 답을 가지는 질문 유형

- □ **secret** 비밀
  → a piece of information that is only known by one person or a few people and should not be told to others
  한 사람이나 몇 사람만 알고 다른 사람에게는 말하지 말아야 하는 정보

- □ **storyline** 줄거리
  → the series of events that happen in a book, film, play, etc.
  책, 영화, 희곡 등에서 일어나는 일련의 사건

서답형

01 다음 짝지어진 두 단어의 관계가 같도록 빈칸에 알맞은 단어를 쓰시오.

> unknown : famous = cowardly : _____

[02~03] 다음 빈칸에 들어갈 말로 가장 적절한 것은?

02

> It's _____. The sun is rising.

① dawn　　② crowd　　③ drought
④ discount　　⑤ aria

03 중요

> Background knowledge will help you to _____ the musical.

① mean　　　　② discount
③ guess　　　　④ appreciate
⑤ celebrate

[04~05] 다음 영영 풀이에 해당하는 단어를 고르시오.

04

> a piece of music in an opera sung by one person

① musical　　　② century
③ storyline　　　④ touch
⑤ aria

05

> causing strong feelings of sadness or sympathy

① riddle　　　　② moving
③ brave　　　　④ cowardly
⑤ difficult

06 중요 밑줄 친 부분의 의미가 잘못된 것은?

① Tonight, we are going to perform a musical. (공연하다)
② Why don't we go out to celebrate the New Year? (축하하다)
③ It's our school's 75th anniversary. (기념일)
④ A brave prince falls in love with her at first sight. (사랑에 빠지다)
⑤ He is nothing more than a stranger to her. (결코 ~가 아닌)

서답형

07 다음 밑줄 친 부분과 의미가 비슷한 것을 주어진 철자로 시작하여 쓰시오.

> He becomes the first man to answer all three puzzles.

➡ r_____

서답형

08 다음 두 문장이 같은 뜻이 되도록 빈칸에 알맞은 말을 쓰시오.

> Turandot is a woman of great beauty.
> = Turandot is a _____ woman.

➡ _____

서답형

09 다음 주어진 우리말에 맞게 빈칸을 채우시오.

(1) 이런, 영화 시간에 늦을 거야.
　➡ Oh, we're going to _____ _____ _____ the movie.
(2) 나는 오후에 일을 쉴 수 있을 것 같구나.
　➡ I guess I can _____ the afternoon _____.

01 다음 우리말에 맞게 빈칸에 알맞은 단어를 쓰시오.

(1) 학교 끝나고 바로, 네 시에 어때?

➡ How about 4 o'clock, _____ _____ school?

(2) 당신이 맞게 대답한다면 나는 죽는 것에 동의하겠습니다.

➡ If you answer _____, I will _____ _____ die.

(3) 그녀와 결혼하길 원하는 왕자는 누구든지 반드시 세 가지 수수께끼에 답해야 합니다.

➡ Any prince who wants to _____ her must answer three _____.

02 영어 설명을 읽고, 문장의 빈칸에 들어갈 알맞은 단어를 쓰시오.

to understand how good something or someone is

(1) Her family doesn't _____ her.

the series of events that happen in a book, film, play, etc.

(2) Having a clear _____ is very important to movies and novels.

03 다음 〈보기〉에서 빈칸에 공통으로 들어갈 단어를 골라 쓰시오.

┌─── 보기 ───┐
take   be   care   look
└─────────────┘

• Can I _____ the afternoon off?
• Why don't we _____ the bus?

04 다음 빈칸에 알맞은 단어를 〈보기〉에서 골라 쓰시오. (형태 변화 가능)

┌─── 보기 ───┐
like   famous   celebrate   perform
└─────────────┘

(1) The prince then sings the _____ _____ aria of the whole opera, "Nessun Dorma."

(2) _____ many other famous operas, *Turandot* is in Italian.

(3) She _____ my birthday last year.

(4) How was our _____?

05 다음 주어진 우리말에 맞게 빈칸을 채우시오. (필요하면 변형하여 쓰시오.)

(1) 수요일에 가면 할인을 받을 수 있어요.

➡ We can get a _____ if we go on a Wednesday.

(2) 그는 그녀에게 단지 낯선 사람일 뿐입니다.

➡ He is _____ _____ _____ a stranger to her.

(3) 만약 실패하면 그는 죽어야 합니다.

➡ If he _____, he must die.

(4) 누군가 그의 이름을 알아낼 때까지 그 누구도 잠들 수 없을 것이다.

➡ No one will go to sleep _____ someone finds out his name.

Conversation

교과서

1 제안하기

> **Why don't we see a magic show?** 마술 쇼 보는 게 어때?

■ 상대방에게 '함께 ~하자'라고 제안이나 권유할 때에는 'Why don't we ~?'를 사용할 수 있다. 'Why don't you ~?'는 함께 하자는 것이 아니고 상대방에게만 권유하는 것이다.

■ **제안하는 다양한 표현**
Why don't we+동사원형 ~? = Let's+동사원형 ~. = Shall we+동사원형 ~? = How[What] about+동사원형+-ing ~? = What do you say to+동사원형+-ing ~?

제안하기와 답하기

- A: Why don't we go on a bike ride? 함께 자전거 타러 가자.
  B: Yes, let's go. 좋아, 가자.

- A: Why don't you get some sleep? 잠을 좀 자렴.
  B: Yes, I think I should. 네, 그래야겠어요.

- A: What shall we do at the park? 우리 공원에서 뭘 할까?
  B: Why don't we see a magic show? 마술 쇼 보는 게 어때?
  A: That's a good idea. 좋은 생각이야.

핵심 Check

1. 다음 대화의 빈칸에 들어갈 말로 알맞은 것은?

   M: _____ The subway will be faster than the bus at this time of day.

   W: That's a good idea.

   ① How do I get to the subway station?
   ② Let's keep our fingers crossed for him.
   ③ Shall we take the subway?
   ④ What happened to the subway?
   ⑤ What's the matter?

2. 다음 대화의 밑줄 친 부분의 의도로 적절한 것은?

   B: Mom, I got only one question wrong on the Korean history exam!

   W: Great! I was sure you would do well. <u>Why don't we go out to celebrate tonight?</u>

   ① 화남 표현하기   ② 제안하기   ③ 설명하기   ④ 의도 표현하기   ⑤ 금지하기

② 약속 정하기

A What time shall we meet? 우리 몇 시에 만날까?

B How about 10 o'clock on Saturday? 토요일 10시는 어때?

- 약속을 정할 때는 What time shall we meet?, 또는 What time should we meet?, Where shall we meet?, Where should we meet? 등의 표현을 써서 몇 시에[어디서] 만날지를 묻고, 시간 및 장소를 제안할 때는 How about ~? What about ~? 등의 표현을 사용한다.

- 시간과 장소 등의 약속을 정할 때 조동사 'should'를 사용하여 '~할까요?'라는 의미를 전달한다.

  - A: What time should we meet? 우리 몇 시에 만날까?
    B: How about 6 o'clock? 6시 어때?
    A: OK. Where should we meet? 좋아. 어디서 만날까?
    B: Let's meet at the subway station. 지하철역에서 만나자.

  - A: Let's go on a picnic this weekend. 이번 주말에 소풍가자.
    B: Good idea! What time shall we meet? 좋은 생각이야. 몇 시에 만날래?
    A: How about 10 o'clock on Saturday? 토요일 10시는 어때?
    B: O.K. Let's meet at the subway station. 좋아. 지하철역에서 만나자.

핵심 Check

3. 다음 빈칸에 들어갈 말로 알맞은 것을 <u>모두</u> 고르시오.

M: Karen, let's practice our parts for the school play today.

G: O.K. _____

B: How about 4 o'clock, right after school?

G: Sounds good.

① Where should we meet?
② How about at the park near your place?
③ What time shall we meet?
④ Please tell me where I should go.
⑤ When should we meet?

4. 다음 밑줄 친 문장과 같은 표현을 주어진 철자로 쓰시오.

Sue: What time shall we meet?

Dan: <u>How about 12?</u>

➡ W _____

Listen & Speak 1-A-1

> M: Liz, hurry up. ❶It's already 6 o'clock.
> W: Oh, ❷we're going to be late for the concert.
> M: ❸Why don't we take the subway? The subway will be ❹faster than the bus at this time of day.
> W: ❺That's a good idea.

M: Liz, 서둘러. 벌써 여섯 시야.
W: 이런, 우린 콘서트에 늦을 거야.
M: 지하철을 타는 게 어때? 지하철은 지금 이 시간에 버스보다 빠를 거야.
W: 좋은 생각이야.

❶ It은 시간을 나타낼 때 사용하는 비인칭 주어.
❷ 'be going to+동사원형'은 '～할 것 같다'는 의미고, 'be late for'는 '～에 늦다'는 뜻이다.
❸ 'Why don't we+동사원형?'은 상대방에게 제안을 할 때 사용하는 표현으로 'Shall we+동사원형?'으로 바꾸어 쓸 수 있다.
❹ '비교급+than' 구문으로 '～보다 더 …한'의 의미이다.
❺ 상대가 제안한 말에 대해 동의하는 표현이다.

Check(√) True or False

(1) Liz and her friend are going to take the bus. T ☐ F ☐

(2) Liz is going to go to the concert. T ☐ F ☐

Listen & Speak 1-A-2

> B: Mom, I got only one question wrong on the Korean history exam!
> W: Great! ❶I was sure you would do well. ❷Why don't we go out to celebrate tonight?
> B: Yes! Can we ❸have pizza for dinner?
> W: Of course, Joe. I'll call your dad.

B: 엄마, 제가 한국사 시험에서 겨우 한 문제만 틀렸어요!
W: 대단해! 네가 잘할 거라고 확신했단다. 오늘밤 축하하러 나가는 건 어때?
B: 좋아요! 저녁으로 피자를 먹어도 되나요?
W: 물론이지, Joe. 아빠에게 전화걸게.

❶ be sure (that) 주어+동사 ～: ～을 확신하다
❷ 'Why don't we+동사원형?'은 상대방에게 제안을 할 때 사용하는 표현으로 'Shall we+동사원형?'으로 바꾸어 쓸 수 있다.
❸ have는 eat의 의미로 사용되었다.

Check(√) True or False

(3) The boy did well on the Korean history exam. T ☐ F ☐

(4) The boy's family are going to go out for dinner. T ☐ F ☐

Listen & Speak 1-B

> A: ❶What shall we do at the park?
> B: ❷Why don't we see a magic show?
> A: That's a good idea.

A: 우리 공원에서 뭘 할까?
B: 마술 쇼를 보는 건 어때?
A: 좋은 생각이야.

❶ What shall we do ～?: 우리 뭘 할까?
❷ 상대방에게 제안을 할 때 사용하는 표현으로 'Shall we+동사원형?', 'Let's+동사원형' 등으로 바꾸어 쓸 수 있다.

Listen & Speak 2-A-1

B: Karen, ❶let's practice our parts for the school play today.
G: O.K. ❷What time shall we meet?
B: ❸How about 4 o'clock, right after school?
G: Sounds good.

❶ Let's+동사원형: '~하자'라는 제안이나 권유의 표현이다.
❷ 시간을 정하는 표현으로 '몇 시에 만날래?'의 뜻이다.
❸ 시간 및 장소를 제안할 때는 'How about ~?', 'What about ~?' 등의 표현을 사용한다.

Listen & Speak 2-A-2

G: Do you want to play badminton together this afternoon, Mark?
B: Sure. ❶Where shall we play?
G: ❷How about at the park near your place?
B: O.K. See you there at 3 o'clock.

❶ 어디서 만날지 장소를 제안하는 표현이다.
❷ 장소를 제안할 때는 'How about ~?', 'What about ~?' 등의 표현을 사용한다.

Listen & Speak 2-B

A: ❶Let's go on a picnic this weekend.
B: Good idea. ❷What time shall we meet?
A: How about 10 o'clock on Saturday?
B: O.K. Let's meet at the subway station. See you there.

❶ Let's+동사원형: '~하자'라는 제안이나 권유의 표현이다.
❷ 몇 시에 만날지 시간을 제안하는 표현이다.

Communicate A

Anna: Dad, ❶guess what! I have no school next Wednesday.
Dad: Really? ❷Why not?
Anna: It's our school's 75th anniversary.
Dad: Oh, I see.
Anna: Can we do something together that day?
Dad: ❸I guess I can take the afternoon off. What do you want to do?
Anna: ❹Why don't we go see a musical at Bravo Theater near your work? We can get a discount if we go on a Wednesday.

Dad: Good idea, Anna! Then, let's just meet at the theater.
Anna: O.K. ❺What time shall we meet?
Dad: How about 12? Then, we can have lunch together, too.
Anna: You're the best, Dad!

❶ 'Guess what!'은 '있잖아'라는 의미로 상대방의 주의를 끌 때 사용하는 표현이다.
❷ 'Why not?'은 Why do you have no school?의 줄임말이다.
❸ 'I guess ~'는 '~할 것 같아'라는 의미다.
❹ 상대방에게 제안을 할 때 사용하는 표현으로 'Shall we+동사원형?', 'Let's+동사원형' 등으로 바꾸어 쓸 수 있다.
❺ 시간을 정하는 표현으로 '몇 시에 만날래?'의 뜻이다.

Communicate B

A: ❶What shall we do this afternoon?
B: ❷Why don't we go see *Wonder Woman*?
A: Good idea! What time shall we meet?
B: How about 4 o'clock?
A: O.K. Let's meet at Moon Theater.

❶ What shall we do ~?: 우리 뭘 할까?
❷ 'Why don't we+동사원형?'은 '~하는 게 어때?'라는 뜻으로 어떤 활동을 함께 하자고 제안할 경우에 사용하는 표현으로 'Let's+동사원형' 등으로 바꾸어 쓸 수 있다.

Progress Check

1. G: Jim, hurry up. It's already 10 o'clock.
   B: Oh, ❶we're going to be late for the movie.
   G: ❷Why don't we take the bus? The bus will be faster than the subway at this time of day.
   B: That's a good idea.
2. B: ❸It's very hot today. ❹Let's go swimming, Julie.
   G: Good idea! Where shall we meet?
   B: ❺How about at the subway station near my place?
   G: O.K. See you there at 11 o'clock.

❶ 'be going to+동사원형'은 '~할 것 같다'는 의미이고, 'be late for'는 '~에 늦다'는 뜻이다.
❷ 'Why don't we+동사원형?'은 '~하는 게 어때?'라는 뜻으로 어떤 활동을 함께 하자고 제안할 경우에 사용한다.
❸ 날씨를 나타내는 비인칭 주어 It이다.
❹ 'Let's+동사원형'은 '~하자'라고 제안을 할 때 사용한다.
❺ 'How about ~?'은 '~는 어때?'라는 표현으로 제안할 때 사용한다.

● 다음 우리말과 일치하도록 빈칸에 알맞은 말을 쓰시오.

Listen & Speak 1-A

1. M: Liz, _____ _____. It's _____ 6 o'clock.

   W: Oh, we're going to _____ _____ _____ the concert.

   M: _____ _____ _____ _____ the subway? The subway will be _____ _____ the bus at this time of day.

   W: That's a good idea.

2. B: Mom, I got only one question _____ on the Korean history exam!

   W: Great! I was _____ you would do _____. _____ _____ _____ go out to _____ tonight?

   B: Yes! Can we have pizza _____ dinner?

   W: _____ _____, Joe. I'll call your dad.

Listen & Speak 1-B

A: What _____ _____ do at the park?

B: _____ _____ _____ see a magic show?

A: That's a _____ _____.

Listen & Speak 2-A

1. B: Karen, _____ practice our _____ for the school _____ today.

   G: O.K. _____ _____ _____ _____ _____?

   B: _____ _____ 4 o'clock, _____ after school?

   G: _____ good.

2. G: Do you want to play badminton together this afternoon, Mark?

   B: Sure. _____ _____ _____ play?

   G: How _____ at the park _____ your place?

   B: O.K. See you there _____ 3 o'clock.

Listen & Speak 2-B

A: _____ go on a picnic this weekend.

B: Good idea. What time _____ we meet?

A: _____ _____ 10 o'clock on Saturday?

B: O.K. _____ _____ at the subway station. See you there.

해석

1. M: Liz, 서둘러. 벌써 여섯 시야.
   W: 이런, 우리 콘서트에 늦을 거야.
   M: 지하철을 타는 게 어때? 지하철은 지금 이 시간에 버스보다 빠를 거야.
   W: 좋은 생각이야.

2. B: 엄마, 제가 한국사 시험에서 겨우 한 문제만 틀렸어요!
   W: 대단해! 네가 잘할 거라고 확신했단다. 오늘 축하하러 나가는 건 어때?
   B: 좋아요! 저녁으로 피자를 먹어도 되나요?
   W: 물론이지, Joe. 아빠에게 전화하마.

A: 우리 공원에서 뭘 할까?
B: 마술 쇼를 보는 건 어때?
A: 좋은 생각이야.

1. B: Karen, 오늘 학교 연극에서 우리 부분을 연습하자.
   G: 좋아. 몇 시에 만날까?
   B: 학교 끝나고 바로, 네 시 어때?
   G: 좋아.

2. G: Mark, 오후에 같이 배드민턴 하지 않을래?
   B: 물론이지. 어디서 할까?
   G: 너희 집 근처 공원은 어때?
   B: 좋아. 세 시에 거기서 보자.

A: 주말에 소풍가자.
B: 좋은 생각이야. 몇 시에 만날래?
A: 토요일 10시는 어때?
B: 좋아. 지하철역에서 만나자. 거기서 봐.

Communicate A

Anna: Dad, _____ what! I have no school next Wednesday.

Dad: Really? _____ _____?

Anna: It's our school's 75th _____.

Dad: Oh, I see.

Anna: Can we do something _____ that day?

Dad: I guess I can _____ the afternoon _____. What do you want to do?

Anna: _____ _____ _____ go see a musical at Bravo Theater near your work? We can _____ a _____ _____ we go on a Wednesday.

Dad: Good idea, Anna! Then, _____ just meet at the theater.

Anna: O.K. What time _____ _____ meet?

Dad: _____ _____ 12? Then, we can have lunch together, too.

Anna: You're the _____, Dad!

Anna: 아빠, 있잖아요! 저는 다음 주 수요일에 수업이 없어요.
아빠: 정말? 왜 없니?
Anna: 75주년 개교 기념일이에요.
아빠: 그렇구나.
Anna: 그날 오후에 같이 뭔가 할 수 있을까요?
아빠: 나는 오후에 휴무를 할 수 있을 것 같구나. 뭘 하고 싶니?
Anna: 아빠 직장 근처 Bravo 극장에서 뮤지컬을 보는 건 어때요? 수요일에 가면 할인을 받을 수 있어요.
아빠: 좋은 생각이구나, Anna! 그럼 바로 극장에서 만나자.
Anna: 좋아요. 몇 시에 만날까요?
아빠: 12시는 어떠니? 그럼 점심도 같이 먹을 수 있단다.
Anna: 최고예요, 아빠!

Communicate B

A: _____ _____ _____ do this afternoon?

B: _____ _____ _____ go see *Wonder Woman*?

A: Good idea! What _____ _____ _____ meet?

B: _____ about 4 o'clock?

A: O.K. _____ meet at Moon Theater.

A: 오늘 오후에 뭘 할까?
B: 원더 우먼을 보러 가는 건 어때?
A: 좋은 생각이야! 몇 시에 만날까?
B: 4시는 어때?
A: 좋아. Moon 극장에서 보자.

Progress Check

1. **G:** Jim, hurry up. It's already 10 o'clock.

   B: Oh, we're going to be late for the movie.

   G: _____ _____ _____ _____ the bus? The bus will be _____ than the subway _____ _____ _____ _____ _____.

   B: That's a good idea.

2. **B:** It's very hot today. _____ _____ _____, Julie.

   G: Good idea! _____ shall we meet?

   B: _____ _____ at the subway station near my place?

   G: O.K. See you there at 11 o'clock.

1. G: Jim, 서둘러. 벌써 10시야.
   B: 이런, 영화 시간에 늦을 거야.
   G: 버스를 타는 게 어때? 지금 이 시간에는 버스가 지하철보다 빠를 거야.
   B: 좋은 생각이야.

2. B: 오늘 굉장히 덥네. 수영하러 가자, Julie.
   G: 좋은 생각이야! 어디서 만날래?
   B: 우리 집 근처 지하철역에서 만나는 게 어때?
   G: 좋아. 11시에 거기서 보자.

[01~03] 다음 대화의 빈칸에 알맞은 말은?

01

B: It's very hot today. Let's go swimming, Julie.
G: Good idea! _____
B: How about at the subway station near my place?
G: O.K. See you there at 11 o'clock.

① Why don't we take the bus?　② What time shall we meet?
③ Let's go there.　④ Where shall we meet?
⑤ Oh, I see.

02

A: Let's go on a picnic this weekend.
B: Good idea. _____
A: How about 10 o'clock on Saturday?
B: O.K. Let's meet at the subway station. See you there.

① Where shall we meet?
② How about at the park near your place?
③ What time shall we meet?
④ What shall we do at the park?
⑤ Why don't we take the subway?

03

M: Liz, hurry up. It's already 6 o'clock.
W: Oh, we're going to be late for the concert.
M: Why don't we take the subway? The subway will be _____ the bus at this time of day.
W: That's a good idea.

① faster than　② more fast than　③ fast than
④ the fastest than　⑤ the faster than

04 자연스러운 대화가 되도록 순서대로 배열하시오.

(A) O.K. See you there at 3 o'clock.
(B) Sure. Where shall we play?
(C) Do you want to play badminton together this afternoon, Mark?
(D) How about at the park near your place?

➡ _____

[01~03] 다음 대화를 읽고 물음에 답하시오.

> A: _____ (A) _____ this afternoon?
> B: Why don't we go see *Wonder Woman*?
> A: Good idea! _____ (B) _____
> B: How ___ (C) ___ 4 o'clock?
> A: O.K. Let's meet at Moon Theater.

01 빈칸 (A)에 알맞은 말을 고르시오.

① What do you do
② What did you do
③ Where shall we meet
④ What shall we do
⑤ What will you make

02 빈칸 (B)에 알맞은 말을 고르시오.

① Shall we make it at 4?
② What time shall we meet?
③ I'm sorry but I can't.
④ Where shall we meet?
⑤ Why don't we go see a musical?

03 빈칸 (C)에 알맞은 말은?

① about ② at ③ for
④ of ⑤ in

04 밑줄 친 부분과 바꾸어 쓸 수 있는 문장을 모두 고르시오.

> B: It's very hot today. <u>Let's go swimming.</u>
> G: Good idea!

① Why don't we go swimming?
② Are you planning to go swimming?
③ Are you going to go swimming?
④ Shall we go swimming?
⑤ What about going swimming?

05 중요 다음 중 짝지어진 대화가 <u>어색한</u> 것은?

① A: Where shall we play?
   B: How about at the park near your place?
② A: Let's go on a picnic this weekend.
   B: Good idea.
③ A: I have no school next Wednesday.
   B: Really? Why not?
④ A: What time shall we meet?
   B: How about 1 o'clock?
⑤ A: Jim, hurry up. It's already 10 o'clock.
   B: What shall we try first?

[06~07] 다음 대화를 읽고 물음에 답하시오.

> B: It's very hot today. ___ⓐ___ go swimming, Julie.
> G: Good idea! ___ⓑ___ shall we meet?
> B: How about at the subway station near my place?
> G: O.K. See you there at 11 o'clock.

06 빈칸 ⓐ, ⓑ에 들어갈 말로 알맞은 것은?

① Let us – What
② Let us – When
③ Let's – What time
④ Let's – Where
⑤ Let's – Whom

07 서답형 다음 영영풀이에 해당하는 단어를 대화에서 찾아 쓰시오.

> a building and the surrounding area where buses or trains stop for people to get on or off

➡ _____

08 다음 대화의 빈칸 (A)에 들어갈 말로 알맞은 것은?

> G: Do you want to play badminton together this afternoon, Mark?
> B: Sure. Where shall we play?
> G: _____(A)_____
> B: O.K. See you there at 3 o'clock.

① How about at the park near your place?
② Let's meet at 3 o'clock.
③ What time shall we meet?
④ I'm playing badminton at the park.
⑤ I'd like to play badminton with you at the park.

[09~12] 다음 대화를 읽고 물음에 답하시오.

> Anna: Dad, guess what! I have no school next Wednesday.
> Dad: Really? Why not?
> Anna: It's our school's 75th anniversary.
> Dad: Oh, I see. (①)
> Anna: Can we do something together that day? (②)
> Dad: ⓐ나는 오후에 휴무를 할 수 있을 것 같구나. What do you want to do?
> Anna: (③) We can get a discount if we go on a Wednesday.
> Dad: Good idea, Anna! Then, let's just meet at the theater. (④)
> Anna: O.K. What time shall we meet?
> Dad: How about 12? Then, we can have lunch together, too. (⑤)
> Anna: You're the best, Dad!

09 위 대화의 ①~⑤ 중 다음 주어진 말이 들어갈 알맞은 곳은?

> Why don't we go see a musical at Bravo Theater near your work?

①   ②   ③   ④   ⑤

10 다음 영영풀이에 해당하는 단어를 대화에서 찾아 쓰시오.

> a day on which you remember or celebrate something that happened on that day in the past

➡ _____

11 밑줄 친 ⓐ의 우리말에 맞게 주어진 단어를 알맞게 배열하시오.

> I, guess, take, off, I, can, the afternoon

➡ _____

12 대화의 내용과 일치하지 않는 것은?

① Anna has no school next Wednesday.
② They are talking about getting a discount for a movie.
③ Bravo Theater provides a discount for people on a Wednesday.
④ They will meet at Bravo Theater.
⑤ They will also have lunch together.

13 대화의 흐름상 빈칸 (A)와 (B)에 들어갈 말로 알맞은 것을 〈보기〉에서 골라 쓰시오.

> ┌ 보기 ┐
> right   guess   appreciate   perform   wrong   suggest   celebrate

> Boy: Mom, I got only one question ___(A)___ on the Korean history exam!
> Woman: Great! I was sure you would do well. Why don't we go out to ___(B)___ tonight?
> Boy: Yes! Can we have pizza for dinner?
> Woman: Of course, Joe. I'll call your dad.

➡ (A) _____ (B) _____

[01~02] 다음 대화를 읽고 물음에 답하시오.

M: Liz, hurry up. It's already 6 o'clock.
W: Oh, we're going to be late for the concert.
M: Why don't we take the subway? (A)지하철은 지금 이 시간에 버스보다 빠를 거야.
W: That's a good idea.

01 What are the speakers going to take?

➡ They _____.

02 밑줄 친 (A)의 우리말에 맞게 주어진 어구를 이용하여 영작하시오.

> this time, day, the subway, the bus, be, will, than, fast, at, of

➡ _____

_____

03 다음 대화의 밑줄 친 부분을 같은 말로 바꾸어 쓸 때, 주어진 철자로 시작하여 쓰시오.

> A: What shall we do at the park?
> B: Why don't we see a magic show?
> A: That's a good idea.

➡ L_____
➡ S_____
➡ W_____

04 다음 대화에서 괄호 안의 단어를 바르게 배열하시오.

> A: (shall, what, meet, time, we)?
> B: How about 4 o'clock?

➡ _____

[05~07] 다음 대화를 읽고 물음에 답하시오.

Anna: Dad, guess what! I have no school next Wednesday.
Dad: Really? Why not?
Anna: It's our school's 75th anniversary.
Dad: Oh, I see.
Anna: Can we do something together that day?
Dad: I guess I can ___(A)___ the afternoon off. What do you want to do?
Anna: Why don't we go see a musical at Bravo Theater near your work? We can get a discount if we go on a Wednesday.
Dad: Good idea, Anna! Then, let's just meet at the theater.
Anna: O.K. What time shall we meet?
Dad: How ___(B)___ 12? Then, (C) we can have a lunch together, too.
Anna: You're the best, Dad!

05 빈칸 (A)와 (B)에 알맞은 단어를 쓰시오.

➡ (A) _____ (B) _____

06 위 대화의 밑줄 친 (C)에서 어법상 틀린 것을 고치시오.

_____ ➡ _____

07 위 대화를 읽고 아래의 표의 빈칸을 완성하시오.

Anna's Next Week Plan		
What: see _____ _____ with _____		
When: _____ Wednesday at _____		
Where: at _____ _____		

Grammar

1 접속사 if

- **You will appreciate it better if you know the story.**
  네가 그 이야기를 안다면 더 잘 감상할 것이다.

- **If he fails, he must die.** 만약 실패한다면, 그는 죽어야만 한다.

- 접속사 if는 '만약 ~한다면'이라는 뜻으로, 조건의 부사절을 이끌며, 'if + 주어 + 동사 ~'의 형태로 쓴다. if절이 주절 앞에 오면 if절 뒤에 콤마(,)를 사용하고, 주절 뒤에 오면 콤마(,)를 사용하지 않는다.
  - **If** you miss the bus, you'll be late for school.
    = You'll be late for school **if** you miss the bus. 네가 버스를 놓친다면, 너는 학교에 늦을 것이다.

- 조건 부사절인 if절에서는 현재시제가 미래시제를 대신한다.
  - **If** it **rains** tomorrow, I will stay at home. (○) 내일 비가 온다면, 나는 집에 머물 것이다.
    If it will rain tomorrow, I will stay at home. (✕)

cf. 시간을 나타내는 부사절도 현재시제가 미래시제를 대신한다. 시간을 나타내는 부사절 접속사는 when(~할 때), until(~까지), before, after, as soon as(~하자마자) 등이 있다.
  - No one will go to sleep **until** someone **finds** out his name. (○)
    No one will go to sleep until someone will find out his name. (✕)

cf. if절이 동사의 목적어 자리에 사용되는 명사절일 경우는 미래시제를 사용할 수 있다.
  - I don't know **if** he **will come** tomorrow. 나는 그가 내일 올지 안 올지 모른다.
  - I wonder **if** she **will tell** you the secret. 그녀가 너에게 그 비밀을 말해 줄지 궁금하다.

핵심 Check

1. 괄호 안에서 알맞은 것을 고르시오.
   (1) If it is fine tomorrow, we (will go / go) on a picnic.
   (2) If you (miss / will miss) the bus, you will be late for the movie.
   (3) If you (will be / are) late for the movie, your friend will be very angry!

2. 다음 문장에서 어법상 틀린 곳이 있다면 바르게 고치오.
   (1) If you will exercise every day, you'll stay healthy.
   ➡ _____
   (2) I don't know if he will come to my house tonight.
   ➡ _____

② as + 형용사/부사의 원급 + as

> • Turandot is **as** cold **as** ice. Turandot는 얼음처럼 차갑다.
> • I can jump **as** high **as** Michael Jordan. 나는 Michael Jordan만큼 높이 점프할 수 있다.

- 형태: as + 형용사/부사의 원급 + as

- 의미: ~만큼 …한/하게 (두 대상의 정도가 같음을 나타냄)

  e.g. She is **as** tall **as** you. 그녀는 너만큼 키가 크다.

  Jane is **as** old **as** Tom. (= Jane and Tom are the same age.)

- 부정문: not as[so] + 형용사/부사의 원급 + as (~만큼 …하지 않은/않게)

  e.g. Tom is **not as** tall **as** Amy. Tom은 Amy만큼 키가 크지 않다.

  My bike is **not so** old **as** his bike. 나의 자전거는 그의 자전거만큼 오래되지 않았다.

  Tom is **not as** old **as** Peter. Tom은 Peter만큼 나이가 많지 않다.

  = Tom is **younger than** Peter. Tom은 Peter보다 어리다.

  = Peter is **older than** Tom. Peter는 Tom보다 나이가 많다.

cf. - **비교급을 이용한 비교**

  두 대상 중 하나가 우위에 있음을 나타낼 때 사용한다.

  형태: 형용사/부사의 비교급 + than ~: ~보다 더 …한/하게

  • Fred is **taller than** I am. Fred는 나보다 더 크다.

  • Cathy is **smarter than** I am. Cathy는 나보다 더 똑똑하다.

- **최상급을 이용한 비교급**

  세 개 이상의 대상 중 어느 하나의 정도가 가장 높을 때 사용한다.

  형태: the + 형용사/부사의 최상급: 가장 ~한/ 하게

  • Sujin is **the tallest** of the three. Sujin은 셋 중에서 가장 크다.

  • Here is **the most interesting** place in Busan. 부산에서 가장 흥미로운 장소가 여기에 있다.

핵심 Check

3. 괄호 안에서 알맞은 것을 고르시오.

(1) A dog is as [cleverer / clever] as a cat.

(2) Science is as [interestingly / interesting] as history.

4. 다음 빈칸에 공통으로 들어갈 말로 알맞은 것은?

This car is ＿＿＿＿ cheap ＿＿＿＿ that one.

① so　　② as　　③ too　　④ such　　⑤ to

01 다음 문장에서 어법상 <u>어색한</u> 부분을 바르게 고치시오.

(1) This new smartphone is as more expensive as a computer.

_____ ➡ _____

(2) This turtle is as small than a coin.

_____ ➡ _____

(3) If you will answer incorrectly, you will have to marry me.

_____ ➡ _____

(4) If you won't run now, you will miss the bus.

_____ ➡ _____

> expensive 비싼
> turtle 거북
> marry 결혼하다
> miss 놓치다

02 다음 빈칸에 공통으로 들어갈 말로 알맞은 것은? (대 · 소문자 무시)

- I asked him _____ he could study with me.
- _____ you watch it, you'll enter a fantasy world.

① whether   ② who   ③ which
④ though   ⑤ if

> enter 들어가다
> fantasy 상상, 공상

03 두 문장을 한 문장으로 만들 때 빈칸에 알맞은 말을 고르시오.

- Sue is 168 cm tall.
- Sam is 168 cm tall, too.
➡ Sue is _____ Sam.

① tall   ② taller than   ③ tall as
④ as tall as   ⑤ as taller as

04 다음 빈칸에 들어갈 말로 알맞은 것은?

- They do not work _____ we do.

① as hard than   ② as hardly as   ③ as hard as
④ hard than   ⑤ as harder as

> hard 열심히
> hardly 거의 ~ 않다

01 다음 중 어법상 <u>어색한</u> 문장은?

① His riddle is as difficult as her.

② This shirt isn't so large as that one.

③ Jenny can speak English as fluently as Maria.

④ Sandra is as heavy as Tom.

⑤ This river is as long as the Han River.

서답형

02 다음 대화를 읽고, 빈칸에 알맞은 말을 쓰시오.

> M: Liz, hurry up. It's already 6 o'clock.
>
> W: Oh, we're going to be late for the concert.
>
> M: Why don't we take the subway? The subway will be _____ than the bus at this time of day.
>
> W: That's a good idea.

➡ _____

03 다음 우리말과 일치하도록 알맞게 영작한 것은?

> 네가 약속을 어긴다면, 아무도 너를 믿지 않을 거야.

① Though you break your promises, nobody will trust you.

② Because you will break your promises, nobody will trust you.

③ If you will break your promises, nobody will trust you.

④ If you break your promises, nobody won't trust you.

⑤ If you break your promises, nobody will trust you.

서답형

04 다음 괄호 안에서 알맞은 단어를 고르시오.

(1) Suji is as pretty (so / as) her sister.

(2) Minji is as (taller / tall) as I.

(3) My room is as big as (yours / you).

서답형

05 다음 우리말에 맞게 주어진 어구를 알맞은 순서로 배열하시오. ((1)과 (2)는 if로 문장을 시작하시오.)

(1) 만약 당신이 이어폰을 사용해야 한다면 음악을 크게 틀지 마시오.

(If / play / have to / do / earphones / use / you / your music / not / loud)

➡ _____

(2) 지하철을 놓친다면, 모임에 늦을 거야.

(If / you / you / will be / miss / late / the subway / the meeting / for)

➡ _____

(3) 내 목소리는 너만큼 크다.

(my voice / as / as / yours / loud / is)

➡ _____

(4) Nick은 Peter만큼 빨리 달릴 수 있다.

(Nick / Peter / run / as / as / can / fast)

➡ _____

중요

06 다음 빈칸에 들어갈 알맞은 것은?

> If your friend _____ very angry, you will have to buy her ice cream.

① will be   ② is

③ won't be   ④ will is

⑤ are

07 〈보기〉의 밑줄 친 부분과 쓰임이 같은 것을 모두 고르시오.

> ┌─ 보기 ─┐
> Tom will be happy <u>if</u> you visit him.

① He asked me <u>if</u> I could play with him.

② I don't know <u>if</u> it will rain tomorrow.

③ I wonder <u>if</u> he will buy a new car.

④ We will play baseball <u>if</u> it doesn't rain tomorrow.

⑤ <u>If</u> he comes back tomorrow, I'll talk to him about the problem.

08 다음 중 어법상 어색한 것은?

① My eyes are as dark as chocolate.

② Fred is as tall as I am.

③ My bike is as old as Tom's bike.

④ Minho speaks English as good as a native speaker.

⑤ Dora is not as fast as I am.

09 다음 우리말을 바르게 영작한 것은?

> ┌─────────────────────────────┐
> 내일 날씨가 맑으면 그들은 바다에 갈 것이다.
> └─────────────────────────────┘

① They will go to the sea if it is sunny tomorrow.

② They go to the sea if it will be sunny tomorrow.

③ They go to the sea if it is sunny tomorrow.

④ If it will be sunny tomorrow, they will go to the sea.

⑤ If it was sunny tomorrow, they went to the sea.

서답형

10 어법상 틀린 부분을 찾아 바르게 고치시오.

(1) Juho doesn't study so hard than Dora.

　　＿＿＿＿＿ ➡ ＿＿＿＿＿

(2) This song sounds as more beautiful as a poem.

　　＿＿＿＿＿ ➡ ＿＿＿＿＿

(3) I can jump as highly as Michael Jordan.

　　＿＿＿＿＿ ➡ ＿＿＿＿＿

(4) If she will miss the bus, she won't get here on time.

　　＿＿＿＿＿ ➡ ＿＿＿＿＿

서답형

11 다음 문장에서 틀린 부분을 찾아 바르게 고치시오.

(1) Your sister is as friend as his.

　　＿＿＿＿＿ ➡ ＿＿＿＿＿

(2) She can't run as faster as Billy.

　　＿＿＿＿＿ ➡ ＿＿＿＿＿

12 다음 중 어법상 어색한 것은?

① If he fails, he must die.

② If you answer correctly, I will agree to die.

③ If you answer incorrectly, you will have to marry me.

④ You will appreciate it better if you know the story.

⑤ If you get up early tomorrow morning, you see the sunrise.

13 다음 두 문장을 한 문장으로 바르게 바꾼 것은?

> • Jomin reads many books.
> • Sumin reads many books, too.

① Jomin reads as much books as Sumin.
② Jomin reads as much as Sumin.
③ Jomin reads as many as Sumin's books.
④ Jomin reads as many books as Sumin.
⑤ Jomin reads more books than Sumin does.

서답형

14 다음 괄호 안에서 알맞은 것을 고르시오.

(1) Anne is not (too / as) tall as Judy.
(2) Sumi speaks English as (well / better) as Minsu.
(3) Your house is as small as (I / mine).

서답형

[15~16] 다음 우리말에 맞게 주어진 어구를 이용하여 영작하시오.

15

> 그녀는 깃털만큼 가볍다.
> (light, a feather)

➡ _____

16

> 호랑이는 코끼리만큼 크지 않다.
> (a tiger, so, big, an elephant)

➡ _____

서답형

17 다음 밑줄 친 부분과 바꿔 쓸 수 있는 말을 한 단어로 쓰시오.

> The bus is not <u>as</u> fast as the subway at this time of day.

➡ _____

[18~19] 주어진 어구들을 사용하여 원급 비교 문장으로 바르게 나타낸 것을 <u>모두</u> 고르시오.

18

> This soldier, brave, a lion

① This soldier is so braver as a lion.
② This soldier isn't as brave as a lion.
③ This soldier is as brave as a lion.
④ This soldier is so brave than a lion.
⑤ This soldier is too brave as a lion.

19

> My father, strong, an ox

① My father isn't so strong as an ox.
② My father is stronger than an ox.
③ My father isn't so stronger as an ox.
④ My father is as stronger as an ox.
⑤ My father is as strong as an ox.

서답형

20 우리말에 맞게 괄호 안에서 알맞은 것을 고르시오.

> • 내가 이탈리아에 간다면 나는 피자와 스파게티를 먹을 것이다.
> • 우리가 내일 만나면 무엇을 할 거니?

➡ If I (will go / go) to Italy, I (will eat / eat) pizza and spaghetti.
➡ When we (will meet / meet) tomorrow, what (will / do) you do?

01 다음 두 문장의 의미가 같도록 빈칸을 완성하시오.

> Mina is bigger than Jenny.
> = Jenny _____ Mina.

02 다음 문장에서 어법상 <u>어색한</u> 부분을 고쳐 문장을 다시 쓰시오.

(1) I can finish the work if you will help me.

➡ _____

_____

(2) If school will finish early tomorrow, I will go see a movie.

➡ _____

(3) If my mom will catch a cold, I will do the dishes for her.

➡ _____

_____

03 다음 그림을 보고 주어진 문장을 완성하시오.

(1)

➡ The dog can _____ the ostrich.

(2)

➡ This turtle is _____ small _____ a coin.

04 다음 문장에서 <u>어색한</u> 부분을 찾아 바르게 고치시오.

(1) Your car is as expensive as me.

_____ ➡ _____

(2) Soccer isn't as more popular as baseball in Korea.

_____ ➡ _____

(3) If it won't rain tomorrow, we'll go on a picnic.

_____ ➡ _____

(4) You will fail if you won't study harder from now on.

_____ ➡ _____

05 두 문장을 'as ~ as'를 이용하여 한 문장으로 쓰시오.

(1) • John is 170cm tall.
   • Susan is 170cm tall, too.

➡ _____

(2) • This apple is sweet.
   • That pineapple is also sweet.

➡ _____

(3) • My bike is old.
   • But his bike is older than mine.

➡ _____

(4) • I watch 5 movies every month.
   • Kate also watches 5 movies every month.

➡ _____

06 다음 표를 보고 원급 비교를 이용하여 다음 빈칸을 완성하시오.

Name	Tom	Eric	Amy
Age	15	14	15
Height	167cm	167cm	163cm
Weight	58kg	52kg	52kg

(1) Eric is _____ Amy.

(2) Tom is _____ Amy.

(3) Tom is _____ Eric.

07 우리말과 일치하도록 주어진 어구를 알맞은 순서로 배열하시오. (부사절로 문장을 시작하시오.)

(1) 만약 당신이 초콜릿을 너무 많이 먹는다면 당신의 치아가 상할 것이다.

(if / too much / you / eat / your / will / teeth / go / bad / chocolate)

➡ _____

_____

(2) 만약 Fred가 학교에 걸어간다면 40분이 걸릴 것이다.

(Fred / to / if / walks / it / take / school / will / 40 minutes)

➡ _____

_____

(3) 만약 네가 지도를 따라간다면 너는 나의 할머니의 집에 도착할 것이다.

(the / follow / you / get / you'll / if / map / to / my grandma's house)

➡ _____

_____

08 다음 주어진 문장에서 어법상 틀린 부분을 찾아 바르게 고쳐 쓰시오.

Turandot must find the answer before dawn, but his riddle is as difficult than her. She says to everyone, "No one will go to sleep until someone will find out his name."

➡ _____

➡ _____

09 다음 표를 보고 수지와 민지를 비교하는 글을 완성하시오. (동등비교 구문을 이용할 것.)

이름	나이	키	100m 기록
Suji	14	167 cm	15초
Minji	14	164 cm	12초

(1) Minji is _____ Suji. (나이)

(2) Minji is _____ Suji. (키)

(3) Suji is _____ Minji. (100m 기록)

10 다음 우리말에 맞게 주어진 어구를 이용하여 영작하시오.

(1) 그녀의 여동생은 고양이만큼 장난꾸러기다. (playful, a kitten)

➡ _____

(2) 우리 집은 묘지만큼이나 조용하다. (home, quiet, a grave)

➡ _____

(3) 나는 내 남동생만큼 키가 크지 않다. (tall, my brother)

➡ _____

Turandot

The Most Dangerous Love in the World!

Welcome, everyone! Tonight, we <u>are going to</u> perform Giacomo
가까운 미래에 확실하게 일어날 일을 표현

Puccini's opera *Turandot*. <u>Like</u> many other famous operas, *Turandot* is
'~과 같이'(전치사)

<u>in Italian</u> because opera started <u>in Italy</u> in the 16th century. Before we
이탈리아어로   이탈리아에서

begin, <u>I'd like to</u> tell you the storyline of the opera *Turandot*. You will
would like to: ~하고 싶다

appreciate it better <u>if</u> you <u>know</u> the story.
'만약 ~한다면'(조건을 나타내는 접속사),   조건을 나타내는 if절에서는 현재형이 미래를 대신

   <u>Turandot, a Chinese princess,</u> is a woman <u>of great beauty</u>, but she is
Turandot와 Chinese princess는 동격으로 같은 사람을 나타낸다.   = very beautiful

<u>as cold as</u> ice. Any prince who wants to marry her must answer three
as+원급+as: 동등비교 표현으로, 두 대상의 동등함을 나타낸다.

riddles. If he fails, he must die. <u>No one has ever been</u> able to answer
부정의 의미인 No one이 주어이므로 문장 전체가 부정의 의미   현재완료: 과거의 시점부터 현재까지 이어지는 상황을 나타낸다.

them. One day, a brave prince falls in love with her at first sight. He

becomes the first man to <u>answer</u> all three riddles.
to부정사의 형용사적 용법

perform 공연하다, 수행하다

Italian 이탈리아어, 이탈리아인; 이탈리아의

century 100년, 세기

storyline (소설 · 연극 · 영화 등의) 줄거리

appreciate 감상하다, 감사하다, 알아주다

riddle 수수께끼

fall in love 사랑에 빠지다, 반하다

 확인문제

● 다음 문장이 본문의 내용과 일치하면 T, 일치하지 <u>않으면</u> F를 쓰시오.

1   Giacomo Puccini composed the opera *Turandot*. ☐

2   *Turandot* is in Italian because Puccini was born in Italy. ☐

3   Many famous operas are in Italian because opera started in Italy. ☐

4   You must appreciate the opera before you know the story. ☐

5   Turandot is a very beautiful Chinese princess. ☐

6   Any prince who wants to marry her must answer four riddles. ☐

7   If the prince fails to answer the riddles, he must die. ☐

8   One day, a brave prince falls in love with her at first sight, but he fails to answer the

    riddles. ☐

However, Turandot does not want to marry the prince. He is nothing
'~에 지나지 않는, ~에 불과한'
more than a stranger to her. He then gives her a riddle of his own. He
자기 자신의
asks her, "What is my name?" He adds, "If you answer correctly, I will
조건절에서는 현재 시제가 미래 시제를 대신한다.
agree to die. If you answer incorrectly, you will have to marry me."
접두사 in-은 반대의 의미를 나타낸다.

Turandot must find the answer before dawn, but his riddle is as
'~ 이전에'(전치사)   as+원급+as: 동등비교
difficult as hers. She says to everyone, "No one will go to sleep until
= her riddles(소유대명사)   아무도 ~하지 않다
someone finds out his name." The prince then sings the most famous
때를 나타내는 부사절에서는 현재형이 미래를 대신   "Nessun Dorma"와 동격
aria of the whole opera, "Nessun Dorma." It means no one sleeps.
앞에 접속사 that 생략

No one sleeps.

No one sleeps, not even you, Princess.
no one은 3인칭 단수 취급하므로 sleeps
…

My secret is safe.

No one will know my name.
…

At dawn, I will win! I will win!

The prince's name is Calaf. Will the princess learn his name in time?

Let's watch the opera and find out.
= How about watching the opera and finding out?

dawn 새벽, 동틀 녘
aria 아리아, 영창
whole 전체; 모든, 전부의
secret 비밀
safe 안전한
in time 제시간에, 늦지 않게
find out 알아내다, 발견하다

📎 **확인문제**

● 다음 문장이 본문의 내용과 일치하면 T, 일치하지 않으면 F를 쓰시오.

1 Turandot wants to marry the prince. ☐

2 The prince is only a stranger to her. ☐

3 The prince gives Turandot a riddle of his own. ☐

4 If Turandot answers correctly, the prince will marry her. ☐

5 The prince's riddle is as difficult as Turandot's. ☐

6 Turandot will learn the prince's name in time. ☐

● 우리말을 참고하여 빈칸에 알맞은 말을 쓰시오.

1 Turandot _____ _____ _____ Love in the World

2 _____, everyone!

3 Tonight, we are going to _____ Giacomo Puccini's opera *Turandot*.

4 _____ many other famous operas, *Turandot* is _____ _____ because opera started _____ _____ in the 16th century.

5 Before we begin, _____ _____ _____ _____ you the storyline of the opera *Turandot*.

6 You will _____ it better _____ you know the story.

7 Turandot, a Chinese princess, is a woman _____ _____ _____, but she is _____ _____ _____ _____.

8 Any prince _____ wants to _____ _____ must answer three riddles.

9 If he _____, he must die.

10 No one _____ _____ _____ able to answer them.

11 One day, a brave prince _____ _____ _____ _____ _____ her at first sight.

12 He becomes _____ _____ _____ to answer all three riddles.

13 _____, Turandot does not want _____ _____ the prince.

14 He is _____ _____ _____ a stranger to her.

15 He then gives her a riddle _____ _____ _____.

1 투란도트, 세상에서 가장 위험한 사랑

2 여러분, 환영합니다!

3 오늘 밤, 우리는 지아코모 푸치니의 오페라 《투란도트》를 공연할 것입니다.

4 다른 많은 유명한 오페라들처럼 《투란도트》는 이탈리아어로 되어 있는데, 오페라가 16세기 이탈리아에서 시작되었기 때문입니다.

5 시작하기 전에 오페라 《투란도트》의 줄거리를 알려 드리려고 합니다.

6 여러분이 줄거리를 알면 이 오페라를 더 잘 감상하게 될 것입니다.

7 중국의 공주 Turandot는 굉장히 아름다운 여인이지만, 그녀는 얼음처럼 차갑습니다.

8 그녀와 결혼하길 원하는 왕자는 누구든지 반드시 세 가지 수수께끼에 답해야 합니다.

9 만약 실패하면 그는 죽어야 합니다.

10 그 누구도 수수께끼에 답할 수 없었습니다.

11 어느 날, 어떤 용감한 왕자가 그녀에게 첫눈에 반합니다.

12 그는 세 수수께끼를 모두 맞힌 첫 번째 사람이 됩니다.

13 그러나 Turandot는 그 왕자와 결혼하길 원하지 않습니다.

14 그는 그녀에게 단지 낯선 사람일 뿐입니다.

15 그러자 그는 그녀에게 자신의 수수께끼를 냅니다.

16 He asks her, "_____ is my name?"

17 He _____, "If you answer correctly, I will agree _____ _____. If you answer _____, you will have to marry me."

18 Turandot must find the answer _____ _____, but his riddle is _____ _____ _____ _____.

19 She says to everyone, "No one will go to sleep _____ someone _____ _____ his name."

20 The prince then sings _____ _____ _____ _____ of the whole opera, "Nessun Dorma."

21 It _____ no one sleeps.

22 No one _____.

23 No one sleeps, _____ _____ _____, Princess.

24 My secret is _____.

25 No one _____ _____ my name.

26 _____ _____, I will win! I will win!

27 The _____ name is Calaf.

28 Will the princess learn his name _____ _____?

29 _____ _____ the opera and find out.

16 그는 그녀에게 "제 이름이 무엇 입니까?"라고 묻습니다.

17 그는 "당신이 맞게 대답한다면 나는 죽는 것에 동의하겠습니 다. 만약 답이 틀리면 당신은 저 와 결혼해야 할 것입니다."라고 덧붙입니다.

18 Turandot는 동이 트기 전에 답 을 찾아야 하지만 그의 수수께 끼는 그녀의 것만큼 어렵습니 다.

19 그녀는 모두에게 "누군가 그의 이름을 알아낼 때까지 그 누구 도 잠들 수 없다."라고 말합니 다.

20 그리고 왕자는 이 오페라 전 체에서 가장 유명한 아리아, Nessun Dorma를 부릅니다.

21 그것은 누구도 잠들지 못한다는 뜻입니다.

22 누구도 잠들지 못하네.

23 누구도 잠들지 못하네, 당신조 차도, 공주여.

24 나의 비밀은 안전하다네.

25 누구도 나의 이름을 알지 못할 것이네.

26 동틀 녘에, 내가 이길 것이라네! 내가 승리할 것이라네!

27 왕자의 이름은 Calaf입니다.

28 공주는 그의 이름을 제때 알아 낼 수 있을까요?

29 오페라를 보고 알아봅시다.

● 우리말을 참고하여 본문을 영작하시오.

1 투란도트, 세상에서 가장 위험한 사랑

➡ _____

2 여러분, 환영합니다!

➡ _____

3 오늘 밤, 우리는 지아코모 푸치니의 오페라 《투란도트》를 공연할 것입니다.

➡ _____

4 다른 많은 유명한 오페라들처럼 《투란도트》는 이탈리아어로 되어 있는데, 오페라가 16세기 이탈리아에서 시작되었기 때문입니다.

➡ _____

5 시작하기 전에 오페라 《투란도트》의 줄거리를 알려 드리려고 합니다.

➡ _____

6 여러분이 줄거리를 알면 이 오페라를 더 잘 감상하게 될 것입니다.

➡ _____

7 중국의 공주 Turandot는 굉장히 아름다운 여인이지만, 그녀는 얼음처럼 차갑습니다.

➡ _____

8 그녀와 결혼하길 원하는 왕자는 누구든지 반드시 세 가지 수수께끼에 답해야 합니다.

➡ _____

9 만약 실패하면 그는 죽어야 합니다.

➡ _____

10 그 누구도 수수께끼에 답할 수 없었습니다.

➡ _____

11 어느 날, 어떤 용감한 왕자가 그녀에게 첫눈에 반합니다.

➡ _____

12 그는 세 수수께끼를 모두 맞힌 첫 번째 사람이 됩니다.

➡ _____

13 그러나 Turandot는 그 왕자와 결혼하길 원하지 않습니다.

➡ _____

14 그는 그녀에게 단지 낯선 사람일 뿐입니다.

➡ _____

15 그러자 그는 그녀에게 자신의 수수께끼를 냅니다.

➡ _____

16 그는 그녀에게 "제 이름이 무엇입니까?"라고 묻습니다.

➡ _____

17 그는 "당신이 맞게 대답한다면 나는 죽는 것에 동의하겠습니다. 만약 답이 틀리면 당신은 저와 결혼해야 할 것입니다."라고 덧붙입니다.

➡ _____

18 Turandot는 동이 트기 전에 답을 찾아야 하지만 그의 수수께끼는 그녀의 것만큼 어렵습니다.

➡ _____

19 그녀는 모두에게 "누군가 그의 이름을 알아낼 때까지 그 누구도 잠들 수 없다."라고 말합니다.

➡ _____

20 그리고 왕자는 이 오페라 전체에서 가장 유명한 아리아, Nessun Dorma를 부릅니다.

➡ _____

21 그것은 누구도 잠들지 못한다는 뜻입니다.

➡ _____

22 누구도 잠들지 못하네.

➡ _____

23 누구도 잠들지 못하네, 당신조차도, 공주여.

➡ _____

24 나의 비밀은 안전하다네.

➡ _____

25 누구도 나의 이름을 알지 못할 것이네.

➡ _____

26 동틀 녘에, 내가 이길 것이라네! 내가 승리할 것이라네!

➡ _____

27 왕자의 이름은 Calaf입니다.

➡ _____

28 공주는 그의 이름을 제때 알아낼 수 있을까요?

➡ _____

29 오페라를 보고 알아봅시다.

➡ _____

[01~03] 다음 글을 읽고 물음에 답하시오.

Welcome, everyone! Tonight, we are going to perform Giacomo Puccini's opera *Turandot*. Like many other famous operas, *Turandot* is in (A)[Italy / Italian] because opera started in Italy in the 16th century. Before we begin, I'd like (B)[to tell / telling] you the storyline of the opera *Turandot*. You will appreciate it better if you (C)[know / will know] the story.

서답형

01 위 글의 괄호 (A)~(C)에서 문맥이나 어법상 알맞은 낱말을 골라 쓰시오.

➡ (A) _____ (B) _____ (C) _____

02 위 글의 뒤에 올 내용으로 가장 알맞은 것을 고르시오.

① 오페라 《투란도트》의 작곡가 소개
② 오페라에 나오는 이탈리아어 이해하기
③ 이탈리아의 유명한 오페라들 소개
④ 오페라 《투란도트》의 줄거리 소개
⑤ 오페라 《투란도트》의 공연 관람 후기

중요

03 위 글의 내용과 일치하지 <u>않는</u> 것은?

① 오늘 밤, 오페라 《투란도트》를 공연할 것이다.
② 오페라 《투란도트》의 작곡가는 지아코모 푸치니 이다.
③ 《투란도트》는 이탈리아어로 되어 있다.
④ 오페라는 16세기 이탈리아에서 시작되었다.
⑤ 이탈리아어를 알면 오페라를 더 잘 감상하게 될 것이다.

[04~06] 다음 글을 읽고 물음에 답하시오.

One day, a brave prince falls in love with her at first sight. He becomes the first man to answer all three riddles.

_____ⒶA, Turandot does not want to marry the prince. (①) He is nothing more than a stranger to ⓐher. (②) He asks her, "What is ⓑmy name?" (③) He adds, "If ⓒyou answer correctly, I will agree to die. (④) If you answer incorrectly, you will have to marry ⓓme." (⑤)

Turandot must find the answer before dawn, but ⓔhis riddle is as difficult as hers. She says to everyone, "No one will go to sleep until someone finds out his name."

04 위 글의 빈칸 Ⓐ에 들어갈 알맞은 말을 고르시오.

① However   ② Therefore
③ In other words   ④ For example
⑤ As a result

05 위 글의 흐름으로 보아, 주어진 문장이 들어가기에 가장 적절한 곳은?

> He then gives her a riddle of his own.

①   ②   ③   ④   ⑤

중요

06 위 글의 밑줄 친 ⓐ~ⓔ 중 가리키는 대상이 같은 것끼리 짝 지어진 것은?

① ⓐ - ⓑ   ② ⓐ - ⓓ
③ ⓑ - ⓔ   ④ ⓒ - ⓓ
⑤ ⓒ - ⓔ

[07~09] 다음 글을 읽고 물음에 답하시오.

Turandot, a Chinese princess, is a woman of great beauty, but she is ⓐas cold as ice. Any prince who wants to marry her must answer three riddles. If he fails, he must die. No one has ever been able to answer them. One day, a brave prince falls in love with her at first sight. He becomes the first man to answer all three riddles.

07 위 글에서 알 수 있는 Turandot의 성격으로 가장 알맞은 것을 고르시오.

① considerate 　② warm-hearted

③ heartless 　④ friendly

⑤ careless

08 위 글의 밑줄 친 ⓐas와 같은 용법으로 쓰인 것은?

① Do as you are told.

② Run as fast as you can.

③ As we go up, the air grows colder.

④ I regarded them as kind helpers.

⑤ As she was tired, she soon fell asleep.

09 위 글을 읽고 대답할 수 없는 질문은?

① Who is Turandot?

② What does Turandot look like?

③ What does the prince who wants to marry Turandot have to do?

④ What are the three riddles that Turandot asks?

⑤ Who becomes the first man to answer all three riddles?

[10~13] 다음 글을 읽고 물음에 답하시오.

Turandot must find the answer ___ⓐ___ dawn, but his riddle is as difficult as hers. She says to everyone, "No one will go to sleep until someone finds out his name."

The prince then sings the most famous aria of the whole opera, "Nessun Dorma." It means no one ___ⓑ___.

No one ___ⓑ___.

No one ___ⓑ___, not even you, Princess.

…

My secret is safe.

No one will know my name.

…

___ⓒ___ dawn, I will win! I will win!

The prince's name is Calaf. Will the princess learn his name in time? Let's watch the opera and ⓓfind out.

10 위 글의 빈칸 ⓐ와 ⓒ에 들어갈 전치사가 바르게 짝지어진 것은?

① at – In 　② before – To

③ before – At 　④ at – To

⑤ on – At

11 위 글의 빈칸 ⓑ에 공통으로 들어갈 알맞은 단어를 고르시오.

① mustn't sleep 　② sleep

③ slept 　④ can't sleep

서답형 ⑤ sleeps

12 다음 질문에 대한 알맞은 대답을 주어진 단어로 시작하여 쓰시오. (6 단어)

Q: Why does the prince say "My secret is safe"?

A: Because _____.

➡ _____

서답형

13 위 글의 밑줄 친 ⓓfind out과 바꿔 쓸 수 있는 단어를 본문에서 찾아 쓰시오.

➡ _____

[14~16] 다음 글을 읽고 물음에 답하시오.

I saw *Beauty and the Beast* last Saturday. It is about a beautiful girl and a beast. I enjoyed it a lot. The songs were great, and the love story was as beautiful as a gem. If you like heart-warming stories about love, you will like it, too.

by Lee Minsu on Aug. 12

14 위 글의 종류로 알맞은 것을 고르시오.

① book report   ② essay
③ article   ④ review
⑤ biography

중요

15 위 글의 내용을 다음과 같이 정리하고자 한다. 다음 빈칸에 들어갈 알맞은 말을 고르시오.

Minsu _____ *Beauty and the Beast* to people who like heart-warming stories about love.

① demands   ② recommends
③ expresses   ④ reports
⑤ advises

16 위 글의 영화에 대해 알 수 없는 것은?

① What's the title of it?
② When did Minsu see it?
③ What is the story about?
④ How did Minsu like it?
⑤ With whom did Minsu see it?

[17~19] 다음 글을 읽고 물음에 답하시오.

ⓐ중국의 공주 Turandot는 굉장히 아름다운 여인이지만, 그녀는 얼음처럼 차갑습니다. Any prince who wants to marry her must answer three riddles. If he fails, he must die. No one has ever been able to answer ⓑthem. One day, a brave prince falls in love with her at first sight. He becomes the first man ⓒto answer all three riddles.

서답형

17 위 글의 밑줄 친 ⓐ의 우리말에 맞게 한 단어를 보충하여, 주어진 어휘를 알맞게 배열하시오. (콤마를 사용할 것.)

beauty / Turandot / she / as / is / but / a Chinese princess / ice / as / a woman / cold / is / great

➡ _____
_____

서답형

18 위 글의 밑줄 친 ⓑthem이 가리키는 것을 본문에서 찾아 쓰시오.

➡ _____

19 위 글의 밑줄 친 ⓒto answer와 to부정사의 용법이 다른 것을 모두 고르시오.

① I want a pen to write it with.
② She was pleased to meet her friend.
③ It was easy for me to do the work.
④ There's not a moment to lose.
⑤ How lucky you are to win the first prize!

[20~23] 다음 글을 읽고 물음에 답하시오.

However, Turandot does not want to marry the prince. He is nothing more than a _____ⓐ_____ to her. He then gives her ⓑa riddle of his own. He asks her, "What is my name?" He adds, "If you answer correctly, I will agree (A)[dying / to die]. If you answer incorrectly, you will have to marry me."

Turandot must find the answer before dawn, but his riddle is as difficult as (B)[her / hers]. She says to everyone, "No one will go to sleep until someone (C)[finds / will find] out his name."

20 위 글의 빈칸 ⓐ에 들어갈 알맞은 말을 고르시오.

① neighbor ② friend
③ husband ④ stranger
⑤ co-worker

서답형

21 위 글의 괄호 (A)~(C)에서 어법상 알맞은 낱말을 골라 쓰시오.

➡ (A) _____ (B) _____ (C) _____

서답형

22 위 글의 밑줄 친 ⓑ가 가리키는 것을 본문에서 찾아 쓰시오.

➡ _____

23 위 글의 마지막 부분에서 알 수 있는 'Turandot'의 심경으로 가장 알맞은 것을 고르시오.

① desperate ② satisfied
③ bored ④ ashamed
⑤ excited

[24~26] 다음 글을 읽고 물음에 답하시오.

Review of *La La Land* ★★★★☆
I saw *La La Land* last Friday. It is about the dreams and love of Mia and Sebastian. I enjoyed its beautiful and ⓐmoving songs. ⓑThe story was also as good as the songs. If you are looking for a good musical movie, you should see this movie.

by Kim Jisu on Aug. 11

24 위 글의 밑줄 친 ⓐmoving과 바꿔 쓸 수 있는 말을 고르시오.

① lively ② cheerful
③ touching ④ energetic
⑤ depressing

서답형

25 To whom does Jisu recommend *La La Land*? Fill in the blank with the suitable words.

➡ To people who _____

_____ .

26 위 글의 밑줄 친 ⓑ와 같은 의미의 문장을 모두 고르시오.

① Not only the story but also the songs were good.
② Not the story but the songs were good.
③ Both the story and the songs were good.
④ Either the story or the songs were good.
⑤ Neither the story nor the songs were good.

[01~03] 다음 글을 읽고 물음에 답하시오.

Welcome, everyone! Tonight, we are going to perform Giacomo Puccini's opera *Turandot*. Like many other famous operas, *Turandot* is in Italian because opera started in Italy in the 16th century. Before we begin, ⓐ I'd like to tell you the storyline of the opera *Turandot*. You will appreciate ⓑit better if you know the story.

01 위 글의 밑줄 친 ⓐ를 우리말로 옮기시오.

➡ _____

02 위 글의 밑줄 친 ⓑ가 가리키는 것을 본문에서 찾아 쓰시오.

➡ _____

03 Why is *Turandot* in Italian? Fill in the blank with the suitable words.

➡ It's because _____
_____.

[04~06] 다음 글을 읽고 물음에 답하시오.

However, Turandot does not want to marry the prince. He is ⓐnothing more than a stranger to her. He then gives her a riddle of his own. He asks her, "What is my name?" He adds, "ⓑIf you answer incorrectly, I will agree to die. If you answer correctly, you will have to marry me."

Turandot must find the answer before dawn, but his riddle is as difficult as hers. She says to everyone, "ⓒNo one will go to sleep until someone finds out his name."

04 위 글의 밑줄 친 ⓐnothing more than과 바꿔 쓸 수 있는 한 단어를 쓰시오.

➡ _____

05 위 글의 밑줄 친 ⓑ에서 흐름상 어색한 부분을 고치시오. (두 군데)

➡ _____, _____

06 위 글의 밑줄 친 ⓒ를 다음과 같이 바꿔 쓸 때 빈칸에 들어갈 알맞은 말을 쓰시오. (5 단어)

➡ People will go to sleep only after
_____.

[07~09] 다음 글을 읽고 물음에 답하시오.

ⓐTurandot, a Chinese princess, is a woman of great beauty, but she is as cold as ice. Any prince ___ⓑ___ wants to marry her must answer three riddles. If he fails, he must die. No one has ever been able to answer them. One day, a brave prince falls in love with her at first sight. He becomes the first man to answer all three riddles.

07 위 글의 밑줄 친 ⓐ를 다음과 같이 바꿔 쓸 때 빈칸에 들어갈 알맞은 말을 쓰시오.

➡ Turandot, a Chinese princess, is a
_____ woman.

08 위 글의 빈칸 ⓑ에 들어갈 알맞은 말을 쓰시오.

➡ _____

09 다음 문장에서 위 글의 내용과 <u>다른</u> 부분을 찾아서 고치시오.

> • Before a brave prince gives answers to all three riddles, a few princes have been able to give correct answers.

_____ ➡ _____

[10~12] 다음 글을 읽고 물음에 답하시오.

> Turandot, a Chinese princess, (A)[is / are] a woman of great beauty, but she is as cold as ice. Any prince who wants to (B)[marry / marry with] her must answer three riddles. If he fails, he must die. No one has ever been able to answer them. One day, a brave prince falls in love with her ⓐ첫눈에. He becomes the first man to (C)[answer / answer to] all three riddles.

10 위 글의 괄호 (A)~(C)에서 어법상 알맞은 낱말을 골라 쓰시오.

➡ (A) _____ (B) _____ (C) _____

11 위 글의 밑줄 친 ⓐ의 우리말을 세 단어로 쓰시오.

➡ _____

12 본문의 내용과 일치하도록 다음 빈칸 (A)와 (B)에 알맞은 단어를 쓰시오.

> Turandot, the Chinese princess, gives (A)_____ _____ to any prince who wants to get married to her. If he doesn't reply to them correctly, he (B)_____ _____ .

[13~14] 다음 글을 읽고 물음에 답하시오.

> Turandot must find the answer before dawn, but his riddle is as difficult as ___ⓐ___ . She says to everyone, "No one will go to sleep until someone finds out his name."
> The prince's name is Calaf. Will the princess learn his name ⓑin time? Let's watch the opera and find out.

13 위 글의 빈칸 ⓐ에 she를 알맞은 형태로 쓰시오.

➡ _____

14 위 글의 밑줄 친 ⓑin time과 바꿔 쓸 수 있는 단어를 본문에서 찾아 쓰시오.

➡ _____

[15~16] 다음 글을 읽고 물음에 답하시오.

> The prince then gives her a riddle of his own. He asks her, "What is my name?" He adds, "ⓐ당신이 맞게 대답한다면 나는 죽는 것에 동의하겠습니다. If you answer incorrectly, you will have to marry me."
> ⓑTurandot must find the answer before dawn, but his riddle is so difficult as hers. She says to everyone, "No one will go to sleep until someone finds out his name."

15 위 글의 밑줄 친 ⓐ의 우리말에 맞게 한 단어를 보충하여, 주어진 어휘를 알맞게 배열하시오.

> die / answer / if / I / correctly / to / you / agree / ,

➡ _____

16 위 글의 밑줄 친 ⓑ에서 어법상 틀린 부분을 고치시오.

_____ ➡ _____

교과서

구석구석

해석

Link

A: How was our performance?
　　　　~은 어땠니?

B: It was amazing! Actually, I've seen the musical *Cats* before, and your song
　　　　　　　　　　　　　　　　　　　　　　현재완료(경험)

was as great as the musical's.
~만큼 ···한(원급 비교)　= the musical's song

구문해설 ・performance 공연 ・amazing 놀라운 ・actually 사실

A: 우리 공연 어땠어?

B: 굉장했어! 사실, 난 뮤지컬 캣츠를 전에 본 적이 있는데, 너희 노래는 그 뮤지컬의 노래만큼 훌륭했어.

Write

Review of *La La Land* ★★★★☆

I saw *La La Land* last Friday. It is about the dreams and love of Mia and
　과거의 일이라 과거시제 사용함　　　　　　　　　　~에 관한 것이다

Sebastian. I enjoyed its beautiful and moving songs. The story was also

as good as the songs. If you are looking for a good musical movie, you should
as+원급+as: ~만큼 좋은　조건의 부사절 접속사　　　　　　　　　　　~해야 한다

see this movie.

by Kim Jisu on Aug. 11

구문해설 ・enjoy 즐기다 ・moving 감동적인 ・look for ~을 찾다

라라랜드에 대한 감상

나는 지난 금요일에 라라랜드를 보았어. 그건 Mia와 Sebastian의 꿈과 사랑에 대한 이야기야. 나는 그것의 아름답고 감동적인 노래를 즐겼어. 이야기도 노래만큼이나 좋았지. 좋은 뮤지컬 영화를 찾고 있다면, 이 영화를 봐야 할 거야.

8월 11일, 김지수 씀

Write

Review of *Beauty and the Beast* ★★★★★

I saw *Beauty and the Beast* last Saturday. It is about a beautiful girl and a beast.
　　　　　　　　　　　　　on last Saturday(×)　*Beauty and the Beast*

I enjoyed it a lot. The songs were great, and the love story was as beautiful as
　Beauty and the Beast　　　　　　　　as+원급+as: 동등비교 표현으로, 두 대상의 동등한 가치를 나타낸다.

a gem. If you like heart-warming stories about love, you will like it, too.
　조건의 부사절에서 미래시제 대신 현재시제를 사용　　　　　　　*Beauty and the Beast*

by Lee Minsu on Aug. 12

구문해설 ・beauty 아름다움, 미녀 ・beast 짐승, 야수 ・gem 보석
　　　　・heart-warming 마음이 따뜻해지는

미녀와 야수에 대한 감상

나는 지난 토요일에 미녀와 야수를 봤어. 그건 예쁜 여자아이와 야수에 대한 이야기야. 나는 그것을 매우 즐겼어. 노래들은 아주 좋았고, 사랑 이야기는 보석만큼 아름다웠어. 마음이 따뜻해지는 사랑 이야기를 좋아한다면, 너도 이걸 좋아할 거야.

8월 12일, 이민수 씀

영역별 핵심문제

01 두 단어의 관계가 나머지 넷과 <u>다른</u> 것은?

① brave – cowardly
② safe – dangerous
③ difficult – easy
④ fail – succeed
⑤ moving – touching

02 밑줄 친 단어와 의미가 같은 것을 고르시오.

A: How was our performance?
B: It was very <u>surprising</u>!

① amazing   ② interesting
③ famous   ④ moving
⑤ popular

03 다음 제시된 단어를 사용하여 자연스러운 문장을 만들 수 <u>없는</u> 것은? (형태 변화 가능)

┌─── 보기 ├───
brave century mean dawn practice
└────────────────

① One day, a _____ prince falls in love with her at first sight.
② Opera started in Italy in the 16th _____.
③ Why don't we _____ the subway?
④ She must find the answer before _____.
⑤ "Nessun Dorma" _____ no one sleeps.

04 사진을 보고 대화의 빈칸에 어울리는 단어를 고르시오.

B: Mom, I got only one question wrong on the Korean history exam!
W: Great! I was sure you would do well. Why don't we go out to _____ tonight?
B: Yes!

① marry   ② appreciate
③ celebrate   ④ leave
⑤ finish

05 우리말에 맞게 빈칸에 알맞은 단어를 쓰시오.

학교 끝나고 바로, 네 시 어때?
How about 4 o'clock, _____ after school?

[06~07] 다음 대화를 읽고 물음에 답하시오.

G: Do you want to play badminton together this afternoon, Mark?
B: Sure. __(A)__ shall we play?
G: __(B)__ about at the park near your place?
B: O.K. See you there at 3 o'clock.

06 빈칸 (A)와 (B)에 들어갈 말을 쓰시오.

➡ (A) _____ (B) _____

07 위 대화의 목적으로 알맞은 것은?

① to advise ② to inform
③ to recommend ④ to make plans
⑤ to appreciate

[08~09] 다음 대화를 읽고 물음에 답하시오.

A: (A)Why don't we eat pizza after school?
B: Good idea. (B)몇 시에 만날까?
A: How about 5 o'clock at the restaurant?
B: O.K. See you then.

08 밑줄 친 (A)와 바꾸어 쓸 수 <u>없는</u> 표현은?

① Let's eat pizza after school.
② Shall we eat pizza after school?
③ Why are we going to eat pizza after school?
④ How about eating pizza after school?
⑤ What about eating pizza after school?

09 밑줄 친 (B)의 우리말에 맞게 주어진 단어를 이용하여 영어로 쓰시오.

what, shall, meet

➡ _____

10 주어진 문장 뒤에 이어질 대화의 순서를 바르게 배열하시오.

What shall we do this afternoon?

(A) Good idea! What time shall we meet?
(B) Why don't we go to the art museum?
(C) How about 2 o'clock?
(D) O.K. Let's meet in front of the museum.

➡ _____

[11~12] 다음 대화를 읽고 물음에 답하시오.

Anna: Dad, guess what! I have no school next Wednesday.
Dad: Really? Why not?
Anna: It's our school's 75th anniversary.
Dad: Oh, I see.
Anna: Can we do something together that day?
Dad: I guess I can take the afternoon ___(A)___. What do you want to do?
Anna: Why don't we go see a musical at Bravo Theater near your work? We can get a discount ___(B)___ we go on a Wednesday.
Dad: Good idea, Anna! Then, let's just meet at the theater.
Anna: O.K. What time ___(C)___ meet?
Dad: How about 12? Then, we can have lunch together, too.
Anna: You're the best, Dad!

11 위 대화의 빈칸 (A)~(C)에 알맞은 말을 쓰시오.

➡ (A) _____ (B) _____ (C) _____

12 위 대화를 읽고 다음 물음에 대해 영어로 답하시오.

Q: Why does Anna have no school next Wednesday?

➡ Because it's _____.

13 우리말에 맞게 주어진 어구를 이용하여 영어로 쓰시오.

세상을 위해 뭔가 특별한 일을 한다면, 세상은 변할 것이다. (if / something / the world / do / change / special / for)

➡ _____

_____

14 다음 우리말을 올바르게 영작한 것은?

> 나는 내가 여배우만큼 예쁘다고 생각해.

① I think I am prettier than an actress.
② I think I am so pretty as an actress.
③ I think I am as pretty as an actress.
④ I think I am the prettiest actress.
⑤ I think I am as pretty than an actress.

15 다음 우리말을 주어진 〈조건〉에 맞게 영작하시오.

> ┌─ 조건 ┐
> • 부정어 'not'을 사용할 것.
> • 'as+원급+as' 구문을 사용할 것.

> 그는 나만큼 TV를 많이 보지 않는다.

➡ _____ I do.

16 다음 빈칸에 공통으로 들어갈 말은? (대 · 소문자 무시)

> (1) You should check _____ it will rain during the trip.
> (2) _____ your bag is too heavy, I'll help you to carry it.

① that　② whether　③ if
④ when　⑤ which

17 다음 중 밑줄 친 부분의 쓰임이 다른 것은?

① Do you know if he is a tailor?
② I am not sure if she is Korean or not.
③ They want to know if the answer is right.
④ He wonders if she likes James.
⑤ We will go swimming if the weather is good.

18 다음 중 주어진 문장을 어법상 바르게 고친 것이 아닌 것은?

① My room is as not large as yours.
→ My room is not as large as yours.
② This donkey is as bigger as that horse.
→ This donkey is so big as that horse.
③ I'll join the club if you will teach me how to snowboard.
→ I'll join the club if you teach me how to snowboard.
④ If you will find something valuable, you should keep it in the safe.
→ If you find something valuable, you should keep it in the safe. *safe: 금고
⑤ Her dress looks as love as mine.
→ Her dress looks as lovely as mine.

19 다음 중 어법상 어색한 문장을 고르시오.

① If my mom catches a cold, I will do the dishes for her.
② I can finish the work if you help me.
③ If you want to succeed in life, you will have to study harder.
④ Bills are not so heavy so coins.
⑤ He kicks the ball as hard as he can.

*bill: 지폐

20 다음 중 어법상 바르지 않은 문장은 몇 개인가?

> • This tool is not so useful as that one.
> • I read as many books as she does.
> • The subway is as faster as the train.
> • We will go swimming if the weather will be fine tomorrow.
> • My mother is as tall as my father.

① 1개　② 2개　③ 3개　④ 4개　⑤ 5개

21 다음 빈칸에 들어갈 형태로 알맞은 것은?

• If my friends _____ their promises, I will talk to them about it.

① breaks　　② will break
③ broken　　④ break
⑤ won't break

22 다음 교통수단에 관한 표를 보고 as ~ as를 이용하여 비교하는 문장을 완성하시오.

Transportation	Subway	Bus	Taxi
Speed	60km	80km	80km
Fare	1,200 won	1,200 won	3,000 won

(1) The subway cannot go _____ the bus. (speed)

(2) The bus is _____ the taxi. (speed)

(3) The subway is _____ the bus. (fare)

23 다음 중 의미가 다른 하나는?

① I'm not as old as you.
② You are older than I.
③ I'm younger than you.
④ I am as young as you.
⑤ You are not as young as I.

24 다음 우리말에 맞게 주어진 단어를 이용하여 빈칸을 채우시오.

(1) 그녀의 얼굴은 CD만큼이나 작다. (small)
➡ Her face is _____ a CD.

(2) 나는 그녀만큼 빨리 달릴 수 있다. (fast)
➡ I can _____ she can.

(3) 나는 너만큼 키가 크고 싶어.
➡ I want to be _____ you.

25 다음 문장에서 틀린 것을 바르게 고치시오.

• Justin will not go if Judy won't go.

_____ ➡ _____

26 다음 문장에서 어법상 틀린 부분을 찾아 바르게 고치시오.

(1) I won't wash my car if it will rain.
_____ ➡ _____

(2) I'm not sure if my grandma comes tomorrow.
_____ ➡ _____

Reading

[27~28] 다음 글을 읽고 물음에 답하시오.

Welcome, everyone! Tonight, we are going to ___ⓐ___ Giacomo Puccini's opera *Turandot*. ⓑLike many other famous operas, *Turandot* is in Italian because opera started in Italy in the 16th century. Before we begin, I'd like to tell you the storyline of the opera *Turandot*. You will appreciate it better if you know the story.

27 위 글의 빈칸 ⓐ에 들어갈 알맞은 말을 고르시오.

① practice　　② perform
③ work　　④ achieve
⑤ complete

28 위 글의 밑줄 친 ⓑLike와 같은 의미로 쓰인 것을 고르시오.

① Do you <u>like</u> vegetables?
② I <u>like</u> playing tennis.
③ Which pen do you <u>like</u> best?
④ I, <u>like</u> everyone else, make mistakes.
⑤ I <u>like</u> my coffee strong.

[29~31] 다음 글을 읽고 물음에 답하시오.

Turandot, a Chinese princess, is a woman of great beauty, but she is as cold as ice. (①) Any prince who wants to marry her must answer three riddles. (②) If he fails, he must die. (③) No one ⓐ<u>has</u> ever <u>been</u> able to answer them. (④) He becomes the first man to answer all three riddles. (⑤)

29 위 글의 흐름으로 보아, 주어진 문장이 들어가기에 가장 적절한 곳은?

One day, a brave prince falls in love with her at first sight.

①   ②   ③   ④   ⑤

30 위 글의 밑줄 친 ⓐ와 현재완료의 용법이 같은 것을 모두 고르시오.

① I <u>have seen</u> a tiger before.
② He <u>has lost</u> his camera.
③ How many times <u>have</u> you <u>read</u> it?
④ She <u>has</u> just <u>arrived</u> here.
⑤ I <u>have known</u> him for five years.

31 위 글의 내용과 일치하지 <u>않는</u> 것은?

① Turandot는 중국의 공주이다.
② Turandot와 결혼하기를 원하는 왕자는 반드시 세 가지 수수께끼에 답해야 한다.
③ 수수께끼에 답하지 못하는 왕자는 죽어야 한다.
④ 지금까지 수수께끼에 답하지 못해 죽은 왕자는 없다.
⑤ 어느 날, 어떤 용감한 왕자가 Turandot에게 첫눈에 반한다.

[32~33] 다음 글을 읽고 물음에 답하시오.

However, Turandot does not want to marry the prince. He is nothing (A)[more / less] than a stranger to her. ⓐ<u>He then gives her a riddle of his own.</u> He asks her, "What is my name?" He adds, "If you answer correctly, I will (B)[agree / refuse] to die. If you answer incorrectly, you will have to marry me."

Turandot must find the answer before dawn, but his riddle is as (C)[different / difficult] as hers. She says to everyone, "No one will go to sleep until someone finds out his name."

32 위 글의 괄호 (A)~(C)에서 문맥이나 어법상 알맞은 낱말을 골라 쓰시오.

➡ (A) _____ (B) _____ (C) _____

33 다음 중 3형식 문장으로 바꿀 때 필요한 전치사가 밑줄 친 ⓐ와 같은 문장을 모두 고르시오.

① Did he buy you the present?
② She sent Tom an email.
③ Mom made me a birthday cake.
④ He asked me a question.
⑤ Who wrote you the thank-you note?

01 출제율 95%

다음 짝지어진 단어의 관계가 같도록 빈칸에 알맞은 말을 쓰시오.

| proposal : suggestion = reply to : _____ |

02 출제율 90%

우리말에 맞게 빈칸에 세 단어의 알맞은 말을 쓰시오.

| 금은 단지 돌에 지나지 않는다. |
| Gold is _____ a stone. |

03 출제율 95%

다음 우리말 해석에 맞게 빈칸을 완성하시오. (철자가 주어진 경우 그 철자로 시작할 것)

(1) 중국의 공주 Turandot는 굉장히 아름다운 여인이지만, 그녀는 얼음처럼 차갑습니다.
➡ Turandot, a Chinese princess, is a woman of great _____, but she is as _____ as ice.

(2) 우리는 지아코모 푸치니의 오페라 《투란도트》를 공연할 것입니다.
➡ We are going to _____ Giacomo Puccini's opera *Turandot*.

(3) 만약 답이 틀리면 당신은 저와 결혼해야 할 것입니다.
➡ If you answer _____, you will have to _____ me.

(4) 어느 날, 어떤 용감한 왕자가 그녀에게 첫눈에 반합니다.
➡ One day, a brave prince _____ _____ _____ with her at first _____.

04 출제율 90%

다음 영영풀이에 해당하는 단어는?

| earlier than the time expected |

① tomorrow   ② already
③ near   ④ hardly
⑤ still

[05~07] 다음 대화를 읽고 물음에 답하시오.

A: ⓐLet's go on a picnic this weekend. ①
B: Good idea. ② What time shall we meet? ③
A: ⓑHow about 10 o'clock on Saturday?
B: ④ O.K. ⑤ See you there.

05 출제율 100%

위 대화의 ①~⑤ 중 주어진 문장이 들어갈 알맞은 곳은?

| Let's meet at the subway station. |

①   ②   ③   ④   ⑤

06 출제율 85%

밑줄 친 ⓐ와 같은 의미를 가진 문장을 쓰고자 한다. 괄호 안에 주어진 어구를 알맞게 배열하시오

(1) (go / why / we / on / don't / a picnic / this weekend / ?)
➡ _____

(2) (going / what / on / this weekend / a picnic / about / ?)
➡ _____

07 출제율 95%

밑줄 친 ⓑ의 목적으로 알맞은 것은?

① 시간 묻기   ② 비교하며 말하기
③ 수정하기   ④ 약속 정하기
⑤ 의도 표현하기

[08~11] 다음 대화를 읽고 물음에 답하시오.

> Anna: Dad, _____(A)_____ I have no school next Wednesday.
>
> Dad: Really? Why not?
>
> Anna: It's our school's 75th anniversary.
>
> Dad: Oh, I see.
>
> Anna: Can we do something together that day?
>
> Dad: I guess I can take the afternoon off. What do you want to do?
>
> Anna: Why don't we go see a musical at Bravo Theater near your work? (B)수요일에 가면 할인을 받을 수 있어요.
>
> Dad: Good idea, Anna! Then, let's just meet at the theater.
>
> Anna: O.K. (C)몇 시에 만날까요?
>
> Dad: How about 12? Then, we can have lunch together, too.
>
> Anna: (D)You're the best, Dad!

08 출제율 95%

다음 영어 설명을 참고하여, 위 대화의 빈칸 (A)에 들어갈 말을 고르시오.

> used before telling someone something interesting or surprising

① you know why?
② what did it say?
③ of course.
④ well done.
⑤ guess what!

09 출제율 90%

밑줄 친 (B)의 우리말과 같도록 다음 문장의 빈칸을 완성하시오.

➡ We can _____ a _____ _____ we go on a Wednesday.

10 출제율 85%

밑줄 친 (C)의 우리말을 괄호 안의 단어를 이용하여 영어로 쓰시오.

➡ _____ (shall, meet)

11 출제율 90%

밑줄 친 (D)에서 추측할 수 있는 Anna의 기분으로 가장 알맞은 것은?

① sad
② lonely
③ happy
④ relaxed
⑤ ashamed

12 출제율 95%

대화의 빈칸에 들어갈 표현으로 적절하지 <u>않은</u> 것은?

> A: Oh, we're going to be late for the concert.
>
> B: _____ The subway will be faster than the bus at this time of the day.

① Let's take the subway.
② How about taking the subway?
③ Are you taking the subway?
④ Why don't we take the subway?
⑤ What about taking the subway?

13 출제율 100%

대화의 흐름상 <u>어색한</u> 곳을 고르시오.

> B: Mom, I got only one question ① <u>wrong</u> on the Korean history exam!
>
> W: ②<u>Great!</u> I was sure you would do ③<u>well</u>. Why don't we go out to ④ <u>appreciate</u> tonight?
>
> B: Yes! Can we have pizza for dinner?
>
> W: ⑤<u>Of course</u>, Joe. I'll call your dad.

① ② ③ ④ ⑤

14 출제율 95%
다음 문장의 빈칸에 공통으로 들어갈 말은?

> • You will be late for the class _____ you miss the subway.
> • _____ the weather is bad, I won't go hiking.

① as[As] ② if[If]
③ because[Because] ④ which[Which]
⑤ though[Though]

15 출제율 85%
다음 표를 보고 틀린 문장을 고르시오.

	Tom	Jane	Mike
나이	15	14	15
키	163	170	170
성적	90	90	70

① Tom is as old as Mike.
② Tom isn't as tall as Jane.
③ Tom is as smart as Jane.
④ Jane is as tall as Mike.
⑤ Jane isn't as smart as Mike.

16 출제율 100%
다음 〈보기〉에서 알맞은 단어를 골라 빈칸에 쓰시오. (필요하면 단어를 변형하시오.)

> ┤ 보기 ├
> study finish rain give
> leave change meet hurry

(1) Can I watch TV if I _____ my homework?
(2) If you _____ this book to him, he will be glad.
(3) If your mom _____ her mind, let me know.

17 출제율 90%
다음 중 어법상 어색한 것은?

① The prince then sings the most famous aria of the whole opera.
② No one will go to sleep until someone will find out his name.
③ My sister is as tall as my father.
④ If you don't give me candy, I will cry!
⑤ If you want to experience something special, come and enjoy the festival.

18 출제율 95%
다음 중 어법상 어색한 것은?

① I can run as fast as Junsu.
② This flower is as pretty as that one.
③ His backpack is as bigger as mine.
④ You are not as smart as I.
⑤ His cell phone is as good as mine.

19 출제율 95%
밑줄 친 부분의 쓰임이 나머지와 다른 것은?

① If he is honest, I'll employ him.
② You can be successful in life if you work hard.
③ I will meet him if he visits you.
④ If you do the work, your parents will be happy.
⑤ Can you tell me if he will come?

20 출제율 90%
다음 〈보기〉의 단어를 이용하여 빈칸에 알맞은 말을 쓰시오.

> ┤ 보기 ├
> well tall kind good big heavy

(1) Jinhee is 150cm tall and I am 170cm tall. Jinhee is _____ me.
(2) Katy doesn't sing as _____ as Jessica.
(3) Subin is 65kg and Jongmin is 65kg, too. Subin is _____ Jongmin.

[21~23] 다음 글을 읽고 물음에 답하시오.

Welcome, everyone! Tonight, we are going to perform Giacomo Puccini's opera *Turandot*. Like many other famous operas, *Turandot* is ___ⓐ___ Italian because opera started ___ⓑ___ Italy ___ⓒ___ the 16th century. Before we begin, I'd like to tell you the storyline of the opera *Turandot*. You will ⓓappreciate it better if you know the story.

출제율 95%

21 위 글의 빈칸 ⓐ~ⓒ에 공통으로 들어갈 전치사를 고르시오.

① for ② from ③ in
④ at ⑤ on

출제율 85%

22 위 글의 밑줄 친 ⓓappreciate와 같은 의미로 쓰인 것을 고르시오.

① This is a great chance to appreciate the architecture of Korea.
② I'd appreciate some help.
③ You won't appreciate how expensive it is.
④ Thanks for coming. I appreciate it.
⑤ I failed to appreciate the distance between the two cities.

출제율 90%

23 다음 질문에 대한 알맞은 대답을 주어진 단어로 시작하여 쓰시오. (3 단어)

Q: How will you be able to appreciate the opera *Turandot* better?
A: By _____ .

➡ _____

[24~26] 다음 글을 읽고 물음에 답하시오.

ⓐTurandot, a Chinese princess, is a woman of great beauty, but she is as sweet as honey. Any prince who wants to marry her must answer three ___ⓑ___ . If he fails, he must die. No one has ever been able to answer them. One day, a brave prince falls in love with her at first sight. He becomes the first man to answer all three ___ⓑ___ .

출제율 95%

24 위 글의 밑줄 친 ⓐ에서 흐름상 어색한 부분을 고치시오.

_____ ➡ _____

출제율 90%

25 주어진 영영풀이를 참고하여 빈칸 ⓑ에 철자 r로 시작하는 단어를 쓰시오.

puzzles or jokes in which you ask a question that seems to be nonsense but which has a clever or amusing answer

➡ _____

출제율 100%

26 위 글을 읽고 알 수 없는 것을 고르시오.

① Turandot의 신분
② Turandot의 외모
③ Turandot와 결혼하려는 왕자들이 통과해야만 하는 절차
④ 절차를 통과하지 못한 왕자들이 감수해야 하는 위험
⑤ 절차를 통과하지 못한 왕자들의 숫자

서술형 실전문제

01 주어진 단어를 이용하여 대화의 빈칸을 완성하시오.

> A: Let's go on a picnic this weekend.
> B: Good idea. _____(A)_____ (time, shall, meet)
> A: How about 10 o'clock on Saturday?
> B: O.K. _____(B)_____ (shall, meet)
> A: Let's meet at the subway station. See you there.

➡ (A) _____
　 (B) _____

02 대화의 빈칸에 제안을 하는 표현을 이용하여 6 단어로 문장을 완성하시오.

> M: _____? The subway will be faster than the bus at this time of day.
> W: That's a good idea.

➡ _____

03 대화의 빈칸 (A)~(C)에 알맞은 표현을 〈보기〉에서 찾아 쓰시오.

> ┤ 보기 ├
> • Why don't we go see *Wonder Woman*?
> • What shall we do this afternoon?
> • How about 4 o'clock?

> A: (A)_____
> B: (B)_____
> A: Good idea! What time shall we meet?
> B: (C)_____
> A: O.K. Let's meet at Moon Theater.

➡ (A) _____
　 (B) _____
　 (C) _____

04 다음 우리말에 맞게 주어진 단어를 이용하여 빈칸에 알맞은 말을 쓰시오.

(1) 그녀의 반지는 나의 것만큼 비싸다.
➡ Her ring is _____. (expensive)

(2) Cathy는 Juliet만큼 친절하지 않다.
➡ Cathy is _____ Juliet. (so, kind)

(3) 그가 내일 여기로 오면, 나에게 데려와.
➡ If he _____ here tomorrow, _____ him _____ me. (come, take)

05 다음 문장에서 어법상 틀린 부분을 찾아 바르게 고치시오.

(1) If it will rain tomorrow, we won't go on a picnic.
_____ ➡ _____

(2) I'll call you if I will need your help.
_____ ➡ _____

06 다음 표를 보고 문장의 빈칸을 채우시오.

조건 1: 번호에 해당하는 표현을 찾아 주어, 동사를 포함한 완전한 문장으로 쓰시오.

조건 2: 동등 비교 표현을 이용하여 쓰시오.

	Minho	Mike	Jane
(1) Age	14	13	14
(2) Height	160	160	165
(3) Weight	50	40	50

(1) Minho is _____ Jane.
　 But Mike is _____ Minho.

(2) Minho is _____ Mike.
　 But _____ Jane.

(3) Minho is _____ Jane.
　 But Mike _____ Minho.

07 다음 문장에서 어법상 **틀린** 부분을 찾아 바르게 고치시오.

> I'll stop talking about it if you won't pay attention to me.

_____ ➡ _____

[08~10] 다음 글을 읽고 물음에 답하시오.

> Turandot, a Chinese princess, is a woman of great beauty, but she is _____ⓐ_____. (A) [Some / Any] prince who wants to marry her must answer three riddles. If he fails, he must die. No one has (B)[ever / never] been able to answer them. One day, a brave prince falls in love with her at first (C)[see / sight]. He becomes the first man to answer all three riddles.

08 다음과 같은 뜻이 되도록 위 글의 빈칸 ⓐ에 들어갈 알맞은 말을 as와 ice를 포함하여 쓰시오.

> very cold

➡ _____

09 위 글의 괄호 (A)~(C)에서 문맥이나 어법상 알맞은 낱말을 골라 쓰시오.

➡ (A) _____ (B) _____ (C) _____

10 본문의 내용과 일치하도록 다음 빈칸에 알맞은 단어를 쓰시오. (본문의 단어를 변형하여 쓰시오.)

> All the princes who tried to answer three riddles at the risk of their lives have _____ to answer them except one prince.

[11~13] 다음 글을 읽고 물음에 답하시오.

> However, Turandot does not want to marry the prince. ⓐ그는 그녀에게 단지 낯선 사람일 뿐입니다. He then gives her a riddle of his own. He asks her, "What is my name?" He adds, "If you answer correctly, I will agree to die. If you answer incorrectly, you will have to marry me."
> Turandot must find the answer before dawn, but his riddle is as difficult as ⓑhers. She says to everyone, "No one will go to sleep until someone finds out his name."

11 위 글의 밑줄 친 ⓐ의 우리말에 맞게 주어진 어휘를 이용하여 9 단어로 영작하시오.

> nothing

➡ _____

12 위 글의 밑줄 친 ⓑhers가 가리키는 것을 영어로 쓰시오.

➡ _____

13 본문의 내용과 일치하도록 다음 빈칸 (A)와 (B)에 알맞은 단어를 쓰시오.

> If Turandot answers the prince's riddle incorrectly, she will have to (A)_____ _____. If Turandot answers correctly, he will agree (B)_____ _____.

창의사고력 서술형 문제

01 다음 그림을 보고 놀이동산에서 해야 할 일을 제안하는 대화를 〈보기〉를 참고하여 완성하시오.

take a train ride
visit the flower garden
watch a musical
ride the water slide
ride the roller coaster

┌─── 보기 ───┐
A: What shall we do at the park?
B: Why don't we see a magic show?
A: That's a good idea.
└───────────┘

02 다음 그림을 보고 지하철과 버스의 속도와 요금을 비교하는 문장을 'as ~ as'를 이용하여 완성하시오. (fast, expensive를 사용할 것)

Transportation	Subway	Bus
Speed	60km	80km
Fare	1,200 won	1,200 won

(1) _____

(2) _____

03 다음 내용을 바탕으로 영화의 감상문을 쓰시오.

┌───┐
• What is the title?   • What did you think about it?
  La La Land   – beautiful and moving songs
• What is it about?   – a good story
  the dreams and love of Mia and Sebastian
└───┘

┌───┐
___(A)___ of *La La Land*   ★ ★ ★ ★ ☆
I saw *La La Land* last Friday. It is about ___(B)___ of Mia and Sebastian. I enjoyed its
___(C)___ songs. The ___(D)___ was also as good as the songs. If you are looking for a
good musical movie, you should see this movie.

                                                    by Kim Jisu on Aug. 11
└───┘

단원별 모의고사

01 다음 단어에 대한 영어 설명이 <u>어색한</u> 것은?

① moving: causing strong feelings of sadness or sympathy

② storyline: the series of events that happen in a book, film, play, etc.

③ marry: to become the legally accepted husband or wife of someone in an official or religious ceremony

④ riddle: a type of question that describes something in a difficult and confusing way and has a clever or funny answer

⑤ appreciate: to do something enjoyable on a special occasion

02 다음 우리말 해석에 맞게 알맞은 단어를 쓰시오.

(1) 나는 오후에 휴무를 할 수 있을 것 같구나.
➡ I guess I can _____ the afternoon _____.

(2) Karen, 오늘 학교 연극의 우리 역할을 연습하자.
➡ Karen, let's _____ our parts for the school _____ today.

(3) 오늘 축하하러 나가는 건 어때?
➡ Why _____ we go out to _____ tonight?

[03~04] 다음 글을 읽고 물음에 답하시오.

I saw *La La Land* last Friday. It is about the dreams and love of Mia and Sebastian. (A)<u>나는 그것의 아름답고 감동적인 이야기가 좋았어.</u> The story was also ___ⓐ___ the songs. If you are looking for a good musical movie, you should see this movie.

03 위 글의 빈칸 ⓐ에 들어갈 말로 알맞은 것은?

① as well as   ② as better as
③ as good as   ④ good as
⑤ the best

04 위 글의 밑줄 친 (A)의 우리말에 맞게 빈칸에 알맞은 단어를 쓰시오. (m으로 시작할 것)

➡ I enjoyed its beautiful and _____ songs.

[05~06] 다음 대화를 읽고 물음에 답하시오.

M: Liz, hurry up. It's already 6 o'clock.
W: Oh, we're going to be late for the concert.
M: Why don't we take the subway? The subway will be faster than the bus at this time of day.
W: That's a good idea.

05 다음 영영풀이에 해당하는 단어를 대화에서 찾아 쓰시오.

happening or arriving after the planned, expected, usual, or necessary time

➡ _____

06 위 대화를 읽고 답할 수 <u>없는</u> 질문을 고르시오.

① What time is it now?
② Where are they going to go?
③ When does the concert begin?
④ What will they take to go to the concert?
⑤ Which is faster, the subway or the bus?

[07~08] 다음 대화를 읽고 물음에 답하시오.

Joe: Mom, I got only one question ①wrong on the Korean history exam!

Mom: Great! I was sure you would ②do poorly. ③Why don't we go out to ④celebrate tonight?

Joe: Yes! Can we ⑤have pizza for dinner?

Mom: Of course, Joe. I'll call your dad.

07 위 대화의 ①~⑤ 중 어휘의 쓰임이 어색한 것은?

①   ②   ③   ④   ⑤

08 위 대화의 내용과 일치하지 않는 것은?

① Joe took the Korean history exam.

② Joe's mom suggests going out tonight.

③ Joe got only one question wrong on the exam.

④ Joe's mom did well on the exam.

⑤ Joe's family will go out for dinner.

09 다음 중 짝지어진 대화가 어색한 것은?

① A: Why don't we see a magic show?
   B: That's a good idea.

② A: Karen, let's practice our parts for the school play today.
   B: O.K. What time shall we meet?

③ A: Where shall we play?
   B: How about at the park near your place?

④ A: What time shall we meet?
   B: How about at the bus stop?

⑤ A: What shall we do this afternoon?
   B: Why don't we go see *Wonder Woman*?

[10~12] 다음 대화를 읽고 물음에 답하시오.

Anna: Dad, guess what! I have no school next Wednesday.

Dad: Really? _____(A)_____

Anna: It's our school's 75th anniversary.

Dad: Oh, I see.

Anna: Can we do something together that day?

Dad: I guess I can take the afternoon off. (B)뭘 하고 싶니?

Anna: Why don't we go see a musical at Bravo Theater near your work? We can get a discount if we go on a Wednesday.

Dad: Good idea, Anna! Then, let's just meet at the theater.

Anna: O.K. What time shall we meet?

Dad: How about 12? Then, we can have lunch together, too.

Anna: You're the best, Dad!

10 빈칸 (A)에 알맞은 말은?

① You know what?   ② I know.

③ Why not?   ④ Excuse me?

⑤ What are you going to do?

11 밑줄 친 (B)의 우리말에 맞게 주어진 단어를 이용하여 영작하시오.

➡ _____(what / want / do)

12 위 대화의 내용과 일치하지 않는 것은?

① Next Wednesday is Anna's school's 75th anniversary.

② Anna won't go to school next Wednesday.

③ Anna and her dad will go see a movie next Wednesday.

④ Anna and her dad will meet at the theater.

⑤ Anna and her dad will have lunch together.

13 다음 괄호 안의 단어를 알맞은 곳에 넣어 문장을 다시 쓰시오.

(1) Anna is as as Julie. (beautiful)

➡ _____

(2) I will let you go out you do finish your job. (if)

➡ _____

14 다음 주어진 문장은 어법상 틀린 문장이다. 바르게 고친 것이 아닌 것은?

① I am not as braver as Jack.
→ I am not as brave as Jack.

② He drove so fast as I.
→ He drove as fast as I

③ Her hair is as long as I.
→ Her hair is as long as me.

④ This bicycle is as not expensive as that one.
→ This bicycle is not as expensive as that one.

⑤ If she will go to the island, she will spend all day swimming.
→ If she goes to the island, she will spend all day swimming.

15 다음 문장에서 어법상 어색한 곳을 찾아 바르게 고치시오.

(1) My room is as not larger as yours.

_____ ➡ _____

(2) This donkey is as bigger as that horse.

_____ ➡ _____

16 다음 그림과 같은 의미가 되도록 'as ~ as'를 이용하여 알맞은 단어를 쓰시오.

Tom   Ann

➡ Ann is _____ Tom.

17 다음 두 문장을 한 문장으로 알맞게 바꾼 것은?

• I will go swimming.
• It will not rain tomorrow.

① I will go swimming if it didn't rain tomorrow.

② I will go swimming if it will not rain tomorrow.

③ I go swimming if it will not rain tomorrow.

④ I will go swimming if it does not rain tomorrow.

⑤ I go swimming if it do not rain tomorrow.

18 다음 중 어법상 어색한 것은?

① If it is sunny tomorrow, how about playing soccer?

② If I'm not busy tomorrow, I will go with you.

③ That tower is as high as this tower.

④ This dog is as big as that dog.

⑤ Tennis is as less popular as soccer.

[19~20] 다음 글을 읽고 물음에 답하시오.

Welcome, everyone! Tonight, we are going to perform Giacomo Puccini's opera *Turandot*. Like many other famous operas, *Turandot* is in ____ⓐ____ because opera started in Italy in the 16th century. Before we begin, I'd like to tell you the ⓑstoryline of the opera *Turandot*. You will appreciate it better if you know the story.

19 본문의 한 단어를 변형하여 위 글의 빈칸 ⓐ에 들어갈 알맞은 말을 쓰시오.

➡ _____

20 위 글의 밑줄 친 ⓑstoryline과 바꿔 쓸 수 있는 말을 고르시오.

① theme　　② setting　　③ plot
④ concept　　⑤ subject

[21~22] 다음 글을 읽고 물음에 답하시오.

Turandot, a Chinese princess, is a woman ____ⓐ____ great beauty, but she is as cold as ice. ⓑAny prince who wants to marry her must ask three riddles. If he fails, he must die. No one has ever been able to answer them. One day, a brave prince falls in love ____ⓒ____ her at first sight. He becomes the first man to answer all three riddles.

21 위 글의 빈칸 ⓐ와 ⓒ에 들어갈 전치사가 바르게 짝지어진 것은?

① for – from　　② of – at
③ of – with　　④ for – at
⑤ on – with

22 위 글의 밑줄 친 ⓑ에서 흐름상 어색한 부분을 찾아 고치시오.

_____ ➡ _____

[23~24] 다음 글을 읽고 물음에 답하시오.

However, Turandot does not want to marry the prince. He is nothing more than a stranger to her. He then gives her a riddle of his own. He asks her, "What is my name?" He adds, "If you answer correctly, I will agree ⓐto die. If you answer incorrectly, you will have to marry me."

Turandot must find the answer before dawn, but his riddle is as difficult as hers. She says to everyone, "No one will go to sleep until someone finds out his name."

23 아래 〈보기〉에서 위 글의 밑줄 친 ⓐto die와 문법적 쓰임이 같은 문장의 개수를 고르시오.

┌─ 보기 ─┐
① I would be happy to be helpful to you.
② She learned to play the piano.
③ This book is too difficult to read.
④ He has a few friends to play with.
⑤ Her plan is to go to the movies tonight.
└────┘

① 1개　② 2개　③ 3개　④ 4개　⑤ 5개

24 위 글의 내용과 일치하지 않는 것은?

① Turandot는 그 왕자와 결혼하기를 원하지 않는다.
② 왕자는 Turandot에게 단지 낯선 사람일 뿐이다.
③ 왕자는 Turandot에게 자신의 수수께끼를 낸다.
④ 만약 Turandot의 답이 틀리면 왕자는 죽는 것에 동의할 것이다.
⑤ Turandot는 동이 트기 전에 수수께끼의 답을 찾아야 한다.

Lesson

6

Food in History

🎤 의사소통 기능

- 선호하는 것 묻고 답하기
  A: Do you prefer summer or winter?
  B: I prefer summer.

- 추천 부탁하기
  Could you recommend a book for me?

🎤 언어 형식

- 수동태
  This dish **was called** tangpyeongchae.

- something/someone+형용사
  King Yeongjo offered them **something special**.

교과서
Words & Expressions

Key Words

- **alone** [əlóun] 튄 혼자, 홀로
- **back** [bæk] 몡 등
- **beginner** [bigínər] 몡 초보자
- **comedy** [kámədi] 몡 희극, 코미디
- **cookbook** [kúkbùk] 몡 요리책
- **culture** [kʌ́ltʃər] 몡 문화
- **dessert** [dizə́ːrt] 몡 후식, 디저트
- **different** [dífərənt] 혱 다른
- **disappointed** [dìsəpɔ́intid] 혱 실망한
- **dish** [diʃ] 몡 음식, 요리
- **fried** [fraid] 혱 튀긴
- **fried fish** 생선 튀김
- **fried vegetables** 채소 볶음
- **fortune teller** 점쟁이
- **funny** [fʌ́ni] 혱 웃긴, 재미있는
- **half** [hæf] 몡 반 혱 반의, 절반의
- **half-moon** [hǽfmùːn] 몡 반달
- **harmony** [háːrməni] 몡 화합, 조화
- **hit** [hit] 몡 성공, 히트작
- **honesty** [ánisti] 몡 정직함
- **however** [hauévər] 튄 하지만
- **imaginary** [imǽdʒənèri] 혱 상상의, 가상의
- **indoor** [índɔr] 혱 실내의
- **ingredient** [ingríːdiənt] 몡 재료
- **interesting** [íntərəstiŋ] 혱 흥미로운
- **Italian** [itǽljən] 혱 이탈리아의
- **kingdom** [kíŋdəm] 몡 왕국
- **mainly** [méinli] 튄 주로
- **mean** [miːn] 동 의미하다
- **meat** [miːt] 몡 육류, 고기
- **offer** [ɔ́ːfər] 동 제안하다, 권하다
- **official** [əfíʃəl] 몡 신하, 관리, 공직자
- **order** [ɔ́ːrdər] 동 주문하다
- **outdoor** [áutdɔr] 혱 실외의
- **party** [páːrti] 몡 정당
- **policy** [páləsi] 몡 정책
- **political** [pəlítikəl] 혱 정치의, 정당의
- **pot** [pat] 몡 냄비, 솥
- **prefer** [prifə́ːr] 동 선호하다
- **recently** [ríːsntli] 튄 최근에
- **recommend** [rèkəménd] 동 추천하다
- **restaurant** [réstərənt] 몡 식당
- **rice flour** 쌀가루
- **scholar** [skálər] 몡 학자
- **seafood** [síːfud] 몡 해산물
- **servant** [sə́ːrvənt] 몡 신하, 하인
- **shape** [ʃeip] 몡 모양
- **since** [sins] 전 ~ 이후로
- **special** [spéʃəl] 혱 특별한
- **symbolize** [símbəlàiz] 동 상징하다
- **table tennis** 탁구
- **traditional** [trədíʃənl] 혱 전통의, 전통적인
- **turtle** [tə́ːrtl] 몡 거북
- **vegetable** [védʒətəbl] 몡 야채, 채소

Key Expressions

- **be afraid of** ~을 두려워하다
- **become worried about** ~에 대해 걱정하게 되다
- **be named after** ~의 이름을 따서 지어지다
- **by oneself** 혼자서, 홀로(= **alone**)
- **dive into** ~으로 뛰어들다
- **have been to**+장소 ~에 가 본 적이 있다
- **How about**+명사/**-ing**? ~은 어때?
- **I'm thinking of ...ing** ~할까 생각 중이야
- **look for** ~을 찾다
- **look like**+명사 ~처럼 보이다
- **on sale** 세일 중
- **on the other hand** 반면에
- **Why don't you**+동사원형 ~? ~하는 게 어때?

Word Power

※ 서로 반대되는 뜻을 가진 어휘

☐ **indoor**(실내의) ↔ **outdoor**(실외의)

☐ **different**(다른) ↔ **same**(같은)

☐ **beginner**(초보자) ↔ **expert**(전문가)

☐ **famous**(유명한) ↔ **unknown**(알려지지 않은)

※ 서로 비슷한 뜻을 가진 단어

☐ **alone** : **by oneself** (혼자)

☐ **offer** : **propose** (제안하다)

☐ **recently** : **lately** (최근에)

☐ **hit** : **success** (성공)

☐ **famous** : **well-known** (유명한)

☐ **imaginary** : **fictional** (가상의, 허구의)

English Dictionary

☐ **beginner** 초보자
→ a person who is starting to do something or learn something for the first time
어떤 것을 하기 시작하거나 처음으로 어떤 것을 배우는 사람

☐ **culture** 문화
→ the way of life, especially the general customs and beliefs, of a particular group of people at a particular time
특정한 시대에 특정한 집단의 사람들이 갖는 삶의 방식으로 특히 일반적인 관습이나 신념

☐ **dessert** 후식
→ sweet food eaten at the end of a meal
식사가 끝났을 때 먹는 단 음식

☐ **disappointed** 실망한
→ unhappy because someone or something was not as good as you hoped or expected
누군가나 무언가가 당신이 희망하거나 기대했던 것만큼 좋지 않았기 때문에 행복하지 않은

☐ **imaginary** 상상의, 가상의
→ created by and existing only in the mind
생각에 의해 만들어지고 생각 속에서만 존재하는

☐ **ingredient** 재료
→ a food that is used with other foods in the preparation of a particular dish
특별한 음식을 준비할 때 다른 음식과 함께 사용되는 음식

☐ **kingdom** 왕국
→ a country ruled by a king or queen
왕이나 여왕이 통치하는 나라

☐ **official** 관리, 신하
→ a person who has a position of responsibility in an organization
조직에서 책임 있는 지위를 가진 사람

☐ **order** 주문하다
→ to ask for something to be made, supplied, or delivered, especially in a restaurant or shop
특히 식당이나 가게에서 만들어지거나, 공급되거나, 배달될 어떤 것을 요청하다

☐ **party** 정당
→ an organization of people with particular political beliefs that competes in elections to try to win positions in local or national government
지방이나 국가 정부에서의 지위를 얻기 위해 선거에서 경쟁하는 특정한 정치적 신념을 가진 사람들의 조직

☐ **policy** 정책
→ a set of ideas or a plan of what to do in particular situations that has been agreed to officially by a group of people, a government, or a political party
특정한 상황에서 무엇을 해야 하는지에 대한 집단이나 정부, 또는 정당이 공식적으로 동의한 일련의 생각이나 계획

☐ **prefer** 선호하다
→ to like, choose, or want one thing rather than another
다른 것보다 하나를 좋아하거나 선택하거나 원하다

☐ **recommend** 추천하다
→ to suggest that someone or something would be good or suitable for a particular job or purpose
어떤 사람이나 어떤 것이 특정 직업이나 목적에 좋거나 적합할 것이라고 제안하다

☐ **scholar** 학자
→ a person who studies a subject in great detail, especially at a university
특히 대학에서 특정한 과목을 매우 세부적으로 공부하는 사람

☐ **servant** 하인, 신하
→ a person who is employed in another person's house, doing jobs such as cooking and cleaning, especially in the past
특히 과거에 다른 사람의 집에 고용되어 요리와 청소와 같은 일을 하는 사람

☐ **symbolize** 상징하다
→ to represent something
어떤 것을 나타내다

서답형

01 다음 짝지어진 두 단어의 관계가 같도록 빈칸에 알맞은 단어를 쓰시오.

> indoor : outdoor = same : _____

[02~03] 다음 빈칸에 들어갈 말로 가장 적절한 것은?

02

> How did tangpyeongchae and sinseollo get their names? Why does songpyeon look like a half moon? There are many interesting stories about our _____ food.

① new   ② popular
③ traditional   ④ foreign
⑤ imaginary

03

> I have added a special _____ to the food.

① policy   ② party
③ guest   ④ honesty
⑤ ingredient

[04~05] 다음 영영풀이에 해당하는 단어를 고르시오.

04

> an organization of people with particular political beliefs that competes in elections to try to win positions in local or national government

① government   ② party
③ kingdom   ④ state
⑤ official

05

> to like, choose, or want one thing rather than another

① offer   ② order   ③ love
④ prefer   ⑤ differ

06 밑줄 친 부분의 의미가 잘못된 것은?

① The color red <u>symbolizes</u> luck in Chinese culture. (상징하다)
② The government has announced a new <u>policy</u>. (정책)
③ Yulgok was a great <u>scholar</u> of Joseon. (학자)
④ My teacher has <u>recommended</u> the book to me. (명령했다)
⑤ I have been very busy <u>recently</u>. (최근에)

서답형

07 다음 〈영어 설명〉을 읽고 빈칸에 알맞은 말을 쓰시오.

> However, the king never listened to him. The scholar was so _____ that he went to live on a mountain.

> <영어 설명> unhappy because someone or something was not as good as you hoped or expected

➡ _____

서답형

08 다음 밑줄 친 단어와 같은 뜻을 가진 두 단어를 쓰시오.

> That is because the scholar lived like a sinseon, an imaginary person who lives <u>alone</u> in nature.

➡ _____

01 영영풀이에 해당하는 단어를 〈보기〉에서 찾아 첫 번째 칸에 쓰고, 두 번째 칸에는 우리말 뜻을 쓰시오.

┌─── 보기 ────
│ recommend / servant / culture / official
│ / symbolize / order / policy
└──────────

(1) _____ : a set of ideas or a plan of what to do in particular situations that has been agreed to officially by a group of people, a government, or a political party: _____

(2) _____ : to suggest that someone or something would be good or suitable for a particular job or purpose: _____

(3) _____ : to represent something: _____

02 다음 빈칸에 알맞은 단어를 〈보기〉에서 골라 쓰시오. (형태 변화 가능)

┌─── 보기 ────
│ mainly / pot / fortune teller / worry
└──────────

(1) The king needs a _____ to know the future of his kingdom.

(2) Add some milk and chicken to the _____.

(3) The king became _____ about his kingdom.

(4) While he lived there by himself, he _____ ate vegetables.

03 영어 설명을 읽고, 문장의 빈칸에 들어갈 알맞은 단어를 쓰시오. (주어진 글자로 시작할 것.)

┌──────────────────────┐
│ not long ago, or at a time that started not │
│ long ago │
└──────────────────────┘

(1) I haven't seen a movie r_____. Could you recommend a good one?

┌──────────────────────┐
│ a person who studies a subject in great │
│ detail, especially at a university │
└──────────────────────┘

(2) In the time of King Yeonsan, there was a s_____ who was famous for his honesty.

04 우리말과 같은 의미가 되도록 빈칸에 알맞은 단어를 쓰시오.

(1) 정직은 최상의 정책이다.
➡ _____ is the best _____.

(2) 정당은 그 문제를 해결해야 한다.
➡ The _____ needs to solve the problem.

05 다음 주어진 우리말에 맞게 빈칸을 채우시오. (필요하면 변형하여 쓰시오.)

(1) 백제는 보름달과 같지만 신라는 반달과 같다.
➡ Baekje is like a full moon, but Silla is like a _____.

(2) 영조는 이 음식처럼 네 당파가 화합을 이루어 일해야 한다는 것을 말하고 싶었다.
➡ Yeongjo wanted to say that the four _____ should work in _____ like this dish.

(3) 그녀는 정부 관리다.
➡ She is an _____ in the government.

Conversation

1 선호하는 것 묻고 답하기

> **A** Do you prefer summer or winter? 넌 여름이 더 좋으니, 겨울이 더 좋으니?
>
> **B** I prefer summer. 나는 여름이 더 좋아.

■ 둘 중 더 좋아하는 것에 대해 물을 때는 'Do you prefer A or B?' 표현을 쓰고, 답할 때는 'I prefer ~.' 형태로 답한다.
A와 B 둘 중에 어떤 것을 더 좋아하는지 물을 때 'Which do you prefer, A or B?'라는 표현도 사용한다. prefer는 'like better[more]'로도 바꿀 수 있으므로 'Which do you like better[more], A or B?'라고도 할 수 있다. which가 뒤의 명사를 수식하는 의문형용사로도 쓰일 수 있으므로 'Which sport do you prefer, baseball or tennis?'라고도 할 수 있다.

■ **선호하는 것 묻기**

선호하는 것을 물을 때는 'Would you prefer A or B?'와 같이 말할 수 있다.

• Would you prefer rice or noodles? 밥을 더 좋아하니, 국수를 더 좋아하니?

• Which do you prefer, dogs or cats? 개와 고양이 중에서 어떤 것을 더 좋아하니?

  = Which do you like better, dogs or cats?

• Would you prefer to buy the books or to borrow them from the library?
  너는 책을 사는 것을 더 좋아하니, 도서관에서 책을 빌리는 것을 더 좋아하니?

■ **선호 표현하기**

선호하는 것을 말할 때는 'B보다 A를 더 좋아한다'는 의미의 'prefer A to B'로 표현할 수 있다.

• I prefer meat to vegetables. 나는 야채보다 고기를 더 좋아해.

  = I would prefer meat to vegetables.

  = I like meat more than vegetables.

• I prefer to stay in my room rather than (to) go out. 외출하는 것보다 방에 있는 게 더 좋아.

핵심 Check

1. 다음 대화의 빈칸에 공통으로 들어갈 알맞은 것은?

A: Which do you _____, baseball or soccer?

B: I _____ soccer to baseball.

① choose   ② prefer   ③ like   ④ have   ⑤ think

② 추천 부탁하기

• **Could you recommend a book for me?** 나한테 책 한 권 추천해 줄 수 있나요?

■ '(제게) ~을 추천해 주시겠어요?'라는 뜻으로 상대방에게 추천을 부탁할 때 'Could you recommend ~ (for me)?' 표현을 쓴다.

A: Could you recommend a book for me? 나에게 책 한 권 추천해 줄래?

B: Well, why don't you read *The Flying Pan*? 음, '플라잉 팬' 어때?

A: Great idea! Thanks. 멋진 생각이야! 고마워.

• Could you recommend one for me? 나에게 하나를 추천해 줄래?

• Which book do you recommend? 어떤 책을 추천하니?

■ **추천하기**

추천을 해줄 때는 동사 recommend를 이용하거나 'Why don't you ~?(~은 어때?)'를 이용하여 답을 한다.

• I recommend reading this article. 이 기사를 읽을 것을 추천해.

• I recommend you take a taxi to go there. 네가 그곳에 택시를 타고 갈 것을 추천해.

• I recommend you watch this movie. 네가 이 영화를 볼 것을 추천해.

핵심 Check

2. 다음 빈칸에 들어갈 말로 알맞은 것은?

G: I haven't seen a movie recently. _____ a good one?

B: Why don't you see *Iron Woman* 2? It's a big hit.

① Where could I see   ② How about
③ Could you recommend   ④ Please tell me where I should see
⑤ Could you show me

3. 다음 밑줄 친 문장의 의도로 알맞은 것은?

W: Excuse me. I'm looking for a skirt. <u>Could you recommend one?</u>

M: What color do you like?

W: Blue and pink are my favorite colors.

① 명령하기   ② 추천 부탁하기   ③ 예약하기
④ 능력 묻기   ⑤ 선호 묻기

Listen & Speak 1-A-1

B: Do you have anything for dessert, Aunt May?

W: Yes, Johnny. ❶Do you prefer pie or cake?

B: ❷I prefer cake.

W: O.K. I have some chocolate cake. I'll get you some.

B: May 이모, 디저트로 먹을 만한 게 있나요?
W: 그럼, Johnny. 파이가 더 좋으니, 케이크가 더 좋으니?
B: 전 케이크가 더 좋아요.
W: 알았어. 초콜릿 케이크가 좀 있네. 좀 갖다 줄게.

❶ 둘 중 더 좋아하는 것에 대해 물을 때 사용하는 표현이다.
❷ 선호하는 것을 답할 때 동사 'prefer'를 사용한다.

Check(√) True or False

(1) Johnny likes cake more than pie. T ☐ F ☐

(2) Aunt May is going to make chocolate cake for Johnny. T ☐ F ☐

Listen & Speak 1-A-2

B: ❶I'm thinking of joining a sports club.

G: ❷Do you prefer indoor or outdoor sports?

B: I prefer indoor sports. I was in the badminton club last year.

G: ❸Why don't you join the table tennis club, then?

B: That's a good idea. Thank you.

B: 나 스포츠 동아리에 가입하려고 생각 중이야.
G: 실내 스포츠가 더 좋아, 야외 스포츠가 더 좋아?
B: 실내 스포츠가 더 좋아. 작년에 배드민턴 동아리에 있었거든.
G: 그럼, 탁구 동아리가 어때?
B: 그게 좋겠다. 고마워.

❶ 'I'm thinking of ...ing'는 '…할 생각 중이야'라는 계획이나 의도를 말할 때 사용하는 표현이다.
❷ A와 B 둘 중에 어떤 것을 더 좋아하는지 물을 때 사용하는 표현으로, 'Which do you prefer, A or B?'라는 표현도 사용한다.
❸ 'Why don't you+동사원형?'은 '…하는 게 어때?'라는 뜻으로 상대방에게 제안할 때 사용한다.

Check(√) True or False

(3) B prefers indoor sports to outdoor sports. T ☐ F ☐

(4) G recommends that B should join the table tennis club. T ☐ F ☐

Listen & Speak 2-A-1

W: Excuse me. I'm looking for an Italian cookbook. ❶Could you recommend one?
M: Well, have you ever cooked Italian food?
W: No, I haven't, but I want to try. I really like spaghetti.
M: Then, ❷how about this Italian cookbook for beginners? It's ❸on sale now.
W: Good! Thank you. I'll take it.

❶ 추천을 부탁하는 표현이다.
❷ 'how about+명사?'로 '~는 어때?'라는 제안의 표현이다.
❸ '세일 중'이라는 표현이다.

 Listen & Speak 2-A-2

G: I haven't seen a movie recently. ❶Could you recommend a good one?
B: ❷Why don't you see *Iron Woman 2*? It's a big hit.
G: Well, I don't like action movies. ❸Can you recommend any good comedies?
B: Then, how about *Funny Families*?
G: That sounds good.

❶ '(제게) ~을 추천해 주시겠어요?'라는 뜻으로 상대방에게 추천을 부탁하는 표현이다.
❷ 'Why don't you+동사원형 ~?'은 '~하는 게 어때?'라는 뜻으로 상대방에게 제안할 때 사용한다.
❸ 상대방에게 추천을 부탁하는 표현이다.

 Listen & Speak B

A: ❶Could you recommend a book for me?
B: Well, why don't you read *The Flying Pan*?
A: Great idea. Thanks.

❶ 상대방에게 추천을 부탁하는 표현이다.

 Communicate A

Jaden: ❶Have you been to the new Chinese restaurant, Ms. Park?
Ms. Park: Are you talking about the one on Main Street, Jaden?
Jaden: Yes, that's the one. They opened about two weeks ago, right?
Ms. Park: I think so. I went there last Friday with my friends.
Jaden: How was the food?

Ms. Park: It was great. We ordered many different dishes. I really liked the fried vegetables.
Jaden: ❷Could you recommend a dish for me? I'm going there for dinner tonight with my family.
Ms. Park: ❸Do you prefer seafood or meat?
Jaden: I prefer seafood.
Ms. Park: Then, you should try their fried fish. You'll love it!

❶ 'Have you been to ~?'는 '~에 가 본 적이 있니?'라는 뜻이다.
❷ '(제게) ~을 추천해 주시겠어요?'라는 뜻으로 상대방에게 추천을 부탁하는 표현이다.
❸ A와 B 둘 중에 어떤 것을 더 좋아하는지 물을 때 사용하는 표현으로, 'Which do you prefer, A or B?'라는 표현도 사용한다.

 Communicate B

M: Could you recommend a Korean restaurant ❶near here?
W: Do you prefer hot or cold food?
M: I prefer cold food.
W: Then, you should ❷try the naengmyeon place at the end of this block.
M: Thank you.

❶ near here: 이 근처에
❷ try: 가 보다

 Progress Check

1. G: I'm thinking of getting a pet.
   B: Do you prefer dogs or cats?
   G: I prefer cats. They're so cute.
   B: Great! I can give you ❶one. I have seven cats at home.
   G: Thank you.
2. W: Excuse me. I'm looking for a skirt. Could you recommend one?
   M: What color do you like?
   W: Blue and pink are my favorite colors.
   M: Then, how about this blue ❷one? It's on sale now.
   W: Good! Thank you. I'll ❸take it.

❶ one = a cat
❷ one = skirt
❸ take = buy

● 다음 우리말과 일치하도록 빈칸에 알맞은 말을 쓰시오.

Listen & Speak 1-A

1. **B:** Do you have _____ for _____, Aunt May?

   W: Yes, Johnny. Do you _____ pie _____ cake?

   B: I _____ cake.

   W: O.K. I have some chocolate cake. I'll _____ you some.

2. **B:** I'm _____ _____ joining a sports club.

   G: Do you _____ _____ _____ _____ sports?

   B: I _____ indoor sports. I was in the badminton club _____ year.

   G: _____ _____ _____ join the table tennis club, then?

   B: That's a good idea. Thank you.

Listen & Speak 2-A

1. **W:** Excuse me. I'm _____ _____ an Italian cookbook. Could you _____ one?

   M: Well, have you ever _____ _____ food?

   W: No, I _____, but I want to try. I really like spaghetti.

   M: Then, _____ _____ this _____ cookbook for _____? It's _____ _____ now.

   W: Good! Thank you. I'll _____ it.

2. **G:** I _____ _____ a movie _____. Could you _____ a good one?

   B: _____ _____ _____ see *Iron Woman 2*? It's a _____ _____.

   G: Well, I don't like _____ movies. Can you _____ any good _____?

   B: Then, _____ about *Funny Families*?

   G: That _____ good.

Listen & Speak B

A: Could you _____ a book for me?

B: Well, _____ _____ _____ read *The Flying Pan*?

A: Great idea. Thanks.

해석

1. **B:** May 이모, 디저트로 먹을 만한 게 있나요?

   W: 그럼, Johnny. 파이가 더 좋으니, 케이크가 더 좋으니?

   B: 전 케이크가 더 좋아요.

   W: 알았어. 초콜릿 케이크가 좀 있네. 좀 갖다 줄게.

2. **B:** 나 스포츠 동아리에 가입하려고 생각 중이야.

   G: 실내 스포츠가 더 좋아, 야외 스포츠가 더 좋아?

   B: 실내 스포츠가 더 좋아. 작년에 배드민턴 동아리에 있었거든.

   G: 그럼, 탁구 동아리가 어때?

   B: 그게 좋겠다. 고마워.

1. **W:** 실례합니다. 이탈리아 요리책을 찾고 있는데요. 추천해 주실 수 있으세요?

   M: 음, 이탈리아 요리를 해 보신 적이 있나요?

   W: 아뇨, 없습니다, 하지만 해 보고 싶어서요. 스파게티를 정말 좋아하거든요.

   M: 그렇다면 초보자들을 위한 이 이탈리아 요리책이 어떨까요? 지금 세일 중이에요.

   W: 좋아요! 감사합니다. 그걸 살게요

2. **G:** 최근에 영화를 한 편도 못 봤어. 좋은 영화 한 편 추천해 줄래?

   B: 《아이언 우먼 2》 어때? 크게 히트를 치고 있는데.

   G: 글쎄, 액션 영화는 안 좋아해. 괜찮은 코미디 영화 추천해 줄 수 있어?

   B: 그렇다면, 《퍼니 패밀리즈》는 어때?

   G: 그게 좋겠다.

A: 나한테 책 한 권 추천해 줄래?

B: 글쎄, '플라잉 팬' 어때?

A: 아주 좋아. 고마워.

Communicate A

Jaden: _____ you _____ _____ the new Chinese restaurant, Ms. Park?

Ms. Park: Are you _____ _____ the one on Main Street, Jaden?

Jaden: Yes, that's _____ _____. They opened about two weeks _____, right?

Ms. Park: I think _____. I _____ there _____ Friday with my friends.

Jaden: _____ _____ the food?

Ms. Park: It was great. We _____ many _____ _____. I really liked the _____ vegetables.

Jaden: Could you _____ a dish _____ me? I'm going there for dinner _____ with my family.

Ms. Park: Do you _____ seafood _____ meat?

Jaden: I _____ _____.

Ms. Park: Then, you _____ _____ their _____ _____. You'll love it!

Communicate B

M: _____ _____ _____ a Korean restaurant near here?

W: _____ you _____ hot _____ cold food?

M: I _____ cold food.

W: Then, you should _____ the naengmyeon place at the end of this block.

M: Thank you.

Progress Check

1. **G:** _____ _____ _____ getting a pet.

   B: Do you _____ dogs _____ cats?

   G: I _____ cats. They're so cute.

   B: Great! I can give you _____. I have seven cats at home.

   G: Thank you.

2. **W:** Excuse me. I'm _____ _____ a skirt. Could you _____ one?

   M: What _____ do you like?

   W: Blue and pink are my _____ colors.

   M: Then, _____ _____ this blue one? It's _____ _____ now.

   W: Good! Thank you. I'll _____ it.

해석

Jaden: 새로 생긴 중국집에 가 보셨어요, 박 선생님?
박 선생님: 메인 가에 있는 거 말하는 거니, Jaden?
Jaden: 네, 거기요. 한 2주 전쯤에 문을 열었어요, 그렇죠?
박 선생님: 그런 것 같아. 지난 금요일에 친구들과 함께 거기에 갔었단다.
Jaden: 음식이 어땠나요?
박 선생님: 훌륭했어. 우린 다양한 음식을 많이 시켰어. 나는 채소볶음이 정말 좋았어.
Jaden: 제게 요리 하나 추천해 주시겠어요? 오늘 저녁에 저녁 식사를 하러 가족들과 함께 그곳에 가거든요.
박 선생님: 너는 해산물을 더 좋아하니, 육류를 더 좋아하니?
Jaden: 전 해산물을 더 좋아해요.
박 선생님: 그럼 그곳의 생선튀김을 먹어 봐. 네가 정말 좋아할 거야!

M: 이 근처에서 한국 음식점 좀 추천해 주실래요?
W: 뜨거운 음식이 더 좋으세요, 차가운 음식이 더 좋으세요?
M: 찬 음식을 더 좋아해요.
W: 그럼, 이 블록 끝에 있는 냉면집에 가 보세요.
M: 감사합니다.

1. G: 애완동물을 키울까 해.
   B: 개가 좋아, 아니면 고양이가 좋아?
   G: 나는 고양이가 좋아. 정말 귀엽잖아.
   B: 잘 됐다! 내가 한 마리 줄 수 있어. 집에 일곱 마리나 있거든.
   G: 고마워.

2. W: 실례합니다. 치마를 찾고 있는데요. 하나 추천해 주실 수 있나요?
   M: 어떤 색을 좋아하세요?
   W: 파란색과 분홍색을 제일 좋아해요.
   M: 그럼, 이 파란 건 어때요? 지금 세일 중이에요.
   W: 좋아요! 감사합니다. 그걸로 할게요.

01 다음 밑줄 친 우리말에 맞게 빈칸에 알맞은 말을 쓰시오.

> A: 나한테 책 한 권 추천해 줄래?
> B: Well, why don't you read *The Flying Pan*?
> A: Great idea. Thanks.

➡ Could you _____ a book _____ me?

[02~03] 대화의 빈칸에 들어갈 말로 알맞은 것은?

02

> B: Do you have anything for dessert, Aunt May?
> W: Yes, Johnny. _____
> B: I prefer cake.
> W: O.K. I have some chocolate cake. I'll get you some.

① Do you want to eat cake?

② Do you have cake?

③ Do you prefer pie or cake?

④ How much do you like chocolate cake?

⑤ Why don't you eat cake?

03

> G: I'm thinking of getting a pet.
> B: Do you prefer dogs or cats?
> G: _____ They're so cute.
> B: Great! I can give you one. I have seven cats at home.
> G: Thank you.

① I prefer cats.　　　② I like dogs most.

③ I don't think so.　　④ How about you?

⑤ I prefer dogs.

04 다음 대화의 밑줄 친 부분의 의도로 알맞은 것은?

> B: We're planning our school's sports day. <u>Do you prefer indoor or outdoor activities?</u>

① 능력 여부 묻기　　② 유감 표현하기　　③ 기대 표현하기

④ 선호 묻기　　　　⑤ 보고하기

[01~02] 다음 대화를 읽고 물음에 답하시오.

> B: _____ (A) _____
> G: Do you prefer indoor or outdoor sports?
> B: I prefer indoor sports. I was in the badminton club last year.
> G: _____ (B) _____, then?
> B: That's a good idea. Thank you.

01 빈칸 (A)에 알맞은 말을 고르시오.

① I'm planning to play tennis.
② I'm considering joining a soccer club.
③ I'm thinking of buying a tennis racket.
④ I'm thinking of joining a sports club.
⑤ I broke my leg in the soccer game.

02 빈칸 (B)에 들어가기에 <u>어색한</u> 말은?

① How about joining the table tennis club
② Why don't you join the table tennis club
③ What about joining the table tennis club
④ What do you say to joining the table tennis
⑤ How do you join the table tennis

03 다음 중 짝지어진 대화가 <u>어색한</u> 것은?

① A: Could you recommend a movie for me?
   B: Well, why don't you watch *Avengers*?
② A: Do you prefer chicken or beef?
   B: I don't like pork.
③ A: I like Chinese food.
   B: Then, I recommend the Chinese restaurant at the Happy Department Store.
④ A: Could you recommend a book for me?
   B: Well, why don't you read *A Good Singer*?
⑤ A: Does Yuna prefer cats or dogs?
   B: She prefers dogs.

서답형

04 대화에서 빈칸에 주어진 〈조건〉대로 문장을 완성하시오.

> B: Do you have anything for dessert, Aunt May?
> W: Yes, Johnny. _____
> B: I prefer cake.

┤ 보기 ├
• 선호를 묻는 표현을 쓸 것
• 'prefer', 'cake', 'pie'를 사용할 것

➡ _____

[05~06] 다음 대화를 읽고 물음에 답하시오.

> W: Excuse me. I'm looking for an Italian cookbook. Could you ⓐ one?
> M: Well, have you ever cooked Italian food?
> W: No, I haven't, but I want to try. I really like spaghetti.
> M: Then, _____ ⓑ this Italian cookbook for beginners? It's on sale now.
> W: Good! Thank you. I'll take it.

05 빈칸 ⓐ, ⓑ에 들어갈 말로 알맞은 것은?

① recommend – where can I buy
② recommend – where did you buy
③ recommend – how about
④ advise – what about
⑤ advise – why don't you

서답형

06 다음 영영풀이에 해당하는 단어를 대화에서 찾아 쓰시오.

> a person who is starting to do something or learn something for the first time

➡ _____

[07~08] 다음 대화를 읽고 물음에 답하시오.

G: I haven't seen a movie recently. Could you recommend a good one?

B: (A)Why don't you see *Iron Woman 2*? It's a big hit.

G: Well, I don't like action movies. _____ (a)

B: Then, how about *Funny Families*?

G: That sounds good.

07 위 대화의 빈칸 (a)에 들어갈 말로 알맞은 것은?

① Can you recommend any good comedies?

② Let's see a movie tonight.

③ Where shall we meet?

④ Do you like action movies?

⑤ I'd like to see action movies.

08 밑줄 친 (A)와 바꾸어 쓸 수 있는 것은?

① Why did you see *Iron Woman 2*?

② Are you planning to see *Iron Woman 2*?

③ Are you going to see *Iron Woman 2*?

④ Shall I see *Iron Woman 2*?

⑤ What about seeing *Iron Woman 2*?

[09~11] 다음 대화를 읽고 물음에 답하시오.

Jaden: (A)새로 생긴 중국집에 가 보셨어요, Ms. Park?

Ms. Park: Are you talking about the one on Main Street, Jaden? (①)

Jaden: Yes, that's the one. (②) They opened about two weeks ago, right?

Ms. Park: I think so. I went there last Friday with my friends.

Jaden: How was the food?

Ms. Park: It was great. (③)

Jaden: _____ (a) I'm going there for dinner tonight with my family. (④)

Ms. Park: Do you prefer seafood or meat?

Jaden: I prefer seafood. (⑤)

Ms. Park: Then, you should try their fried fish. You'll love it!

09 위 대화의 (①)~(⑤) 중 다음 주어진 말이 들어갈 알맞은 곳은?

> We ordered many different dishes. I really liked the fried vegetables.

① ② ③ ④ ⑤

10 위 대화의 빈칸 (a)에 들어갈 말로 알맞은 것은?

① Could you recommend a Japanese restaurant near here?

② Do you prefer sushi or udong?

③ Do you prefer Chinese or Japanese food?

④ Could you recommend a dish for me?

⑤ Why don't you try the new Chinese restaurant?

서답형

11 위 대화의 밑줄 친 (A)의 우리말에 맞게 주어진 단어를 배열하시오.

> (been / the / new / restaurant / have / you / to / Chinese)

➡ _____

[01~02] 다음 대화를 읽고 물음에 답하시오.

> Man: Could you recommend a Korean restaurant near here?
>
> Woman: (A)뜨거운 음식이 더 좋으세요, 차가운 음식이 더 좋으세요?
>
> Man: I prefer cold food.
>
> Woman: Then, you should try the naengmyeon place at the end of this block.
>
> Man: Thank you.

01 What food is the man going to eat?

➡ _____

02 밑줄 친 (A)의 우리말에 맞게 주어진 단어를 이용하여 영작하시오.

> (prefer / hot / cold / food)

➡ _____

03 다음 그림을 보고 주어진 단어를 이용하여 (1)은 선호하는 것을 묻는 말을, (2)는 선호하는 말을 쓰시오.

> A: (1)_____
>   (rainy days / sunny days)
> B: I (2)_____ (sunny days)

04 다음 문장의 우리말에 맞게 단어를 바르게 배열하시오.

> 나한테 책 한 권 추천해 줄 수 있나요?
> (recommend / a / book / could / me / for / you / ?)

➡ _____

[05~06] 다음 대화를 읽고 물음에 답하시오.

> Jaden: Have you been to the new Chinese restaurant, Ms. Park?
>
> Ms. Park: Are you talking about the one on Main Street, Jaden?
>
> Jaden: Yes, that's the one. They opened about two weeks ago, right?
>
> Ms. Park: I think so. I went there last Friday with my friends.
>
> Jaden: How was the food?
>
> Ms. Park: It was great. We ordered many different dishes. I really liked the fried vegetables.
>
> Jaden: _____(A)_____ I'm going there for dinner tonight with my family.
>
> Ms. Park: _____(B)_____
>
> Jaden: I prefer seafood.
>
> Ms. Park: Then, you should try their fried fish. You'll love it!

05 위 대화의 빈칸 (A)에 주어진 어구를 이용하여 '제게 요리 하나 추천해 주시겠어요?'라는 표현을 영어로 쓰시오.

> (could / a dish / me)

➡ _____

06 위 대화의 빈칸 (B)에 주어진 조건에 맞게 한 문장을 쓰시오.

> ┤ 조건 ├
> • 선호하는 것을 묻는 표현을 쓸 것.
> • 'seafood'와 'meat'를 사용할 것.

➡ _____
   _____

Grammar

① 수동태

- They **called** this dish tangpyeongchae. 〈능동태〉 그들은 이 음식을 탕평채라고 불렀다.
- This dish **was called** tangpyeongchae. 〈수동태〉 이 음식은 탕평채라고 불렸다.

■ 수동태는 주어가 동작의 대상인 문장으로 '주어+be동사+과거분사(+by 행위자)'의 형식을 가지며 '~해지다, …에 의해 ~되다[당하다]'라는 의미이다. 수동태 문장의 주어 자리에는 능동태 문장의 목적어가 오고, by 다음에는 능동태 문장의 주어를 쓴다. 누가 그 동작을 했는지 중요하지 않거나 잘 모를 때, 수동태 문장으로 표현하며 'by+행위자'를 생략한다. 수동태는 현재, 과거, 미래 시제로 쓸 수 있고, 'be동사+과거분사'에서 be동사로 시제를 나타낸다.

■ 4형식 문장의 수동태는 간접목적어와 직접목적어 각각을 주어로 하는 수동태가 가능하다. 직접목적어를 주어로 한 수동태에서는 간접목적어 앞에 특정한 전치사를 써야 한다.
전치사 to를 쓰는 동사는 'bring, give, show, send, tell, teach' 등이고, 전치사 for를 쓰는 동사는 'buy, choose, cook, get, make' 등이며, 전치사 of를 쓰는 동사는 'ask' 등이 있다. 또한 'buy, make, read, write' 등은 직접목적어를 주어로 하는 수동태만 가능하다.

- Her mom **made** her a dress.
  → A dress **was made** for her by her mom. 옷이 그녀의 엄마에 의해 그녀에게 만들어졌다.
  → She was made a dress by her mom. (×)

■ 조동사가 있는 문장의 수동태는 '조동사+be+p.p.' 형식을 갖는다.

- Jake **will send** her an e-mail.
  → An e-mail **will be sent** to her by Jake. 이메일이 Jake에 의해 그녀에게 보내질 것이다.

■ 5형식 문장의 수동태는 목적어와 목적격 보어 자리에 모두 명사가 오더라도 목적어만 수동태의 주어 자리에 올 수 있으며, 목적격 보어 자리에 동사원형이 쓰이면 수동태 문장에서는 to부정사 형태로 바뀌어야 한다.

- The teacher **made** him **do** his homework. 선생님이 그에게 숙제를 하도록 시켰다.
  → He **was made to do** his homework by the teacher.

■ by 이외의 전치사를 사용하는 수동태에 유의한다.

- be interested in: ~에 흥미가 있다
- be filled with: ~로 가득 차다
- be covered with: ~로 덮여 있다
- be surprised at: ~에 놀라다
- be made of: ~로 만들어지다(물리적 변화)
- be made from: ~로 만들어지다(화학적 변화)

핵심 Check

1. 다음 괄호 안에서 알맞은 말을 고르시오.
   (1) The gate (painted / was painted) by John.
   (2) Social studies was taught (for / to) us by Mr. Min.
   (3) They were pleased (for / with) the news.

② something/someone+형용사

- King Yeongjo offered them something **special**. 영조가 그들에게 특별한 무언가를 권했다.
- I want to eat something **cold**. 나는 시원한 무언가를 먹고 싶다.

■ 형용사는 보통 명사 앞에 오지만, '-thing, -one, -body'로 끝나는 대명사는 형용사가 뒤에서 수식한다. 이러한 대명사에는 something, someone, somebody, anything, anyone, anybody, nothing, no one, nobody 등이 있다.

- I want something **big** and **baggy**. 크고 헐렁한 것으로 주십시오.
- Did you meet anyone **nice** last weekend? 지난 주말 괜찮은 사람을 만났니?

■ '-thing, -one, -body'로 끝나는 대명사를 to부정사와 형용사가 동시에 수식할 때 어순은 '대명사+형용사+to부정사'이다.

- I have something **important to tell** you. 너에게 할 중요한 이야기가 있다.
- She didn't have anything **nice to say** about him. 그녀는 그에 대해 좋게 말할 게 없었어.

핵심 Check

2. 다음 괄호 안에서 알맞은 말을 고르시오.

(1) Do you have (long anything / anything long)?

(2) (Terrible something / Something terrible) happened last night.

(3) Dr. Ian couldn't find (anyone nice to talk with / anyone to talk with nice).

01 다음 빈칸에 알맞은 것은?

> • J. K. Rowling wrote it.
> → It _____ by J. K. Rowling.

① writes   ② wrote   ③ has written
④ is written   ⑤ was written

02 괄호 안의 단어를 바르게 배열한 것은?

> We (special, need, something).

① need special something   ② need something special
③ special something need   ④ something special need
⑤ something need special

03 다음 우리말에 맞게 빈칸에 알맞은 말을 쓰시오.

(1) 그 학교는 10년 전에 세워졌다.
  ➡ The school _____ _____ ten years ago.
(2) 'Romeo and Juliet'은 Shakespeare에 의해 쓰여졌다.
  ➡ Romeo and Juliet _____ _____ by Shakespeare.
(3) 우리는 어떤 재미있는 사람을 찾고 있다. (funny와 someone을 이용할 것.)
  ➡ We are looking for _____ _____.
(4) 그는 어떤 중요한 사람임에 틀림없다. (important와 somebody를 이용할 것.)
  ➡ He must be _____ _____.

04 다음 문장에서 어법상 어색한 부분을 바르게 고쳐 쓰시오.

(1) His room cleans every day by him.
  _____ ➡ _____
(2) Give me something to read interesting.
  _____ ➡ _____

01 다음 빈칸에 알맞은 것은?

> This toy _____ by my dad.

① makes   ② made
③ to make   ④ was made
⑤ was making

 02 다음 중 어법상 어색한 것을 고르시오.

① We need a special plan.
② Is it something good?
③ King Yeongjo offered them something special.
④ Is there anything interesting to buy?
⑤ I don't have reliable anyone.

03 다음 중 수동태로의 전환이 어색한 것은?

① Thomas Edison invented the light bulb.
  → The light bulb was invented by Thomas Edison.
② Her mother often made it for the family.
  → It was often made for the family by her mother.
③ The teacher made us do homework.
  → We were made do homework by the teacher.
④ Her mom chose her a beautiful dress.
  → A beautiful dress was chosen for her by her mom.
⑤ They sold shirts and pants at the shop.
  → Shirts and pants were sold at the shop.

 04 다음 중 어법상 옳은 것은?

① My family eats something special on Chuseok.
② How were tangpyeongchae and sinseollo got their names?
③ *The Mona Lisa* painted by Leonardo da Vinci.
④ There was wrong something with my bill.
⑤ The dress will be bought to her by Mary.

05 다음 우리말을 바르게 영작한 것은?

> 오직 33명 만이 그녀에 의해 최종 오디션에 선발되었다.

① Only 33 were chosen with the final audition by her.
② Only 33 were chosen for the final audition by her.
③ Only 33 were chosen of the final audition by her.
④ The final audition was chosen for only 33 by her.
⑤ Only 33 were chosen for her by the final audition.

 06 다음 빈칸에 공통으로 들어갈 말로 가장 적절한 것은?

> • The box was filled _____ chocolate bars.
> • I'm not satisfied _____ the customer service.

① at   ② in   ③ of
④ for   ⑤ with

07 다음 대화의 빈칸에 들어갈 말이 바르게 짝지어진 것은?

> M: Did you go to the party last night? Who hold the party? And how was it?
>
> W: It _____ by Dave. It was great and I met _____ there.

① was held – someone funny
② held – someone funny
③ was held – funny someone
④ held – funny someone
⑤ holds – anyone funny

서답형

08 다음 괄호 안에서 알맞은 것을 고르시오.

(1) Beautiful flowers were sent (to / for) her by an old man.

(2) A new type of character was made (to / for) the Horde, too.

(3) A lot of questions were asked (to / of) the singer by her fans.

서답형

09 다음 그림을 참고하여 주어진 문장의 빈칸을 알맞게 채우시오.

> A: Did you find _____ at the store?
> B: Yes, I found some funny hats.

➡ _____

중요

10 다음 중 두 문장의 의미가 <u>다른</u> 것은?

① They advised him to leave the place as soon as possible.
   → He was advised to leave the place as soon as possible by them.

② He made William finish the work by the next day.
   → William was made to finish the work by the next day by him.

③ Gibson gave Jane a present.
   → A present was given for Jane by Gibson.

④ Someone stole my bag.
   → My bag was stolen.

⑤ Mom bought me a smartphone.
   → A smartphone was bought for me by mom.

서답형

11 다음 문장에서 어법상 <u>어색한</u> 부분을 찾아 바르게 고치시오.

(1) In 1964, China's first nuclear test was taken place.

   ➡ _____

(2) *Two Sisters* painted Auguste Renoir in 1881.

   ➡ _____

(3) Give me something to drink cold.

   ➡ _____

(4) They will see her as respectable someone.

   ➡ _____

12 주어진 문장을 영어로 바르게 옮긴 것은?

> 나는 어젯밤에 아주 놀라운 일이 발생했다고 들었다.

① I heard very surprising anything was happened last night.

② I heard very surprising something happened last night.

③ I heard very surprising something was happened last night.

④ I heard something very surprising happened last night.

⑤ I heard something very surprising was happened last night.

서답형

13 다음 문장을 수동태로 바꿔 쓰시오.

(1) He bought me a nice cap.

➡ _____

_____

(2) They speak French in France.

➡ _____

_____

(3) Who draw the picture *The Sunflowers*?

➡ _____

_____

(4) Marianne made Sam delicious spaghetti last night.

➡ _____

_____

(5) I heard Emily talking to her friend in class.

➡ _____

_____

14 다음 문장에서 something이 들어갈 위치로 알맞은 곳은?

> • People avoid others' notice ① when ② they ③ do ④ bad ⑤.

①   ②   ③   ④   ⑤

15 다음 문장을 수동태로 바르게 바꾼 것은?

> She gave it up in order to support her family.

① It gave up by her in order to support her family.

② It given up by her in order to support her family.

③ It was given up her in order to support her family.

④ It was given by her in order to support her family.

⑤ It was given up by her in order to support her family.

서답형

16 다음 빈칸에 들어갈 말이 바르게 짝지어진 것은?

> • The storyline of the opera *Turandot* will _____ to you by me. (tell)
> • Many fancy cars _____ in Korea. (make) (현재 시제)
> • I _____ the number of side dishes. (surprise) (과거 시제)
> • Susan _____ acting. (interest) (과거 시제)
> • He _____ dust while walking along the road. (cover) (과거 시제)
> • His heart _____ pride at that time. (fill) (과거 시제)

01 다음 문장을 수동태로 바꿔 쓰시오.

(1) Each ingredient symbolized a different political party.

➡ _____

_____

(2) The king never listened to him.

➡ _____

_____

(3) Dan made his son a small sandcastle.

➡ _____

_____

(4) They throw away many computers every year in the United States.

➡ _____

_____

(5) Who wrote the novel, *Christmas Carol*?

➡ _____

_____

02 다음 괄호 안에 주어진 단어를 넣어 문장을 다시 쓰시오.

(1) I want to show something to you. (wonderful)

➡ _____

_____

(2) I want to work with somebody for our business. (honest)

➡ _____

_____

(3) There was nobody at the meeting. (important)

➡ _____

_____

03 다음 문장에서 어법상 어색한 부분을 찾아 바르게 고쳐 다시 쓰시오.

(1) The bench painted the man.

➡ _____

_____

(2) Spicy food is loving by all of my family members.

➡ _____

_____

(3) The bookshelf was made from wood.

➡ _____

_____

(4) Amy was heard sing in front of all the classmates by us.

➡ _____

_____

(5) She was written a long letter by him.

➡ _____

_____

(6) A wedding ring with a small ruby will be bought to her.

➡ _____

_____

04 주어진 말을 이용하여 대화의 빈칸을 채우시오.

A: Are there any interesting programs on TV tonight?
B: No, there is _____ on TV. (nothing)

➡ _____

05 다음 우리말을 괄호 안에 주어진 어휘를 이용하여 영작하시오.

(1) 그것의 등에 무언가가 쓰여 있었다.
(something, write, back)

➡ _____

_____

(2) 로마는 하루아침에 이루어지지 않았다.
(Rome, build, a day)

➡ _____

(3) 제가 그에게 전화를 해보았지만, 그의 전화기는 꺼져 있었습니다. (call him, his phone, turn off)

➡ _____

(4) 내 숙제는 나에 의해 일요일까지는 끝내져야 한다. (my homework, by Sunday, must, finish)

➡ _____

(5) 나는 Tom에게서 흥미로운 무언가를 들었다.
(interesting, something)

➡ _____

(6) 그 집에는 아무도 행복한 사람이 없을 것이다.
(nobody, that house, there, will)

➡ _____

06 다음 문장에서 어법상 <u>어색한</u> 부분을 찾아 바르게 고치시오.

(1) I'm looking for funny someone.

_____ ➡ _____

(2) Is it always hard to try new something?

_____ ➡ _____

(3) Can I have cold to drink something?

_____ ➡ _____

(4) I could find new nobody there.

_____ ➡ _____

07 다음 문장을 수동태는 능동태로, 능동태는 수동태로 고치시오.

(1) Thomas Edison invented the light bulb.

➡ _____

_____

(2) Mahatma Gandhi is respected by many people.

➡ _____

_____

(3) They canceled all the flights due to the bad weather.

➡ _____

_____

08 주어진 단어를 활용하여 빈칸에 알맞은 말을 쓰시오.

• Artist: Vincent Van Gogh
• Title: *The Starry Night*
• Year: 1889

This picture _____ _____ (paint) by Vincent Van Gogh. It _____ _____ (title) *The Starry Night* and _____ _____ (complete) in 1889.

Reading

A Bite of Korean History

How did tangpyeongchae and sinseollo get their names? Why does
songpyeon look like a half moon? There are many interesting stories
look like+명사: ~처럼 보이다
about our traditional food. Let's dive into the fun history of our food.
~에 관한   *재미있는*

bite: 한 입, 소량의 음식
half: 반, 절반; 절반의
dive into: ~으로 뛰어들다
official: 신하, 관리, 공무원
offer: 제의[제안]하다, 권하다
ingredient: (특히 요리 등의) 재료, 성분
symbolize: 상징하다
political: 정치의, 정당의
party: 정당
policy: 정책

Tangpyeongchae

One day, King Yeongjo was having dinner with his officials and
과거진행형 having = eating   *영조*
offered them something special. It was a dish with four colorful
영조의 신하들   *something과 같이 -thing으로 끝나는 대명사를 수식할 때 형용사가 뒤에 온다.*
ingredients. Each ingredient symbolized a different political party.
각각의(+단수명사)   *정파*
Yeongjo wanted to say that the four parties should work in harmony
that 이하는 영조가 말하고 싶었던 것이 무엇인지를 나타내는 목적어   *화합을 이루어*
like this dish. This dish was called tangpyeongchae. The name came
~와 같이   *be동사+과거분사: ~라고 불렸다(수동의 의미)*
from Yeongjo's policy tangpyeongchaek.

확인문제

● 다음 문장이 본문의 내용과 일치하면 T, 일치하지 <u>않으면</u> F를 쓰시오.

1 There are many interesting stories about our traditional food. ☐

2 One day, King Yeongjo was having dinner with his sons. ☐

3 Tangpyeongchae was a dish with four colorful ingredients. ☐

4 Yeongjo said that the four parties should work in harmony by his policy

tangpyeongchaek. ☐

Sinseollo

In the time of King Yeonsan, there was a scholar who was famous
for his honesty. When the king did something wrong, the scholar was
never afraid of telling him so. However, the king never listened to him.
The scholar was so disappointed that he went to live on a mountain.
While he lived there by himself, he mainly ate vegetables. He made a
special pot to cook many different vegetables together. People called
this pot and the food in it sinseollo. That is because the scholar lived
like a sinseon, an imaginary person who lives alone in nature.

Songpyeon

It was the time of the last king of Baekje. One day, the king and his
servants found a strange turtle. Something was written on its back. It
said, "Baekje is like a full moon, but Silla is like a half moon."
The king asked a fortune teller, "What does this mean?"
The fortune teller answered, "A full moon will soon become smaller.
On the other hand, a half moon will grow bigger and become a full
moon."

The king became worried about his kingdom. However, people of
Silla were very happy to learn this and made rice cakes in the shape of
a half moon. Since then, people have enjoyed these half-moon shaped
rice cakes, songpyeon.

scholar: 학자

honesty: 정직함 *cf.* honest: 정직한

disappointed: 실망한

by oneself 혼자서, 홀로 (= alone)

mainly: 주로

pot: 냄비, 솥

imaginary: 상상의

servant: 하인, 시종

turtle: 거북

fortune teller: 점술가, 역술인, 점쟁이

kingdom: 왕국

확인문제

● 다음 문장이 본문의 내용과 일치하면 T, 일치하지 <u>않으면</u> F를 쓰시오.

1 In the time of King Yeonsan, there was a servant who was famous for his
honesty. ☐

2 King Yeonsan made a special pot to cook many different vegetables together. ☐

3 The last king of Silla and his servants found a strange turtle. ☐

4 People of Silla made rice cakes in the shape of a half moon. ☐

● 우리말을 참고하여 빈칸에 알맞은 말을 쓰시오.

1 A _____ of Korean History

2 _____ did tangpyeongchae and sinseollo _____ _____ _____?

3 _____ does songpyeon _____ _____ a half moon?

4 There are many interesting stories about our _____ _____.

5 Let's _____ _____ the fun history of our food.

Tangpyeongchae

6 One day, King Yeongjo _____ _____ _____ with his officials and offered them _____ _____.

7 It was a dish with _____ _____ _____.

8 Each ingredient symbolized _____ _____ _____ _____.

9 Yeongjo wanted to say that the four parties should work _____ _____ like this dish.

10 This dish _____ _____ tangpyeongchae.

11 The name _____ _____ Yeongjo's policy tangpyeongchaek.

Sinseollo

12 In the time of King Yeonsan, there was a scholar who _____ _____ _____ his honesty.

13 When the king did _____ _____, the scholar was never _____ _____ _____ him so.

14 _____, the king never listened to him.

15 The scholar was _____ disappointed _____ he went to live on a mountain.

16 While he lived there _____ _____, he mainly ate vegetables.

17 He made _____ _____ _____ to cook many different vegetables together.

18 People _____ this pot and _____ _____ _____ _____ sinseollo.

19 That is _____ the scholar lived _____ a sinseon, an _____ person who lives alone in nature.

Songpyeon

20 It was the time of _____ _____ _____ of Baekje.

21 One day, the king and his servants found _____ _____ _____.

22 Something _____ _____ on its back.

23 It said, "Baekje _____ _____ a full moon, but Silla _____ _____ a half moon."

24 The king asked a fortune teller, "_____ does this _____?"

25 The fortune teller answered, "A full moon will soon become _____.

26 _____ _____ _____ _____, a half moon will _____ _____ and become a full moon."

27 The king became _____ about his kingdom.

28 _____, people of Silla were very happy to learn this and made rice cakes _____ _____ _____ _____ a half moon.

29 _____ _____, people _____ _____ these half-moon shaped rice cakes, songpyeon.

15 학자는 너무 실망하여 산속으로 살러 들어갔다.

16 그곳에서 혼자 사는 동안, 그는 주로 채소를 먹었다.

17 그는 여러 다양한 채소들을 함께 요리하기 위해 특별한 솥을 만들었다.

18 사람들은 이 솥과 그 안의 음식을 신선로라고 불렀다.

19 그것은 그 학자가 마치 자연 속에 홀로 사는 상상의 인물인 신선처럼 살았기 때문이다.

송편

20 백제의 마지막 왕 때였다.

21 어느 날, 왕과 신하들은 이상한 거북을 한 마리 발견했다.

22 그 거북의 등에 무언가 쓰여 있었다.

23 그것은 "백제는 보름달과 같지만 신라는 반달과 같다."였다.

24 왕은 점술가에게 "이게 무슨 뜻인가?"라고 물었다.

25 점술가는 "보름달은 곧 작아질 것입니다.

26 반면에, 반달은 점점 커져서 보름달이 될 것입니다."라고 답했다.

27 왕은 자신의 왕국이 걱정되었다.

28 그러나 신라 사람들은 이것을 알고 매우 기뻐하며 반달 모양의 떡을 만들었다.

29 그 후로 사람들은 이 반달 모양의 떡인 송편을 즐겨 먹고 있다.

● 우리말을 참고하여 본문을 영작하시오.

1 한국 역사 한 입

➡ _____

2 탕평채와 신선로는 어떻게 해서 그런 이름을 얻게 되었을까?

➡ _____

3 송편은 왜 반달 모양일까?

➡ _____

4 우리의 전통 음식에 대한 재미있는 이야기들이 많이 있다.

➡ _____

5 우리 음식의 재미있는 역사 속으로 들어가 보자.

➡ _____

Tangpyeongchae 탕평채

6 어느 날, 영조가 그의 신하들과 저녁을 먹다가 그들에게 특별한 무언가를 권했다.

➡ _____

7 그것은 네 가지의 다채로운 재료로 만든 음식이었다.

➡ _____

8 각 재료는 서로 다른 당파를 상징했다.

➡ _____

9 영조는 이 음식처럼 네 당파가 화합을 이루어 일해야 한다는 것을 말하고 싶었다.

➡ _____

10 이 음식은 탕평채라고 불렸다.

➡ _____

11 그 이름은 영조의 정책인 탕평책에서 왔다.

➡ _____

Sinseollo 신선로

12 연산군 시대에 정직하기로 유명한 한 학자가 있었다.

➡ _____

13 왕이 무언가를 잘못하면, 그 학자는 왕에게 그렇게 말하는 것을 절대 두려워하지 않았다.

➡ _____

14 그러나 왕은 그의 말에 전혀 귀 기울이지 않았다.

➡ _____

15 학자는 너무 실망하여 산속으로 살러 들어갔다.

➡ _____

16 그곳에서 혼자 사는 동안, 그는 주로 채소를 먹었다.

➡ _____

17 그는 여러 다양한 채소들을 함께 요리하기 위해 특별한 솥을 만들었다.

➡ _____

18 사람들은 이 솥과 그 안의 음식을 신선로라고 불렀다.

➡ _____

19 그것은 그 학자가 마치 자연 속에 홀로 사는 상상의 인물인 신선처럼 살았기 때문이다.

➡ _____

Songpyeon 송편

20 백제의 마지막 왕 때였다.

➡ _____

21 어느 날, 왕과 신하들은 이상한 거북을 한 마리 발견했다.

➡ _____

22 그 거북의 등에 무언가가 쓰여 있었다.

➡ _____

23 그것은 "백제는 보름달과 같지만 신라는 반달과 같다."였다.

➡ _____

24 왕은 점술가에게 "이게 무슨 뜻인가?"라고 물었다.

➡ _____

25 점술가는 "보름달은 곧 작아질 것입니다.

➡ _____

26 반면에, 반달은 점점 커져서 보름달이 될 것입니다."라고 답했다.

➡ _____

27 왕은 자신의 왕국이 걱정되었다.

➡ _____

28 그러나 신라 사람들은 이것을 알고 매우 기뻐하며 반달 모양의 떡을 만들었다.

➡ _____

29 그 후로 사람들은 이 반달 모양의 떡인 송편을 즐겨 먹고 있다.

➡ _____

[01~04] 다음 글을 읽고 물음에 답하시오.

(A)[How / What] did tangpyeongchae and sinseollo get their names? Why does songpyeon (B)[look / look like] a half moon? There are many (C)[interesting / interested] stories about our traditional _____ⓐ_____. ⓑLet's dive into the fun history of our food.

01 위 글의 빈칸 ⓐ에 들어갈 알맞은 말을 고르시오.

① ceremony   ② food
③ culture   ④ holiday
⑤ custom

서답형

02 위 글의 괄호 (A)~(C)에서 문맥이나 어법상 알맞은 낱말을 골라 쓰시오.

➡ (A) _____ (B) _____ (C) _____

03 위 글의 밑줄 친 ⓑ와 의미가 다른 문장을 고르시오.

① How about diving into the fun history of our food?
② Why don't we dive into the fun history of our food?
③ Shall we dive into the fun history of our food?
④ Why do you dive into the fun history of our food?
⑤ What about diving into the fun history of our food?

04 위 글의 뒤에 올 내용으로 가장 알맞은 것을 고르시오.

① 우리 음식을 즐기는 방법
② 전통 문화 계승의 소중함
③ 우리 음식의 재미있는 역사
④ 우리 음식의 조리법
⑤ 미풍양속을 지키는 사례들

[05~07] 다음 글을 읽고 물음에 답하시오.

Tangpyeongchae

One day, King Yeongjo was having dinner with his officials and (a)그들에게 특별한 무언가를 권했다. It was a dish with four colorful ingredients. Each ingredient symbolized a different political ⓐparty. Yeongjo wanted to say that the four parties should work in harmony like this dish. This dish was called tangpyeongchae. The name came from Yeongjo's ___(A)___ tangpyeongchaek.

05 위 글의 빈칸 (A)에 들어갈 알맞은 말을 고르시오.

① recipe   ② justice   ③ custom
④ policy   ⑤ dessert

06 위 글의 밑줄 친 ⓐparty와 같은 의미로 쓰인 것을 고르시오.

① Did you go to the birthday party?
② She belongs to the Democratic Party.
③ She held a dinner party yesterday.
④ He was a third party.
⑤ The school will take a party of 40 children to France.

서답형

07 위 글의 밑줄 친 (a)의 우리말에 맞게 주어진 어휘를 알맞게 배열하시오.

special / them / offered / something

➡ _____

[08~10] 다음 글을 읽고 물음에 답하시오.

Tangpyeongchae

One day, King Yeongjo was having dinner with his officials and offered them something (A)[ordinary / special]. It was a dish with four colorful ingredients. Each (B)[ingredient / ingredients] symbolized (C)[a different / the same] political party. Yeongjo wanted to say that the four parties should work ___(A)___ harmony like this dish. This dish was called tangpyeongchae. The name came ___(B)___ Yeongjo's policy tangpyeongchaek.

08 위 글의 빈칸 (A)와 (B)에 들어갈 전치사가 바르게 짝지어진 것은?

① to – from   ② on – by
③ in – from   ④ to – for
⑤ in – for

서답형

09 위 글의 괄호 (A)~(C)에서 문맥이나 어법상 알맞은 낱말을 골라 쓰시오.

➡ (A) _____ (B) _____ (C) _____

10 위 글의 내용과 일치하지 않는 것은?

① 어느 날, 영조가 그의 신하들과 저녁을 먹다가 그들에게 특별한 무언가를 권했다.
② 영조가 권한 것은 네 가지 종류의 음식이었다.
③ 음식의 각 재료는 당파를 상징했다.
④ 영조는 이 음식처럼 네 당파가 화합을 이루어 일해야 한다는 것을 말하고 싶었다.
⑤ 탕평채의 이름은 탕평책을 따서 지어졌다.

[11~13] 다음 글을 읽고 물음에 답하시오.

Sinseollo

In the time of King Yeonsan, there was a scholar who was famous for his honesty. When the king did something wrong, the scholar was never afraid of telling ①him so. However, the king never listened to ②him. The scholar was ___ⓐ___ disappointed ___ⓑ___ he went to live on a mountain. While he lived there by ③himself, ④he mainly ate vegetables. ⑤He made a special pot to cook many different vegetables together. People called this pot and the food in it sinseollo. That is because the scholar lived like a sinseon, an imaginary person who lives alone in nature.

11 위 글의 빈칸 ⓐ와 ⓑ에 들어갈 말이 바르게 짝지어진 것은?

① so – as   ② such – that
③ too – as   ④ so – that
⑤ too – that

12 밑줄 친 ①~⑤ 중에서 가리키는 대상이 나머지 넷과 다른 것은?

①   ②   ③   ④   ⑤

13 위 글의 주제로 알맞은 것을 고르시오.

① a scholar who was famous for his honesty
② King Yeonsan who never listened to the scholar
③ the disappointment of the scholar
④ a sinseon, an imaginary person
⑤ a story behind the food, Sinseollo

[14~16] 다음 글을 읽고 물음에 답하시오.

Songpyeon

It was the time of the last king of Baekje. One day, the king and his servants found a strange turtle. Something was written on its back. It said, "Baekje is like a full moon, but Silla is like a half moon."

The king asked a fortune teller, "What does this mean?"

The fortune teller answered, "A full moon will soon become smaller. On the other hand, a half moon will grow bigger and become a full moon."

The king became worried about his kingdom. However, people of Silla were very happy to learn this and made rice cakes in the shape of a half moon. Since then, people ⓐhave enjoyed these half-moon shaped rice cakes, songpyeon.

14 위 글의 밑줄 친 ⓐhave enjoyed와 현재완료의 용법이 다른 것을 모두 고르시오.

① She has lost her book.
② He has played basketball for two hours.
③ I have learned English since 2013.
④ She hasn't cleaned her room yet.
⑤ I have never seen a whale.

서답형

15 Why did the last king of Baekje become worried about his kingdom? Fill in the blanks with suitable words.

➡ That's because some letters written on a turtle's back said "Baekje is like a _____ _____," and a fortune teller said, "A _____ _____ will soon become _____."

16 위 글을 읽고 대답할 수 없는 질문은?

① Who found a strange turtle?
② What did the letters on the turtle's back mean?
③ Was the last king of Baekje satisfied with the letters on the turtle's back?
④ In what shape did people of Silla make rice cakes?
⑤ What fillings for songpyeon did people of Silla use?

[17~19] 다음 글을 읽고 물음에 답하시오.

Sinseollo

In the time of King Yeonsan, there was a scholar who was famous for his honesty. When the king did something wrong, the scholar was never afraid of telling him so. ___ⓐ___, the king never listened to him. (①) The scholar was so disappointed that he went to live on a mountain. (②) While he lived there by himself, he mainly ate vegetables. (③) People called this pot and the food in it sinseollo. (④) That is because the scholar lived like a sinseon, an imaginary person who lives alone in nature. (⑤)

17 위 글의 빈칸 ⓐ에 들어갈 알맞은 말을 고르시오.

① Therefore   ② However
③ For example   ④ In addition
⑤ Moreover

18 위 글의 흐름으로 보아, 주어진 문장이 들어가기에 가장 적절한 곳은?

He made a special pot to cook many different vegetables together.

①   ②   ③   ④   ⑤

19 위 글의 'the scholar'에 대한 설명으로 옳지 <u>않은</u> 것은?

① 연산군 시대에 살았던 정직하기로 유명한 학자였다.

② 왕이 무언가를 잘못하면, 왕에게 그것에 대해 말하는 것을 절대 두려워하지 않았다.

③ 왕이 그의 말에 전혀 귀 기울이지 않자 그는 너무 실망하여 산속으로 들어갔다.

④ 여러 다양한 채소들을 함께 요리하기 위해 특별한 솥을 만들었다.

⑤ 자연 속에 홀로 살면서 신선이 되었다.

[20~22] 다음 글을 읽고 물음에 답하시오.

Songpyeon

It was the time of the last king of Baekje. One day, the king and his servants found a strange turtle. Something was written on ⓐ<u>its</u> back. It said, "Baekje is like a full moon, but Silla is like a half moon."

The king asked a fortune teller, "What does this mean?"

The fortune teller answered, "A full moon will soon become smaller. On the other hand, a half moon will grow bigger and become a full moon."

The king became ___(A)___ about his kingdom. However, people of Silla were very happy to learn this and made rice cakes in the shape of a half moon. Since then, people have enjoyed these half-moon shaped rice cakes, songpyeon.

20 위 글의 빈칸 (A)에 들어갈 알맞은 말을 고르시오.

① satisfied ② bored

③ worried ④ interested

⑤ comfortable

서답형

21 위 글의 밑줄 친 ⓐits가 가리키는 것을 본문에서 찾아 쓰시오.

➡ _____

22 위 글의 제목으로 알맞은 것을 고르시오.

① Something Was Written on a Turtle's Back!

② Baekje Is Like a Full Moon!

③ Silla Is Like a Half Moon!

④ Don't Worry! A Half Moon Becomes a Full Moon!

⑤ Why Does Songpyeon Look Like a Half moon?

[23~24] 다음 글을 읽고 물음에 답하시오.

Fish Skin Sundae

My family eats something special on Chuseok. (①) It is made of rice, vegetables, and fish skin. (②) It is a kind of sundae. (③) She is from North Korea. (④) When she was young, her mother often made it for the family. (⑤) The food gives us a chance to think about my grandma's home.

23 위 글의 흐름으로 보아, 주어진 문장이 들어가기에 가장 적절한 곳은?

When I eat this food, I always think of my grandma.

① ② ③ ④ ⑤

서답형

24 What are the ingredients of fish skin sundae? Answer in English in a full sentence. (7 words)

➡ _____

[01~03] 다음 글을 읽고 물음에 답하시오.

Tangpyeongchae

One day, King Yeongjo was having dinner with his officials and offered ⓐthem something special. It was a dish with four colorful ingredients. Each ingredient symbolized a different political party. Yeongjo wanted to say that the four parties should work ⓑin harmony like this dish. This dish was called tangpyeongchae. The name came from Yeongjo's policy tangpyeongchaek.

01 위 글의 밑줄 친 ⓐthem이 가리키는 것을 본문에서 찾아 쓰시오.

➡ _____

02 위 글의 밑줄 친 ⓑin harmony를 한 단어로 고치시오.

➡ _____

⭐중요
03 본문의 내용과 일치하도록 다음 빈칸 (A)와 (B)에 알맞은 단어를 쓰시오.

> Tangpyeongchae was a dish with (A)_____ colorful ingredients, and each of them symbolized a different (B)_____ _____.

[04~06] 다음 글을 읽고 물음에 답하시오.

Sinseollo

In the time of King Yeonsan, there was a scholar who was famous for his honesty. When the king did something wrong, the scholar was never afraid of telling him ⓐso. However, the king never listened to him.

ⓑ학자는 너무 실망하여 산속으로 살러 들어갔다. While he lived there ⓒby himself, he mainly ate vegetables. He made a special pot to cook many different vegetables together. People called this pot and the food in it sinseollo. That is because the scholar lived like a sinseon, an imaginary person who lives alone in nature.

⭐중요
04 위 글의 밑줄 친 ⓐso가 가리키는 것을 본문에서 찾아 쓰시오.

➡ _____

05 위 글의 밑줄 친 ⓑ의 우리말에 맞게 한 단어를 보충하여, 주어진 어휘를 알맞게 배열하시오.

> on a mountain / he / to live / that / was / went / disappointed / the scholar

➡ _____

_____

06 위 글의 밑줄 친 ⓒby himself와 바꿔 쓸 수 있는 단어를 본문에서 찾아 쓰시오.

➡ _____

[07~09] 다음 글을 읽고 물음에 답하시오.

Songpyeon

It was the time of the last king of Baekje. One day, the king and his servants found a strange turtle. Something was written on its back. It said, "Baekje is ___ⓐ___ a full moon, but Silla is ___ⓑ___ a half moon."

The king asked a fortune teller, "What does this mean?"

The fortune teller answered, "A full moon will soon become smaller. ⓒOn the other hand, a half moon will grow smaller and become a full moon."

The king became worried about his kingdom. However, people of Silla were very happy to learn this and made rice cakes in the shape of a half moon. Since then, people have enjoyed these half-moon shaped rice cakes, songpyeon.

07 위 글의 빈칸 ⓐ와 ⓑ에 공통으로 들어갈 알맞은 말을 쓰시오.

➡ _____

08 위 글의 밑줄 친 ⓒ에서 흐름상 어색한 부분을 찾아 고치시오.

_____ ➡ _____

09 위 글의 보름달과 반달이 상징하는 것을 우리말로 쓰시오.

➡ 보름달: _____
　반달: _____

[10~11] 다음 글을 읽고 물음에 답하시오.

Tangpyeongchae

One day, King Yeongjo was having dinner with his officials and offered them something special. It was a dish with four colorful ingredients. ⓐ각 재료는 서로 다른 당파를 상징했다. Yeongjo wanted to say that the four parties should work in harmony like this dish. ⓑThis dish was called tangpyeongchae. The name came from Yeongjo's policy tangpyeongchaek.

10 위 글의 밑줄 친 ⓐ의 우리말에 맞게 주어진 어휘를 이용하여 7단어로 영작하시오.

each, symbolized, party

➡ _____

11 위 글의 밑줄 친 ⓑ를 능동태로 고치시오.

➡ _____

[12~13] 다음 글을 읽고 물음에 답하시오.

Songpyeon

It was the time of the last king of Baekje. One day, the king and his servants found a strange turtle. Something was written on its back. It said, "Baekje is like a full moon, but Silla is like a half moon."

The king asked a fortune teller, "What does ⓐthis mean?"

The fortune teller answered, "A full moon will soon become smaller. On the other hand, a half moon will grow bigger and become a full moon."

The king became worried about his kingdom. However, people of Silla were very happy to learn this and made rice cakes in the shape of a half moon. Since then, people have enjoyed these half-moon shaped rice cakes, songpyeon.

12 위 글의 밑줄 친 ⓐthis가 가리키는 것을 영어로 쓰시오.

➡ _____

_____

13 Why did people of Silla make rice cakes in the shape of a half moon? Fill in the blanks with suitable words.

➡ That's because some letters written on a turtle's back said "Silla is like a _____ moon," and a fortune teller said, "A _____ moon will grow _____ and become a _____ moon."

구석구석

Work Together

A: <u>Could you recommend</u> a salad for me?
　　추천을 부탁하는 표현

B: We have two salads today. <u>Do you prefer</u> chicken salad <u>or</u> green salad?
　　　둘 중 더 좋아하는 것에 대해 물을 때는 Do you prefer A or B?를 사용한다.

A: <u>I prefer</u> green salad.
　선호하는 것을 답할 때

B: O.K. <u>Here you are.</u>
　　　물건을 건네줄 때 쓰는 표현

A: Thank you.

구문해설 • recommend: 추천하다

A: 샐러드 좀 추천해 주시겠습니까?

B: 저희는 오늘 두 가지 샐러드가 있습니다. 닭고기 샐러드가 더 좋으신가요, 야채 샐러드가 더 좋으신가요?

A: 야채 샐러드가 더 좋아요.

B: 네. 여기 나왔습니다.

A: 감사합니다.

Write

Chocolate Songpyeon

My family eats <u>something special</u> on Chuseok. It <u>is made of</u> rice flour,
　　　　　　　　–thing으로 끝나는 대명사를 수식할 때는 형용사가 뒤에 온다.　　　　　　　～으로 만들어진다

chocolate, and nuts. It is a kind of tteok. When I eat this food, I <u>always</u> think
　　　　　　　　　　　　　　　　　　　　　　　　　빈도부사: 일반동사 앞에 위치

of my little brother. Three years ago, he ate all the fillings for songpyeon,

so we <u>decided to make</u> chocolate songpyeon. This food gives us a chance
　　　decide는 to부정사를 목적어로 취한다.

<u>to remember</u> that funny day.
to부정사의 형용사적 용법

구문해설 • rice flour: 쌀가루　• nut: 견과　• filling: (음식의) 소, 속　• remember: 기억하다

초콜릿 송편

나의 가족은 추석에 특별한 것을 먹는다. 그것은 쌀가루, 초콜릿, 그리고 견과로 만들어진다. 그것은 일종의 떡이다. 내가 이 음식을 먹을 때, 나는 항상 나의 남동생을 생각한다. 3년 전, 그가 송편의 모든 소를 먹어서, 우리는 초콜릿 송편을 만들기로 결심했다. 이 음식은 우리에게 그 재미있던 날을 기억할 기회를 준다.

Culture Project

The word *dongporou* <u>comes from</u> the name of the famous Chinese poet Su
　└─ 동격 ─┘　　～에서 생겨나다

Dongpo. <u>During</u> his time in Hangzhou, he invented a way <u>to keep pork fresh</u>
　　　　during+명사(구), while+절　　　　　　　　　　　　형용사적 용법 keep의 보어로 형용사

for a long time. He <u>made</u> the pork <u>sweet and salty</u>. Afterwards, dongporou <u>or</u>
　　　　　　　　　　　made의 보어로 형용사　　　　　　　　　　　　　즉

dongpo pork became popular <u>across China</u>.
　　　　　　　　　　　　　～의 전역에서

구문해설 • poet: 시인　• pork: 돼지고기　• salty: 짠, 소금기가 있는　• afterwards: 뒤[나중]에, 그후

동파육이라는 단어는 중국의 유명한 시인인 소동파의 이름에서 나왔다. 그의 시대에 항저우에서. 그는 돼지고기를 오랫동안 신선하게 유지하는 방법을 창안했다. 그는 돼지고기를 달고 짜게 만들었다. 나중에 동파육, 즉 동파 돼지고기는 중국 전역에서 인기 있게 되었다.

영역별 핵심문제

Words & Expressions

01 다음 두 단어의 관계가 같도록 빈칸에 알맞은 단어를 쓰시오.

> different : same = indoor : _____

02 우리말 해석에 맞게 주어진 글자로 시작하여 문장을 완성하시오.

> 우리 음식의 재미있는 역사 속으로 들어가 보자.
> Let's d_____ _____ the fun history of our food.

03 대화의 빈칸에 어울리는 단어를 고르시오.

> One day, King Yeongjo was having dinner with his officials and offered them something special. It was a dish with four colorful ingredients. Each ingredient _____ a different political party.

① offered
② appreciated
③ symbolized
④ included
⑤ tasted

04 다음 〈보기〉의 단어를 사용하여 자연스러운 문장을 만들 수 없는 것은?

> ┌─ 보기 ─┐
> afraid / policy / prefer / servant / shape

① Do you _____ indoor or outdoor sports?
② One day, the king and his _____ found a strange turtle.
③ When the king did something wrong, the scholar was never _____ of telling him so.
④ This dish came from Yeongjo's _____ tangpyeongchaek.
⑤ The story is based on an _____ animal.

05 다음 우리말에 해당하는 단어를 쓰시오. (2 words)

> 송편은 왜 반달 모양일까?
> Why does songpyeon _____ a half moon?

➡ _____

Conversation

[06~07] 다음 대화를 읽고 물음에 답하시오.

> W: Excuse me. I'm looking for a skirt.
> _____(A)_____
> M: What color do you like?
> W: Blue and pink are my favorite colors.
> M: Then, how about this blue one? (B)그것은 지금 세일 중이에요. (sale / now) (4 words)
> W: Good! Thank you. I'll take it.

06 빈칸 (A)에 들어갈 말로 알맞은 것은?

① Do you know where to buy one?
② What's wrong?
③ Can you recommend any good comedies?
④ Could you recommend one?
⑤ Which do you prefer?

07 밑줄 친 (B)의 우리말에 맞게 주어진 단어를 이용하여 쓰시오.

➡ _____

[08~09] 다음 대화를 읽고 물음에 답하시오.

> G: _____(A)_____
> B: (①) Do you prefer dogs or cats?
> G: (②) They're so cute. (③)
> B: Great! (④) I can give you one. (⑤) I have seven cats at home.
> G: Thank you.

08 빈칸 (A)에 들어갈 말로 알맞은 것은?

① I'm looking for a dog.
② Do you like pets?
③ Why are you getting a pet?
④ Could you recommend a movie for me?
⑤ I'm thinking of getting a pet.

09 위 대화의 (①)~(⑤) 중 주어진 문장이 들어갈 위치로 알맞은 것은?

> I prefer cats.

①   ②   ③   ④   ⑤

10 다음 중 두 사람의 대화가 어색한 것은?

① A: What color do you like?
　 B: Blue and pink are my favorite colors.
② A: Do you prefer hot or cold food?
　 B: I prefer cold food.
③ A: How was the food?
　 B: It was great.
④ A: Excuse me. I'm looking for a skirt. Could you recommend one?
　 B: What color do you like?
⑤ A: Could you recommend a restaurant near here?
　 B: O.K. I'll try it. Thanks.

[11~12] 다음 대화를 읽고 물음에 답하시오.

Jaden: Have you been to the new Chinese restaurant, Ms. Park?
Ms. Park: Are you talking about the one on Main Street, Jaden?
Jaden: Yes, that's the one. They opened about two weeks ago, right?
Ms. Park: I think so. I went there last Friday with my friends.

Jaden: How was the food?
Ms. Park: It was great. We ordered many different dishes. I really liked the fried vegetables.
Jaden: Could you recommend a dish for me? I'm going there for dinner tonight with my family.
Ms. Park: Do you prefer seafood or meat?
Jaden: I prefer seafood.
Ms. Park: Then, you should try their fried fish. You'll love it!

11 위 대화를 읽고 다음 물음에 대해 영어로 답하시오.

> Q: What food does Ms. Park recommend?

➡ _____

12 위 대화의 내용과 일치하지 <u>않는</u> 것은?

① The new Chinese restaurant opened about two weeks ago.
② Ms. Park has been to the new Chinese restaurant.
③ Ms. Park went to the new restaurant with her friends.
④ Ms. Park really liked fried fish.
⑤ Jaden likes seafood more than meat.

Grammar

13 주어진 어휘를 이용하여 다음 우리말에 맞게 빈칸을 채우시오.

> 우리는 특별한 누군가를 찾고 있다.
> We are _____. (someone, look, special)

➡ _____

14 다음 주어진 문장과 같은 뜻이 되도록 빈칸을 채우시오.

(1) He chose his son an interesting storybook.

➡ An interesting storybook _____

_____.

(2) A lady asked me the way to the bus stop.

➡ The way to the bus stop _____

_____.

15 다음 중 어법상 올바른 것은?

① The National Museum of Korea built in 1945.

② My wallet had stolen on the crowded subway.

③ She was made leave her family by him.

④ Are you going to do anything special after school?

⑤ Is there available anybody this weekend?

16 다음 빈칸에 들어갈 말을 순서대로 바르게 짝지어진 것을 고르시오.

• Did you see _____?

• We _____ 45 minutes to solve all the problems by the teacher.

① anything red – gave

② red something – were given

③ something red – were given

④ red something – gave

⑤ something red – gave

17 다음 중 어법상 어색한 문장은?

① *The Mona Lisa* was painted by Leonardo da Vinci.

② The soup is smelled good.

③ I am called Big Deer by my classmates because I am good at running.

④ He was seen to dance by his friends.

⑤ Sand castles were built by some children on the beach.

18 다음 빈칸에 공통으로 알맞은 것은?

• I have _____ great for you.

• There's _____ wrong with your computer. It doesn't work well.

① anyone　　② nobody

③ something　④ anything

⑤ nothing

19 다음 빈칸에 들어갈 전치사가 나머지와 다른 것은?

① Do you think I'll be satisfied _____ small potatoes?

② These cookies were made _____ my mother.

③ The singer of the year was chosen _____ online voters.

④ This room was cleaned _____ him.

⑤ The mouse was caught _____ the cat.

20 어법상 어색한 것을 찾아 바르게 고쳐 다시 쓰시오.

(1) Ann was seen walk on the street by Jack yesterday.

➡ Ann _____

_____.

21 우리말과 같은 의미가 되도록 빈칸에 알맞은 말을 쓰시오.

어젯밤 많은 사람이 하늘에서 이상한 무엇인가를 보았다. (see, strange)
Last night many people _____ in the sky.

➡ _____

Reading

[22~23] 다음 글을 읽고 물음에 답하시오.

Tangpyeongchae

One day, King Yeongjo was ___ⓐ___ dinner with his officials and offered them something special. It was a dish with four colorful ingredients. Each ingredient symbolized a different political party. Yeongjo wanted to say that the four parties should work in harmony like this dish. This dish was called tangpyeongchae. The name came from Yeongjo's policy tangpyeongchaek.

22 다음 문장의 빈칸 중에 위 글의 빈칸 ⓐ에 들어갈 단어를 쓸 수 없는 문장을 고르시오.

① We are _____ a good time.
② I'm _____ a book.
③ They are _____ a fight.
④ My mother is _____ trouble with the computer.
⑤ He is _____ a walk.

23 본문의 내용과 일치하도록 다음 빈칸에 알맞은 단어를 쓰시오.

Yeongjo wanted to say that like the four ingredients of tangpyeongchae, the _____ _____ should work in harmony.

[24~26] 다음 글을 읽고 물음에 답하시오.

Songpyeon

It was the time of the last king of Baekje. One day, the king and his servants found a strange turtle. Something was written on its back. It said, "ⓐ백제는 보름달과 같지만 신라는 반달과 같다."

The king asked a fortune teller, "What does this mean?"

The fortune teller answered, "A full moon will soon become smaller. ___(A)___, a half moon will grow bigger and become a full moon."

The king became worried about his kingdom. However, people of Silla were very happy to learn this and made rice cakes in the shape of a half moon. Since then, people have enjoyed these half-moon shaped rice cakes, songpyeon.

24 위 글의 빈칸 (A)에 들어갈 알맞은 말을 고르시오.

① Likewise ② Thus
③ In other words ④ Therefore
⑤ On the other hand

25 위 글의 밑줄 친 ⓐ의 우리말에 맞게 주어진 어휘를 이용하여 13단어로 영작하시오.

is like, a half moon

➡ _____

26 위 글의 주제로 알맞은 것을 고르시오.

① to tell the fortune with a turtle's back

② the origin of songpyeon shaped the half-moon

③ the important role of a fortune teller

④ the meaning of the shape of the moon

⑤ how to make rice cakes well

[27~29] 다음 글을 읽고 물음에 답하시오.

Sinseollo

In the time of King Yeonsan, there was a scholar who was famous for his honesty. When the king did something wrong, the scholar was never afraid of ⓐtelling him so. However, the king never listened to him. The scholar was so disappointed that he went to live on a mountain. While he lived there by himself, he mainly ate vegetables. He made a special pot to cook many different vegetables together. People called this pot and the food in it sinseollo. ⓑThat is because the scholar lived like a sinseon, an imaginary person who lives alone in nature.

27 위 글의 밑줄 친 ⓐtelling과 문법적 쓰임이 같은 것을 모두 고르시오.

① She smelled something burning.

② I'm proud of being Korean.

③ John is yelling at the dog.

④ I saw him entering the room.

⑤ How about playing outside?

28 위 글의 밑줄 친 ⓑThat이 가리키는 것을 본문에서 찾아 쓰시오.

➡ _____

29 위 글의 내용과 일치하지 <u>않는</u> 것은?

① In the time of King Yeonsan, there was a very honest scholar.

② The king never listened to the advice of the scholar.

③ The scholar went to live on a mountain because he was so disappointed.

④ The scholar made a special pot to cook many different vegetables together with people.

⑤ This pot and the food in it were called sinseollo.

[30~31] 다음 글을 읽고 물음에 답하시오.

Fish Skin Sundae

My family eats something special on Chuseok. It is made ⓐ____ rice, vegetables, and fish skin. It is a kind of sundae. When I eat this food, I always think of my grandma. She is ⓑ____ North Korea. When she was young, her mother often made it for the family. The food gives us a chance ⓒto think about my grandma's home.

30 위 글의 빈칸 ⓐ와 ⓑ에 들어갈 전치사가 바르게 짝지어진 것은?

① from – in   ② from – by

③ of – from   ④ into – from

⑤ of – in

31 위 글의 밑줄 친 ⓒto think와 to부정사의 용법이 <u>다른</u> 것을 모두 고르시오.

① We go to school to learn many things.

② I have nothing particular to do today.

③ He was too tired to work any longer.

④ It is good for your health to get up early.

⑤ It is high time to finish your work.

✏️ 출제율 85%

01 다음 두 단어의 관계가 같도록 빈칸에 알맞은 말을 쓰시오.

recently : lately = fictional : _____

✏️ 출제율 95%

02 우리말에 맞게 빈칸에 알맞은 단어를 쓰시오.

- 점술가는 "보름달은 곧 작아질 것입니다."라고 답했다.
  The (A)_____ answered, "A full moon will soon become smaller."
- 어느 날, 영조가 그의 신하들과 저녁을 먹다가 그들에게 특별한 무언가를 권했다.
  One day, King Yeongjo was having dinner with his officials and (B)_____ them something special.

[03~04] 다음 영영풀이에 해당하는 단어를 고르시오.

✏️ 출제율 95%

03

unhappy because someone or something was not as good as you hoped or expected

① pleased   ② funny
③ disappointed   ④ alone
⑤ interested

✏️ 출제율 90%

04

sweet food eaten at the end of a meal

① dish   ② dessert
③ fried   ④ ingredient
⑤ desert

[05~06] 다음 대화를 읽고 물음에 답하시오.

Girl: I ①haven't seen a movie recently. Could you recommend a good one?
Boy: ②Why don't you seeing Iron Woman 2? It's ③a big hit.

Girl: Well, I don't like action movies. Can you recommend ④any good comedies?
Boy: Then, how about Funny Families?
Girl: That ⑤sounds good.

✏️ 출제율 100%

05 대화의 ①~⑤ 중 어법상 어색한 것은?

①   ②   ③   ④   ⑤

✏️ 출제율 95%

06 다음은 위 대화를 요약한 문장이다. 빈칸에 들어갈 알맞은 말을 쓰시오.

Because the girl hasn't seen a movie recently, she asks the boy to _____ a movie. The girl _____ comedies _____ action movies, so the boy recommends a _____ movie, Funny Families.

✏️ 출제율 95%

07 빈칸에 들어갈 말로 알맞은 것은?

M: Could you recommend a Korean restaurant near here?
W: Do you prefer hot or cold food?
M: _____
W: Then, you should try the naengmyeon place at the end of this block.
M: Thank you.

① I like Korean food more than Chinese food.
② I like hot food more than cold food.
③ How about you?
④ I prefer cold food.
⑤ Blue and pink are my favorite colors.

[08~09] 다음 대화를 읽고 물음에 답하시오.

Jaden: Have you been to the new Chinese restaurant, Ms. Park? (①)

Ms. Park: Are you talking about the one on Main Street, Jaden? (②)

Jaden: Yes, that's the one. (③)

Ms. Park: I think so. I went there last Friday with my friends. (④)

Jaden: How was the food?

Ms. Park: It was great. We ordered many different dishes. I really liked the fried vegetables. (⑤)

Jaden: _____(A)_____ I'm going there for dinner tonight with my family.

Ms. Park: Do you prefer seafood or meat?

Jaden: I prefer seafood.

Ms. Park: Then, you should try their fried fish. You'll love it!

출제율 95%

08 위 대화의 (①)~(⑤) 중 주어진 문장이 들어갈 위치로 알맞은 것은?

They opened about two weeks ago, right?

①   ②   ③   ④   ⑤

출제율 90%

09 대화의 빈칸 (A)에 들어갈 표현을 주어진 조건에 맞게 쓰시오.

┌── 보기 ──
• '제게 ~을 추천해 주시겠어요?'라는 뜻으로 상대방에게 추천을 부탁하는 표현을 쓸 것.
• 'could', 'a dish', 'me'를 사용할 것.

➡ _____

출제율 90%

10 다음 대화의 빈칸에 들어갈 말로 알맞은 것은?

W: Excuse me. I'm looking for an Italian cookbook. Could you recommend one?

M: Well, have you ever cooked Italian food?

W: No, I haven't, but I want to try. I really like spaghetti.

M: Then, _____ It's on sale now.

W: Good! Thank you. I'll take it.

① how about this cookbook for experts?

② why don't you try the new Indian restaurant in front of the school?

③ I want to know more about Italian food.

④ why don't you go to another bookstore?

⑤ how about this Italian cookbook for beginners?

[11~12] 다음 중 어법상 어색한 것은?

출제율 100%

11 ① This teddy bear was made by my father.

② The room was filled with the smell of roses.

③ The baby was named Thomas by the parents.

④ The baby will be looked after my mom while I'm away.

⑤ Ann was made to wash the dishes by her aunt.

출제율 95%

12 ① It's something red.

② Is it something small?

③ I hope to meet new somebody.

④ I met someone beautiful today.

⑤ There was not anyone strange there.

13 다음 문장에서 틀린 것을 고쳐 다시 쓰시오.

(1) My father is resembled by me.

➡ _____

(2) I want hot something to eat.

➡ _____

14 우리말 의미에 맞도록 괄호 안의 단어를 이용하여 영작하시오.

(1) 카드에 이상한 무언가가 적혀 있었다. (something, write)

➡ _____
_____

(2) 한국의 역사와 문화는 그것의 전통 음식에서 발견될 수 있다. (find, food)

➡ _____
_____

(3) 그것은 쌀, 야채 그리고 생선 껍질로 만들어진다. (make, fish skin)

➡ _____
_____

[15~16] 다음 글을 읽고 물음에 답하시오.

Tangpyeongchae

One day, King Yeongjo was having dinner with his officials and ⓐoffered them something special. It was a dish with four colorful ingredients. Each ingredient ⓑsymbolized a different political party. Yeongjo wanted to say that the four parties should work in harmony like this dish. This dish was called tangpyeongchae. The name came from Yeongjo's policy tangpyeongchaek.

15 위 글의 밑줄 친 ⓐ를 3형식 문장으로 고치시오.

➡ _____

16 위 글의 밑줄 친 ⓑsymbolized와 바꿔 쓸 수 있는 말을 모두 고르시오.

① represented   ② accepted

③ discussed   ④ mentioned

⑤ stood for

[17~19] 다음 글을 읽고 물음에 답하시오.

Sinseollo

In the time of King Yeonsan, there was a scholar who was famous for his honesty. When the king did something wrong, the scholar was never afraid of telling him so. However, the king never listened to him. The scholar was so disappointed that he went ⓐto live on a mountain. While he lived there by himself, he mainly ate vegetables. He made a special pot to cook many different vegetables together. People called this pot and the food in it sinseollo. That is because the scholar lived like a sinseon, an imaginary person who lives alone in nature.

17 위 글의 밑줄 친 ⓐto live와 to부정사의 용법이 같은 것을 모두 고르시오.

① I need a house to live in.

② He didn't tell us what to do.

③ She grew up to be a famous musician.

④ It is difficult to understand her feelings.

⑤ I am sorry to give you trouble.

18 위 글의 제목으로 알맞은 것을 고르시오.

① The Cruelty of King Yeonsan

② How Did Sinseollo Get Its Name?

③ The Difficulty of Giving the King Advice

④ The Good Point of Eating Vegetables

⑤ How to Cook Many Different Vegetables Together

19 다음 빈칸 (A)와 (B)에 알맞은 단어를 넣어 신선로에 대한 소개를 완성하시오. 출제율 90%

> It was a special pot which was made to cook many (A)_____ _____ together by a scholar who lived (B)_____ on a mountain.

[20~22] 다음 글을 읽고 물음에 답하시오.

Songpyeon

(①) It was the time of the (A)[last / latest] king of Baekje. (②) One day, the king and his servants found a strange turtle. (③) It said, "Baekje is like a full moon, but Silla is like a half moon." (④)

The king asked a fortune teller, "What does this mean?" (⑤)

The fortune teller answered, "A full moon will soon become smaller. On the other hand, a half moon will grow bigger and become a full moon."

The king became (B)[worrying / worried] about his kingdom. ___ⓐ___, people of Silla were very happy to learn this and made rice cakes in the shape of a half moon. Since then, people have enjoyed these half-moon (C)[shaping / shaped] rice cakes, songpyeon.

20 위 글의 빈칸 ⓐ에 들어갈 알맞은 말을 고르시오. 출제율 95%

① For example   ② However
③ Besides   ④ That is
⑤ On the one hand

21 위 글의 흐름으로 보아, 주어진 문장이 들어가기에 가장 적절한 곳은? 출제율 100%

> Something was written on its back.

①   ②   ③   ④   ⑤

22 위 글의 괄호 (A)~(C)에서 문맥이나 어법상 알맞은 낱말을 골라 쓰시오. 출제율 90%

➡ (A) _____ (B) _____ (C) _____

[23~25] 다음 글을 읽고 물음에 답하시오.

Chocolate Songpyeon

ⓐ나의 가족은 추석에 특별한 것을 먹는다. It is made of rice flour, chocolate, and nuts. It is a kind of tteok. When I eat this food, I always think of my little brother. Three years ago, he ate all the fillings for songpyeon, so we decided ___(A)___ chocolate songpyeon. This food gives us a chance to remember that funny day.

23 위 글의 빈칸 (A)에 make를 알맞은 형태로 쓰시오. 출제율 95%

➡ _____

24 위 글의 밑줄 친 ⓐ의 우리말에 맞게 주어진 어휘를 이용하여 7단어로 영작하시오. 출제율 90%

> eats, something, on

➡ _____

25 위 글을 읽고 알 수 없는 것을 고르시오. 출제율 100%

① 필자의 가족이 추석에 먹는 특별한 음식
② 초콜릿 송편의 재료
③ 초콜릿 송편을 먹을 때 생각나는 사람
④ 송편소로 준비했던 견과의 종류
⑤ 초콜릿 송편을 만들게 된 계기

01 다음 대화를 읽고 물음에 답하시오.

> Jaden: Have you been to the new Chinese restaurant, Ms. Park?
>
> Ms. Park: Are you talking about the one on Main Street, Jaden?
>
> Jaden: Yes, that's the one. They opened about two weeks ago, right?
>
> Ms. Park: I think so. I went there last Friday with my friends.
>
> Jaden: How was the food?
>
> Ms. Park: It was great. We ordered many different dishes. I really liked the fried vegetables.
>
> Jaden: Could you recommend a dish for me? I'm going there for dinner tonight with my family.
>
> Ms. Park: Do you prefer seafood or meat?
>
> Jaden: I prefer seafood.
>
> Ms. Park: Then, you should try their fried fish. You'll love it!

(1) Where is the new Chinese restaurant?

   ➡ _____

(2) Who will Jaden go to the restaurant with?

   ➡ _____

02 다음 대화의 빈칸에 들어갈 말을 주어진 조건에 맞게 영어로 쓰시오.

> G: I haven't seen a movie recently. Could you recommend a good one?
>
> B: _____ It's a big hit.
>
> G: Well, I don't like action movies. Can you recommend any good comedies?
>
> B: Then, how about *Funny Families*?
>
> G: That sounds good.

┤ 조건 ├
- '*Iron Woman 2*'를 제안하는 표현을 사용할 것.
- 숫자와 **see**를 포함하여 7단어로 쓰시오.

➡ _____

03 다음 대화의 빈칸에 들어갈 말을 주어진 조건에 맞게 영어로 쓰시오.

> B: I'm thinking of joining a sports club.
>
> G: _____
>
> B: I prefer indoor sports. I was in the badminton club last year.
>
> G: Why don't you join the table tennis club, then?
>
> B: That's a good idea. Thank you.

┤ 조건 ├
- 둘 중 더 좋아하는 것에 대해 묻는 표현을 쓸 것.
- 'indoor'와 'outdoor'를 사용하여 7단어로 쓸 것.

➡ _____

04 다음 문장에서 틀린 것을 고쳐 다시 쓰시오.

(1) BTS was appeared on TV last night.

   ➡ _____

(2) It was made run on city streets and highways.

   ➡ _____

(3) Sinseollo was called this pot and the food in it by people.

   ➡ _____

(4) There was new nothing in this magazine.

   ➡ _____

Sinseollo

In the time of King Yeonsan, there was a scholar who was famous for his honesty. When the king did something wrong, the scholar was never afraid of telling him so. However, the king never listened to him. The scholar was so (A)[disappointing / disappointed] that he went to live on a mountain. While he lived there by himself, he mainly ate vegetables. He made a special pot to cook many different vegetables together. ⓐPeople called this pot and the food in it sinseollo. That is (B)[because / why] the scholar lived like a sinseon, an (C)[imaginary / imaginative] person who lives alone in nature.

05 위 글의 괄호 (A)~(C)에서 문맥이나 어법상 알맞은 낱말을 골라 쓰시오.

➡ (A) _____ (B) _____ (C) _____

06 Why did the scholar make a special pot? Fill in the blanks with suitable words.

➡ He made a special pot in order that he _____ _____ many different vegetables together.

07 위 글의 밑줄 친 ⓐ를 수동태로 고치시오.

➡ _____

_____

Songpyeon

It was the time of the last king of Baekje. One day, the king and his servants found a strange turtle. Something was written on its back. It said, "Baekje is like a full moon, but Silla is like a half moon."

The king asked a fortune teller, "What does this mean?"

The fortune teller answered, "A full moon will soon become smaller. On the other hand, a half moon will grow bigger and become a full moon."

The king became worried about his kingdom. However, people of Silla were very happy to learn ⓐthis and made rice cakes in the shape of a half moon. Since then, people have enjoyed these half-moon shaped rice cakes, songpyeon.

08 위 글의 밑줄 친 ⓐthis가 가리키는 것을 영어로 쓰시오.

➡ _____

_____

09 Why were people of Silla very happy? Fill in the blanks with the same word.

➡ That's because they believed that the power of Silla would grow _____ like a half moon which will grow _____ and become a full moon.

10 다음 빈칸에 알맞은 단어를 넣어 반달 모양의 송편에 대한 소개를 완성하시오.

People have enjoyed the half-moon shaped rice cakes, songpyeon, since it was made in the shape of a half moon by _____ _____ _____ .

창의사고력 서술형 문제

01 다음 그림을 보고 음식을 추천하는 말과 선호하는 것을 묻고 답하는 대화를 〈보기〉와 같이 자신의 경우에 맞게 쓰시오.

SALAD	MAIN DISH	DESSERT
chicken salad	seafood spaghetti	chocolate ice cream
green salad	bibimbap	patbingsu

> 보기
>
> A: Could you recommend a salad for me?
>
> B: Do you prefer chicken salad or green salad?
>
> A: I prefer green salad.

02 주어진 동사와 수동태를 사용하여 다양한 문장을 완성하시오.

These pictures/paint	These dresses/make
Hangeul/invent	*Harry Potter*/write

(1) _____

(2) _____

(3) _____

(4) _____

03 다음 내용을 바탕으로 우리 집의 특별한 음식을 소개하는 글을 쓰시오.

> 1. My family enjoys fish skin sundae on Chuseok.
> 2. It is made of rice, vegetables, and fish skin.
> 3. It has a story about my grandma and her home in North Korea.
> 4. It is special because it gives us a chance to think about my grandma's home.

> **Fish Skin Sundae**
>
> My family eats something special on (A)_____. It is made of rice, vegetables, and (B)_____. It is a kind of sundae. When I eat this food, I always think of my grandma. She is from (C)_____. When she was young, her mother often made it for the family. The food gives us a chance to think about (D)_____.

단원별 모의고사

01 다음 단어에 대한 영어 설명이 <u>어색한</u> 것은?

① culture: the way of life, especially the general customs and beliefs, of a particular group of people at a particular time

② order: to ask for something to be made, supplied, or delivered, especially in a restaurant or shop

③ servant: a person who is employed in another person's house, doing jobs such as cooking and cleaning, especially in the past

④ beginner: a person who is starting to do something or learn something for the first time

⑤ dessert: a food that is used with other foods in the preparation of a particular dish

02 다음 우리말 해석에 맞게 알맞은 단어를 쓰시오.

(1) 학생들은 과학 실험에 몰두했다.
➡ The students _____ into the science experiment.

(2) 우리의 전통 음식에 대한 재미있는 이야기들이 많이 있다.
➡ There are many i_____ stories about our traditional food.

03 다음 영영풀이에 해당하는 단어를 고르시오.

> a country ruled by a king or queen

① tradition   ② policy
③ kingdom   ④ scholar
⑤ official

04 다음 글의 빈칸에 들어갈 단어를 영어 설명을 보고 쓰시오.

> While the scholar lived there by himself, he mainly ate vegetables. He made a special _____ to cook many different vegetables together.
> <영어 설명>
> any of various types of container, usually round, especially one used for cooking food

05 대화의 빈칸에 공통으로 들어갈 말은?

> B: Do you have anything for dessert, Aunt May?
> W: Yes, Johnny. Do you _____ pie or cake?
> B: I _____ cake.
> W: O.K. I have some chocolate cake. I'll get you some.

① agree   ② think   ③ have
④ recommend   ⑤ prefer

06 주어진 문장에 이어질 글의 순서로 알맞은 것은?

> A: Excuse me. I'm looking for a skirt. Could you recommend one?

> (A) Then, how about this blue one? It's on sale now.
> (B) Blue and pink are my favorite colors.
> (C) What color do you like?
> (D) Good! Thank you. I'll take it.

① (A) – (B) – (C) – (D)
② (B) – (C) – (A) – (D)
③ (C) – (A) – (D) – (B)
④ (C) – (B) – (A) – (D)
⑤ (D) – (B) – (C) – (A)

07 대화의 밑줄 친 ①~⑤ 중 어휘의 쓰임이 어색한 것은?

> W: Excuse me. I'm ①<u>looking</u> for an Italian cookbook. Could you ②<u>command</u> one?
> M: Well, have you ever cooked Italian food?
> W: No, I haven't, but I ③<u>want to try</u>. I really ④<u>like</u> spaghetti.
> M: Then, how about this Italian cookbook for ⑤<u>beginners</u>? It's on sale now.
> W: Good! Thank you. I'll take it.

①   ②   ③   ④   ⑤

08 다음 중 짝지어진 대화가 어색한 것은?

① A: Do you prefer pie or cake?
  B: I prefer cake.
② A: What kind of restaurant do you like to go to?
  B: I like to go to Chinese restaurants.
③ A: Why don't you join the table tennis club, then?
  B: That's a good idea. Thank you.
④ A: I'm thinking of joining a sports club.
  B: I prefer action movies.
⑤ A: Could you recommend a book for me?
  B: Why don't you read *The Flying Pan*?

09 다음 대화의 빈칸에 공통으로 들어갈 말로 알맞은 것은?

> G: I haven't seen a movie recently. Could you _____ a good one?
> B: Why don't you see *Iron Woman 2*? It's a big hit.
> G: Well, I don't like action movies. Can you _____ any good comedies?
> B: Then, how about *Funny Families*?
> G: That sounds good.

① have   ② commend   ③ advise
④ bring   ⑤ recommend

[10~12] 다음 대화를 읽고 물음에 답하시오.

> Jaden: Have you been to the new Chinese restaurant, Ms. Park?
> Ms. Park: Are you talking about the one on Main Street, Jaden?
> Jaden: Yes, that's the one. They opened about two weeks ago, right?
> Ms. Park: I think so. I went there last Friday with my friends.
> Jaden: How was the food?
> Ms. Park: It was great. We ordered many different dishes. I really liked the fried vegetables.
> Jaden: Could you recommend a dish for me? I'm going there for dinner tonight with my family.
> Ms. Park: Do you prefer seafood or meat?
> Jaden: I prefer seafood.
> Ms. Park: _____(A)_____ You'll love it!

10 빈칸 (A)에 알맞은 말은?

① Well, why don't you watch *Avengers*?
② I've never been to the Chinese restaurant.
③ Then, you should try their fried fish.
④ Why don't you try the fried vegetables?
⑤ I'd like to order some seafood.

11 다음 질문에 대해 영어로 답하시오.

> Q: What food did Ms. Park like at the restaurant?

➡ She _____.

12 위 대화를 읽고 답할 수 <u>없는</u> 질문은?

① Where is the new Chinese restaurant?
② When did the restaurant open?
③ When did Ms. Park go to the restaurant?
④ How many dishes will Jaden's family order?
⑤ When will Jaden go to the restaurant with his family?

13 다음 주어진 문장을 능동태는 수동태로, 수동태는 능동태로 바꾸시오.

(1) Songpyeon was made in the shape of a half moon by people of Silla.

➡ _____

(2) Did John paint the picture?

➡ _____

(3) Mariel told her daughter a funny story. (2가지로 쓸 것.)

➡ _____

(4) English is spoken in many countries.

➡ _____

14 다음 중 어법상 <u>어색한</u> 것은?

① The tree will be planted by them tomorrow.
② We are waiting for special someone.
③ The scholar was so disappointed that he went to live on a mountain.
④ When the king did something wrong, the scholar was never afraid of telling him so.
⑤ I found this book while I was looking for something interesting at a bookstore.

15 밑줄 친 부분 중 생략할 수 있는 것은?

① This book was read <u>by many children</u>.
② What are you called <u>by your classmates</u>?
③ These flowers were planted <u>by my mom</u>.
④ Is French spoken in Canada <u>by them</u>?
⑤ The book was written <u>by Mina</u>.

16 괄호 안의 어구를 바르게 배열하여 문장을 완성하시오.

(1) I think that (I, something, the class, can, new, learn, at).

➡ _____

(2) (you, today, interesting, heard, have, anything)?

➡ _____

17 다음 중 어법상 적절한 것은?

① The food is made from rice flour, chocolate, and nuts.
② Is there anything new in this magazine?
③ This song wrote a famous musician.
④ I want to drink cold something.
⑤ I want to do special something for my brother's birthday party.

[18~19] 다음 글을 읽고 물음에 답하시오.

Tangpyeongchae
One day, King Yeongjo was having dinner with his officials and offered them something special. It was a dish with four ⓐcolor ingredients. Each ingredient symbolized a different political party. Yeongjo wanted to say that the four parties should work in harmony ⓑlike this dish. This dish was called tangpyeongchae. The name came from Yeongjo's policy tangpyeongchaek.

18 밑줄 친 ⓐ를 알맞은 형태로 고치시오.

➡ _____

19 위 글의 밑줄 친 ⓑlike와 같은 의미로 쓰인 것을 고르시오.

① Look for the things of <u>like</u> shape.
② I <u>like</u> playing the piano.
③ Please make it <u>like</u> this.
④ He studied painting, music, and the <u>like</u>.
⑤ Do as you <u>like</u>.

[20~21] 다음 글을 읽고 물음에 답하시오.

Sinseollo

In the time of King Yeonsan, there was a scholar ___ⓐ___ was famous for his honesty. When the king did something wrong, the scholar was never afraid of telling him so. However, the king never listened to him. The scholar was so disappointed that he went to live on a mountain. While he lived there by himself, he mainly ate vegetables. He made a special pot to cook many different vegetables together. ⓑ<u>사람들은 이 솥과 그 안의 음식을 신선로라고 불렀다.</u> That is because the scholar lived like a sinseon, an imaginary person ___ⓒ___ lives alone in nature.

20 위 글의 빈칸 ⓐ와 ⓒ에 공통으로 들어갈 알맞은 말을 고르시오. (2개)

① who   ② which   ③ whom
④ that   ⑤ what

21 밑줄 친 ⓑ의 우리말에 맞게 주어진 어휘를 이용하여 10단어로 영작하시오.

┌─────────────────────────────┐
│   People, the food, sinseollo   │
└─────────────────────────────┘

➡ _____

[22~23] 다음 글을 읽고 물음에 답하시오.

Songpyeon

It was the time of the last king of Baekje. One day, the king and his servants found a strange turtle. Something was written on its back. It said, "Baekje is like a full moon, but Silla is like a half moon."

The king asked a fortune teller, "What does this mean?"

The fortune teller answered, "A full moon will soon become smaller. ⓐ<u>On the other hand</u>, a half moon will grow bigger and become a full moon."

The king became worried about his kingdom. However, people of Silla were very happy to learn this and made rice cakes in the shape of a half moon. Since then, people have enjoyed these half-moon shaped rice cakes, songpyeon.

22 위 글의 밑줄 친 ⓐOn the other hand와 바꿔 쓸 수 있는 말을 고르시오.

① Otherwise   ② Whereas
③ Besides   ④ Nevertheless
⑤ In addition

23 위 글의 내용과 일치하지 <u>않는</u> 것은?

① 어느 날, 백제의 마지막 왕과 신하들은 이상한 거북을 한 마리 발견했다.
② 그 거북의 등에 "백제는 보름달과 같지만 신라는 반달과 같다."라는 말이 쓰여 있었다.
③ 왕은 점술가에게 거북의 등에 쓰여 있는 말의 뜻을 물었다.
④ 점술가의 말을 듣고 왕은 자신의 왕국이 걱정되었다.
⑤ 백제 사람들은 반달 모양의 떡을 만들었다.

Lesson 7

Think Big, Start Small

🎙 의사소통 기능

- 알고 있음 표현하기
  I've heard our music teacher is getting married.

- 상기시켜 주기
  A: I'm going to go hiking.
  B: Don't forget to take a bottle of water.

🎙 언어 형식

- 5형식 동사+목적어+형용사
  Add some bleach to **keep the water clear**.

- 사역동사
  Let me just **put** your phone in a glass.

Words & Expressions

Key Words

- **actress** [金ktris] 명 여배우
- **amazing** [əméiziŋ] 형 놀라운
- **amusement park** 놀이공원
- **bend**(–bent–bent) [bend] 동 구부리다, 휘다
- **blackout** [blǽkaut] 명 대규모 정전 사태
- **bleach** [bli:tʃ] 명 표백제
- **bottle** [bátl] 명 병
- **ceiling** [síːliŋ] 명 천장
- **charity** [tʃǽrəti] 명 자선단체
- **chief** [tʃiːf] 형 주요한 명 우두머리, 부장
- **darkness** [dáːrknis] 명 어둠, 암흑
- **difficult** [dífikʌlt] 형 어려운
- **dim sum** 딤섬(중국식 작은 만두 요리)
- **electricity** [ilektrísəti] 명 전기
- **enough** [inʌ́f] 형 충분한
- **exciting** [iksáitiŋ] 형 흥미로운
- **favorite** [féivərit] 형 가장 좋아하는
- **foundation** [faundéiʃən] 명 재단
- **impossible** [impásəbl] 형 불가능한
- **install** [instɔ́ːl] 설치하다
- **interesting** [íntərəstiŋ] 형 흥미로운
- **invent** [invént] 동 발명하다
- **last** [læst] 동 지속되다
- **leave**(–left–left) [liːv] 동 떠나다
- **leftover** [léftouvər] 명 남은 음식
- **less** [les] 형 더 적은
- **magic** [mǽdʒik] 형 마법의, 신기한
- **meal** [miːl] 명 식사
- **packed** [pækt] 형 꽉 들어찬
- **popular** [pápjulər] 형 인기 있는
- **remain** [riméin] 동 남아 있다
- **roof** [ruːf] 명 지붕
- **safe** [seif] 형 안전한
- **save** [seiv] 동 구하다
- **shake**(–shook–shaken) [ʃeik] 동 흔들다, 털다
- **shelter** [ʃéltər] 명 주거지, 쉼터
- **shout** [ʃaut] 동 외치다
- **single** [síŋgl] 형 단 하나의
- **spread**(–spread–spread) [spred] 동 퍼지다
- **surprisingly** [sərpráiziŋli] 부 놀랍게도
- **teach**(–taught–taught) [tiːtʃ] 동 가르치다
- **thing** [θiŋ] 명 (복수형으로) 상황
- **times** [taimz] 명 (반복되는 행위의) ~번
- **village** [vílidʒ] 명 마을
- **whole** [houl] 형 전체의
- **widely** [wáidli] 부 널리, 폭넓게
- **winter break** 겨울 방학
- **work** [wəːrk] 동 작동하다

Key Expressions

- **at least** 최소한, 적어도
- **because of**+명사 ~ 때문에
- **be going to**부정사 ~할 예정이다
- **not ~ anymore** 더 이상 ~ 않다
- **dry off** ~을 말리다
- **get married** 결혼하다
- **I can't wait to**부정사 빨리 ~하고 싶다
- **just like** ~와 꼭 마찬가지로
- **forget to**부정사 ~할 것을 잊다
- **how to**부정사 ~하는 방법
- **fill A with B** A를 B로 채우다
- **come up with** ~을 생각해 내다, ~을 만들어 내다
- **have to**+동사원형 ~해야 한다
- **light up** ~을 환하게 밝히다
- **pay for** 지불하다
- **thanks to** ~ 덕분에
- **thousands of** 수천의
- **too**+형용사+**to**부정사 너무 ~해서 …할 수 없다
- **turn off** ~을 끄다
- **turn up** (소리 등을) 높이다

Word Power

※ 서로 반대되는 뜻을 가진 어휘

□ **difficult** (어려운) ↔ **easy** (쉬운)

□ **popular** (인기 있는) ↔ **unpopular** (인기 없는)

□ **possible** (가능한) ↔ **impossible** (불가능한)

□ **exciting** (흥미로운) ↔ **boring** (지루한)

□ **safe** (안전한) ↔ **dangerous** (위험한)

□ **whole** (전체의) ↔ **partial** (일부분의)

※ 서로 비슷한 뜻을 가진 단어

□ **shout** : **yell** (외치다)

□ **save** : **rescue** (구하다)

□ **last** : **continue** (지속하다)

□ **install** : **set up** (설치하다)

□ **work** : **operate** (작동하다)

□ **chief** : **main** (주요한)

English Dictionary

□ **blackout** 정전
→ a time when there is no light or power because of an electricity failure
전기 시스템의 고장으로 빛이나 전력이 없는 때

□ **bleach** 표백제
→ a strong chemical used for cleaning things or removing colour from things
물건을 청소하거나 사물에서 색을 제거하기 위해 사용되는 강한 화학물질

□ **charity** 자선, 자선단체
→ a system of giving money, food, or help free to those who are in need because they are ill, poor, or have no home, or any organization that has the purpose of providing money or helping in this way
병들거나 가난하거나 집이 없기 때문에 어려움에 처한 사람들에게 무료로 돈, 음식 또는 도움을 주는 시스템, 또는 이런 식으로 돈과 도움을 제공할 목적을 가지고 있는 단체

□ **ceiling** 천장
→ the inside surface of a room that you can see when you look above you
위쪽을 바라볼 때 볼 수 있는 방의 안쪽 표면

□ **daytime** 낮
→ the period between the time when the sun rises and the time it goes down, or the part of the day that is neither evening nor night
해가 뜨는 시간과 지는 시간 사이의 기간이나 저녁도 밤도 아닌 하루의 부분

□ **electricity** 전기
→ a form of energy that can be produced in several ways and that provides power to devices that create light, heat, etc
여러 가지 방법으로 생산될 수 있고 빛, 열 등을 만드는 장치에 동력을 제공하는 에너지의 형태

□ **install** 설치하다
→ to put furniture, a machine, or a piece of equipment into position and make it ready to use
가구, 기계 또는 장비를 제 위치에 놓고 사용할 준비가 되게 하다

□ **invent** 발명하다
→ to design and/or create something that has never been made before
이전에 만들어진 적이 없는 어떤 것을 디자인하거나 만들다

□ **lamp** 램프, 등
→ a device for giving light, especially one that has a covering
특히 덮개가 있는 빛을 제공하는 장치

□ **last** 지속되다
→ to continue to exist
계속해서 존재하다

□ **roof** 지붕
→ the covering that forms the top of a building, vehicle, etc
건물이나 차량의 상부를 형성하는 덮개

□ **spread** 퍼지다
→ to cover, reach, or have an effect on a wider or increasing area
더 넓은 또는 증가하는 영역을 덮거나, 도달하거나, 영향을 미치다

서답형

01 다음 짝지어진 두 단어의 관계가 같도록 빈칸에 알맞은 단어를 쓰시오.

> difficult : easy = partial : _____

[02~03] 다음 빈칸에 들어갈 말로 가장 적절한 것은?

02
> "I can't read a book in my room!" shouted Marco, a boy in a village in the Philippines. His house has no _____ just like all the other houses in the village.

① sunlight　　　② roof
③ tradition　　　④ electricity
⑤ ceiling

중요

03
> This amazing plastic bottle is called a Moser lamp because it was _____ by Alfredo Moser.

① invited　　　② saved
③ taught　　　④ interested
⑤ invented

[04~05] 다음 영영풀이에 해당하는 단어를 고르시오.

04
> a device for giving light, especially one that has a covering

① lamp　　　② wheel
③ ceiling　　　④ roof
⑤ bottle

05
> a form of energy that can be produced in several ways and that provides power to devices that create light, heat, etc

① device　　　② daytime
③ electricity　　　④ bleach
⑤ charity

중요

06 밑줄 친 부분의 의미가 잘못된 것은?

① Bend the straw to use it easily. (굽히다)
② Strong lightning can cause a blackout.(정전)
③ Use bleach to make your clothes clean. (표백제)
④ His father is the chief of police. (주요한)
⑤ The daytime gets longer in the summer. (낮)

서답형

[07~08] 우리말 해석에 맞게 주어진 문장의 빈칸에 세 단어의 영어를 쓰시오.

07
> 이 정전들은 그가 집을 밝히는 새로운 방법을 생각해 내도록 만들었다.
> ➡ These blackouts made him _____ a new way to light his house.

08
> 병의 3분의 1은 지붕 위에 남아 있도록 한다.
> ➡ Let _____ the bottle remain above the roof.

01 영영풀이에 해당하는 단어를 〈보기〉에서 찾아 첫 번째 칸에 쓰고, 두 번째 칸에는 우리말 뜻을 쓰시오.

┌─ 보기 ┐
ceiling / roof / daytime / blackout / bleach
└─────────────┘

(1) _____ : the period between the time when the sun rises and the time it goes down, or the part of the day that is neither evening nor night: _____

(2) _____ : the inside surface of a room that you can see when you look above you: _____

(3) _____ : a time when there is no light or power because of an electricity failure: _____

02 다음 주어진 우리말에 맞게 빈칸을 채우시오. (필요하면 변형하여 쓰시오.)

(1) Moser 램프는 앞으로 오랫동안 많은 사람들의 삶을 밝혀 줄 것이다.
➡ Moser lamps will _____ the lives of many people for many years to come. (두 단어로 쓰시오)

(2) 햇빛이 병 속의 물에 의해 굴절되어 방에 퍼진다.
➡ Sunlight is _____ by the water in the bottle and _____ around the room.

03 우리말 해석을 읽고, 주어진 철자를 알맞은 순서로 배열하여 빈칸을 채우시오.

(1) 남은 음식을 집에 가져가시겠어요?
➡ Do you want to take the _____ home? (e, o, t, e, l, f, r, v)

(2) 필리핀에서 Moser 램프는 My Shelter 재단에 의해 널리 사용된다.
➡ In the Philippines, Moser lamps are widely used by the My Shelter _____. (t, d, o, a, f, i, u, n, n, o)

04 다음 빈칸에 알맞은 단어를 〈보기〉에서 골라 쓰시오. (형태 변화 가능)

┌─ 보기 ┐
wide / chief / bleach / whole
└─────────────┘

(1) She played the _____ scientist in the movie *Jupiter*.
(2) Add some _____ to keep the water clear.
(3) Today, gas is _____ used for cooking.

05 영어 설명을 읽고, 문장의 빈칸에 들어갈 알맞은 단어를 쓰시오.

┌─────────────────────────┐
an empty space in an object, usually with an opening to the object's surface, or an opening that goes completely through an object
└─────────────────────────┘

(1) Make a _____ in the roof, and push the bottle into the _____.

┌─────────────────────────┐
with special powers or happening in an unusual or unexpected way, or easily or quickly
└─────────────────────────┘

(2) Surprisingly, it is very easy to make this _____ lamp.

Conversation

① 알고 있음 표현하기

• **I've heard our music teacher is getting married.** 우리 음악 선생님께서 결혼하신다고 들었어.

■ 어떤 사실을 들어서 알고 있음을 말할 때 'I've heard (that) ~.' 표현을 쓴다.

알고 있는지 묻기

• Do you know about ~? / You know ~, don't you?
  "~에 관해 알고 있니?" / "너는 ~을 알고 있지, 그렇지 않니?"

• Are you aware of ~? / Have you heard ~? "~을 알고 있니? / ~을 들었니?"

알고 있음 표현하기

• I've heard that ~. / I heard ~. / I know ~. "나는 ~라고 들었어 / 나는 알고 있어"

• A: Are you aware of today's lunch menu? 오늘의 점심 메뉴가 뭔지 알고 있니?
  B: I've heard that today's lunch menu is Kimchi fried rice.
      나는 오늘 점심이 김치 볶음밥이라고 들었어.

• I heard you didn't come to school yesterday. 나는 네가 어제 학교에 오지 않았다고 들었어.

핵심 Check

1. 다음 대화의 빈칸에 들어갈 알맞은 것은?

A: Do you know why Ted was absent from school yesterday?

B: _____

① I know he is very healthy.
② I've heard he was sick.
③ He likes to study in his room.
④ I wanted to go to school.
⑤ He feels good today.

② 상기시켜 주기

A I'm going to go hiking. 나는 하이킹을 하러 갈 거야.

B Don't forget to take a bottle of water. 물 한 병 챙기는 것을 잊지 마.

■ '~하는 것을 잊지 마'라는 뜻으로 상대방에게 해야 할 일을 상기시켜 줄 때 'Don't forget to부정사'나 'Remember to부정사'를 사용한다.

- A: Are you ready for your trip to Jejudo? 너는 제주도로 여행 갈 준비되었니?

  B: Not yet. What should I bring? 아직. 내가 무엇을 가져가야만 하니?

  A: Don't forget to bring a camera and a map of Jejudo.

    = Remember to bring a camera and a map of Jejudo.

    카메라와 제주도 지도를 가져가야 할 것을 잊지 마[기억해라].

- A: Don't forget to be quiet in the library. 도서관에서 조용히 하는 것 잊지 마.

  B: I won't forget. 잊지 않을게요.

- A: What will you take with you to a deserted island? 너는 무인도에 무엇을 가져갈 것이니?

  B: I will take a pen and some paper to write a diary. 나는 일기를 쓸 펜과 종이를 가져갈 거야.

  A: Don't forget to take some matches. 성냥을 가져가야 할 것도 잊지 마.

핵심 Check

2. 다음 빈칸에 들어갈 말로 알맞은 것은?

A: I'm going bike riding.

B: Have fun and _____.

A: Okay, I won't.

① it's fine today
② I think we should not make fun of others
③ don't forget to wear a helmet
④ I'm interested in baseball
⑤ I'm going to go on a trip to Jejudo

Listen & Speak 1-A-1

G: ❶Can you turn up the volume on your phone? I like this song.

B: ❷I can't turn it up anymore. It's the highest volume.

G: ❸Let me just put your phone in a glass. ❹I've heard a glass works like a speaker.

B: ❺What an interesting idea! Let's try it now.

G: 네 휴대폰 소리를 키워줄 수 있겠니? 이 노래가 좋아.
B: 소리를 더는 키울 수 없어. 음량이 이미 가장 높은데.
G: 그냥 네 휴대폰을 유리잔 안에 넣게 해 줘. 유리잔이 스피커처럼 쓰인다고 들었어.
B: 재미있는 생각이야! 지금 해보자.

❶ 상대방에게 요청할 때 사용하는 표현으로 '~해 줄 수 있니?'의 의미다.
❷ 'turn up'은 '볼륨을 높이다'는 의미로 목적어가 대명사(it)일 때 '동사+대명사+부사'의 어순을 취한다. not ~ anymore는 '더 이상 ~ 않다'는 의미다.
❸ 'Let+목적어+동사원형'은 '…가 ~하게 하다'는 의미다.
❹ 어떤 사실을 들어서 알고 있음을 말할 때 'I've heard (that) ~.' 표현을 쓴다. 'work'는 '작동하다'는 의미다.
❺ 감탄문으로 'What+a(n)+형용사+명사+주어+동사 ~!'의 어순을 취한다.

Check(√) True or False

(1) G likes the song in B's phone.　　T ☐　F ☐

(2) G suggests that B should use a speaker to listen to the song.　　T ☐　F ☐

Listen & Speak 1-A-2

B: ❶I've heard that a movie star is coming to our school.

G: That's right. She's my favorite actress.

B: Oh, who is she?

G: Miranda Kim. She played the chief scientist in the movie *Jupiter*.

B: Wow, ❷I can't wait to see her!

B: 우리 학교에 영화 배우가 온다고 들었어.
G: 맞아. 내가 가장 좋아하는 여배우야.
B: 오, 누군데?
G: Miranda Kim이야. 영화 《주피터》에서 책임 과학자를 연기했어.
B: 우와, 빨리 만나보고 싶은데!

❶ 어떤 사실을 들어서 알고 있음을 말할 때 사용하는 표현으로 '~을 들었다'는 뜻이다. 'is coming'은 현재진행형으로 미래의 일을 나타낸다.
❷ 'I can't wait to부정사'는 '빨리 ~하고 싶어'라는 뜻이다.

Check(√) True or False

(3) B knows a movie star is coming to his school.　　T ☐　F ☐

(4) B saw the movie in which Miranda Kim played the chief scientist the actress coming to his school.

　　T ☐　F ☐

Listen & Speak 2-A-1

W: Excuse me, ❶are you finished with your meal?

M: Yes, it was really good.

W: Do you want to take the leftovers home?

M: Yes, please.

W: ❷Don't forget to eat the leftovers by tomorrow.

❶ 'be finished with'는 '~을 마치다, ~을 끝내다'는 의미다.

❷ '~하는 것을 잊지 마'라는 뜻으로 상대방에게 해야 할 일을 상기시켜 줄 때 사용하는 표현이다. 이때 'forget to부정사'는 '~할 것을 잊다'는 미래의 일을 나타낸다.

Listen & Speak 2-A-2

B: ❶What's your plan for this winter break?

G: ❷I'm going to visit Hong Kong with my parents.

B: That sounds exciting. What are you going to do there?

G: I'm going to go to an amusement park. I'm also going to try all kinds of food.

B: Good. ❸Don't forget to try some dim sum.

❶ 미래의 계획을 물어볼 때 사용하는 표현이다.

❷ 'be going to부정사'는 '~할 예정이다'는 뜻으로 미래 계획을 말할 때 사용한다.

❸ '~하는 것을 잊지 마'라는 뜻으로 상대방에게 해야 할 일을 상기시켜 줄 때 사용하는 표현이다.

Communicate A

Yuri: What's wrong, Jaden?

Jaden: My science homework is too difficult.

Yuri: ❶What do you have to do?

Jaden: I need to find a way ❷to save trees.

Yuri: That's easy. ❸I've heard that we can save trees ❹by using less paper.

Jaden: Oh, I think I've heard that, too. Then, I can just ❺stop using paper cups.

Yuri: Yes! You can also use just one paper towel to dry off your hands.

Jaden: That's impossible. I need at least two or three paper towels.

Yuri: Just shake your hands before you use a paper towel. Then, one will be ❻more than enough.

Jaden: Oh, that's a good idea, Yuri! I'll try that next time.

Yuri: Good! Just ❼don't forget to shake your hands at least 10 times.

❶ 'have to부정사'는 '~해야 한다'는 의미다.

❷ 'to save'는 명사 'a way'를 꾸며주는 형용사 용법이다.

❸ 어떤 사실을 들어서 알고 있음을 말할 때 사용하는 표현으로 '~을 들었다'는 뜻이다.

❹ 'by -ing'는 '~함으로써'의 뜻이다.

❺ 'stop -ing'는 '~하는 것을 멈추다'라는 뜻이다.

❻ 'more than enough'는 '충분하고도 남을 거야'라는 뜻이다.

❼ '~하는 것을 잊지 마'라는 뜻으로 상대방에게 해야 할 일을 상기시켜 줄 때 사용하는 표현이다.

Communicate B

A: ❶I've heard that saving electricity is the best way to save the Earth.

B: I've heard that, too. What can we do to save electricity?

A: ❷Why don't we turn off the light when we're not using it?

B: That's a good idea. ❸Don't forget to turn off the light when you leave your room.

❶ 어떤 사실을 들어서 알고 있음을 말할 때 사용하는 표현으로 '~을 들었다'라는 뜻이다.

❷ '~하는 게 어때?'라는 뜻으로 상대방에게 제안할 때 사용한다.

❸ '~하는 것을 잊지 마'라는 뜻으로 상대방에게 해야 할 일을 상기시켜 줄 때 사용하는 표현이다.

Progress Check

1. B: ❶I've heard that a famous baseball player is coming to our school.

   G: That's right. He's my favorite player.

   B: Oh, who is he?

   G: I'm not going to tell you. It's a surprise!

2. B: What's your plan for this winter break?

   G: I'm going to visit Vietnam with my parents.

   B: That sounds exciting. What are you going to do there?

   G: I'm going to spend some time on the beach and eat lots of seafood.

   B: Good. ❷Don't forget to try the fruit there, too.

   G: O.K., I won't forget.

❶ 어떤 사실을 들어서 알고 있음을 말할 때 사용하는 표현이다.

❷ '~하는 것을 잊지 마'라는 뜻으로 상대방에게 해야 할 일을 상기시켜 줄 때 사용하는 표현이다.

● 다음 우리말과 일치하도록 빈칸에 알맞은 말을 쓰시오.

Listen & Speak 1-A

1. **G:** Can you _____ _____ the volume on your phone? I like this song.

   B: I can't _____ _____ _____ _____. It's the _____ volume.

   G: _____ me just _____ your phone in a glass. _____ _____ a glass _____ _____ a speaker.

   B: _____ _____ _____ _____! _____ try it now.

2. **B:** _____ _____ that a movie star _____ _____ to our school.

   G: That's right. She's my _____ _____.

   B: Oh, who is she?

   G: Miranda Kim. She _____ the _____ scientist in the movie *Jupiter*.

   B: Wow, I _____ _____ _____ see her!

해석

1. G: 네 휴대폰 소리를 키워줄 수 있겠니? 이 노래가 좋아.
   B: 소리를 더는 키울 수 없어. 음량이 이미 가장 높은데.
   G: 그냥 네 휴대폰을 유리잔 안에 넣게 해 줘. 유리잔이 스피커처럼 쓰인다고 들었어.
   B: 재미있는 생각이야! 지금 해 보자.

2. B: 우리 학교에 영화 배우가 온다고 들었어.
   G: 맞아. 내가 가장 좋아하는 여배우야.
   B: 오, 누군데?
   G: Miranda Kim이야. 영화 《주피터》에서 책임 과학자를 연기했어.
   B: 우와, 빨리 만나보고 싶은데!

Listen & Speak 2-A

1. **W:** Excuse me, are you _____ with your meal?

   M: Yes, it was really _____.

   W: Do you _____ _____ _____ the _____ home?

   M: Yes, please.

   W: _____ _____ _____ _____ the leftovers by tomorrow.

2. **B:** What's _____ _____ _____ this _____ _____?

   G: _____ _____ _____ visit Hong Kong with my parents.

   B: That sounds _____. What are you _____ _____ _____ there?

   G: I'm _____ _____ _____ to an _____ park. I'm also going to try _____ _____ of food.

   B: Good. _____ _____ _____ _____ some dim sum.

1. W: 실례합니다, 식사를 마치셨나요?
   M: 네, 정말 좋았어요.
   W: 남은 음식을 집에 가져가시겠어요?
   M: 네, 부탁합니다.
   W: 내일까지는 남은 음식을 다 드시는 걸 잊지 마세요.

2. B: 이번 겨울 방학에는 뭘 할 거야?
   G: 부모님과 홍콩에 갈 거야.
   B: 신나겠는걸. 거기서 뭘 할 거니?
   G: 놀이공원에 갈 거야. 그리고 온갖 음식들을 먹어 볼 거야.
   B: 좋은데. 딤섬을 먹어 보는 걸 잊지 마.

Communicate A

Yuri: What's _____, Jaden?

Jaden: My science homework is too _____.

Yuri: What do you _____ _____ do?

Jaden: I need to find a way _____ _____ trees.

Yuri: That's easy. _____ _____ _____ we can save trees _____ _____ _____ paper.

Jaden: Oh, I think _____ _____ _____, _____. Then, I can just _____ _____ paper cups.

Yuri: Yes! You can also use just one paper towel _____ _____ _____ your hands.

Jaden: That's _____. I need _____ _____ two or three paper towels.

Yuri: Just _____ your hands _____ you use a paper towel. Then, one will be _____ _____ _____.

Jaden: Oh, that's a good idea, Yuri! I'll _____ that _____ _____.

Yuri: Good! Just _____ _____ _____ _____ your hands _____ _____ 10 _____.

Communicate B

A: _____ _____ that _____ _____ is the best way _____ _____ the Earth.

B: I've _____ _____, _____. What can we do to _____ electricity?

A: Why don't we _____ _____ the light _____ we're not using it?

B: That's a good idea. _____ _____ to _____ _____ the light _____ you _____ your room.

Progress Check

1. **B:** _____ _____ _____ a famous baseball player _____ _____ to our school.

   G: That's right. He's my _____ player.

   B: Oh, who is he?

   G: I'm not going to tell you. It's a _____!

2. **B:** What's your _____ _____ this winter break?

   G: I'm going _____ _____ Vietnam with my parents.

   B: That _____ _____. What are you going to do there?

   G: I'm going to _____ some time on the _____ and eat lots of _____.

   B: Good. _____ _____ _____ _____ the fruit there, too.

   G: O.K., I _____ _____.

해석

유리: 무슨 일 있니, Jaden?
Jaden: 과학 숙제가 너무 어려워.
유리: 뭘 해야 하는데?
Jaden: 나무들을 살리는 방법을 찾아야 해.
유리: 그건 쉬워. 나는 종이를 덜 사용함으로써 나무들을 살릴 수 있다고 들었어.
Jaden: 아, 나도 들어 본 것 같아. 그럼, 종이컵 쓰는 걸 멈추면 되겠네.
유리: 맞아! 그리고 손을 말리는 데 종이 수건을 한 장만 쓸 수도 있지.
Jaden: 그건 불가능해. 나는 종이 수건이 적어도 두세 장은 필요해.
유리: 종이 수건을 쓰기 전에 손을 털어 봐. 그럼, 한 장으로 충분하고도 남을 거야.
Jaden: 오, 좋은 생각이야, 유리야! 다음에 해 봐야겠어.
유리: 좋아! 손을 적어도 열 번은 털어야 한다는 걸 잊지 마.

A: 전기를 절약하는 게 지구를 살리는 데 가장 좋은 방법이라고 들었어.
B: 나도 들었어. 전기를 절약하기 위해 무엇을 할 수 있을까?
A: 사용하지 않을 때는 전기를 끄는 게 어때?
B: 좋은 생각이야. 방을 나갈 때 불 끄는 것을 잊지 마.

1. B: 유명한 야구 선수가 우리 학교로 온다고 들었어.
   G: 맞아. 그는 내가 가장 좋아하는 선수야.
   B: 오, 누군데?
   G: 말해주지 않을 거야. 놀라게 할 거야!

2. B: 이번 겨울 방학에 무슨 계획이 있니?
   G: 부모님과 함께 베트남에 갈 거야.
   B: 재미있겠다. 거기서 뭘 할 거야?
   G: 바닷가에서 시간을 좀 보내고 해산물을 많이 먹을 거야.
   B: 좋아. 거기 과일을 먹어 보는 것도 잊지 마.
   G: 알겠어, 잊지 않을게.

01 다음 대화의 빈칸에 들어갈 말로 알맞은 것은?

B: _____
G: That's right. He's my favorite player.
B: Oh, who is he?
G: I'm not going to tell you. It's a surprise!

① I heard you didn't come to school yesterday.
② I've heard the car was invented earlier than the bicycle.
③ I've heard that a famous baseball player is coming to our school.
④ I heard chocolate isn't good for dogs.
⑤ Ted, I've been told Mr. Brown is going back to Canada.

[02~03] 다음 대화를 읽고, 물음에 답하시오.

W: Excuse me, (A)식사를 마치셨나요?
M: Yes, it was really good.
W: Do you want to take the leftovers home?
M: Yes, please.
W: _____ (B)

02 (A)의 우리말에 맞게 주어진 단어를 알맞은 순서로 배열하시오.

(finished / you / with / are / your / meal / ?)

➡ _____

03 빈칸 (B)에 들어갈 말로 알맞은 것은?

① Don't remember to eat the leftovers by tomorrow.
② Don't forget eating the leftovers by tomorrow.
③ Remember eating the leftovers by tomorrow.
④ Don't forget to come home until 7.
⑤ Don't forget to eat the leftovers by tomorrow.

01 다음 중 짝지어진 대화가 <u>어색한</u> 것은?

① A: What's your plan for this winter break?
B: I'm going to visit Hong Kong with my parents.

② A: What's wrong, Jaden?
B: Don't forget to bring my science homework tomorrow.

③ A: You can also use just one paper towel to dry off your hands.
B: That's impossible.

④ A: What can we do to save electricity?
B: Why don't we turn off the light when we're not using it?

⑤ A: Don't forget to try the fruit there, too.
B: O.K., I won't forget.

[02~03] 다음 대화를 읽고 물음에 답하시오.

G: _____(A)_____ I like this song.
B: I can't turn it up anymore. It's the highest volume.
G: Let me just put your phone in a glass. _____(B)_____
B: What an interesting idea! Let's try it now.

02 빈칸 (A)에 알맞은 말을 고르시오.

① Can I play soccer with my friends after school?
② Would you turn down the volume on your phone?
③ I think the volume of your phone is high.
④ Can you turn up the volume on your phone?
⑤ What are you interested in?

03 빈칸 (B)에 들어갈 알맞은 말은?

① Be carful to put your phone in a glass
② Do you know about my latest cell phone?
③ I've heard a glass works like a speaker.
④ I've heard you have a nice speaker.
⑤ I use a phone to take pictures.

[04~05] 다음 대화를 읽고 물음에 답하시오.

B: What's your plan for this winter break?
G: _____(A)_____ visit Hong Kong with my parents.
B: That sounds exciting. What are you going to do there?
G: I'm going to go to an amusement park. I'm also going to try all kinds of food.
B: Good. _____(B)_____ some dim sum.

04 빈칸 (A), (B)에 들어갈 말로 알맞은 것은?

① I'm going to – Don't remember to try
② I was going to – Don't forget trying
③ I'm going to – Don't forget trying
④ I was going to – Remember trying
⑤ I'm going to – Don't forget to try

 05 다음 영영풀이에 해당하는 단어를 대화에서 찾아 쓰시오.

a Chinese meal or snack of small dishes including different foods fried or cooked in steam

➡ _____

[06~07] 다음 대화를 읽고 물음에 답하시오.

Yuri: What's wrong, Jaden?

Jaden: My science homework is too difficult.

Yuri: What do you have to do? (①)

Jaden: I need to find a way to save trees.

Yuri: That's easy. I've heard that we can save trees by using less paper. (②)

Jaden: Oh, I think I've heard that, too. Then, I can just stop using paper cups. (③)

Yuri: Yes! You can also use just one paper towel to dry off your hands.

Jaden: That's impossible. (④)

Yuri: Just shake your hands before you use a paper towel. Then, one will be more than enough. (⑤)

Jaden: Oh, that's a good idea, Yuri! I'll try that next time.

Yuri: Good! Just don't forget to shake your hands at least 10 times.

06 위 대화의 (①)~(⑤) 중 다음 주어진 말이 들어갈 알맞은 곳은?

> I need at least two or three paper towels.

①   ②   ③   ④   ⑤

07 위 대화의 내용과 일치하지 <u>않는</u> 것은?

① They are talking about an easy way to save trees.

② Jaden thinks that his science homework is difficult.

③ Jaden has to find a way to save trees.

④ Yuri suggests that Jaden should stop using paper cups and use just one paper towel to dry off his hands.

⑤ Yuri suggests to Jaden that he should shake his hands at least 10 times before he uses a paper towel.

[08~09] 다음 대화를 읽고 물음에 답하시오.

A: I've heard that _____(A)_____ is the best way to save the Earth.

B: I've heard that, too. What can we do to save electricity?

A: _____(B)_____ when we're not using it?

B: That's a good idea. Don't forget to turn off the light when you leave your room.

08 위 대화의 빈칸 (A)에 들어갈 말로 알맞은 것은?

① saving electricity

② saving water

③ using less paper

④ washing hands

⑤ using paper towels

09 빈칸 (B)에 들어갈 말로 알맞은 것은?

① Why did you turn off the light

② Are you planning to turn off the light

③ Why don't we turn off the light

④ Shall I turn off the light

⑤ Don't forget turning off the light

[01~02] 다음 대화를 읽고 물음에 답하시오.

Boy: What's your plan for this winter break?

Girl: I'm going to visit Vietnam with my parents.

Boy: That sounds exciting. What are you going to do there?

Girl: I'm going to spend some time on the beach and eat lots of seafood.

Boy: Good. Don't forget to try the fruit there, too.

Girl: O.K., (A)잊지 않을게(forget).

01 Read the dialogue above and write what the boy suggests the girl do on her trip? (Write 5 words.)

➡ He suggests that _____.

02 밑줄 친 (A)의 우리말에 맞게 주어진 단어를 이용하여 영작하시오. (3단어로 쓸 것)

➡ _____

[03~04] 다음 대화를 읽고 물음에 답하시오.

Yuri: What's wrong, Jaden?

Jaden: My science homework is too difficult.

Yuri: What do you have to do?

Jaden: I need to find a way to save trees.

Yuri: That's easy. (A)나는 종이를 덜 사용함으로써 나무들을 살릴 수 있다고 들었어.

Jaden: Oh, I think I've heard that, too. Then, I can just stop using paper cups.

Yuri: Yes! You can also use just one paper towel to dry off your hands.

Jaden: That's impossible. I need at least two or three paper towels.

Yuri: Just shake your hands before you use a paper towel. Then, one will be more than enough.

Jaden: Oh, that's a good idea, Yuri! I'll try that next time.

Yuri: Good! Just _____ (B)

03 밑줄 친 (A)의 우리말에 맞게 주어진 단어를 이용하여 영어로 쓰시오.

> I've / that / can / by / use / little

➡ _____

04 대화의 빈칸 (B)에 주어진 조건과 우리말 해석에 맞게 한 문장을 쓰시오.

┌─ 조건 ─┐
'forget'을 이용하여 상기시켜 주는 표현을 쓸 것.

┌─ 해석 ─┐
'손을 적어도 열 번은 털어야 한다는 걸 잊지 마'

➡ _____

05 Read the sentence below and fill in the blank to complete the advice that the boy gives to the girl.

> Girl: I'm going to go hiking tomorrow, but I'm worried about bad weather.

➡ Boy: _____ take an umbrella with you.

06 다음 우리말에 맞게 주어진 어휘를 바르게 배열하시오.

> 우리 학교에 영화배우가 온다고 들었어.
> (I've / a movie / heard / star / that / is / to / our school / coming)

➡ _____

Grammar

1 5형식 동사+목적어+형용사

> • Add some bleach to **keep** the water **clear.** 물을 깨끗이 유지하기 위해 표백제를 조금 넣어라.
>
> • You'll **find** it **interesting.** 너는 그게 재미있다는 걸 알 거야.

■ '주어+동사+목적어+목적격보어'의 어순으로 이루어진 문장을 5형식 문장이라고 하며, 목적격보어 자리에는 명사, 형용사, to부정사, 현재분사, 과거분사, 동사원형 등 다양한 형태가 올 수 있다. 이때, 목적격보어는 목적어의 특징이나 상태 등을 설명하는 역할을 한다. 형용사를 목적격보어로 취하는 동사에는 find, get, keep, leave, make, paint, think 등이 있다.

   • He **made** his daughter a **teacher.** 〈명사〉 그는 그의 딸을 교사로 만들었다.

   • She **makes** me **happy.** 〈형용사〉 그녀는 나를 행복하게 해.

■ 목적격 보어를 형용사가 아닌 부사로 쓰지 않도록 주의해야 한다.

   • Do you **think** him **honest**? 너는 그가 정직하다고 생각하니?

   • This jacket will **keep** you **warm.** 이 재킷이 너를 따뜻하게 해 줄 거야.

■ 5형식 문장과 4형식 문장 비교

   5형식 문장: 주어+동사+목적어+목적격보어

   • He **kept** his room **clean.** (his room = clean) 그는 그의 방을 깨끗하게 유지했다.

   4형식 문장: 주어+동사+간접목적어+직접목적어

   • Her mom **made** her a **dress.** (her ≠ a dress) 그녀의 엄마는 그녀에게 옷을 만들어 주었다.

핵심 Check

1. 다음 우리말에 맞게 빈칸에 알맞은 말을 쓰시오.

   (1) 그는 그녀가 유명하게 만들었다.

   ➡ He made her _____ .

   (2) 아름다운 꽃들은 그녀를 행복하게 만든다.

   ➡ Beautiful flowers make her _____ .

② 사역동사

> • **Let** me just **put** your phone in a glass. 그냥 네 휴대폰을 유리잔 안에 넣게 해 줘.

■ 사역동사
  - 의미: (목적어)가 ~하게 하다/~하도록 시키다
  - 형태: 사역동사(let/make/have)+목적어+동사원형

■ 사역동사는 '사역동사+목적어+목적격보어'의 형태로 '(목적어)가 ~하게 하다/~하도록 시키다'의 뜻을 가지며 사역동사에는 make, have, let이 있다.
  - Mom **made** me **do** the dishes. 엄마는 내게 설거지를 하도록 시켰다.
  - She **let** me **go** home early. 그녀는 내가 집에 일찍 가도록 해 주었다.

■ 목적격보어로 동사원형이 오면 능동의 의미로 '~(목적어)가 …(목적격보어)을 하게 하다'의 뜻을 가지며, 과거분사가 오면 수동의 의미로 '~(목적어)가 …(목적격보어)을 당하게[되게] 하다'의 뜻을 갖는다.
  - I **had** him **call** her. 〈능동〉 나는 그가 그녀에게 전화하도록 했다. (그가 전화하는 것으로 능동)
  - He **had** his computer **repaired**. 〈수동〉 그는 그의 컴퓨터가 수리되도록 했다. (컴퓨터가 수리되는 것으로 수동)

■ 'help'와 'get'
  - help는 목적격보어로 동사원형이나 to부정사가 나오며 뜻의 차이는 없다.
  - It **helped** her **forget** life on the streets.
    = It **helped** her **to forget** life on the streets. 그것은 그녀로 하여금 거리에서의 삶을 잊는 데 도움이 되었다.
  - get이 '~하게 하다'라는 사역동사의 뜻으로 쓰일 때 목적격보어로 능동의 의미일 때는 to부정사를, 수동의 의미일 때는 과거분사를 쓴다.
  - He **got** her **to finish** her homework. 〈능동〉 그는 그녀가 숙제를 끝내도록 시켰다.
    = He **had** her **finish** her homework.
  - He **got** his computer **repaired**. 〈수동〉 그는 그의 컴퓨터가 수리되도록 했다.
    = He **had** his computer **repaired**.

핵심 Check

2. 다음 괄호 안에서 알맞은 것을 고르시오.
  (1) Dad had me (wash / to wash) his car.
  (2) Carol got her house (paint / painted).
  (3) Minhee helped me (to do / doing) my homework.
  (4) They got him (sign / to sign) the contract.

01 다음 문장에서 어법상 <u>어색한</u> 부분을 바르게 고쳐 쓰시오.

(1) The funny movie made me to laugh.

_____ ➡ _____

(2) I let him finishing cleaning his room.

_____ ➡ _____

(3) The song made me sadly.

_____ ➡ _____

(4) Too much homework makes me tiring.

_____ ➡ _____

02 주어진 단어를 어법에 맞게 빈칸에 쓰시오.

(1) She had her son _____ the trash away. (throw)

(2) She had the trash _____ away. (throw)

(3) She got him _____ her at the station. (meet)

(4) He helped his sister _____ her homework. (do)

03 다음 우리말을 영어로 바르게 옮긴 것은?

> 그 소설은 그녀를 유명하게 만들었다.

① The novel made her famously.

② The novel made her famous.

③ The novel had her famous.

④ She made the novel famous.

⑤ She made the novel famously.

04 주어진 단어를 바르게 배열하여 다음 우리말을 영어로 쓰시오.

> • 제게 그녀의 이름을 알게 해 주세요.
> (me / name / know / let / her)

➡ _____

01 다음 빈칸에 알맞은 말이 순서대로 바르게 짝지어진 것은?

> • His parents let him _____ a pet.
> • We had a math test yesterday and found it _____.

① to have – difficultly
② having – difficultly
③ having – difficult
④ have – difficultly
⑤ have – difficult

02 다음 빈칸에 들어갈 말로 적절한 것을 모두 고르시오.

> His neighbor helped him _____ his roof.

① fix   ② fixes   ③ fixed
④ fixing   ⑤ to fix

03 ⭐중요 다음 빈칸에 알맞은 말을 고르시오.

> Merriam _____ the garden in the backyard very beautiful.

① found   ② called   ③ asked
④ ordered   ⑤ begged

04 서답형 주어진 어구를 이용하여 다음 우리말을 영어로 쓰시오. (7단어)

> 그 항아리는 과일을 차갑게 유지할 수 있다. (the pot, keep, the fruit)

➡ _____

05 ⭐중요 다음 중 어법상 어색한 것은?

① Could you let Cindy know that I'll call her later?
② Finally we got the little child to sit still long enough for photo.
③ Her wish was to have her son's name mention at graduation.
④ It helped him to forget other things.
⑤ I'll make my robot clean my room.

06 서답형 괄호 안에서 알맞은 것을 고르시오.

(1) Catherine wanted to have her son (learn / to learn) Chinese.
(2) Let me (see / seeing) if I can get there on time.
(3) Amy got her room (to clean / cleaned).
(4) Did the coach (make / help) the team to win the soccer match?
(5) The teacher gets us (read / to read) many books.
(6) I found the movie (interesting / interestingly).
(7) I tried to do exercise (regular / regularly) and it made me (health / healthy).

07 다음 중 어법상 올바른 문장을 고르시오.

① Add some bleach to keep the water clearly.
② This food will make me healthily.
③ What made you so angry last Saturday?
④ Reading a lot of books will make me well at English.
⑤ This heater will make us stay warmly in winter.

08 다음 중 어법상 바르지 <u>않은</u> 것은?

I ①had the beef ②cook and ③put ④it ⑤into sandwiches.

①   ②   ③   ④   ⑤

09 다음 문장에서 어법상 틀린 부분을 찾아 바르게 고쳐 쓰시오.

When I arrived at home, I found my wallet steal.

_____ ➡ _____

[10~11] 다음 우리말을 영어로 바르게 옮긴 것을 고르시오.

10 (2개)

Ben은 Marie가 의자에 앉도록 도와주었다.

① Ben helped Marie sits on the chair.
② Ben helped Marie sat on the chair.
③ Ben helped Marie sit on the chair.
④ Ben helped Marie to sit on the chair.
⑤ Ben helped Marie sitting on the chair.

11

내가 아기를 안전하게 지킬 것이다.

① The baby will keep me safe.
② The baby will keep me safely.
③ The baby will keep I safe.
④ I'll keep the baby safe.
⑤ I'll keep the baby safely.

12 다음 문장의 빈칸에 알맞지 <u>않은</u> 것은?

Venus _____ her daughter be on a healthy diet.

① made   ② had   ③ let
④ helped   ⑤ got

13 밑줄 친 부분과 용법이 <u>다른</u> 것은?

Eating vegetables every day will <u>make</u> me healthy.

① She always <u>makes</u> me happy.
② His lie <u>made</u> her angry.
③ She <u>made</u> her son sad.
④ My dad <u>made</u> me a model train.
⑤ The comedy <u>made</u> them laugh.

14 다음 중 어법상 어색한 문장을 <u>모두</u> 고르시오.

① He helped her to carry her cases up the stairs.
② Elizabeth had the meat roast in the garden.
③ Morris got the girl stand up in front of students.
④ Alicia had her daughter take care of her cats.
⑤ Playing soccer always makes Beckham feel excited.

15 다음 중 (A)~(C)에서 어법상 옳은 것끼리 바르게 짝지은 것은?

> • Charlotte made Tom (A)(bake / baking) some cookies for her.
> • Angelina got him (B)(take / to take) some photos of her.
> • Richard had his bike (C)(fix / fixed).

	(A)	(B)	(C)
①	baking	take	fixed
②	baking	to take	fix
③	bake	to take	fix
④	bake	take	fix
⑤	bake	to take	fixed

서답형

16 두 문장의 뜻이 같도록 빈칸에 알맞은 말을 쓰시오.

(1) Kirk found the test difficult.
 = Kirk found that _____ _____ _____ difficult.

(2) I think him silly.
 = I think that _____ _____ _____.

서답형

17 다음 문장에서 어법상 <u>어색한</u> 부분을 바르게 고치시오.

(1) The police made the thief to wear handcuffs.
 _____ ➡ _____

(2) Julie got the man write down 25 things he wanted to do.
 _____ ➡ _____

(3) The girl had her purse steal on the train.
 _____ ➡ _____

서답형

18 다음 괄호 안에 주어진 어구를 이용하여 우리말을 영어로 옮기시오.

(1) 우리 아버지는 차를 깨끗이 유지하신다. (my father, keep, clean)
 ➡ _____

(2) 비 오는 날은 나를 슬프게 한다. (rainy days, sad, make)
 ➡ _____

(3) 그녀의 새 책은 그녀를 유명하게 만들었다. (make, famous)
 ➡ _____

(4) 나는 내 아이들이 TV를 보게 하지 않을 것이다. (let, watch, TV)
 ➡ _____

(5) 재미있는 이야기가 나를 웃게 했다. (the funny story, make)
 ➡ _____

(6) 나는 그 남자에게 내 컴퓨터를 고치도록 했다. (have, the man, fix)
 ➡ _____

[19~20] 다음 빈칸에 알맞은 말을 고르시오.

19

> My brother _____ my room dirty.

① made ② ordered ③ did
④ asked ⑤ have

20 중요

> My boss _____ a meeting.

① got me arrange
② made me arranged
③ got me arranged
④ made me arrange
⑤ makes I arranged

01 다음 중 어법상 어색한 부분을 찾아 바르게 고쳐 다시 쓰시오.

(1) She made him to finish his work by the next day.

➡ _____

_____

(2) She doesn't let her children playing online games.

➡ _____

_____

(3) I must go to the dry cleaner's to have my suit clean.

➡ _____

_____

(4) Mom got me help my sister with her homework.

➡ _____

_____

(5) I helped him calming down before playing the guitar on the stage.

➡ _____

_____

02 다음 문장의 빈칸에 한 단어씩을 채워 비슷한 뜻을 갖는 문장으로 바꿔 쓰시오.

(1) As I read the book, I felt sad.

= The book made _____ _____.

(2) When he did exercise regularly, he became healthy.

= Regular exercise _____ _____

_____.

03 다음 두 문장을 주어진 〈조건〉에 맞춰 〈보기〉와 같이 한 문장으로 완성하시오.

┤ 보기 ├
• My mom was busy today.
• So, she asked me to prepare dinner tonight.
→ My mom had me prepare dinner tonight.

┤ 조건 ├
1. 동사 have와 repair를 이용할 것.
2. 5 단어로 쓸 것.

• Eric had a broken camera.
• So, he brought it to a repair shop and asked a repairman to repair it.

➡ _____

04 다음 중 어법상 어색한 부분을 찾아 바르게 고쳐 다시 쓰시오.

(1) A strange man broke into my house, but he stole nothing and left it cleanly.

➡ _____

_____

(2) They made Stacy happiness by saying white lies.

➡ _____

(3) He found his new smartphone broke.

➡ _____

(4) At first, Samanda thought William honestly.

➡ _____

(5) This thick blanket will keep you warmly.

➡ _____

05 다음 그림을 참고하여 단어 turn의 알맞은 형태를 빈칸에 채우시오.

➡ I made him _____ up the volume of his smartphone.

06 〈보기〉에서 의미상 적절한 단어를 골라 빈칸에 알맞은 형태로 쓰시오.

┌─ 보기 ├─
be   watch   carry   find   clean
└─────────────┘

(1) The teacher made the students _____ their desks yesterday.

(2) Mom had the heavy box _____ upstairs.

(3) They got him _____ in the prison for a while.

(4) Yesterday I helped Jaden _____ his lost keys.

(5) His parents let him _____ TV after he finishes his homework.

07 그림을 보고 괄호 안에 주어진 단어들을 바르게 배열하여 문장을 완성하시오.

(holidays, year, her, lots, next, makes, having, excited, of)

➡ _____
   _____

08 다음 문장을 〈보기〉와 같이 사역동사를 이용하여 바꿔 쓰시오.

┌─ 보기 ├─
Mr. Kim got Jack to open the window.
= Mr. Kim had Jack open the window.
└─────────────┘

(1) Eve allowed Adam to use her pen.

➡ _____

(2) She forced Dan to follow her advice.

➡ _____

09 다음 괄호 안에 주어진 단어를 이용하여 우리말을 영어로 옮기시오.

(1) 그는 어제 그의 차가 닦여지게 했다. (have, wash)

➡ _____

(2) 우리는 램프를 더 밝게 만들 수 있었다. (the lamp, make, bright.)

➡ _____

One-Dollar Magic Lamps

"Wow, I can read a book in my room now!" shouted Marco, a boy in a village in the Philippines. His house has no electricity just like all the other houses in the village. People in the village are too poor to pay for electricity. Even during the daytime, they live in darkness because the houses are packed close together. Now things are changing because of a single plastic bottle. One plastic bottle in the ceiling can light up a whole room without using any electricity.

This amazing plastic bottle is called a Moser lamp because it was invented by Alfredo Moser. In 2002, there were many blackouts in his town in Brazil. These blackouts made him come up with a new way to light his house.

A Moser lamp can be made for about one dollar and lasts for about 10 years. It is also very safe. It can never start a house fire. Surprisingly, it is very easy to make this magic lamp.

---

magic: 마법의, 신기한
lamp: 램프, 등
shout: 외치다
electricity: 전기
village 마을
daytime: 낮, 주간
packed 꽉 들어찬
ceiling: 천장
whole 전체의
blackout 정전 사태
last 지속되다

● 다음 문장이 본문의 내용과 일치하면 T, 일치하지 <u>않으면</u> F를 쓰시오.

1 Marco's house has no electricity just like all the other houses in the village. ☐

2 During the daytime, they live in the bright room. ☐

3 A Moser lamp can be made for about one dollar and lasts for about 10 years. ☐

4 It is not easy to make this magic lamp. ☐

How to make a Moser lamp from a bottle
how to+동사원형: ~하는 방법

1. Fill a clear plastic bottle with water.
~으로

2. Add some bleach to keep the water clear.
keep+목적어+목적격 보어(5형식): 목적격 보어의 자리에 형용사를 씀. to keep: 부사적 용법

3. Make a hole in the roof, and push the bottle into the hole.

4. Let a third of the bottle remain above the roof.
사역동사 let+목적어+목적격 보어(동사원형): ~이 …하게 하다

5. Sunlight is bent by the water in the bottle and spreads around the
and로 연결된 병렬 구조. spreads 앞에 주어 sunlight가 생략됨.

room.

In the Philippines, Moser lamps are widely used by the My Shelter
수동태

Foundation. The charity also teaches local people how to make and

install the lamps. Thanks to the charity, thousands of homes in the
thousands of+명사: 수천의 ~. cf. hundred. thousand. million 등의 단어가
숫자 뒤에서 단위로 사용될 때: 단수형으로만 사용 e.g. two hundred. three million

Philippines now have Moser lamps. It has also made Moser lamps
= The charity   현재완료 계속 용법   5형식 동사+목적어+목적격보어(형용사)

popular in other countries, such as Argentina, India, and Fiji. Moser
~와 같은

lamps will light up the lives of many people for many years to come.
life의 복수형   앞으로 오랫동안

bleach: 표백제

hole: 구멍

bend: 구부러지다. 휘다 (bend-
bent-bent)

spread: 펼치다, (여러 장소로) 퍼뜨리다

thanks to: ~ 덕분에

charity: 자선 단체

install: 설치하다

life: 삶. 생활

확인문제

● 다음 문장이 본문의 내용과 일치하면 T, 일치하지 않으면 F를 쓰시오.

1   To make a Moser lamp from a bottle, you must fill a clear plastic bottle with
water. ☐

2   You need to add some bleach to keep the water cool. ☐

3   You must let two thirds of the bottle remain above the roof. ☐

4   Sunlight is bent by the water in the bottle and spreads around the room. ☐

5   The My Shelter Foundation teaches local people how to make and install Moser
lamps. ☐

6   Thanks to the My Shelter Foundation, thousands of homes in the Philippines now
have Moser lamps. ☐

● 우리말을 참고하여 빈칸에 알맞은 말을 쓰시오.

1 _____ Magic Lamps

2 "Wow, I can read a book in my room now!" shouted Marco, a boy in a village _____ _____ _____.

3 His house _____ _____ _____ just like _____ _____ _____ _____ in the village.

4 People in the village are _____ poor _____ pay for electricity.

5 Even during the daytime, they live in darkness because the houses _____ _____ _____ _____.

6 Now things are changing _____ _____ a single plastic bottle.

7 One plastic bottle in the ceiling can _____ _____ a whole room _____ _____ any electricity.

8 This amazing plastic bottle _____ _____ a Moser lamp _____ it _____ _____ _____ Alfredo Moser.

9 In 2002, there were _____ _____ in his town in Brazil.

10 These blackouts made him _____ _____ _____ a new way to light his house.

11 A Moser lamp can _____ _____ _____ about one dollar and _____ _____ about 10 years.

12 It is also _____ _____.

1 1달러짜리 마법의 전구

2 "우와, 이젠 제 방에서 책을 읽을 수 있어요!" 필리핀의 한 마을에 사는 소년인 Marco가 외쳤다.

3 그의 집은 마을의 다른 모든 집들과 마찬가지로 전기가 없다.

4 마을 사람들은 너무나 가난해서 전기세를 낼 수가 없다.

5 심지어 낮 동안에도, 집들이 빽빽하게 들어차 있어서 그들은 어둠 속에 살아간다.

6 이제 플라스틱병 하나 때문에 상황이 바뀌고 있다.

7 천장에 있는 플라스틱병 하나는 전기를 쓰지 않고 방 전체를 밝힐 수 있다.

8 이 놀라운 플라스틱병은 Moser 램프라고 불리는데, 그것이 Alfredo Moser에 의해 발명되었기 때문이다.

9 2002년, 브라질에 있는 그의 마을에는 정전이 잦았다.

10 이 정전들은 그가 집을 밝히는 새로운 방법을 생각해 내도록 만들었다.

11 Moser 램프는 1달러 정도로 만들 수 있고 10년 정도 지속된다.

12 그것은 또한 매우 안전하다.

13 It can _____ _____ a house fire.

14 Surprisingly, it is very easy _____ _____ this magic lamp.

15 _____ _____ _____ a Moser lamp from a bottle

16 1. _____ a clear plastic bottle _____ water.

17 2. _____ some bleach _____ _____ the water _____.

18 3. Make a hole in the roof, and _____ the bottle _____ the hole.

19 4. Let _____ _____ of the bottle _____ above the roof.

20 5. Sunlight _____ _____ by the water in the bottle and _____ around the room.

21 In the Philippines, Moser lamps _____ _____ _____ by the My Shelter Foundation.

22 _____ _____ also teaches local people _____ _____ _____ and _____ the lamps.

23 _____ _____ the charity, _____ _____ homes in the Philippines now have Moser lamps.

24 It _____ also _____ Moser lamps popular in other countries, _____ _____ Argentina, India, and Fiji.

25 Moser lamps will light up the lives of many people _____ _____ _____ _____ _____.

13 그것은 절대 집에 불을 낼 수 없다.

14 놀랍게도, 이 신기한 램프를 만드는 것은 매우 쉽다.

15 병으로 Moser 램프를 만드는 법

16 1. 투명한 플라스틱병에 물을 채운다.

17 2. 물을 깨끗이 유지하기 위해 표백제를 조금 넣는다.

18 3. 지붕에 구멍을 내고, 병을 구멍 안으로 넣는다.

19 4. 병의 3분의 1은 지붕 위에 남아 있도록 한다.

20 5. 햇빛이 병 속의 물에 의해 굴절되어 방에 퍼진다.

21 필리핀에서 Moser 램프는 My Shelter 재단에 의해 널리 사용된다.

22 또한 그 자선단체는 지역 사람들에게 램프를 만들고 설치하는 법을 가르친다.

23 이 자선단체 덕분에, 필리핀의 수천 가구가 이제 Moser 램프를 갖고 있다.

24 그 단체는 아르헨티나, 인도, 피지와 같은 다른 나라들에서도 Moser 램프가 유명해 지도록 만들었다.

25 Moser 램프는 앞으로 오랫동안 많은 사람들의 삶을 밝혀 줄 것이다.

● 우리말을 참고하여 본문을 영작하시오.

1 1달러짜리 마법의 전구

➡ _____

2 "우와, 이젠 제 방에서 책을 읽을 수 있어요!" 필리핀의 한 마을에 사는 소년인 Marco가 외쳤다.

➡ _____

3 그의 집은 마을의 다른 모든 집들과 마찬가지로 전기가 없다.

➡ _____

4 마을 사람들은 너무나 가난해서 전기세를 낼 수가 없다.

➡ _____

5 심지어 낮 동안에도, 집들이 빽빽하게 들어차 있어서 그들은 어둠 속에 살아간다.

➡ _____

6 이제 플라스틱병 하나 때문에 상황이 바뀌고 있다.

➡ _____

7 천장에 있는 플라스틱병 하나는 전기를 쓰지 않고 방 전체를 밝힐 수 있다.

➡ _____

8 이 놀라운 플라스틱병은 Moser 램프라고 불리는데, 그것이 Alfredo Moser에 의해 발명되었기 때문이다.

➡ _____

9 2002년, 브라질에 있는 그의 마을에는 정전이 잦았다.

➡ _____

10 이 정전들은 그가 집을 밝히는 새로운 방법을 생각해 내도록 만들었다.

➡ _____

11 Moser 램프는 1달러 정도로 만들 수 있고 10년 정도 지속된다.

➡ _____

12 그것은 또한 매우 안전하다.

➡ _____

13 그것은 절대 집에 불을 낼 수 없다.

➡ _____

14 놀랍게도, 이 신기한 램프를 만드는 것은 매우 쉽다.

➡ _____

15 병으로 Moser 램프를 만드는 법

➡ _____

16 1. 투명한 플라스틱병에 물을 채운다.

➡ _____

17 2. 물을 깨끗이 유지하기 위해 표백제를 조금 넣는다.

➡ _____

18 3. 지붕에 구멍을 내고, 병을 구멍 안으로 넣는다.

➡ _____

19 4. 병의 3분의 1은 지붕 위에 남아 있도록 한다.

➡ _____

20 5. 햇빛이 병 속의 물에 의해 굴절되어 방에 퍼진다.

➡ _____

21 필리핀에서 Moser 램프는 My Shelter 재단에 의해 널리 사용된다.

➡ _____

22 또한 그 자선단체는 지역 사람들에게 램프를 만들고 설치하는 법을 가르친다.

➡ _____

23 이 자선단체 덕분에, 필리핀의 수천 가구가 이제 Moser 램프를 갖고 있다.

➡ _____

24 그 단체는 아르헨티나, 인도, 피지와 같은 다른 나라들에서도 Moser 램프가 유명해 지도록 만들었다.

➡ _____

25 Moser 램프는 앞으로 오랫동안 많은 사람들의 삶을 밝혀 줄 것이다.

➡ _____

[01~04] 다음 글을 읽고 물음에 답하시오.

"Wow, I can read a book in my room now!" shouted Marco, a boy in a village in the Philippines. (①) His house has no electricity just like all the other houses in the village. (②) People in the village are too poor to pay _____ⓐ_____ electricity. (③) Even during the daytime, they live _____ⓑ_____ darkness because the houses are packed close together. (④) One plastic bottle in the ceiling can light up a whole room without using any _____ⓒ_____. (⑤)

01 위 글의 빈칸 ⓐ와 ⓑ에 들어갈 전치사가 바르게 짝지어진 것은?

① for – on
② to – in
③ in – from
④ for – in
⑤ to – from

02 위 글의 빈칸 ⓒ에 들어갈 말로 가장 옳은 것을 고르시오.

① source
② electricity
③ chemicals
④ gas
⑤ resource

03 위 글의 흐름으로 보아, 주어진 문장이 들어가기에 가장 적절한 곳은?

> Now things are changing because of a single plastic bottle.

① ② ③ ④ ⑤

04 위 글의 내용과 일치하지 않는 것은?

① Marco의 집은 마을의 다른 모든 집들과 마찬가지로 전기가 없다.
② Marco의 마을 사람들은 너무나 가난해서 전기세를 낼 수가 없다.
③ 낮 동안에는 대부분의 마을 사람들의 집안에 햇빛이 들어온다.
④ 이제 플라스틱병 하나 때문에 어둠 속에서 살아가던 상황이 바뀌고 있다.
⑤ 천장에 있는 플라스틱병 하나로 방 전체를 밝힐 수 있다.

[05~07] 다음 글을 읽고 물음에 답하시오.

How to make a Moser lamp from a bottle

1. _____ⓐ_____ a clear plastic bottle with water.
2. _____ⓑ_____ some bleach to _____ⓒ_____ the water clear.
3. _____ⓓ_____ a hole in the roof, and _____ⓔ_____ the bottle into the hole.
4. (A)Let a third of the bottle remain above the roof.
5. (B)Sunlight is bent by the water in the bottle and spreads around the room.

05 위 글의 빈칸 ⓐ~ⓔ에 들어갈 수 없는 단어를 고르시오. (대·소문자 무시)

① push
② make
③ give
④ fill
⑤ add

서답형

06 위 글의 밑줄 친 (A)를 다음과 같이 바꿔 쓸 때 빈칸에 들어갈 알맞은 말을 쓰시오.

➡ Let _____ of the bottle remain below the roof.

서답형

07 위 글의 밑줄 친 (B)를 능동태로 고치시오.

➡ _____

[08~10] 다음 글을 읽고 물음에 답하시오.

This amazing plastic bottle is called a Moser lamp because it was invented by Alfredo Moser. In 2002, there were many blackouts in his town in Brazil. These blackouts made him come up with a new way ⓐto light his house.

A Moser lamp can be made for about one dollar and ___(A)___ for about 10 years. It is also very safe. It can never start a house fire. Surprisingly, it is very easy to make this magic lamp.

서답형

08 주어진 영영풀이를 참고하여 빈칸 (A)에 철자 l로 시작하는 단어를 알맞은 형태로 쓰시오.

> to continue to be able to be used for a particular length of time

➡ _____

09 위 글의 밑줄 친 ⓐto light와 to부정사의 용법이 **다른** 것을 **모두** 고르시오.

① To take a walk is good for the health.
② John needed someone to help him.
③ He stopped his car to check the engine.
④ She was sad to hear the news.
⑤ I have much homework to finish by tomorrow.

중요

10 위 글의 제목으로 알맞은 것을 고르시오.

① Various Uses of a Plastic Bottle
② Alfredo Moser, the Inventor of the Moser Lamp
③ The Cheap and Safe Magic Lamp
④ Blackouts Caused the Invention of a Lamp
⑤ The Amazing Effect of a Creative Idea

[11~14] 다음 글을 읽고 물음에 답하시오.

In the Philippines, Moser lamps are widely used by the My Shelter Foundation. The charity also teaches local people how to make and install the lamps. ___ⓐ___ the charity, ⓑ필리핀의 수천 가구 now have Moser lamps. It has also made Moser lamps popular in other countries, ⓒsuch as Argentina, India, and Fiji. Moser lamps will light ___ⓓ___ the lives of many people for many years to come.

중요

11 위 글의 빈칸 ⓐ에 들어갈 알맞은 말을 고르시오.

① Instead of   ② Without
③ In place of   ④ Thanks to
⑤ Unlike

서답형

12 위 글의 밑줄 친 ⓑ의 우리말을 다음 주어진 단어를 이용하여 여섯 단어로 쓰시오.

> of, home

➡ _____

서답형

13 위 글의 밑줄 친 ⓒsuch as와 바꿔 쓸 수 있는 단어를 쓰시오.

➡ _____

14 위 글의 빈칸 ⓓ에 들어갈 알맞은 말을 고르시오.

① up   ② to
③ for   ④ from
⑤ with

[15~18] 다음 글을 읽고 물음에 답하시오.

How to make a Moser lamp from a bottle

1. Fill a clear plastic bottle ___ⓐ___ water.
2. Add some bleach ⓑ<u>to keep</u> the water clear.
3. Make a hole in the roof, and push the bottle ___ⓒ___ the hole.
4. ⓓ<u>Let a third of the bottle to remain above the roof.</u>
5. Sunlight is bent by the water in the bottle and spreads around the room.

15 위 글의 빈칸 ⓐ와 ⓒ에 들어갈 전치사가 바르게 짝지어진 것은?

① in – from　② with – from
③ in – into　④ to – by
⑤ with – into

16 아래 보기에서 위 글의 밑줄 친 ⓑ<u>to keep</u>과 to부정사의 용법이 <u>다른</u> 것의 개수를 고르시오.

┌─ 보기 ─┐
① Give me something <u>to write</u> on.
② I went to London <u>to meet</u> my uncle.
③ She worked hard <u>to be</u> a professor.
④ She is planning <u>to visit</u> her uncle.
⑤ You had better come early <u>to get</u> seats.
└─────┘

① 1개　② 2개　③ 3개　④ 4개　⑤ 5개

서답형

17 위 글의 밑줄 친 ⓓ에서 어법상 틀린 부분을 찾아 고치시오.

➡ _____　➡　_____

18 다음 중 '플라스틱병으로 Moser 램프를 만드는 법'을 올바르게 이해하지 <u>못한</u> 사람을 고르시오.

① 성민: 불투명한 플라스틱병에 물을 채워 넣어야 한다.

② 재희: 표백제를 조금 넣는 이유는 물을 깨끗이 유지하기 위해서이다.
③ 보람: 지붕에 구멍을 내고, 병을 구멍 안으로 넣어야 한다.
④ 형규: 병의 3분의 1은 지붕 위에 남아 있도록 해야 한다.
⑤ 민수: 햇빛이 병 속의 물에 의해 굴절되어 방에 퍼지게 된다.

[19~21] 다음 글을 읽고 물음에 답하시오.

In the Philippines, Moser lamps are widely used by the My Shelter Foundation. The charity also teaches local people how to make and ⓐ<u>install</u> the lamps. Thanks to the charity, thousands of homes in the Philippines now have Moser lamps. It has also made Moser lamps popular in other countries, such as Argentina, India, and Fiji. Moser lamps will light up the lives of many people for many years ⓑ<u>to come</u>.

서답형

19 위 글의 밑줄 친 ⓐinstall 앞에 생략된 말을 쓰시오.

➡ _____

20 아래 〈보기〉에서 위 글의 밑줄 친 ⓑ<u>to come</u>과 문법적 쓰임이 <u>다른</u> 것의 개수를 고르시오.

┌─ 보기 ─┐
① I think it necessary <u>to do</u> the work now.
② Sujin is happy <u>to meet</u> her old friends.
③ We are ready <u>to leave</u> for London.
④ He promised me <u>to send</u> a postcard to me from Paris.
⑤ This apron has no pocket <u>to put</u> things in.
└─────┘

① 1개　② 2개　③ 3개　④ 4개　⑤ 5개

21 위 글의 주제로 알맞은 것을 고르시오.

① the strong points of the Moser lamps
② people who work for the My Shelter Foundation
③ the remarkable activities of the My Shelter Foundation
④ the popularity of the Moser lamps
⑤ the long-lasting power of the Moser lamps

24 위 글을 읽고 대답할 수 <u>없는</u> 질문은?

① What's the name of the amazing plastic bottle?
② Why did Alfredo Moser come up with a new way to light his house?
③ Is it expensive to make a Moser lamp?
④ How long does a Moser lamp last?
⑤ How long does it take to make a Moser lamp?

[25~27] 다음 글을 읽고 물음에 답하시오.

You can make ⓐa lot of things with a CD case. You can even make a grass container. First, fill half of the CD case with soil and water, and put grass seeds into the soil. Second, close the case and tape all of the sides. Finally, leave it in the sun (A)[during / for] about ten days. Now, your grass container is ready. It will make you (B)[happy / happily] when the grass (C)[grows / will grow].

[22~24] 다음 글을 읽고 물음에 답하시오.

This amazing plastic bottle is called a Moser lamp because it was invented by Alfredo Moser. In 2002, there were many blackouts in his town in Brazil. These blackouts made him come up with a new way to light his house.

A Moser lamp can be made for ⓐabout one dollar and lasts for about 10 years. It is also very safe. ⓑIt can never start a house fire. Surprisingly, it is very easy to make this magic lamp.

서답형

25 위 글의 괄호 (A)~(C)에서 어법상 알맞은 낱말을 골라 쓰시오.

➡ (A) _____ (B) _____ (C) _____

22 위 글의 밑줄 친 ⓐabout과 같은 의미로 쓰인 것을 고르시오.

① Tell me all about it.
② It costs about $10.
③ The film is about poor boys.
④ There is nobody about.
⑤ What is he about?

26 위 글의 밑줄 친 ⓐa lot of와 바꿔 쓸 수 없는 말을 고르시오.

① lots of   ② many
③ plenty of   ④ a number of
⑤ much

서답형

27 CD 케이스로 잔디를 기르는 용기를 만드는 법을 우리말로 설명하시오.

➡ (1) _____
   (2) _____
   (3) _____

서답형

23 위 글의 밑줄 친 ⓑIt이 가리키는 것을 본문에서 찾아 쓰시오.

➡ _____

[01~03] 다음 글을 읽고 물음에 답하시오.

"Wow, I can read a book in my room now!" shouted Marco, a boy in a village in the Philippines. His house has no electricity just like all the other houses in the village. ⓐ People in the village are too poor to pay for electricity. Even during the daytime, they live in darkness ⓑ집들이 빽빽하게 들어차 있어서. Now things are changing because of a single plastic bottle. One plastic bottle in the ceiling can light up a whole room without using any electricity.

01 위 글의 밑줄 친 ⓐ를 다음과 같이 바꿔 쓸 때 빈칸에 들어갈 알맞은 말을 쓰시오.

➡ People in the village are _____ poor _____ they _____ pay for electricity.

02 위 글의 밑줄 친 ⓑ의 우리말에 맞게 한 단어를 보충하여, 주어진 어휘를 알맞게 배열하시오.

together / packed / the houses / close / because

➡ _____

03 다음 문장에서 위 글의 내용과 다른 부분을 찾아서 고치시오.

Now people in Marco's village can light up a whole room with using some electricity by installing one plastic bottle in the ceiling.

_____ ➡ _____

[04~06] 다음 글을 읽고 물음에 답하시오.

This amazing plastic bottle is called a Moser lamp because it was invented by Alfredo Moser. In ⓐ2002, there were many blackouts in his town in Brazil. These blackouts made him come up with ⓑa new way to light his house.

A Moser lamp can be made for about one dollar and lasts for about 10 years. It is also very safe. It can never start a house fire. Surprisingly, ⓒit is very easy to make this magic lamp.

04 위 글의 밑줄 친 ⓐ2002를 영어로 읽는 법을 쓰시오.

➡ _____

05 위 글의 밑줄 친 ⓑa new way to light his house가 가리키는 것을 본문에서 찾아 쓰시오.

➡ _____

06 위 글의 밑줄 친 ⓒ를 다음과 같이 바꿔 쓸 때 빈칸에 들어갈 알맞은 말을 쓰시오.

➡ (1) _____ _____ this magic lamp is very easy

(2) _____ this magic lamp is very easy

(3) _____ _____ _____ is very easy to make

[07~08] 다음 글을 읽고 물음에 답하시오.

In the Philippines, ⓐMoser lamps are widely used by the My Shelter Foundation. The charity also teaches local people how to make and install the lamps. Thanks to the charity, thousands of homes in the Philippines now have Moser lamps. ⓑIt has also made Moser lamps popularly in other countries, such as Argentina, India, and Fiji. Moser lamps will light up the lives of many people for many years to come.

07 위 글의 밑줄 친 ⓐ를 능동태로 고치시오.

➡ _____

또는 _____

08 위 글의 밑줄 친 ⓑ에서 어법상 틀린 부분을 찾아 고치시오.

_____ ➡ _____

[09~11] 다음 글을 읽고 물음에 답하시오.

This amazing plastic bottle is called a Moser lamp because it was invented by Alfredo Moser. In 2002, there were many blackouts in his town in Brazil. ⓐThese blackouts made him come up with a new way to light his house.

ⓑMoser 램프는 1달러 정도로 만들 수 있고 10년 정도 지속된다. It is also very safe. It can never start a house fire. Surprisingly, it is very easy to make this magic lamp.

09 위 글의 밑줄 친 ⓐ를 다음과 같이 바꿔 쓸 때 빈칸에 들어갈 알맞은 말을 쓰시오.

➡ _____ these blackouts, he came up with a new way to light his house.

10 위 글의 밑줄 친 ⓑ의 우리말에 맞게 한 단어를 보충하여, 주어진 어휘를 알맞게 배열하시오.

| lasts / a Moser lamp / for about 10 years / about one dollar / can be made / and |

➡ _____

_____

11 위 글에 나타난 Moser lamp의 장점 네 가지를 우리말로 �시오.

➡ (1) _____ (2) _____
(3) _____ (4) _____

[12~13] 다음 글을 읽고 물음에 답하시오.

In the Philippines, Moser lamps are (A)[wide / widely] used by the My Shelter Foundation. The charity also teaches local people (B)[how / what] to make and install the lamps. ⓐThanks to the charity, thousands of homes in the Philippines now have Moser lamps. It has also made Moser lamps popular in other countries, such as Argentina, India, and Fiji. Moser lamps will (C)[light up / lighten up] the lives of many people for many years to come.

12 위 글의 괄호 (A)~(C)에서 문맥이나 어법상 알맞은 낱말을 골라 쓰시오.

➡ (A) _____ (B) _____ (C) _____

13 위 글의 밑줄 친 ⓐ를 다음과 같이 바꿔 쓸 때 빈칸에 들어갈 알맞은 말을 쓰시오.

➡ The charity makes it possible for thousands of homes in the Philippines _____ now.

구석구석

Link - Share

We thought we could make the lamp brighter with a glass bottle. We made one
<u>we 앞에 접속사 that 생략</u>   <u>[도구·수단] ~으로, ~을 사용하여</u>

lamp out of a plastic bottle and another lamp out of a glass bottle. All the other
<u>~으로 (= from)</u>   <u>another+단수 명사</u>   <u>다른 모든 단계들(복수에 주의)</u>

steps were the same. We learned that the glass bottle lamp was brighter than
<u>알았다</u>   <u>비교급</u>

the plastic bottle lamp.

구문해설 • make A out of B: B로 A를 만들다

우리는 우리가 램프를 유리병으로 더 밝게 만들 수 있다고 생각했다. 우리는 플라스틱병으로 램프를 하나 만들고 유리병으로 또 다른 하나를 만들었다. 다른 모든 단계는 똑같았다. 우리는 유리병 램프가 플라스틱병 램프보다 더 밝다는 것을 알았다.

Write

You can make a lot of things with a CD case. You can even make a grass
<u>= many</u>

container. First, fill half of the CD case with soil and water, and put grass
<u>fill A with B: A를 B로 채우다</u>

seeds into the soil. Second, close the case and tape all of the sides. Finally,
<u>(동사) 닫다</u>   <u>= Lastly</u>

leave it in the sun for about ten days. Now, your grass container is ready.
<u>= the case</u>   <u>약</u>

It will make you happy when the grass grows.
5형식 구문으로, 목적격보어의 자리에 형용사 happy를 쓰는 것이 적절하다.

구문해설 • container: 그릇, 용기 • seed: 씨, 씨앗 • tape: (테이프로) 붙이다; 테이프

당신은 CD 케이스로 많은 것들을 만들 수 있다. 당신은 심지어 잔디를 기르는 용기를 만들 수도 있다. 먼저 CD 케이스의 절반을 흙과 물로 채우고, 잔디 씨앗을 흙 안에 넣어라. 두 번째, 케이스를 닫고 모든 옆면에 테이프를 붙여라. 마지막으로, 햇빛이 비치는 곳에 약 10일 동안 놓아 두어라. 이제, 당신의 잔디를 기르는 용기가 준비되었다. 잔디가 자랄 때 그것은 당신을 행복하게 만들어 줄 것이다.

Culture Project - Share

We'd like to talk about a pot-in-pot cooler. It keeps food fresh without
<u>~하고 싶다(= want to)</u>   <u>keep+목적어+목적격보어(형용사)</u>

electricity. It's very easy to make one. First, put a pot inside a larger pot. Then,
<u>가주어</u>   <u>진주어</u>

pour sand and water between these pots. Just let the water dry off, and it'll
<u>let(사역동사)+목적어+동사원형</u>

cool the food.

구문해설 • cooler 냉장고 • fresh 신선한 • electricity 전기 • pot 항아리 • inside ~ 안에
• pour 붓다 • dry off 마르다

우리는 pot-in-pot cooler (항아리 냉장고)에 대해 이야기하고 싶다. 그것은 전기 없이 식품을 신선하게 유지할 수 있다. 그것을 만드는 것은 매우 쉽다. 우선, 항아리 하나를 더 큰 항아리에 넣는다. 그리고 항아리들 사이에 모래와 물을 넣는다. 물이 그저 마르게 두면, 그것이 음식을 시원하게 할 것이다.

영역별 핵심문제

01 다음 주어진 두 단어의 관계가 같도록 빈칸에 주어진 철자로 단어를 쓰시오.

> shout : yell = set up : i_____

02 우리말에 맞게 밑줄 친 'hang'을 이용하여 빈칸을 완성하시오.

> 옷걸이에 옷을 거는 것을 잊지 마.
> Don't forget to <u>hang</u> your clothes on the
> _____.

03 다음 〈보기〉의 단어를 사용하여 자연스러운 문장을 만들 수 없는 것은?

> ┌─ 보기 ├─
> volume / install / leftovers / lamp /
> forward

① Can you turn down the _____, please?
② Don't _____ rumors about other people.
③ It is good to take the _____ home to avoid waste.
④ Turn on the _____ when it gets dark.
⑤ Let's step _____ to take a closer look.

04 다음 빈칸에 어울리는 단어를 고르시오.

> His house has no electricity just like all the other houses in the village. People in the village are too poor to _____ electricity.

① save ② invent
③ turn off ④ dry off
⑤ pay for

05 다음 우리말에 해당하는 단어를 주어진 철자로 시작하여 쓰시오.

> 이제 플라스틱병 하나 때문에 상황이 바뀌고 있다.
> Now t_____ are changing because of a single plastic bottle.

[06~07] 다음 대화를 읽고 물음에 답하시오.

> W: Excuse me, ⓐ<u>are you finished</u> with your meal?
> M: Yes, it was ⓑ<u>really good</u>.
> W: Do you want to ⓒ<u>take the leftovers home</u>?
> M: Yes, please.
> W: ⓓ<u>Don't forget eating the leftovers</u> ⓔ<u>by tomorrow</u>.

06 위 대화의 ⓐ~ⓔ 중 어법상 어색한 것은?

① ⓐ ② ⓑ ③ ⓒ ④ ⓓ ⑤ ⓔ

07 다음에 주어진 영어 설명에 해당하는 단어를 위 대화에서 찾아 그 단어와 뜻을 쓰시오.

> <영어 설명> food remaining after a meal

➡ _____

[08~09] 다음 대화를 읽고 물음에 답하시오.

B: What's your plan for this winter break? (①)

G: I'm going to visit Hong Kong with my parents. (②)

B: That sounds exciting. (③)

G: I'm going to go to an amusement park. (④) I'm also going to try all kinds of food. (⑤)

B: Good. _____ (A)

08 위 대화의 (①)~(⑤) 중 주어진 문장이 들어갈 위치로 알맞은 것은?

> What are you going to do there?

①   ②   ③   ④   ⑤

09 빈칸 (A)에 들어갈 말로 알맞은 것은?

① Don't forget to bring your lunch.

② Don't forget to return those books.

③ Don't forget to try some dim sum

④ Don't forget to visit my grandma.

⑤ Don't forget to go hiking.

10 다음 중 두 사람의 대화가 <u>어색한</u> 것은?

① A: Excuse me, are you finished with your meal?

   B: Yes, it was really good.

② A: I've heard that a movie star is coming to our school.

   B: That's right. She's my favorite actress.

③ A: Don't forget to recycle the cans and bottles.

   B: Sure, I will.

④ A: I've heard you didn't come to school yesterday.

   B: I got a bad cold.

⑤ A: I've heard the car was invented earlier than the bicycle.

   B: Really? That's interesting.

[11~12] 다음 대화를 읽고 물음에 답하시오.

Yuri: What's wrong, Jaden?

Jaden: My science homework is too difficult.

Yuri: What do you have to do?

Jaden: I need to find a way to save trees.

Yuri: That's easy. I've heard that we can save trees by using less paper.

Jaden: Oh, I think I've heard that, too. Then, I can just stop using paper cups.

Yuri: Yes! You can also use just one paper towel to dry off your hands.

Jaden: That's impossible. I need at least two or three paper towels.

Yuri: Just shake your hands before you use a paper towel. Then, one will be more than enough.

Jaden: Oh, that's a good idea, Yuri! I'll try that next time.

Yuri: Good! Just don't forget to shake your hands at least 10 times.

11 다음 물음에 대한 답을 대화에서 찾아 9단어의 영어로 답하시오.

> Q: What does Yuri suggest to Jaden?

➡ _____

12 위 대화를 읽고 답할 수 <u>없는</u> 질문은?

① What are the speakers talking about?

② What does Jaden have to do for his science homework?

③ How can we use only one paper towel to dry off our hands?

④ According to Yuri, how can we save trees?

⑤ How many paper towels does Yuri use a day?

Grammar

13 다음 중 어법상 바르지 <u>않은</u> 것은?

① Please let me go.

② I had my hair cut at a famous salon last week.

③ I saw him getting on a bus.

④ Mom made me wash the dishes after dinner.

⑤ He got his car wash yesterday.

14 다음 그림을 보고 괄호 안에 주어진 어휘를 이용하여 빈칸에 알맞은 말을 쓰시오.

My father made me _____ the tree.
(plant)

15 주어진 어휘를 알맞게 배열하여 다음 우리말을 영어로 옮기시오.

그녀는 텔레비전이 시간 낭비라고 생각해서 그녀의 아이들이 TV를 보게 하지 않는다.
(she, she, her children, a waste, television, TV, time, is, watch, doesn't, thinks, let, so, of)

➡ _____

_____

16 다음 문장을 주어진 어휘로 시작하는 문장으로 바꿔 쓰시오.

(1) When my daughter was born, I was really happy.

➡ My daughter's birth made _____. (2단어)

(2) When she heard about the accident, she got nervous.

➡ Hearing about the accident made _____. (2단어)

17 다음 빈칸에 공통으로 들어갈 말로 가장 알맞은 것은?

| • She couldn't _____ them silent. |
| • Mike, _____ your room clean. |

① ask   ② find   ③ keep
④ take   ⑤ tell

18 다음 중 어법상 바른 문장의 개수는?

ⓐ My brother got his robot to do his homework.

ⓑ I heard my name called.

ⓒ My parents won't let me to go out late at night.

ⓓ It will help me improving my English.

ⓔ I'll make my robot tell funny stories.

ⓕ Being sick makes me sad.

ⓖ Eating an apple a day can make us healthily.

ⓗ My father always keeps his car clean and shiny.

ⓘ I like the music because it always makes me relaxed.

① 2개   ② 3개   ③ 4개   ④ 5개   ⑤ 6개

19 다음 빈칸에 공통으로 들어갈 말은?

> • Sunny days _____ me happy.
> • I'll _____ my robot cook for me.

① have   ② find   ③ let
④ make   ⑤ take

[20~21] 다음 빈칸에 알맞은 것은?

20

> Eddie's room is not tidy. I'll make him keep it _____.

① clean   ② cleans   ③ cleaned
④ cleaning   ⑤ to clean

21

> Emily had her boy friend _____ some games with her sisters.

① play   ② plays   ③ played
④ playing   ⑤ to play

22 다음 밑줄 친 단어의 쓰임이 주어진 문장과 같은 것은?

> He made me wash his car yesterday.

① Harry wanted to make me a bowl of spaghetti.
② The heavy snowstorm made us stay at home.
③ They wonder if taking a foot bath can make us relaxed.
④ We made him captain.
⑤ Do you know what made her upset?

Reading

[23~24] 다음 글을 읽고 물음에 답하시오.

"Wow, I can read a book in my room now!" shouted Marco, a boy in a village in the Philippines. His house has no electricity just ⓐlike all the other houses in the village. People in the village are too poor to pay for electricity. Even during the daytime, they live in darkness because the houses are packed close together. Now things are changing because of a single plastic bottle. One plastic bottle in the ceiling can light up a whole room without __(A)__ any electricity.

23 위 글의 빈칸 (A)에 use를 알맞은 형태로 쓰시오.

➡ _____

24 위 글의 밑줄 친 ⓐlike와 같은 의미로 쓰인 것을 모두 고르시오.

① He ran like the wind.
② They responded in like manner.
③ I like to paint in my spare time.
④ What do you like about him?
⑤ She acts like a fool.

[25~27] 다음 글을 읽고 물음에 답하시오.

This amazing plastic bottle is called a Moser lamp because it was invented by Alfredo Moser. In 2002, there were many blackouts in his town in Brazil. These blackouts made him come up with a new way to light his house.
A Moser lamp can be made for about one dollar and lasts for about 10 years. It is also very safe. It can never start a house fire. Surprisingly, it is very easy ⓐto make this magic lamp.

25 What made Alfredo Moser come up with a new way to light his house? Fill in the blanks with suitable words.

➡ _____ in his town in Brazil in 2002 made him do so.

26 위 글의 밑줄 친 ⓐto make와 to부정사의 용법이 다른 것을 모두 고르시오.

① He decided to sell his car.
② He is looking for friends to go camping with.
③ My dream is to become a famous actor.
④ That club is not easy to join.
⑤ I found it useless to teach him math.

27 위 글의 내용과 일치하지 않는 것은?

① 이 놀라운 플라스틱병은 발명가의 이름을 따서 Moser 램프라고 불린다.
② 2002년, 브라질에 있는 Alfredo Moser의 마을에는 정전이 잦았다.
③ Moser 램프는 1달러 정도로 만들 수 있고 10년 정도 지속된다.
④ Moser 램프는 매우 안전해서 절대 집에 불을 낼 수 없다.
⑤ 이 신기한 램프를 만드는 것은 다소 어렵다.

[28~30] 다음 글을 읽고 물음에 답하시오.

1. Fill a clear plastic bottle with water.
2. Add some ____ⓐ____ to keep the water (A)[clear / clearly].
3. Make a hole in the roof, and push the bottle into the hole.
4. Let (B)[a third / a thirds] of the bottle remain above the roof.
5. Sunlight (C)[bends / is bent] by the water in the bottle and spreads around the room.

28 주어진 영영풀이를 참고하여 빈칸 ⓐ에 철자 b로 시작하는 단어를 쓰시오.

> a chemical that is used to make cloth white

➡ _____

29 위 글의 괄호 (A)~(C)에서 어법상 알맞은 낱말을 골라 쓰시오.

➡ (A) _____ (B) _____ (C) _____

30 위 글의 제목으로 가장 알맞은 것을 고르시오.

① How to Use a Clear Plastic Bottle
② Are There Any Ways to Use Natural Resources?
③ Is It Easy to Make a Hole in the Roof?
④ How to Make a Moser Lamp from a Bottle
⑤ We Must Use Sunlight Effectively!

[31~32] 다음 글을 읽고 물음에 답하시오.

You can make a lot of things with a wire hanger. You can even make a book holder. First, bend a wire hanger in the middle. Second, bend both ends up and forward. ____ⓐ____, bend down the top part of the hanger. Now, your book holder is ready. ⓑIt will keep your hands free.

31 위 글의 빈칸 ⓐ에 들어갈 알맞은 말을 모두 고르시오.

① Lastly   ② At last
③ In the end   ④ Finally
⑤ As a result

32 위 글의 밑줄 친 ⓑIt이 가리키는 것을 본문에서 찾아 쓰시오.

➡ _____

01 출제율 85%

다음 두 단어의 관계가 같도록 빈칸에 알맞은 말을 쓰시오.

| popular : unpopular = dangerous : _____ |

02 출제율 95%

우리말에 맞게 빈칸 (A), (B)에 알맞은 단어를 쓰시오.

- 심지어 낮 동안에도, 집들이 빽빽하게 들어차 있어서 그들은 어둠 속에 살아간다.
  Even during the daytime, they live in darkness because the houses are (A)_____ close together.
- 이 자선단체 덕분에, 필리핀의 수천 가구가 이제 Moser 램프를 갖고 있다.
  (B)_____ the charity, thousands of homes in the Philippines now have Moser lamps.

[03~04] 다음 영영풀이에 해당하는 단어를 찾으시오.

03 출제율 90%

| a strong chemical used for cleaning things or removing colour from things |

① lamp　　　　② thing
③ bleach　　　④ magic
⑤ paint

04 출제율 90%

| to cover, reach, or have an effect on a wider or increasing area |

① cross　　　　② last
③ shout　　　　④ spend
⑤ spread

[05~06] 다음 대화를 읽고 물음에 답하시오.

G: Can you ①turn up the volume on your phone? I like this song.
B: I can't ②turn up it anymore. It's ③the highest volume.
G: Let me just put your phone in a glass. ④I've heard a glass works like a speaker.
B: ⑤What an interesting idea! Let's (A)try it now.

05 출제율 100%

위 대화의 ①~⑤ 중 어법상 어색한 것은?

①　　　②　　　③　　　④　　　⑤

06 출제율 90%

위 대화의 밑줄 친 (A)try it이 의미하는 것을 본문에서 찾아 6단어로 쓰시오.

➡ _____

07 출제율 95%

다음 대화의 빈칸에 들어갈 말로 알맞은 것은?

B: I've heard that a movie star is coming to our school.
G: That's right. She's my favorite actress.
B: Oh, who is she?
G: Miranda Kim. She played the chief scientist in the movie *Jupiter*.
B: Wow, _____

① I can't wait to see her!
② don't forget to take something to eat.
③ don't forget to take lots of rest.
④ I know that.
⑤ how wonderful you are!

08 다음 대화의 밑줄 친 우리말에 맞게 주어진 단어를 알맞은 순서로 배열하시오.

> A: I've heard that saving electricity is the best way to save the Earth.
>
> B: I've heard that, too. What can we do to save electricity?
>
> A: Why don't we turn off the light when we're not using it?
>
> B: That's a good idea. 방을 나갈 때 불 끄는 것을 잊지 마. (turn off / when / don't / to / you / leave / forget / the light / your room)

➡ _____

_____

[09~10] 다음 대화를 읽고 물음에 답하시오.

Yuri: What's wrong, Jaden?

Jaden: My science homework is too difficult.

Yuri: What do you have to do?

Jaden: I need to find a way to ⓐsave trees.

Yuri: That's easy. I've heard that we can save trees by using ⓑless paper.

Jaden: Oh, I think I've heard that, too. Then, I can just ⓒstop using paper cups.

Yuri: Yes! You can also use just one paper towel to dry off your hands.

Jaden: That's ⓓpossible. I need at least two or three paper towels.

Yuri: Just shake your hands before you use a paper towel. Then, _____(A)_____.

Jaden: Oh, that's a good idea, Yuri! I'll try that next time.

Yuri: Good! Just ⓔdon't forget to shake your hands at least 10 times.

09 위 대화의 빈칸 (A)에 들어갈 말로 알맞은 것은?

① you will have to save trees

② you will need more paper towels

③ you will stop using paper cups

④ your hands will be dried up faster

⑤ one will be more than enough

10 위 대화의 밑줄 친 ⓐ~ⓔ 중, 어휘의 쓰임이 어색한 것은?

① ⓐ   ② ⓑ   ③ ⓒ   ④ ⓓ   ⑤ ⓔ

[11~12] 어법상 바른 문장을 모두 고르시오.

11 ① You'd better have the tooth pulled out.

② Let him joining your club.

③ He made me to introduce myself.

④ She had Mike called me.

⑤ She got me to walk her dog.

12 ① We found the window break.

② I saw him sang in front of students.

③ She left him alone.

④ The novel made her famous.

⑤ Let's keep the room clean.

13 다음 우리말을 주어진 어휘를 이용하여 영작하시오.

(1) 이 영화는 그 배우들을 유명하게 만들었다.
(make, famous)

➡ _____

(2) 내 부모님은 내가 열심히 공부하도록 시키신다.
(make, hard)

➡ _____

14 다음 문장에서 어법상 틀린 부분을 찾아 바르게 고치시오.

> He got me wash the dishes.

_____ ➡ _____

[15~16] 다음 글을 읽고 물음에 답하시오.

> "Wow, I can read a book in my room now!" shouted Marco, a boy in a village in the Philippines. His house has no electricity just like all the other houses in the village. ⓐ마을 사람들은 너무나 가난해서 전기세를 낼 수가 없다. Even (A)[during / while] the daytime, they live in darkness because the houses are (B)[packing / packed] close together. Now things are changing because of a single plastic bottle. One plastic bottle in the ceiling can light up a whole room without using (C)[any / no] electricity.

15 위 글의 밑줄 친 ⓐ의 우리말에 맞게 주어진 어휘를 이용하여 11단어로 영작하시오.

> people, too, pay for

➡ _____

16 위 글의 괄호 (A)~(C)에서 어법상 알맞은 낱말을 골라 쓰시오.

➡ (A) _____ (B) _____ (C) _____

[17~19] 다음 글을 읽고 물음에 답하시오.

> (A)This amazing plastic bottle is called a Moser lamp because it was invented ① by Alfredo Moser. ②In 2002, there were many blackouts in his town in Brazil. These blackouts made him come up ③with a new way to light his house.
>
> A Moser lamp can be made ④by about one dollar and lasts ⑤for about 10 years. It is also very safe. It can never start a house fire. Surprisingly, ⓐit is very easy to make this magic lamp.

17 위 글의 밑줄 친 ①~⑤ 중 전치사의 쓰임이 어색한 것을 찾아 고치시오.

_____ 번 ➡ _____

18 위 글의 밑줄 친 ⓐit과 문법적 쓰임이 다른 것을 모두 고르시오.

① I gave it to her.
② It is impossible to master English in a month or two.
③ They considered it impossible for us to climb the mountain.
④ How far is it from here to the station?
⑤ It is strange that he says so.

19 위 글을 읽고 밑줄 친 (A)This amazing plastic bottle에 대해 알 수 없는 것을 고르시오.

① 이름   ② 발명가   ③ 발명 동기
④ 제작비   ⑤ 제작 방법

[20~21] 다음 글을 읽고 물음에 답하시오.

How to make a Moser lamp from a bottle

1. Fill a clear plastic bottle with water.
2. Add some bleach ⓐ물을 깨끗이 유지하기 위해.
3. Make a hole in the roof, and push the bottle into the hole.
4. Let a third of the bottle remain above the roof.
5. Sunlight is bent by the water in the bottle and spreads around the room.

출제율 90%

20 위 글의 밑줄 친 ⓐ의 우리말을 다섯 단어로 쓰시오.

➡ _____

출제율 100%

21 위 글을 읽고 대답할 수 없는 질문은?

① What do you need to make a Moser lamp?
② Why do you need to add some bleach?
③ Where do you install a Moser lamp?
④ How long does it take to install a Moser lamp?
⑤ How does a Moser lamp operate?

[22~24] 다음 글을 읽고 물음에 답하시오.

In the Philippines, Moser lamps are widely used by the My Shelter ⓐFoundation. ⓑ또한 그 자선단체는 지역 사람들에게 램프를 만들고 설치하는 법을 가르친다. Thanks to the charity, thousands of homes in the Philippines now have Moser lamps. It has also made Moser lamps popular in other countries, such as Argentina, India, and Fiji. Moser lamps will light up the lives of many people for many years to come.

출제율 85%

22 위 글의 밑줄 친 ⓐFoundation과 같은 의미로 쓰인 것을 고르시오.

① These stories have no foundation.
② They are getting enough financial support from a religious foundation.
③ The organization has grown enormously since its foundation in 1955.
④ The rumour is totally without foundation.
⑤ The holiday is also called the National Foundation Day of Korea.

출제율 95%

23 위 글의 밑줄 친 ⓑ의 우리말에 맞게 한 단어를 보충하여, 주어진 어휘를 알맞게 배열하시오.

to make / also / the lamps / local people / teaches / and / the charity / install

➡ _____

_____

출제율 100%

24 다음 중 'My Shelter Foundation'의 활동에 대한 설명으로 옳지 않은 것을 고르시오.

① 필리핀에서 My Shelter Foundation에 의해 Moser 램프가 널리 사용된다.
② 지역 사람들에게 램프를 만드는 법을 가르친다.
③ 지역 사람들에게 램프를 설치하는 법을 가르친다.
④ 필리핀의 수만 가구가 이제 Moser 램프를 갖게 해주었다.
⑤ 아르헨티나, 인도, 피지와 같은 다른 나라들에서도 Moser 램프가 유명해지도록 만들었다.

[01~02] 다음 대화를 읽고 물음에 답하시오.

Yuri: What's wrong, Jaden?

Jaden: My science homework is too difficult.

Yuri: What do you have to do?

Jaden: I need to find a way to save trees.

Yuri: That's easy. _____(A)

Jaden: Oh, I think I've heard that, too. Then, I can just stop using paper cups.

Yuri: Yes! You can also use just one paper towel to dry off your hands.

Jaden: That's impossible. I need at least two or three paper towels.

Yuri: (B)종이 수건을 쓰기 전에 손을 털어 봐. Then, one will be more than enough.

Jaden: Oh, that's a good idea, Yuri! I'll try that next time.

Yuri: Good! Just don't forget to shake your hands at least 10 times.

01 위 대화의 빈칸 (A)에 들어갈 표현을 주어진 〈조건〉에 맞게 영어로 쓰시오.

┌── 조건 ──┐
• 어떤 사실을 들어서 알고 있음을 말할 때 사용하는 표현을 쓸 것
• 'hear'를 이용하여 현재완료로 표현할 것
• 'that'절에 'save trees', 'by', 'less'를 이용하여 '우리가 종이를 덜 사용함으로써 나무들을 살릴 수 있다'는 우리말에 맞게 쓸 것

➡ _____

02 위 대화의 밑줄 친 우리말에 맞게 주어진 단어를 알맞은 순서로 배열하시오.

┌─────────────────────────────┐
hands / before / shake / just / your / you / a / use / paper / towel
└─────────────────────────────┘

➡ _____

03 다음 문장의 빈칸에 들어갈 말을 주어진 〈조건〉에 맞게 영어로 쓰시오.

┌─────────────────────────────┐
B: What's your plan for this winter break?

G: I'm going to visit Vietnam with my parents.

B: That sounds exciting. What are you going to do there?

G: I'm going to spend some time on the beach and eat lots of seafood.

B: Good. _____, too.

G: O.K., I won't forget.
└─────────────────────────────┘

┌── 조건 ──┐
• 상대방에게 상기시키는 표현을 쓸 것
• '~할 것을 잊지 마'라는 뜻으로 쓸 것
• 'try the fruit there'라는 표현을 사용할 것

➡ _____

04 다음 우리말을 주어진 어휘를 이용하여 영작하시오.

(1) 나는 사촌의 생일잔치에 가고 싶지 않았으나 엄마가 나를 가도록 하셨다. (my cousin, my mom, make)

➡ _____

(2) 그들은 그들의 집이 칠해지도록 시켰다. (have, their house, paint)

➡ _____

(3) 그 선물은 그 아이들을 종일 행복하게 해 주었다. (present, make, all day long)

➡ _____

★ 중요
05 다음 문장에서 어법상 어색한 것을 고쳐 다시 쓰시오.

(1) The noise kept me wake.

➡ _____

(2) He found the exam difficultly.

➡ _____

(3) These blackouts made him to come up with a new way to light his house.

➡ _____
_____

(4) He had his computer repair yesterday.

➡ _____

(5) Help me taking some pictures of them.

➡ _____

07 주어진 영영풀이에 해당하는 단어를 위 글에서 찾아 쓰시오.

> periods of time during which the electricity supply to a place is temporarily cut off

➡ _____

08 본문의 내용과 일치하도록 다음 빈칸에 알맞은 단어를 쓰시오.

> We can say that a Moser lamp is _____ _____ because it can never start a house fire.

[06~08] 다음 글을 읽고 물음에 답하시오.

ⓐThis amazing plastic bottle is called a Moser lamp because it was invented by Alfredo Moser. In 2002, there were many blackouts in his town in Brazil. These blackouts made him come up with a new way to light his house.

A Moser lamp can be made for about one dollar and lasts for about 10 years. It is also very safe. It can never start a house fire. Surprisingly, it is very easy to make this magic lamp.

06 위 글의 밑줄 친 ⓐ를 능동태로 고치시오.

➡ _____
_____

[09~10] 다음 글을 읽고 물음에 답하시오.

In the Philippines, Moser lamps are widely used by the My Shelter Foundation. ⓐThe charity also teaches local people how to make and install the lamps. ⓑThanks to the charity, thousand of homes in the Philippines now have Moser lamps. It has also made Moser lamps popular in other countries, such as Argentina, India, and Fiji. Moser lamps will light up the lives of many people for many years to come.

09 위 글의 밑줄 친 ⓐThe charity가 가리키는 것을 본문에서 찾아 쓰시오.

➡ _____

10 위 글의 밑줄 친 ⓑ에서 어법상 틀린 부분을 찾아 고치시오.

_____ ➡ _____

01 상자 안의 Plan과 Advice를 읽고 어울리는 것끼리 연결하여, 계획과 조언을 말하는 대화를 〈보기〉와 같이 작성하시오.

Plan
go to Gyeongju go on a field trip

Advice
visit the National Museum take something to eat

보기

• Plan: go hiking   • Advice: take a bottle of water

A: I'm going to go hiking.

B: Don't forget to take a bottle of water.

A: O.K., I won't forget.

02 다음 문장을 make를 이용하여 비슷한 의미의 문장으로 바꿔 쓰시오.

(1) Mom told me to do the dishes this morning.

(2) The doctor ordered him to stop smoking.

(3) Miranda asked her husband to buy some fruit.

(1) _____

(2) _____

(3) _____

03 다음 내용을 바탕으로 자신이 만들고 싶은 물건에 관한 글을 쓰시오.

a book holder

1. Bend a wire hanger in the middle.

2. Bend both ends up and forward.

3. Bend down the top part of the hanger.

4. Put your book on the book holder.

You can make a lot of things with a (A)_____. You can even make a book holder. First, (B)_____ a wire hanger in the middle. Second, bend (C)_____ up and forward. Finally, bend down the (D)_____ of the hanger. Now, your book holder is ready. It will keep your hands (E)_____.

단원별 모의고사

01 다음 단어에 대한 영어 설명이 <u>어색한</u> 것은?

① roof: the covering that forms the top of a building, vehicle, etc
② last: to continue to exist
③ invent: to design and/or create something that has never been made before
④ install: to put furniture, a machine, or a piece of equipment into position and make it ready to use
⑤ surprisingly: including a lot of different places, people, subjects, etc

02 다음 우리말에 맞게 빈칸에 알맞은 단어를 쓰시오.

(1) 나는 나무를 심기 위해 구멍을 파고 있다.
➡ I am digging a _____ to plant a tree.

(2) 전선을 구부릴 때 적절한 도구를 사용해라.
➡ Use the right tools when you bend a _____.

03 다음 영영풀이에 해당하는 단어를 고르시오.

a system of giving money, food, or help free to those who are in need because they are ill, poor, or have no home, or any organization that has the purpose of providing money or helping in this way

① company   ② charity
③ kingdom   ④ government
⑤ foundation

04 빈칸에 들어갈 단어를 영어 설명을 보고 주어진 철자로 시작하여 쓰시오.

This a_____ plastic bottle is called a Moser lamp because it was invented by Alfredo Moser.
<영어 설명>
extremely surprising

05 대화의 빈칸에 들어갈 말은?

B: I've heard that a famous baseball player is coming to our school.
G: That's right. He's my favorite player.
B: Oh, who is he?
G: I'm not going to tell you. _____

① I won't forget.
② I've heard that, too.
③ Sorry to hear that.
④ It's a surprise!
⑤ I had a great time there.

06 주어진 문장에 이어질 글의 순서로 알맞은 것은?

W: Excuse me, are you finished with your meal?

(A) Yes, please.
(B) Do you want to take the leftovers home?
(C) Yes, it was really good.
(D) Don't forget to eat the leftovers by tomorrow.

① (A) – (B) – (C) – (D)
② (B) – (C) – (A) – (D)
③ (C) – (A) – (D) – (B)
④ (C) – (B) – (A) – (D)
⑤ (D) – (B) – (C) – (A)

07 대화의 밑줄 친 ①~⑤ 중 어휘의 쓰임이 <u>어색한</u> 것은?

A: I've heard that ①saving electricity is the best way to ②save the Earth.

B: I've heard that, too. What can we do to save electricity?

A: Why don't we ③turn off the light when we're not using it?

B: That's a good idea. Don't ④forget to turn off the light when you ⑤enter your room.

①   ②   ③   ④   ⑤

08 다음 중 짝지어진 대화가 <u>어색한</u> 것은?

① A: I'm going to the supermarket.
   B: Don't forget to buy some toilet paper. We're running out of it.

② A: Tom, are you finished with your art homework?
   B: Yes, I'm almost done.

③ A: I've heard the school soccer team won the soccer match.
   B: Really? That's nice.

④ A: I've heard the school gym is going to open next month.
   B: I will, thanks.

⑤ A: You know what? I've heard the car was invented earlier than the bicycle.
   B: Really? That's interesting.

[09~10] 다음 대화를 읽고 요약문의 빈칸을 완성하시오.

09

B: What's your plan for this winter break?

G: I'm going to visit Hong Kong with my parents.

B: That sounds exciting. What are you going to do there?

G: I'm going to go to an amusement park. I'm also going to try all kinds of food.

B: Good. Don't forget to try some dim sum.

⬇

The girl is going to visit Hong Kong with _____ during this _____. She is going to go to an _____, and she will also try all kinds of _____. And the boy suggests that she try some _____.

10

B: I've heard that a movie star is coming to our school.

G: That's right. She's my favorite actress.

B: Oh, who is she?

G: Miranda Kim. She played the chief scientist in the movie *Jupiter*.

B: Wow, I can't wait to see her!

⬇

The boy has _____ that a _____ is coming to their school. Actually, the movie star is the girl's _____ _____. Her name is Miranda Kim, and she _____ the _____ scientist in the movie *Jupiter*.

[11~12] 다음 대화를 읽고 물음에 답하시오.

Yuri: What's wrong, Jaden?

Jaden: My science homework is too difficult.

Yuri: What do you have to do?

Jaden: I need to find a way to save trees.

Yuri: That's easy. _____ (A)

Jaden: Oh, I think I've heard that, too. Then, I can just stop using paper cups.

Yuri: Yes! You can also use just one paper towel to dry off your hands.

Jaden: That's impossible. I need at least two or three paper towels.

Yuri: Just shake your hands before you use a paper towel. Then, one will be more than enough.

Jaden: Oh, that's a good idea, Yuri! I'll try that next time.

Yuri: Good! Just don't forget to shake your hands at least 10 times.

11 빈칸 (A)에 알맞은 말은?

① I've heard that drinking coffee very often isn't good for our health.

② I've never been to the Chinese restaurant.

③ I've heard that we can save trees by using less paper.

④ I've heard that we have to plant as many trees as possible.

⑤ I've heard that using paper cups is a way to save the earth.

12 위 대화를 읽고 다음 질문에 대해 영어로 답하시오.

> Q: How can we use only one paper towel to dry off our hands?

➡ We can _____

_____.

13 다음 그림을 보고 괄호 안에 주어진 어휘를 이용하여 주어진 대화의 빈칸을 한 단어씩 알맞게 채우시오.

A: Did you like the sandwich?

B: Yes, I did. Having delicious sandwiches always makes _____

_____. (happy)

14 다음 중 어법상 바르지 <u>않은</u> 것은?

① I don't want to have my picture take by a stranger.

② Don't make me say that again.

③ I won't let the cake be touched.

④ Let's keep the classroom clean.

⑤ The song has made him popular.

15 다음 중 어법상 <u>어색한</u> 부분을 바르게 고치시오.

(1) They took care of the apartment and kept it tidily.

_____ ➡ _____

(2) Dad had the tree plant.

_____ ➡ _____

16 주어진 문장의 밑줄 친 부분과 용법이 <u>다른</u> 하나는?

> My brother always <u>makes</u> me clean the room.

① It <u>makes</u> me pleased.

② Playing the game <u>made</u> me excited.

③ Her mom <u>made</u> her a dress.

④ I will <u>make</u> her call you tomorrow.

⑤ He <u>made</u> me buy the book.

17 다음 글에서 어법상 <u>틀린</u> 부분을 찾아 바르게 고쳐 쓰시오.

> Sam really wanted a dog, but his parents didn't let him to have a pet.

_____ ➡ _____

[18~20] 다음 글을 읽고 물음에 답하시오.

"Wow, I can read a book in my room now!" shouted Marco, a boy in a village in (A) [Philippines / the Philippines]. His house has no electricity just like all the other houses in the village. People in the village are _____ ⓐ _____ poor _____ ⓑ _____ pay for electricity. Even during the daytime, they live in darkness (B) [because / because of] the houses are packed close together. Now things are changing (C) [because / because of] a single plastic bottle. One plastic bottle in the ceiling can light up a whole room without using any electricity.

18 위 글의 빈칸 ⓐ와 ⓑ에 들어갈 알맞은 말을 고르시오.

① so – that
② too – to
③ such – that
④ so – as to
⑤ enough – to

19 위 글의 괄호 (A)~(C)에서 어법상 알맞은 낱말을 골라 쓰시오.

➡ (A) _____ (B) _____

   (C) _____

20 Does a plastic bottle in the ceiling need any electricity to light up a whole room? Answer in English in a full sentence. (3 words)

➡ _____

[21~22] 다음 글을 읽고 물음에 답하시오.

This amazing plastic bottle is called a Moser lamp ⓐbecause it was invented by Alfredo Moser. In 2002, there were many blackouts in his town in Brazil. ⓑThese blackouts made him to come up with a new way to light his house.

A Moser lamp can be made for about one dollar and lasts for about 10 years. It is also very safe. It can never start a house fire. Surprisingly, it is very easy to make this magic lamp.

21 위 글의 밑줄 친 ⓐ를 능동태로 고치시오.

➡ _____

22 위 글의 밑줄 친 ⓑ에서 어법상 틀린 부분을 찾아 고치시오.

_____ ➡ _____

[23~24] 다음 글을 읽고 물음에 답하시오.

In the Philippines, Moser lamps are widely used by the My Shelter Foundation. The charity also teaches local people how to make and install the lamps. Thanks to the charity, thousands of homes in the Philippines now have Moser lamps. It has also made Moser lamps popular in other countries, such as Argentina, India, and Fiji. Moser lamps will light up the lives of many people for many years to come.

23 What enables thousands of homes in the Philippines to have Moser lamps now? Answer in English. (5 words)

➡ _____

24 위 글의 내용과 일치하지 않는 것은?

① In the Philippines, the My Shelter Foundation widely uses Moser lamps.
② The My Shelter Foundation teaches local people how to make the lamps.
③ The My Shelter Foundation teaches local people how to install the lamps.
④ Thousands of homes in the Philippines now have Moser lamps by the help of the My Shelter Foundation.
⑤ Many people of the Philippines have made Moser lamps popular in other countries.

INSIGHT
on the textbook
교과서 파헤치기

※ 다음 영어를 우리말로 쓰시오.

01 practice		22 incorrectly	
02 subway		23 stranger	
03 appreciate		24 discount	
04 brave		25 difficult	
05 century		26 mean	
06 actually		27 amazing	
07 marry		28 ostrich	
08 dawn		29 add	
09 perform		30 anniversary	
10 fail		31 right	
11 storyline		32 safe	
12 riddle		33 theater	
13 princess		34 whole	
14 celebrate		35 hurry up	
15 already		36 be late for ~	
16 performance		37 Why don't you+동사원형 ~?	
17 secret		38 would like to+동사원형	
18 correctly		39 as+형용사+as ~	
19 suggestion		40 fall in love with ~	
20 famous		41 nothing more than ~	
21 guess		42 in time	
		43 find out	

※ 다음 우리말을 영어로 쓰시오.

01	비밀		22	지하철	
02	추측하다		23	(말을) 덧붙이다, 더하다	
03	세기		24	기념하다	
04	정확하지 않게		25	유명한	
05	실은, 사실은		26	안전한	
06	공주		27	공연	
07	용감한		28	제안	
08	타조		29	연습하다	
09	할인		30	감동적인	
10	감상하다, 감사하다		31	어려운	
11	낯선 사람, 이방인		32	놀라운	
12	정확하게, 바르게		33	수수께끼	
13	동의하다		34	아름다움, 미	
14	연극, 극, 희곡		35	~에 늦다, 지각하다	
15	줄거리		36	제시간에, 늦지 않게	
16	이미, 벌써		37	알아내다, 발견하다	
17	기념일		38	서두르다	
18	~와 결혼하다		39	~와 사랑에 빠지다	
19	공연하다, 수행하다		40	(일을) 쉬다	
20	실패하다		41	어느 날	
21	전체, 모든, 전부의		42	첫눈에	
			43	~하고 싶다	

※ 다음 영영풀이에 알맞은 단어를 <보기>에서 골라 쓴 후, 우리말 뜻을 쓰시오.

1 _____ : a period of 100 years: _____

2 _____ : earlier than the time expected: _____

3 _____ : to do an action or piece of work: _____

4 _____ : very surprising: _____

5 _____ : the series of events that happen in a book, film, play, etc.: _____

6 _____ : a piece of music in an opera sung by one person: _____

7 _____ : showing no fear of dangerous or difficult things: _____

8 _____ : a reduction in the normal price: _____

9 _____ : to understand how good something or someone is: _____

10 _____ : to do something enjoyable on a special occasion: _____

11 _____ : causing strong feelings of sadness or sympathy: _____

12 _____ : to give an answer to a particular question when you do not have all the facts and so cannot be certain if you are correct: _____

13 _____ : a piece of information that is only known by one person or a few people and should not be told to others: _____

14 _____ : to become the legally accepted husband or wife of someone in an official or religious ceremony: _____

15 _____ : a day on which you remember or celebrate something that happened on that day in the past: _____

16 _____ : a type of question that describes something in a difficult and confusing way and has a clever or funny answer: _____

보기			
marry	celebrate	secret	moving
amazing	discount	century	aria
guess	anniversary	appreciate	perform
riddle	storyline	already	brave

대화문 Test

Step1

※ 다음 우리말과 일치하도록 빈칸에 알맞은 말을 쓰시오.

 해석

Listen & Speak 1-A

1. **M:** Liz, _____ _____. It's _____ 6 o'clock.

 W: Oh, we're _____ the concert.

 M: _____ _____ _____ _____ the subway? The subway will be _____ _____ the bus at this time of day.

 W: That's a _____ _____.

2. **B:** Mom, I _____ _____ one question _____ on the Korean history exam!

 W: Great! I was _____ you would do _____. _____ _____ _____ _____ _____ _____ tonight?

 B: Yes! Can we _____ _____ _____ dinner?

 W: _____ _____, Joe. I'll call your dad.

1. M: Liz, 서둘러. 벌써 여섯 시야.
   W: 이런, 우린 콘서트에 늦을 거야.
   M: 지하철을 타는 게 어때? 지하철은 지금 이 시간에 버스보다 빠를 거야.
   W: 좋은 생각이야.

2. B: 엄마, 제가 한국사 시험에서 겨우 한 문제만 틀렸어요!
   W: 대단해! 네가 잘할 거라고 확신했단다. 오늘 축하하러 나가는 건 어때?
   B: 좋아요! 저녁으로 피자를 먹어도 되나요?
   W: 물론이지, Joe. 아빠에게 전화하마.

Listen & Speak 1-B

A: _____ _____ _____ _____ at the park?

B: _____ _____ _____ _____ a magic show?

A: That's _____ _____ _____.

A: 우리 공원에서 뭘 할까?
B: 마술 쇼를 보는 건 어때?
A: 좋은 생각이야.

Listen & Speak 2-A

1. **B:** Karen, _____ _____ our _____ for the _____ _____ today.

 G: O.K. _____ _____ _____ _____ _____ _____?

 B: _____ _____ 4 o'clock, _____ _____ _____?

 G: _____ good.

2. **G:** Do you want to _____ _____ together this afternoon, Mark?

 B: Sure. _____ _____ _____ _____ play?

 G: _____ _____ at the park _____ your place?

 B: O.K. _____ _____ _____ _____ 3 o'clock.

1. B: Karen, 오늘 학교 연극에서 우리 부분을 연습하자.
   G: 좋아. 몇 시에 만날까?
   B: 학교 끝나고 바로, 네 시 어때?
   G: 좋아.

2. G: Mark, 오후에 같이 배드민턴 하지 않을래?
   B: 물론이지. 어디서 할까?
   G: 너희 집 근처 공원은 어때?
   B: 좋아. 세 시에 거기서 보자.

Listen & Speak 2-B

A: _____ this weekend.

B: Good idea. _____ _____ _____ _____ _____ _____?

A: _____ _____ 10 o'clock _____ Saturday?

B: O.K. _____ _____ at the subway station. See you there.

A: 주말에 소풍가자.
B: 좋은 생각이야. 몇 시에 만날래?
A: 토요일 10시는 어때?
B: 좋아. 지하철역에서 만나자. 거기서 봐.

Communicate A

Anna: Dad, _____ _____! I _____ _____ _____ _____ next Wednesday.

Dad: Really? _____ _____?

Anna: It's our school's 75th _____.

Dad: Oh, I see.

Anna: Can we do something _____ that day?

Dad: I guess I can _____ the afternoon _____. _____ do you _____ _____ do?

Anna: _____ _____ _____ _____ _____ _____ a musical at Bravo Theater _____ _____ _____? We can _____ a _____ we _____ _____ _____ _____.

Dad: Good idea, Anna! Then, _____ _____ _____ at the theater.

Anna: O.K. What time _____ _____ meet?

Dad: _____ _____ 12? Then, we can _____ _____ together, too.

Anna: You're the _____, Dad!

Communicate B

A: _____ _____ _____ _____ do this afternoon?

B: _____ _____ _____ go see *Wonder Woman*?

A: Good idea! What _____ _____ _____ _____?

B: _____ _____ 4 o'clock?

A: O.K. _____ _____ at Moon Theater.

Progress Check

1. **G:** Jim, _____ _____. It's _____ 10 o'clock.

   B: Oh, we're going to _____ _____ _____ the movie.

   G: _____ _____ _____ _____ the bus? The bus will be _____ _____ the subway _____ _____ _____ _____ _____.

   B: That's a _____ _____.

2. **B:** It's very _____. _____ _____ _____, Julie.

   G: Good idea! _____ _____ we _____?

   B: _____ _____ at the subway station near my place?

   G: O.K. _____ you _____ at 11 o'clock.

Anna: 아빠, 있잖아요! 저는 다음 주 수요일에 수업이 없어요.
아빠: 정말? 왜 없니?
Anna: 75주년 개교 기념일이에요.
아빠: 그렇구나.
Anna: 그날 오후에 같이 뭔가 할 수 있을까요?
아빠: 나는 오후에 휴무를 할 수 있을 것 같구나. 뭘 하고 싶니?
Anna: 아빠 직장 근처 Bravo 극장에서 뮤지컬을 보는 건 어때요? 수요일에 가면 할인을 받을 수 있어요.
아빠: 좋은 생각이구나, Anna! 그럼 바로 극장에서 만나자.
Anna: 좋아요. 몇 시에 만날까요?
아빠: 12시는 어떠니? 그럼 점심도 같이 먹을 수 있단다.
Anna: 최고예요, 아빠!

A: 오늘 오후에 뭘 할까?
B: 원더 우먼을 보러 가는 건 어때?
A: 좋은 생각이야! 몇 시에 만날까?
B: 4시는 어때?
A: 좋아. Moon 극장에서 보자.

1. G: Jim, 서둘러. 벌써 10시야.
   B: 이런, 영화 시간에 늦을 거야.
   G: 버스를 타는 게 어때? 지금 이 시간에는 버스가 지하철보다 빠를 거야.
   B: 좋은 생각이야.

2. B: 오늘 굉장히 덥네. 수영하러 가자, Julie.
   G: 좋은 생각이야! 어디서 만날래?
   B: 우리 집 근처 지하철역에서 만나는 게 어때?
   G: 좋아. 11시에 거기서 보자.

Step2

※ 다음 우리말에 맞도록 대화를 영어로 쓰시오.

Listen & Speak 1-A

1. M: _____
   W: _____
   M: _____
   _____
   W: _____

2. B: _____
   W: _____
   _____
   B: _____
   W: _____

Listen & Speak 1-B

A: _____
B: _____
A: _____

Listen & Speak 2-A

1. B: _____
   G: _____
   B: _____
   G: _____

2. G: _____
   B: _____
   G: _____
   B: _____

Listen & Speak 2-B

A: _____
B: _____
A: _____
B: _____

해석

1. M: Liz, 서둘러. 벌써 여섯 시야.
   W: 이런, 우린 콘서트에 늦을 거야.
   M: 지하철을 타는 게 어때? 지하철은 지금 이 시간에 버스보다 빠를 거야.
   W: 좋은 생각이야.

2. B: 엄마, 제가 한국사 시험에서 겨우 한 문제만 틀렸어요!
   W: 대단해! 네가 잘할 거라고 확신했단다. 오늘 축하하러 나가는 건 어때?
   B: 좋아요! 저녁으로 피자를 먹어도 되나요?
   W: 물론이지, Joe. 아빠에게 전화하마.

A: 우리 공원에서 뭘 할까?
B: 마술 쇼를 보는 건 어때?
A: 좋은 생각이야.

1. B: Karen, 오늘 학교 연극에서 우리 부분을 연습하자.
   G: 좋아. 몇 시에 만날까?
   B: 학교 끝나고 바로, 네 시 어때?
   G: 좋아.

2. G: Mark, 오후에 같이 배드민턴 하지 않을래?
   B: 물론이지. 어디서 할까?
   G: 너희 집 근처 공원은 어때?
   B: 좋아. 세 시에 거기서 보자.

A: 주말에 소풍가자.
B: 좋은 생각이야. 몇 시에 만날래?
A: 토요일 10시는 어때?
B: 좋아. 지하철역에서 만나자. 거기서 봐.

Communicate A

Anna: _____

Dad: _____

Anna: _____

Dad: _____

Anna: _____

Dad: _____

Anna: _____

Dad: _____

Anna: _____

Dad: _____

Anna: _____

Anna: 아빠, 있잖아요! 저는 다음 주 수요일에 수업이 없어요.
아빠: 정말? 왜 없니?
Anna: 75주년 개교 기념일이에요.
아빠: 그렇구나.
Anna: 그날 오후에 같이 뭔가 할 수 있을까요?
아빠: 나는 오후에 휴무를 할 수 있을 것 같구나. 뭘 하고 싶니?
Anna: 아빠 직장 근처 Bravo 극장에서 뮤지컬을 보는 건 어때요? 수요일에 가면 할인을 받을 수 있어요.
아빠: 좋은 생각이구나, Anna! 그럼 바로 극장에서 만나자.
Anna: 좋아요. 몇 시에 만날까요?
아빠: 12시는 어떠니? 그럼 점심도 같이 먹을 수 있단다.
Anna: 최고예요, 아빠!

Communicate B

A: _____

B: _____

A: _____

B: _____

A: _____

A: 오늘 오후에 뭘 할까?
B: 원더 우먼을 보러 가는 건 어때?
A: 좋은 생각이야! 몇 시에 만날까?
B: 4시는 어때?
A: 좋아. Moon 극장에서 보자.

Progress Check

1. G: _____

   B: _____

   G: _____

   _____

   B: _____

2. B: _____

   G: _____

   B: _____

   G: _____

1. G: Jim, 서둘러. 벌써 10시야.
   B: 이런, 영화 시간에 늦을 거야.
   G: 버스를 타는 게 어때? 지금 이 시간에는 버스가 지하철보다 빠를 거야.
   B: 좋은 생각이야.

2. B: 오늘 굉장히 덥네. 수영하러 가자, Julie.
   G: 좋은 생각이야! 어디서 만날래?
   B: 우리 집 근처 지하철역에서 만나는 게 어때?
   G: 좋아. 11시에 거기서 보자.

Step1

※ 다음 우리말과 일치하도록 빈칸에 알맞은 것을 골라 쓰시오.

1 Turandot The _____ _____ Love in the _____

A. Dangerous   B. Most   C. World

2 _____, _____!

A. everyone   B. welcome

3 Tonight, we are _____ to _____ Giacomo Puccini's _____ *Turandot*.

A. perform   B. going   C. opera

4 _____ many _____ famous operas, *Turandot* is in _____ _____ opera started in Italy in the 16th century.

A. because   B. like   C. Italian   D. other

5 _____ we begin, I'd _____ to tell you the _____ of the opera *Turandot*.

A. like   B. before   C. storyline

6 You will _____ it _____ _____ you know the story.

A. better   B. if   C. appreciate

7 Turandot, a Chinese princess, is a woman _____ great _____, but she is as _____ _____ ice.

A. of   B. cold   C. beauty   D. as

8 Any prince _____ wants to _____ her _____ answer three riddles.

A. marry   B. who   C. must

9 If he _____, he must _____.

A. die   B. fails

10 No one _____ ever _____ _____ to answer them.

A. able   B. been   C. has

11 _____ day, a brave prince _____ in love with her _____ first _____.

A. falls   B. sight   C. one   D. at

12 He _____ the first man to _____ all three _____.

A. answer   B. becomes   C. riddles

13 _____, Turandot does not want to _____ the _____.

A. marry   B. however   C. prince

14 He is _____ _____ _____ a stranger to her.

A. than   B. nothing   C. more

15 He _____ gives her a riddle _____ his _____.

A. of   B. then   C. own

---

1 투란도트, 세상에서 가장 위험한 사랑

2 여러분, 환영합니다!

3 오늘 밤, 우리는 지아코모 푸치니의 오페라 《투란도트》를 공연할 것입니다.

4 다른 많은 유명한 오페라들처럼 《투란도트》는 이탈리아어로 되어 있는데, 오페라가 16세기 이탈리아에서 시작되었기 때문입니다.

5 시작하기 전에 오페라 《투란도트》의 줄거리를 알려 드리려고 합니다.

6 여러분이 줄거리를 알면 이 오페라를 더 잘 감상하게 될 것입니다.

7 중국의 공주 Turandot는 굉장히 아름다운 여인이지만, 그녀는 얼음처럼 차갑습니다.

8 그녀와 결혼하길 원하는 왕자는 누구든지 반드시 세 가지 수수께끼에 답해야 합니다.

9 만약 실패하면 그는 죽어야 합니다.

10 그 누구도 수수께끼에 답할 수 없었습니다.

11 어느 날, 어떤 용감한 왕자가 그녀에게 첫눈에 반합니다.

12 그는 세 수수께끼를 모두 맞힌 첫 번째 사람이 됩니다.

13 그러나 Turandot는 그 왕자와 결혼하길 원하지 않습니다.

14 그는 그녀에게 단지 낯선 사람일 뿐입니다.

15 그러자 그는 그녀에게 자신의 수수께끼를 냅니다.

16 He _____ her, "_____ is my name?"
    A. what   B. asks

17 He _____, "If you answer _____, I will agree to _____. If you answer _____, you will have to marry me."
    A. correctly   B. die   C. adds   B. incorrectly

18 Turandot must find the answer _____ _____, but his riddle is _____ difficult as _____.
    A. dawn   B. hers   C. as   D. before

19 She says to everyone, "No one will go _____ sleep _____ someone _____ _____ his name."
    A. out   B. finds   C. until   D. to

20 The prince then sings the _____ _____ _____ of the _____ opera, "Nessun Dorma."
    A. most   B. whole   C. famous   D. aria

21 It _____ no one _____.
    A. sleeps   B. means

22 _____ one _____.
    A. sleeps   B. no

23 No _____ sleeps, _____ _____ you, Princess.
    A. even   B. one   C. not

24 My _____ is _____.
    A. safe   B. secret

25 _____ one _____ _____ my name.
    A. know   B. will   C. no

26 _____ _____, I _____ win! I will win!
    A. will   B. at   C. dawn

27 The _____ name _____ Calaf.
    A. is   B. prince's

28 Will the princess _____ his name _____ _____?
    A. time   B. learn   C. in

29 Let's _____ the opera and _____ _____.
    A. out   B. watch   C. find

16 그는 그녀에게 "제 이름이 무엇입니까?"라고 묻습니다.

17 그는 "당신이 맞게 대답한다면 나는 죽는 것에 동의하겠습니다. 만약 답이 틀리면 당신은 저와 결혼해야 할 것입니다."라고 덧붙입니다.

18 Turandot는 동이 트기 전에 답을 찾아야 하지만 그의 수수께끼는 그녀의 것만큼 어렵습니다.

19 그녀는 모두에게 "누군가 그의 이름을 알아낼 때까지 그 누구도 잠들 수 없다."라고 말합니다.

20 그리고 왕자는 이 오페라 전체에서 가장 유명한 아리아, Nessun Dorma를 부릅니다.

21 그것은 누구도 잠들지 못한다는 뜻입니다.

22 누구도 잠들지 못하네.

23 누구도 잠들지 못하네, 당신조차도, 공주여.

24 나의 비밀은 안전하다네.

25 누구도 나의 이름을 알지 못할 것이네.

26 동틀 녘에, 내가 이길 것이라네! 내가 승리할 것이라네!

27 왕자의 이름은 Calaf입니다.

28 공주는 그의 이름을 제때 알아낼 수 있을까요?

29 오페라를 보고 알아봅시다.

※ 다음 우리말과 일치하도록 빈칸에 알맞은 말을 쓰시오.

1   Turandot _____ _____ _____ Love in the _____

2   _____, _____!

3   Tonight, we _____ _____ _____ _____ Giacomo Puccini's opera *Turandot*.

4   _____ many _____ _____ _____, *Turandot* is _____ _____ _____ opera started _____ _____ in the _____.

5   Before we begin, _____ _____ _____ _____ you the _____ _____ _____ *Turandot*.

6   You will _____ it _____ _____ you know the story.

7   Turandot, a Chinese princess, is a woman _____ _____ _____, but she is _____ _____ _____ _____.

8   Any prince _____ wants to _____ _____ must answer _____ _____.

9   If he _____, he _____ _____.

10   No one _____ _____ answer them.

11   One day, a brave prince _____ _____ _____ _____ her _____ _____ _____.

12   He becomes _____ _____ _____ _____ _____ all three riddles.

13   _____, Turandot does not want _____ _____ the prince.

14   He is _____ _____ _____ a stranger to her.

15   He then gives _____ _____ _____ _____ _____ _____.

1 투란도트, 세상에서 가장 위험한 사랑

2 여러분, 환영합니다!

3 오늘 밤, 우리는 지아코모 푸치니의 오페라 《투란도트》를 공연할 것입니다.

4 다른 많은 유명한 오페라들처럼 《투란도트》는 이탈리아어로 되어 있는데, 오페라가 16세기 이탈리아에서 시작되었기 때문입니다.

5 시작하기 전에 오페라 《투란도트》의 줄거리를 알려 드리려고 합니다.

6 여러분이 줄거리를 알면 이 오페라를 더 잘 감상하게 될 것입니다.

7 중국의 공주 Turandot는 굉장히 아름다운 여인이지만, 그녀는 얼음처럼 차갑습니다.

8 그녀와 결혼하길 원하는 왕자는 누구든지 반드시 세 가지 수수께끼에 답해야 합니다.

9 만약 실패하면 그는 죽어야 합니다.

10 그 누구도 수수께끼에 답할 수 없었습니다.

11 어느 날, 어떤 용감한 왕자가 그녀에게 첫눈에 반합니다.

12 그는 세 수수께끼를 모두 맞힌 첫 번째 사람이 됩니다.

13 그러나 Turandot는 그 왕자와 결혼하길 원하지 않습니다.

14 그는 그녀에게 단지 낯선 사람일 뿐입니다.

15 그러자 그는 그녀에게 자신의 수수께끼를 냅니다.

16 He _____ _____, "_____ is my name?"

17 He _____, "If you answer _____, I will _____ _____

_____. If you answer _____, you will _____ _____

_____ me."

18 Turandot must find the answer _____ _____, but his riddle is

_____ _____ _____ _____.

19 She says to everyone, "No one will _____ _____ _____

_____ someone _____ _____ his name."

20 The prince then sings _____ _____ _____ _____ of the

_____ _____, "Nessun Dorma."

21 It _____ no one _____.

22 _____ one _____.

23 No one sleeps, _____ _____ _____, Princess.

24 _____ _____ is _____.

24 _____ _____ _____ _____ my name.

26 _____ _____, I _____ _____! I will win!

27 The _____ _____ is Calaf.

28 _____ the princess _____ his name _____ _____?

29 _____ _____ the opera and _____ _____.

16 그는 그녀에게 "제 이름이 무엇입니까?"라고 묻습니다.

17 그는 "당신이 맞게 대답한다면 나는 죽는 것에 동의하겠습니다. 만약 답이 틀리면 당신은 저와 결혼해야 할 것입니다."라고 덧붙입니다.

18 Turandot는 동이 트기 전에 답을 찾아야 하지만 그의 수수께끼는 그녀의 것만큼 어렵습니다.

19 그녀는 모두에게 "누군가 그의 이름을 알아낼 때까지 그 누구도 잠들 수 없다."라고 말합니다.

20 그리고 왕자는 이 오페라 전체에서 가장 유명한 아리아, Nessun Dorma를 부릅니다.

21 그것은 누구도 잠들지 못한다는 뜻입니다.

22 누구도 잠들지 못하네.

23 누구도 잠들지 못하네, 당신조차도, 공주여.

24 나의 비밀은 안전하다네.

25 누구도 나의 이름을 알지 못할 것이네.

26 동틀 녘에, 내가 이길 것이라네! 내가 승리할 것이라네!

27 왕자의 이름은 Calaf입니다.

28 공주는 그의 이름을 제때 알아낼 수 있을까요?

29 오페라를 보고 알아봅시다.

※ 다음 문장을 우리말로 쓰시오.

1 Turandot The Most Dangerous Love in the World

➡ _____

2 Welcome, everyone!

➡ _____

3 Tonight, we are going to perform Giacomo Puccini's opera *Turandot*.

➡ _____

4 Like many other famous operas, *Turandot* is in Italian because opera started in Italy in the 16th century.

➡ _____

5 Before we begin, I'd like to tell you the storyline of the opera *Turandot*.

➡ _____

6 You will appreciate it better if you know the story.

➡ _____

7 Turandot, a Chinese princess, is a woman of great beauty, but she is as cold as ice.

➡ _____

8 Any prince who wants to marry her must answer three riddles.

➡ _____

9 If he fails, he must die.

➡ _____

10 No one has ever been able to answer them.

➡ _____

11 One day, a brave prince falls in love with her at first sight.

➡ _____

12 He becomes the first man to answer all three riddles.

➡ _____

13 However, Turandot does not want to marry the prince.

➡ _____

14 He is nothing more than a stranger to her.

➡ _____

15 He then gives her a riddle of his own.

➡ _____

16 ▷ He asks her, "What is my name?"

➡ _____

17 ▷ He adds, "If you answer correctly, I will agree to die. If you answer incorrectly, you will have to marry me."

➡ _____

_____

18 ▷ Turandot must find the answer before dawn, but his riddle is as difficult as hers.

➡ _____

19 ▷ She says to everyone, "No one will go to sleep until someone finds out his name."

➡ _____

20 ▷ The prince then sings the most famous aria of the whole opera, "Nessun Dorma."

➡ _____

21 ▷ It means no one sleeps.

➡ _____

22 ▷ No one sleeps.

➡ _____

23 ▷ No one sleeps, not even you, Princess.

➡ _____

24 ▷ My secret is safe.

➡ _____

25 ▷ No one will know my name.

➡ _____

26 ▷ At dawn, I will win! I will win!

➡ _____

27 ▷ The prince's name is Calaf.

➡ _____

28 ▷ Will the princess learn his name in time?

➡ _____

29 ▷ Let's watch the opera and find out.

➡ _____

Step4

※ 다음 괄호 안의 단어들을 우리말에 맞도록 바르게 배열하시오.

1 (Turandot / Most / The / Love / Dangerous / the / in / World)
➡ _____

2 (everyone! / welcome,)
➡ _____

3 (we / tonight, / going / are / perform / to / Puccini's / Giacomo / Turandot. / opera)
➡ _____

4 (many / like / famous / other / operas, / is / Turandot / Italian / in / opera / because / in / started / Italy / the / century. / 16th / in)
➡ _____

5 (we / before / begin, / like / I'd / tell / to / the / you / of / storyline / Turandot. / opera / the)
➡ _____

6 (will / you / it / appreciate / better / you / if / know / story. / the)
➡ _____

7 (a / Turandot, / princess, / Chinese / a / is / woman / great / of / beauty, / but / is / she / cold / as / ice. / as)
➡ _____

8 (prince / any / wants / who / marry / to / her / answer / must / riddles. / three)
➡ _____

9 (he / if / fails, / he / die. / must)
➡ _____

10 (one / no / ever / has / been / to / able / them. / answer)
➡ _____

11 (day, / one / brave / a / prince / falls / love / in / her / with / sight. / first / at)
➡ _____

12 (becomes / he / first / the / to / man / answer / all / riddles. / three)
➡ _____

13 (Turandot / however / not / does / to / want / prince. / the / marry)
➡ _____

14 (is / he / more / nothing / a / than / stranger / her. / to)
➡ _____

15 (then / he / gives / a / her / riddel / own. / his / of)
➡ _____

1 투란도트, 세상에서 가장 위험한 사랑

2 여러분, 환영합니다!

3 오늘 밤, 우리는 지아코모 푸치니의 오페라 《투란도트》를 공연할 것입니다.

4 다른 많은 유명한 오페라들처럼 《투란도트》는 이탈리아어로 되어 있는데, 오페라가 16세기 이탈리아에서 시작되었기 때문입니다.

5 시작하기 전에 오페라 《투란도트》의 줄거리를 알려 드리려고 합니다.

6 여러분이 줄거리를 알면 이 오페라를 더 잘 감상하게 될 것입니다.

7 중국의 공주 Turandot는 굉장히 아름다운 여인이지만, 그녀는 얼음처럼 차갑습니다.

8 그녀와 결혼하길 원하는 왕자는 누구든지 반드시 세 가지 수수께끼에 답해야 합니다.

9 만약 실패하면 그는 죽어야 합니다.

10 그 누구도 수수께끼에 답할 수 없었습니다.

11 어느 날, 어떤 용감한 왕자가 그녀에게 첫눈에 반합니다.

12 그는 세 수수께끼를 모두 맞힌 첫 번째 사람이 됩니다.

13 그러나 Turandot는 그 왕자와 결혼하길 원하지 않습니다.

14 그는 그녀에게 단지 낯선 사람일 뿐입니다.

15 그러자 그는 그녀에게 자신의 수수께끼를 냅니다.

16 (asks / he / her, / is / "what / name?" / my)

➡ _____

17 (adds, / he / you / "if / answer / correctly, / will / I / die. to / agree / you / if / incorrectly, / answer / will / you / to / have / me." / marry)

➡ _____

18 (must / Turandot / find / answer / the / dawn, / before / his / but / as / is / riddle / difficult / hers. / as)

➡ _____

➡ _____

19 (says / she / everyone, / to / one / "no / go / will / sleep / to / someone / until / out / finds / name." / his)

➡ _____

➡ _____

20 (prince / the / sings / then / most / the / aria / famous / of / opera, / whole / the / Dorma." / "Nessun)

➡ _____

➡ _____

21 (means / it / one / sleeps. / no)

➡ _____

22 (sleeps. / one / no)

➡ _____

23 (one / no / sleeps, even / not / Princess. / you,)

➡ _____

24 (secret / safe. / is / my)

➡ _____

25 (one / no / know / will / name. / my)

➡ _____

26 (dawn, / at / will / I / win! / will / I / win!)

➡ _____

27 (prince's / the / is / Calaf. / name)

➡ _____

28 (the / will / learn / princess / name / his / time? / in)

➡ _____

29 (watch / let's / opera / the / out. / find / and)

➡ _____

16 그는 그녀에게 "제 이름이 무엇입니까?"라고 묻습니다.

17 그는 "당신이 맞게 대답한다면 나는 죽는 것에 동의하겠습니다. 만약 답이 틀리면 당신은 저와 결혼해야 할 것입니다."라고 덧붙입니다.

18 Turandot는 동이 트기 전에 답을 찾아야 하지만 그의 수수께끼는 그녀의 것만큼 어렵습니다.

19 그녀는 모두에게 "누군가 그의 이름을 알아낼 때까지 그 누구도 잠들 수 없다."라고 말합니다.

20 그리고 왕자는 이 오페라 전체에서 가장 유명한 아리아, Nessun Dorma를 부릅니다.

21 그것은 누구도 잠들지 못한다는 뜻입니다.

22 누구도 잠들지 못하네.

23 누구도 잠들지 못하네, 당신조차도, 공주여.

24 나의 비밀은 안전하다네.

25 누구도 나의 이름을 알지 못할 것이네.

26 동틀 녘에, 내가 이길 것이라네! 내가 승리할 것이라네!

27 왕자의 이름은 Calaf입니다.

28 공주는 그의 이름을 제때 알아낼 수 있을까요?

29 오페라를 보고 알아봅시다.

※ 다음 우리말을 영어로 쓰시오.

1 투란도트, 세상에서 가장 위험한 사랑

➡ _____

2 여러분, 환영합니다!

➡ _____

3 오늘 밤, 우리는 지아코모 푸치니의 오페라 《투란도트》를 공연할 것입니다.

➡ _____

4 다른 많은 유명한 오페라들처럼 《투란도트》는 이탈리아어로 되어 있는데, 오페라가 16세기 이탈리아에서 시작되었기 때문입니다.

➡ _____

5 시작하기 전에 오페라 《투란도트》의 줄거리를 알려 드리려고 합니다.

➡ _____

6 여러분이 줄거리를 알면 이 오페라를 더 잘 감상하게 될 것입니다.

➡ _____

7 중국의 공주 Turandot는 굉장히 아름다운 여인이지만, 그녀는 얼음처럼 차갑습니다.

➡ _____

8 그녀와 결혼하길 원하는 왕자는 누구든지 반드시 세 가지 수수께끼에 답해야 합니다.

➡ _____

9 만약 실패하면 그는 죽어야 합니다.

➡ _____

10 그 누구도 수수께끼에 답할 수 없었습니다.

➡ _____

11 어느 날, 어떤 용감한 왕자가 그녀에게 첫눈에 반합니다.

➡ _____

12 그는 세 수수께끼를 모두 맞힌 첫 번째 사람이 됩니다.

➡ _____

13 그러나 Turandot는 그 왕자와 결혼하길 원하지 않습니다.

➡ _____

14 그는 그녀에게 단지 낯선 사람일 뿐입니다.

➡ _____

15 그러자 그는 그녀에게 자신의 수수께끼를 냅니다.

➡ _____

16 그는 그녀에게 "제 이름이 무엇입니까?"라고 묻습니다.

➡ _____

17 그는 "당신이 맞게 대답한다면 나는 죽는 것에 동의하겠습니다. 만약 답이 틀리면 당신은 저와 결혼해야 할 것입니다."라고 덧붙입니다.

➡ _____

_____

18 Turandot는 동이 트기 전에 답을 찾아야 하지만 그의 수수께끼는 그녀의 것만큼 어렵습니다.

➡ _____

19 그녀는 모두에게 "누군가 그의 이름을 알아낼 때까지 그 누구도 잠들 수 없다."라고 말합니다.

➡ _____

20 그리고 왕자는 이 오페라 전체에서 가장 유명한 아리아, Nessun Dorma를 부릅니다.

➡ _____

21 그것은 누구도 잠들지 못한다는 뜻입니다.

➡ _____

22 누구도 잠들지 못하네.

➡ _____

23 누구도 잠들지 못하네, 당신조차도, 공주여.

➡ _____

24 나의 비밀은 안전하다네.

➡ _____

25 누구도 나의 이름을 알지 못할 것이네.

➡ _____

26 동틀 녘에, 내가 이길 것이라네! 내가 승리할 것이라네!

➡ _____

27 왕자의 이름은 Calaf입니다.

➡ _____

28 공주는 그의 이름을 제때 알아낼 수 있을까요?

➡ _____

29 오페라를 보고 알아봅시다.

➡ _____

※ 다음 우리말과 일치하도록 빈칸에 알맞은 말을 쓰시오.

Link

1. A: _____ was _____ _____?

2. B: It was _____! Actually, I've _____ the musical *Cats* before, and your song was _____ _____ _____ the _____.

1. A: 우리 공연 어땠어?
2. B: 굉장했어. 사실, 뮤지컬 캣츠를 전에 본 적이 있는데, 너희 노래는 뮤지컬의 노래만큼 대단했어.

Write

1. _____ _____ *La La Land*

2. I _____ *La La Land* _____ _____.

3. It _____ _____ the _____ and _____ of Mia and Sebastian.

4. I enjoyed _____ _____ and _____ _____.

5. The story _____ _____ _____ _____ _____ the songs.

6. If you _____ _____ _____ a good musical movie, you _____ _____ this movie.

7. _____ Kim Jisu _____ Aug. 11

1. 라라랜드에 대한 감상
2. 나는 지난 금요일에 라라랜드를 보았다.
3. 그건 Mia와 Sebastian의 꿈과 사랑에 대한 이야기야.
4. 나는 그것의 아름답고 감동적인 노래를 즐겼어.
5. 이야기도 노래만큼이나 좋았지.
6. 좋은 뮤지컬 영화를 찾고 있다면, 이 영화를 봐야 할 거야.
7. 8월 11일, 김지수 씀

Write

1. _____ _____ *Beauty and the Beast*

2. I _____ *Beauty and the Beast* _____ _____.

3. It is about a _____ _____ and a _____.

4. I enjoyed _____ _____ _____.

5. The songs were great, and the love story was _____ _____ _____ _____ _____.

6. If you _____ _____ _____ about love, you _____ _____ it, _____.

7. _____ Lee Minsu _____ _____. 12

1. 미녀와 야수에 대한 감상
2. 나는 지난 토요일에 미녀와 야수를 봤어.
3. 그건 예쁜 여자아이와 야수에 대한 이야기야.
4. 나는 그것을 매우 즐겼어.
5. 노래들은 아주 좋았고, 사랑 이야기는 보석만큼 아름다웠어.
6. 마음이 따뜻해지는 사랑 이야기를 좋아한다면, 너도 이걸 좋아할 거야.
7. 8월 12일, 이민수 씀

※ 다음 우리말을 영어로 쓰시오.

Link

1. A: 우리 공연 어땠어?
   ➡ _____

2. B: 굉장했어. 사실, 뮤지컬 캣츠를 전에 본적이 있는데, 너희 노래는 뮤지컬의 노래만큼 대단했어.
   ➡ _____

Write

1. 라라랜드에 대한 감상
   ➡ _____

2. 나는 지난 금요일에 라라랜드를 보았다.
   ➡ _____

3. 그건 Mla와 Sebastian의 꿈과 사랑에 대한 이야기야.
   ➡ _____

4. 나는 그것의 아름답고 감동적인 노래를 즐겼어.
   ➡ _____

5. 이야기도 노래만큼이나 좋았지.
   ➡ _____

6. 좋은 뮤지컬 영화를 찾고 있다면, 이 영화를 봐야 할 거야.
   ➡ _____

7. 8월 11일, 김지수 씀
   ➡ _____

Write

1. 미녀와 야수에 대한 감상
   ➡ _____

2. 나는 지난 토요일에 미녀와 야수를 봤어.
   ➡ _____

3. 그건 예쁜 여자아이와 야수에 대한 이야기야.
   ➡ _____

4. 나는 그것을 매우 즐겼어.
   ➡ _____

5. 노래들은 아주 좋았고, 사랑 이야기는 보석만큼 아름다웠어.
   ➡ _____

6. 마음이 따뜻해지는 사랑 이야기를 좋아한다면, 너도 이걸 좋아할 거야.
   ➡ _____

7. 8월 12일, 이민수 씀
   ➡ _____

※ 다음 영어를 우리말로 쓰시오.

01	beginner	22	symbolize
02	seafood	23	servant
03	disappointed	24	dish
04	fortune teller	25	harmony
05	alone	26	special
06	back	27	kingdom
07	prefer	28	order
08	half-moon	29	shape
09	policy	30	mainly
10	culture	31	official
11	funny	32	different
12	meat	33	outdoor
13	scholar	34	political
14	honesty	35	on sale
15	traditional	36	on the other hand
16	imaginary	37	be afraid of
17	offer	38	look like+명사
18	indoor	39	by oneself
19	recently	40	dive into
20	ingredient	41	become worried about
21	recommend	42	have been to+장소
		43	be named after

※ 다음 우리말을 영어로 쓰시오.

01 전통의, 전통적인

02 문화

03 해산물

04 주로

05 제안하다, 권하다

06 신하, 관리, 공직자

07 다른

08 신하, 하인

09 실내의

10 특별한

11 재료

12 혼자, 홀로

13 등

14 선호하다

15 초보자

16 웃긴, 재미있는

17 정치의, 정당의

18 점쟁이

19 반의, 절반(의)

20 실망한

21 추천하다

22 상징하다

23 화합, 조화

24 정책

25 주문하다

26 성공, 히트작

27 정직함

28 반달

29 상상의, 가상의

30 학자

31 왕국

32 실외의

33 정당

34 최근에

35 세일 중

36 ~처럼 보이다

37 ~을 두려워하다

38 ~으로 뛰어들다

39 반면에

40 혼자서, 홀로

41 ~의 이름을 따서 지어지다

42 ~할까 생각 중이다

43 ~에 대해 걱정하다

※ 다음 영영풀이에 알맞은 단어를 <보기>에서 골라 쓴 후, 우리말 뜻을 쓰시오.

1 _____ : sweet food eaten at the end of a meal: _____

2 _____ : a country ruled by a king or queen: _____

3 _____ : to represent something: _____

4 _____ : created by and existing only in the mind: _____

5 _____ : a person who is starting to do something or learn something for the first time: _____

6 _____ : to like, choose, or want one thing rather than another: _____

7 _____ : a food that is used with other foods in the preparation of a particular dish: _____

8 _____ : a person who has a position of responsibility in an organization: _____

9 _____ : a person who studies a subject in great detail, especially at a university: _____

10 _____ : to suggest that someone or something would be good or suitable for a particular job or purpose: _____

11 _____ : a person who is employed in another person's house, doing jobs such as cooking and cleaning, especially in the past: _____

12 _____ : the way of life, especially the general customs and beliefs, of a particular group of people at a particular time: _____

13 _____ : unhappy because someone or something was not as good as you hoped or expected: _____

14 _____ : an organization of people with particular political beliefs that competes in elections to try to win positions in local or national government: _____

15 _____ : to ask for something to be made, supplied, or delivered, especially in a restaurant or shop: _____

16 _____ : a set of ideas or a plan of what to do in particular situations that has been agreed to officially by a group of people, a government, or a political party: _____

보기			
servant	kingdom	prefer	recommend
policy	order	culture	ingredient
dessert	scholar	beginner	party
symbolize	disappointed	official	imaginary

※ 다음 우리말과 일치하도록 빈칸에 알맞은 말을 쓰시오.

Listen & Speak 1-A

1. **B:** Do you have _____ for _____, Aunt May?

   W: Yes, Johnny. Do you _____ pie _____ cake?

   B: I _____ cake.

   W: O.K. I have some chocolate cake. I'll _____ you _____.

2. **B:** I'm _____ _____ _____ a sports club.

   G: Do you _____ _____ _____ _____ sports?

   B: I _____ indoor sports. I was in the badminton club _____ year.

   G: _____ _____ _____ _____ the table tennis club, then?

   B: That's a _____ _____. Thank you.

1. **B:** May 이모, 디저트로 먹을 만한 게 있나요?
   W: 그럼, Johnny. 파이가 더 좋으니, 케이크가 더 좋으니?
   B: 전 케이크가 더 좋아요.
   W: 알았어. 초콜릿 케이크가 좀 있네. 좀 갖다 줄게.

2. **B:** 나 스포츠 동아리에 가입하려고 생각 중이야.
   G: 실내 스포츠가 더 좋아, 야외 스포츠가 더 좋아?
   B: 실내 스포츠가 더 좋아. 작년에 배드민턴 동아리에 있었거든.
   G: 그럼, 탁구 동아리가 어때?
   B: 그게 좋겠다. 고마워.

Listen & Speak 2-A

1. **W:** _____ me. I'm _____ _____ an Italian cookbook. Could you _____ one?

   M: Well, _____ you ever _____ _____ food?

   W: No, I _____, but I want _____ _____. I really like spaghetti.

   M: Then, _____ _____ this _____ cookbook for _____? It's _____ _____ now.

   W: Good! Thank you. I'll _____ it.

2. **G:** I _____ _____ a movie _____. Could you _____ a good one?

   B: _____ _____ _____ see *Iron Woman 2*? It's a _____ _____.

   G: Well, I don't like _____ movies. Can you _____ any good _____?

   B: Then, _____ _____ *Funny Families*?

   G: That _____ good.

1. **W:** 실례합니다. 이탈리아 요리책을 찾고 있는데요. 추천해 주실 수 있으세요?
   M: 음, 이탈리아 요리를 해 보신 적이 있나요?
   W: 아뇨, 없습니다. 하지만 해 보고 싶어서요. 스파게티를 정말 좋아하거든요.
   M: 그렇다면 초보자들을 위한 이 이탈리아 요리책이 어떨까요? 지금 세일 중이에요.
   W: 좋아요! 감사합니다. 그걸 살게요

2. **G:** 최근에 영화를 한 편도 못 봤어. 좋은 영화 한 편 추천해 줄래?
   B: 《아이언 우먼 2》 어때? 크게 히트를 치고 있는데.
   G: 글쎄, 액션 영화는 안 좋아해. 괜찮은 코미디 영화 추천해 줄 수 있어?
   B: 그렇다면, 《퍼니 패밀리즈》는 어때?
   G: 그게 좋겠다.

Listen & Speak B

A: Could you _____ a book _____ _____?

B: Well, _____ _____ _____ _____ *The Flying Pan*?

A: Great idea. Thanks.

A: 나한테 책 한 권 추천해 줄래?
B: 글쎄, '플라잉 팬' 어때?
A: 아주 좋아. 고마워.

Communicate A

Jaden: _____ you _____ _____ the new Chinese restaurant, Ms. Park?

Ms. Park: Are you _____ _____ the one on Main Street, Jaden?

Jaden: Yes, that's _____ _____. They opened _____ two weeks _____, _____?

Ms. Park: I think _____. I _____ there _____ Friday with my friends.

Jaden: _____ _____ the food?

Ms. Park: It was great. We _____ many _____ _____. I really liked the _____ vegetables.

Jaden: Could you _____ a dish _____ me? I'm going there for dinner _____ _____ my family.

Ms. Park: Do you _____ seafood _____ meat?

Jaden: I _____ _____.

Ms. Park: Then, you _____ _____ their _____ _____. You'll love it!

Communicate B

M: _____ _____ _____ a Korean restaurant _____ here?

W: _____ you _____ hot _____ cold food?

M: I _____ cold food.

W: Then, you should _____ the naengmyeon place _____ _____ _____ _____ this block.

M: Thank you.

Progress Check

1. **G:** _____ _____ _____ _____ a pet.

   B: Do you _____ dogs _____ cats?

   G: I _____ cats. They're so _____.

   B: Great! I can _____ _____ _____. I have seven cats at home.

   G: Thank you.

2. **W:** Excuse me. I'm _____ _____ a skirt. Could you _____ one?

   M: _____ _____ do you _____?

   W: Blue and pink are my _____ _____.

   M: Then, _____ _____ this blue one? It's _____ _____ now.

   W: Good! Thank you. I'll _____ it.

Jaden: 새로 생긴 중국집에 가 보셨어요, 박 선생님?

박 선생님: 메인 가에 있는 거 말하는 거니, Jaden?

Jaden: 네, 거기요. 한 2주 전쯤에 문을 열었어요, 그렇죠?

박 선생님: 그런 것 같아. 지난 금요일에 친구들과 함께 거기에 갔었단다.

Jaden: 음식이 어땠나요?

박 선생님: 훌륭했어. 우린 다양한 음식을 많이 시켰어. 나는 채소볶음이 정말 좋았어.

Jaden: 제게 요리 하나 추천해 주시겠어요? 오늘 저녁에 저녁 식사를 하러 가족들과 함께 그곳에 가거든요.

박 선생님: 너는 해산물을 더 좋아하니, 육류를 더 좋아하니?

Jaden: 전 해산물을 더 좋아해요.

박 선생님: 그럼 그곳의 생선튀김을 먹어 봐. 네가 정말 좋아할 거야!

M: 이 근처에서 한국 음식점 좀 추천해 주실래요?

W: 뜨거운 음식이 더 좋으세요, 차가운 음식이 더 좋으세요?

M: 찬 음식을 더 좋아해요.

W: 그럼, 이 블록 끝에 있는 냉면집에 가 보세요.

M: 감사합니다.

1. G: 애완동물을 키울까 해.

   B: 개가 좋아, 아니면 고양이가 좋아?

   G: 나는 고양이가 좋아. 정말 귀엽잖아.

   B: 잘 됐네! 내가 한 마리 줄 수 있어. 집에 일곱 마리나 있거든.

   G: 고마워.

2. W: 실례합니다. 치마를 찾고 있는데요. 하나 추천해 주실 수 있나요?

   M: 어떤 색을 좋아하세요?

   W: 파란색과 분홍색을 제일 좋아해요.

   M: 그럼, 이 파란 건 어때요? 지금 세일 중이에요.

   W: 좋아요! 감사합니다. 그걸로 할게요.

※ 다음 우리말에 맞도록 대화를 영어로 쓰시오.

 해석

Listen & Speak 1-A

1. B: _____
   W: _____
   B: _____
   W: _____

2. B: _____
   G: _____
   B: _____
   G: _____
   B: _____

1. B: May 이모, 디저트로 먹을 만한 게 있나요?
   W: 그럼, Johnny. 파이가 더 좋으니, 케이크가 더 좋으니?
   B: 전 케이크가 더 좋아요.
   W: 알았어. 초콜릿 케이크가 좀 있네. 좀 갖다 줄게.

2. B: 나 스포츠 동아리에 가입하려고 생각 중이야.
   G: 실내 스포츠가 더 좋아, 야외 스포츠가 더 좋아?
   B: 실내 스포츠가 더 좋아. 작년에 배드민턴 동아리에 있었거든.
   G: 그럼, 탁구 동아리가 어때?
   B: 그게 좋겠다. 고마워.

Listen & Speak 2-A

1. W: _____
   M: _____
   W: _____
   M: _____
   W: _____

2. G: _____
   B: _____
   G: _____
   B: _____
   G: _____

1. W: 실례합니다. 이탈리아 요리책을 찾고 있는데요. 추천해 주실 수 있으세요?
   M: 음, 이탈리아 요리를 해 보신 적이 있나요?
   W: 아뇨, 없습니다. 하지만 해 보고 싶어서요. 스파게티를 정말 좋아하거든요.
   M: 그렇다면 초보자들을 위한 이 이탈리아 요리책이 어떨까요? 지금 세일 중이에요.
   W: 좋아요! 감사합니다. 그걸 살게요

2. G: 최근에 영화를 한 편도 못 봤어. 좋은 영화 한 편 추천해 줄래?
   B: 《아이언 우먼 2》 어때? 크게 히트를 치고 있는데.
   G: 글쎄, 액션 영화는 안 좋아해. 괜찮은 코미디 영화 추천해 줄 수 있어?
   B: 그렇다면, 《퍼니 패밀리즈》는 어때?
   G: 그게 좋겠다.

Listen & Speak B

A: _____
B: _____
A: _____

A: 나한테 책 한 권 추천해 줄래?
B: 글쎄, '플라잉 팬' 어때?
A: 아주 좋아. 고마워.

Communicate A

Jaden: _____

Ms. Park: _____

Jaden: _____

Ms. Park: _____

Jaden: _____

Ms. Park: _____
_____

Jaden: _____
_____

Ms. Park: _____

Jaden: _____

Ms. Park: _____

Jaden: 새로 생긴 중국집에 가 보셨어
요, 박 선생님?

박 선생님: 메인 가에 있는 거 말하는 거
니, Jaden?

Jaden: 네, 거기요. 한 2주 전쯤에 문을
열었어요, 그렇죠?

박 선생님: 그런 것 같아. 지난 금요일에
친구들과 함께 거기에 갔었단다.

Jaden: 음식이 어땠나요?

박 선생님: 훌륭했어. 우린 다양한 음식
을 많이 시켰어. 나는 채소볶음이
정말 좋았어.

Jaden: 제게 요리 하나 추천해 주시겠
어요? 오늘 저녁에 저녁 식사를 하
러 가족들과 함께 그곳에 가거든요.

박 선생님: 너는 해산물을 더 좋아하니,
육류를 더 좋아하니?

Jaden: 전 해산물을 더 좋아해요.

박 선생님: 그럼 그곳의 생선튀김을 먹
어 봐. 네가 정말 좋아할 거야!

Communicate B

M: _____

W: _____

M: _____

W: _____

M: _____

M: 이 근처에서 한국 음식점 좀 추천해
주실래요?

W: 뜨거운 음식이 더 좋으세요, 차가운
음식이 더 좋으세요?

M: 찬 음식을 더 좋아해요.

W: 그럼, 이 블록 끝에 있는 냉면집에
가 보세요.

M: 감사합니다.

Progress Check

1. G: _____

B: _____

G: _____

B: _____

G: _____

2. W: _____

M: _____

W: _____

M: _____

W: _____

1. G: 애완동물을 키울까 해.
   B: 개가 좋아, 아니면 고양이가 좋
   아?
   G: 나는 고양이가 좋아. 정말 귀엽잖
   아.
   B: 잘 됐다! 내가 한 마리 줄 수 있
   어. 집에 일곱 마리나 있거든.
   G: 고마워.

2. W: 실례합니다. 치마를 찾고 있는
   데요. 하나 추천해 주실 수 있나
   요?
   M: 어떤 색을 좋아하세요?
   W: 파란색과 분홍색을 제일 좋아해
   요.
   M: 그럼, 이 파란 건 어때요? 지금
   세일 중이에요.
   W: 좋아요! 감사합니다. 그걸로 할게
   요.

※ 다음 우리말과 일치하도록 빈칸에 알맞은 것을 골라 쓰시오.

1 A _____ of _____ _____
  A. History   B. Bite   C. Korean

2 _____ did tangpyeongchae and sinseollo _____ their _____?
  A. get   B. how   C. names

3 Why does songpyeon _____ _____ a _____ moon?
  A. like   B. half   C. look

4 _____ _____ many interesting stories about our _____
  _____.
  A. are   B. food   C. traditional   D. there

5 _____ _____ _____ the fun history of our food.
  A. into   B. dive   C. let's

Tangpyeongchae

6 One day, King Yeongjo was _____ dinner with his _____
  and offered them _____ _____.
  A. something   B. having   C. special   D. officials

7 It was a _____ with four _____ _____.
  A. colorful   B. dish   C. ingredients

8 _____ ingredient _____ a different _____ party.
  A. symbolized   B. political   C. each

9 Yeongjo wanted to say _____ the four parties should work
  _____ _____ _____ this dish.
  A. harmony   B. that   C. like   D. in

10 This dish _____ _____ tangpyeongchae.
  A. called   B. was

11 The name _____ _____ Yeongjo's _____ tangpyeongchaek.
  A. policy   B. from   C. came

Sinseollo

12 In the _____ of King Yeonsan, there _____ a scholar who was
  _____ _____ his honesty.
  A. famous   B. for   C. time   D. was

13 When the king did _____ _____, the scholar was never
  _____ of _____ him so.
  A. afraid   B. something   C. telling   D. wrong

14 _____, the king never _____ _____ him.
  A. listened   B. however   C. to

---

1 한국 역사 한 입

2 탕평채와 신선로는 어떻게 해서 그런 이름을 얻게 되었을까?

3 송편은 왜 반달 모양일까?

4 우리의 전통 음식에 대한 재미있는 이야기들이 많이 있다.

5 우리 음식의 재미있는 역사 속으로 들어가 보자.

탕평채

6 어느 날, 영조가 그의 신하들과 저녁을 먹다가 그들에게 특별한 무언가를 권했다.

7 그것은 네 가지의 다채로운 재료로 만든 음식이었다.

8 각 재료는 서로 다른 당파를 상징했다.

9 영조는 이 음식처럼 네 당파가 화합을 이루어 일해야 한다는 것을 말하고 싶었다.

10 이 음식은 탕평채라고 불렸다.

11 그 이름은 영조의 정책인 탕평책에서 왔다.

신선로

12 연산군 시대에 정직하기로 유명한 한 학자가 있었다.

13 왕이 무언가를 잘못하면, 그 학자는 왕에게 그렇게 말하는 것을 절대 두려워하지 않았다.

14 그러나 왕은 그의 말에 전혀 귀기울이지 않았다.

15 The scholar was _____ disappointed _____ he went to live _____ a mountain.

A. that   B. on   C. so

16 _____ he lived there _____ _____, he _____ ate vegetables.

A. himself   B. mainly   C. while   D. by

17 He made a _____ _____ to cook many _____ vegetables together.

A. pot   B. different   C. special

18 People _____ this _____ and the food _____ it sinseollo.

A. in   B. pot   C. called

19 That is _____ the scholar lived _____ a sinseon, an _____ person who lives _____ in nature.

A. like   B. alone   C. because   D. imaginary

Songpyeon

20 It was the _____ of the _____ _____ of Baekje.

A. last   B. time   C. king

21 _____ day, the king and his _____ found a _____ turtle.

A. strange   B. one   C. servants

22 _____ was _____ on its _____.

A. back   B. something   C. written

23 It said, "Baekje is _____ a _____ moon, but Silla is like a _____ moon."

A. like   B. half   C. full

24 The king asked a _____, "_____ does this _____?"

A. fortune   B. mean   C. teller   D. what

25 The _____ teller answered, "A _____ moon will soon _____ _____.

A. become   B. full   C. fortune   D. smaller

26 _____ the _____ hand, a half moon will _____ _____ and become a full moon."

A. grow   B. other   C. on   D. bigger

27 The king _____ _____ _____ his kingdom.

A. worried   B. became   C. about

28 _____, people of Silla were very happy _____ learn this and made rice cakes _____ the _____ of a half moon.

A. shape   B. to   C. in   D. however

29 _____ _____, people _____ enjoyed these half-moon _____ rice cakes, songpyeon.

A. shaped   B. since   C. have   D. then

15 학자는 너무 실망하여 산속으로 살러 들어갔다.

16 그곳에서 혼자 사는 동안, 그는 주로 채소를 먹었다.

17 그는 여러 다양한 채소들을 함께 요리하기 위해 특별한 솥을 만들었다.

18 사람들은 이 솥과 그 안의 음식을 신선로라고 불렀다.

19 그것은 그 학자가 마치 자연 속에 홀로 사는 상상의 인물인 신선처럼 살았기 때문이다.

송편

20 백제의 마지막 왕 때였다.

21 어느 날, 왕과 신하들은 이상한 거북을 한 마리 발견했다.

22 그 거북의 등에 무언가가 쓰여 있었다.

23 그것은 "백제는 보름달과 같지만 신라는 반달과 같다."였다.

24 왕은 점술가에게 "이게 무슨 뜻인가?"라고 물었다.

25 점술가는 "보름달은 곧 작아질 것입니다.

26 반면에, 반달은 점점 커져서 보름달이 될 것입니다."라고 답했다.

27 왕은 자신의 왕국이 걱정되었다.

28 그러나 신라 사람들은 이것을 알고 매우 기뻐하며 반달 모양의 떡을 만들었다.

29 그 후로 사람들은 이 반달 모양의 떡인 송편을 즐겨 먹고 있다.

※ 다음 우리말과 일치하도록 빈칸에 알맞은 말을 쓰시오.

1 A _____ of _____ _____

2 _____ did tangpyeongchae and sinseollo _____ _____ _____?

3 _____ does songpyeon _____ _____ a _____ _____?

4 _____ _____ many interesting stories about our _____ _____.

5 Let's _____ _____ the fun history of our food.

Tangpyeongchae

6 One day, King Yeongjo _____ _____ _____ with his _____ and _____ them _____ _____.

7 It was a dish _____ _____ _____ _____.

8 Each ingredient symbolized _____ _____ _____.

9 Yeongjo wanted to say that the four parties should work _____ _____ _____ this dish.

10 This dish _____ _____ tangpyeongchae.

11 The name _____ _____ Yeongjo's policy tangpyeongchaek.

Sinseollo

12 In the time of King Yeonsan, there _____ _____ _____ who _____ _____ _____ his honesty.

13 When the king did _____ _____, the scholar _____ _____ _____ _____ _____ him so.

14 _____, the king never _____ _____ him.

1 한국 역사 한 입

2 탕평채와 신선로는 어떻게 해서 그런 이름을 얻게 되었을까?

3 송편은 왜 반달 모양일까?

4 우리의 전통 음식에 대한 재미 있는 이야기들이 많이 있다.

5 우리 음식의 재미있는 역사 속 으로 들어가 보자.

탕평채

6 어느 날, 영조가 그의 신하들과 저녁을 먹다가 그들에게 특별한 무언가를 권했다.

7 그것은 네 가지의 다채로운 재 료로 만든 음식이었다.

8 각 재료는 서로 다른 당파를 상 징했다.

9 영조는 이 음식처럼 네 당파가 화합을 이루어 일해야 한다는 것을 말하고 싶었다.

10 이 음식은 탕평채라고 불렸다.

11 그 이름은 영조의 정책인 탕평 책에서 왔다.

신선로

12 연산군 시대에 정직하기로 유명 한 한 학자가 있었다.

13 왕이 무언가를 잘못하면, 그 학 자는 왕에게 그렇게 말하는 것 을 절대 두려워하지 않았다.

14 그러나 왕은 그의 말에 전혀 귀 기울이지 않았다.

15 The scholar was _____ disappointed _____ he went to live on a mountain.

16 _____ he lived there _____ _____, he mainly ate vegetables.

17 He made _____ _____ _____ to cook many different vegetables _____.

18 People _____ this pot and _____ _____ _____ _____ sinseollo.

19 That is _____ the scholar lived _____ a sinseon, an _____ person who _____ _____ in nature.

Songpyeon

20 It was the time of _____ _____ _____ of Baekje.

21 One day, the king and his _____ found _____ _____ _____.

22 Something _____ _____ _____ _____ _____ _____.

23 It said, "Baekje _____ a _____ _____, but Silla _____ _____ a _____ _____."

24 The king asked a fortune teller, "_____ does this _____?"

25 The _____ _____ answered, "A full moon will soon _____ _____.

26 _____ _____ _____, a half moon will _____ _____ and _____ a _____ _____."

27 The king _____ _____ _____ his kingdom.

28 _____, people of Silla were very happy to learn this and made rice cakes _____ _____ _____ _____ a half moon.

29 _____ _____, people _____ _____ these half-moon _____ _____ _____, songpyeon.

15 학자는 너무 실망하여 산속으로 살러 들어갔다.

16 그곳에서 혼자 사는 동안. 그는 주로 채소를 먹었다.

17 그는 여러 다양한 채소들을 함께 요리하기 위해 특별한 솥을 만들었다.

18 사람들은 이 솥과 그 안의 음식을 신선로라고 불렀다.

19 그것은 그 학자가 마치 자연 속에 홀로 사는 상상의 인물인 신선처럼 살았기 때문이다.

송편

20 백제의 마지막 왕 때였다.

21 어느 날. 왕과 신하들은 이상한 거북을 한 마리 발견했다.

22 그 거북의 등에 무언가가 쓰여 있었다.

23 그것은 "백제는 보름달과 같지만 신라는 반달과 같다."였다.

24 왕은 점술가에게 "이게 무슨 뜻인가?"라고 물었다.

25 점술가는 "보름달은 곧 작아질 것입니다.

26 반면에. 반달은 점점 커져서 보름달이 될 것입니다."라고 답했다.

27 왕은 자신의 왕국이 걱정되었다.

28 그러나 신라 사람들은 이것을 알고 매우 기뻐하며 반달 모양의 떡을 만들었다.

29 그 후로 사람들은 이 반달 모양의 떡인 송편을 즐겨 먹고 있다.

※ 다음 문장을 우리말로 쓰시오.

1 ▶ A Bite of Korean History

➡ _____

2 ▶ How did tangpyeongchae and sinseollo get their names?

➡ _____

3 ▶ Why does songpyeon look like a half moon?

➡ _____

4 ▶ There are many interesting stories about our traditional food.

➡ _____

5 ▶ Let's dive into the fun history of our food.

➡ _____

Tangpyeongchae

6 ▶ One day, King Yeongjo was having dinner with his officials and offered them something special.

➡ _____

7 ▶ It was a dish with four colorful ingredients.

➡ _____

8 ▶ Each ingredient symbolized a different political party.

➡ _____

9 ▶ Yeongjo wanted to say that the four parties should work in harmony like this dish.

➡ _____

10 ▶ This dish was called tangpyeongchae.

➡ _____

11 ▶ The name came from Yeongjo's policy tangpyeongchaek.

➡ _____

Sinseollo

12 ▶ In the time of King Yeonsan, there was a scholar who was famous for his honesty.

➡ _____

13 ▶ When the king did something wrong, the scholar was never afraid of telling him so.

➡ _____

14 ▶ However, the king never listened to him.

➡ _____

15 The scholar was so disappointed that he went to live on a mountain.

➡ _____

16 While he lived there by himself, he mainly ate vegetables.

➡ _____

17 He made a special pot to cook many different vegetables together.

➡ _____

18 People called this pot and the food in it sinseollo.

➡ _____

19 That is because the scholar lived like a sinseon, an imaginary person who lives alone in nature.

➡ _____

Songpyeon

20 It was the time of the last king of Baekje.

➡ _____

21 One day, the king and his servants found a strange turtle.

➡ _____

22 Something was written on its back.

➡ _____

23 It said, "Baekje is like a full moon, but Silla is like a half moon."

➡ _____

24 The king asked a fortune teller, "What does this mean?"

➡ _____

25 The fortune teller answered, "A full moon will soon become smaller.

➡ _____

26 On the other hand, a half moon will grow bigger and become a full moon."

➡ _____

27 The king became worried about his kingdom.

➡ _____

28 However, people of Silla were very happy to learn this and made rice cakes in the shape of a half moon.

➡ _____

29 Since then, people have enjoyed these half-moon shaped rice cakes, songpyeon.

➡ _____

※ 다음 괄호 안의 단어들을 우리말에 맞도록 바르게 배열하시오.

1 (Bite / A / History / of / Korean)
➡ _____

2 (did / how / sinseollo / and / tangpyeongchae / their / get / names?)
➡ _____

3 (does / why / look / songpyeon / like / half / moon? / a)
➡ _____

4 (are / there / interesting / many / about / stories / traditional / our / food.)
➡ _____

5 (dive / let's / into / fun / the / of / history / food. / our)
➡ _____

Tangpyeongchae

6 (day, / one / Yeongjo / King / having / was / with / dinner / officials / his / and / them / offered / special. / something)
➡ _____

7 (was / it / dish / a / four / with / ingredients. / colorful)
➡ _____

8 (ingredient / each / a / symbolized / political / different / party.)
➡ _____

9 (Yeongjo / to / wanted / say / that / four / the / parties / work / should / harmony / in / this / like / dish.)
➡ _____

10 (dish / this / called / was / tangpyeongchae.)
➡ _____

11 (name / the / from / came / policy / Yeongjo's / tangpyeongchaek.)
➡ _____

Sinseollo

12 (the / in / of / time / Yeonsan, / King / was / there / who / a / scholar / was / for / famous / his / for / honesty.)
➡ _____

13 (the / when / king / something / did / wrong, / scholar / the / never / was / of / afraid / telling / so. / him)
➡ _____

14 (the / however, / king / listened / never / him. / to)
➡ _____

1 한국 역사 한 입

2 탕평채와 신선로는 어떻게 해서 그런 이름을 얻게 되었을까?

3 송편은 왜 반달 모양일까?

4 우리의 전통 음식에 대한 재미 있는 이야기들이 많이 있다.

5 우리 음식의 재미있는 역사 속 으로 들어가 보자.

탕평채

6 어느 날, 영조가 그의 신하들과 저녁을 먹다가 그들에게 특별한 무언가를 권했다.

7 그것은 네 가지의 다채로운 재 료로 만든 음식이었다.

8 각 재료는 서로 다른 당파를 상 징했다.

9 영조는 이 음식처럼 네 당파가 화합을 이루어 일해야 한다는 것을 말하고 싶었다.

10 이 음식은 탕평채라고 불렸다.

11 그 이름은 영조의 정책인 탕평 책에서 왔다.

신선로

12 연산군 시대에 정직하기로 유명 한 한 학자가 있었다.

13 왕이 무언가를 잘못하면, 그 학 자는 왕에게 그렇게 말하는 것 을 절대 두려워하지 않았다.

14 그러나 왕은 그의 말에 전혀 귀 기울이지 않았다.

15 (scholar / the / so / was / disappointed / he / that / to / went / live / on / mountain. / a)

➡ _____

16 (he / while / there / lived / himself, / by / mainly / he / vegetables. / ate)

➡ _____

17 (made / he / special / a / to / pot / many / cook / vegetables / different / together.)

➡ _____

18 (called / people / pot / this / and / food / the / it / in / sinseollo.)

➡ _____

19 (is / that / because / scholar / the / like / lived / sinseon, / a / imaginary / an / person / who / alone / lives / nature. / in)

➡ _____

Songpyeon

20 (was / it / time / the / of / last / the / Baekje. / king / of)

➡ _____

21 (day, / one / king / the / and / servants / his / a / found / turtle. / strange)

➡ _____

22 (was / something / on / written / back. / its)

➡ _____

23 (said, / it "Baekje / like / is / full / a / moon, / but / is / Silla / half / a / moon." / like)

➡ _____

24 (king / the / a / asked / teller, / fortune / "what / this / does / mean?")

➡ _____

25 (fortune / the / teller / answered, / "full / a / moon / soon / will / smaller. / become)

➡ _____

26 (the / on / hand, / other / half / a / moon / grow / will / and / bigger / become / moon." / full / a)

➡ _____

27 (king / the / worried / became / about / kingdom. / his)

➡ _____

28 (people / however, / Silla / of / very / were / to / happy / this / learn / and / rice / made / cakes / the / in / shape / a / of / moon. / half)

➡ _____

29 (then, / since / have / people / these / enjoyed / shaped / half-moon / rice / songpyeon. / cakes,)

➡ _____

15 학자는 너무 실망하여 산속으로 살러 들어갔다.

16 그곳에서 혼자 사는 동안, 그는 주로 채소를 먹었다.

17 그는 여러 다양한 채소들을 함께 요리하기 위해 특별한 솥을 만들었다.

18 사람들은 이 솥과 그 안의 음식을 신선로라고 불렀다.

19 그것은 그 학자가 마치 자연 속에 홀로 사는 상상의 인물인 신선처럼 살았기 때문이다.

송편

20 백제의 마지막 왕 때였다.

21 어느 날, 왕과 신하들은 이상한 거북을 한 마리 발견했다.

22 그 거북의 등에 무언가 쓰여 있었다.

23 그것은 "백제는 보름달과 같지만 신라는 반달과 같다."였다.

24 왕은 점술가에게 "이게 무슨 뜻인가?"라고 물었다.

25 점술가는 "보름달은 곧 작아질 것입니다.

26 반면에, 반달은 점점 커져서 보름달이 될 것입니다."라고 답했다.

27 왕은 자신의 왕국이 걱정되었다.

28 그러나 신라 사람들은 이것을 알고 매우 기뻐하며 반달 모양의 떡을 만들었다.

29 그 후로 사람들은 이 반달 모양의 떡인 송편을 즐겨 먹고 있다.

※ **다음 우리말을 영어로 쓰시오.**

1 한국 역사 한 입

➡ _____

2 탕평채와 신선로는 어떻게 해서 그런 이름을 얻게 되었을까?

➡ _____

3 송편은 왜 반달 모양일까?

➡ _____

4 우리의 전통 음식에 대한 재미있는 이야기들이 많이 있다.

➡ _____

5 우리 음식의 재미있는 역사 속으로 들어가 보자.

➡ _____

Tangpyeongchae 탕평채

6 어느 날, 영조가 그의 신하들과 저녁을 먹다가 그들에게 특별한 무언가를 권했다.

➡ _____

7 그것은 네 가지의 다채로운 재료로 만든 음식이었다.

➡ _____

8 각 재료는 서로 다른 당파를 상징했다.

➡ _____

9 영조는 이 음식처럼 네 당파가 화합을 이루어 일해야 한다는 것을 말하고 싶었다.

➡ _____

10 이 음식은 탕평채라고 불렸다.

➡ _____

11 그 이름은 영조의 정책인 탕평책에서 왔다.

➡ _____

Sinseollo 신선로

12 연산군 시대에 정직하기로 유명한 한 학자가 있었다.

➡ _____

13 왕이 무언가를 잘못하면, 그 학자는 왕에게 그렇게 말하는 것을 절대 두려워하지 않았다.

➡ _____

14 그러나 왕은 그의 말에 전혀 귀 기울이지 않았다.

➡ _____

15 학자는 너무 실망하여 산속으로 살러 들어갔다.

➡ _____

16 그곳에서 혼자 사는 동안, 그는 주로 채소를 먹었다.

➡ _____

17 그는 여러 다양한 채소들을 함께 요리하기 위해 특별한 솥을 만들었다.

➡ _____

18 사람들은 이 솥과 그 안의 음식을 신선로라고 불렀다.

➡ _____

19 그것은 그 학자가 마치 자연 속에 홀로 사는 상상의 인물인 신선처럼 살았기 때문이다.

➡ _____

Songpyeon 송편

20 백제의 마지막 왕 때였다.

➡ _____

21 어느 날, 왕과 신하들은 이상한 거북을 한 마리 발견했다.

➡ _____

22 그 거북의 등에 무언가가 쓰여 있었다.

➡ _____

23 그것은 "백제는 보름달과 같지만 신라는 반달과 같다."였다.

➡ _____

24 왕은 점술가에게 "이게 무슨 뜻인가?"라고 물었다.

➡ _____

25 점술가는 "보름달은 곧 작아질 것입니다.

➡ _____

26 반면에, 반달은 점점 커져서 보름달이 될 것입니다."라고 답했다.

➡ _____

27 왕은 자신의 왕국이 걱정되었다.

➡ _____

28 그러나 신라 사람들은 이것을 알고 매우 기뻐하며 반달 모양의 떡을 만들었다.

➡ _____

29 그 후로 사람들은 이 반달 모양의 떡인 송편을 즐겨 먹고 있다.

➡ _____

※ 다음 우리말과 일치하도록 빈칸에 알맞은 말을 쓰시오.

Work Together

1. A: _____ _____ _____ a salad for me?

2. B: We have two salads today. _____ _____ _____ chicken salad _____ green salad?

3. A: I _____ green salad.

4. B: O.K. _____ _____ _____ .

5. A: _____ you.

1. A: 샐러드 좀 추천해 주시겠습니까?
2. B: 저희는 오늘 두 가지 샐러드가 있습니다. 닭고기 샐러드가 더 좋으신가요, 야채 샐러드가 더 좋으신가요?
3. A: 야채 샐러드가 더 좋아요.
4. B: 네. 여기 나왔습니다.
5. A: 감사합니다.

Write

1. _____ Songpyeon

2. My family eats _____ _____ on Chuseok.

3. It _____ _____ rice _____ , chocolate, and _____ .

4. It is _____ _____ _____ tteok.

5. _____ I eat this food, I _____ _____ _____ my little brother.

6. Three years _____ , he ate all the _____ for songpyeon, so we _____ _____ _____ chocolate songpyeon.

7. This food gives us a _____ _____ _____ that funny day.

1. 초콜릿 송편
2. 나의 가족은 추석에 특별한 것을 먹는다.
3. 그것은 쌀가루, 초콜릿, 그리고 견과로 만들어진다.
4. 그것은 일종의 떡이다.
5. 내가 이 음식을 먹을 때, 나는 항상 나의 남동생을 생각한다.
6. 3년 전, 그가 송편의 모든 소를 먹어서, 우리는 초콜릿 송편을 만들기로 결심했다.
7. 이 음식은 우리에게 그 재미있던 날을 기억할 기회를 준다.

Culture Project

1. The word *dongporou* _____ _____ the name of the _____ _____ _____ Su Dongpo.

2. _____ his time in Hangzhou, he invented a way _____ _____ pork fresh _____ _____ _____ _____ .

3. He made the pork _____ _____ _____ .

4. _____ , dongporou _____ dongpo pork _____ _____ _____ China.

1. 동파육이라는 단어는 중국의 유명한 시인인 소동파의 이름에서 나왔다.
2. 그의 시대에 항저우에서, 그는 돼지고기를 오랫동안 신선하게 유지하는 방법을 창안했다.
3. 그는 돼지고기를 달고 짜게 만들었다.
4. 나중에 동파육, 즉 동파 돼지고기는 중국 전역에서 인기 있게 되었다.

※ 다음 우리말을 영어로 쓰시오.

Work Together

1. A: 샐러드 좀 추천해 주시겠습니까?
➡ _____

2. B: 저희는 오늘 두 가지 샐러드가 있습니다. 닭고기 샐러드가 더 좋으신가요, 야채 샐러드가 더 좋으신가요?
➡ _____

3. A: 야채 샐러드가 더 좋아요.
➡ _____

4. B: 네. 여기 나왔습니다.
➡ _____

5. A: 감사합니다.
➡ _____

Write

1. 초콜릿 송편
➡ _____

2. 나의 가족은 추석에 특별한 것을 먹는다.
➡ _____

3. 그것은 쌀가루, 초콜릿, 그리고 견과로 만들어진다.
➡ _____

4. 그것은 일종의 떡이다.
➡ _____

5. 내가 이 음식을 먹을 때, 나는 항상 나의 남동생을 생각한다.
➡ _____

6. 3년 전, 그가 송편의 모든 소를 먹어서, 우리는 초콜릿 송편을 만들기로 결심했다.
➡ _____

7. 이 음식은 우리에게 그 재미있던 날을 기억할 기회를 준다.
➡ _____

Culture Project

1. 동파육이라는 단어는 중국의 유명한 시인인 소동파의 이름에서 나왔다.
➡ _____

2. 그의 시대에 항저우에서, 그는 돼지고기를 오랫동안 신선하게 유지하는 방법을 창안했다.
➡ _____

3. 그는 돼지고기를 달고 짜게 만들었다.
➡ _____

4. 나중에 동파육, 곧 동파 돼지고기는 중국 전역에서 인기 있게 되었다.
➡ _____

※ 다음 영어를 우리말로 쓰시오.

01 single

02 chief

03 darkness

04 spread

05 electricity

06 foundation

07 amusement park

08 blackout

09 shelter

10 impossible

11 ceiling

12 widely

13 bend

14 charity

15 install

16 shout

17 invent

18 shake

19 magic

20 leftover

21 whole

22 bleach

23 enough

24 packed

25 popular

26 surprisingly

27 remain

28 roof

29 safe

30 village

31 work

32 save

33 less

34 amazing

35 pay for

36 at least

37 light up

38 not ~ anymore

39 forget to부정사

40 turn up

41 thanks to

42 come up with

43 just like

※ 다음 우리말을 영어로 쓰시오.

01 구부리다, 휘다 _____

02 천장 _____

03 흔들다, 털다 _____

04 자선단체 _____

05 어둠, 암흑 _____

06 어려운 _____

07 전체의 _____

08 대규모 정전 사태 _____

09 널리, 폭넓게 _____

10 남은 음식 _____

11 주요한; 우두머리, 부장 _____

12 더 적은 _____

13 불가능한 _____

14 외치다 _____

15 전기 _____

16 단 하나의 _____

17 작동하다 _____

18 구하다 _____

19 놀이공원 _____

20 재단 _____

21 지붕 _____

22 마법의, 신기한 _____

23 주거지, 쉼터 _____

24 마을 _____

25 인기 있는 _____

26 설치하다 _____

27 남아 있다 _____

28 안전한 _____

29 지속되다 _____

30 놀랍게도 _____

31 표백제 _____

32 꽉 들어찬 _____

33 충분한 _____

34 발명하다 _____

35 ~을 환하게 밝히다 _____

36 ~ 덕분에 _____

37 더 이상 ~ 않다 _____

38 ~을 말리다 _____

39 지불하다 _____

40 ~할 것을 잊다 _____

41 ~을 생각해 내다, ~을 만들어 내다 _____

42 (소리 등을) 높이다 _____

43 A를 B로 채우다 _____

※ 다음 영영풀이에 알맞은 단어를 <보기>에서 골라 쓴 후, 우리말 뜻을 쓰시오.

1 _____ : to continue to exist: _____

2 _____ : a very small town located in a country area: _____

3 _____ : the covering that forms the top of a building, vehicle, etc.: _____

4 _____ : food that has not been finished at a meal: _____

5 _____ : a time when there is no light or power because of an electricity failure: _____

6 _____ : to keep someone or something safe from death, harm, loss, etc.: _____

7 _____ : the inside surface of a room that you can see when you look above you: _____

8 _____ : liked or enjoyed by a large number of people: _____

9 _____ : a device for giving light, especially one that has a covering: _____

10 _____ : to cover, reach, or have an effect on a wider or increasing area: _____

11 _____ : to design and/or create something that has never been made before: _____

12 _____ : a strong chemical used for cleaning things or removing colour from things: _____

13 _____ : to put furniture, a machine, or a piece of equipment into position and make it ready to use: _____

14 _____ : the period between the time when the sun rises and the time it goes down, or the part of the day that is neither evening nor night: _____

15 _____ : a form of energy that can be produced in several ways and that provides power to devices that create light, heat, etc.: _____

16 _____ : a system of giving money, food, or help free to those who are in need because they are ill, poor, or have no home, or any organization that has the purpose of providing money or helping in this way _____

보기			
charity	blackout	roof	village
bleach	install	spread	leftover
ceiling	electricity	daytime	save
last	lamp	invent	popular

※ 다음 우리말과 일치하도록 빈칸에 알맞은 말을 쓰시오.

Listen & Speak 1-A

1. G: Can you _____ _____ the volume on your phone? I like this song.

   B: I can't _____ _____ _____ _____. It's the _____ volume.

   G: _____ me just _____ your phone in a glass. _____ _____ a glass _____ _____ a speaker.

   B: _____ _____ _____ _____ _____! _____ try it now.

2. B: _____ _____ that a movie star _____ _____ to our school.

   G: That's _____. She's my _____ _____.

   B: Oh, who is she?

   G: Miranda Kim. She _____ the _____ _____ in the movie *Jupiter*.

   B: Wow, I _____ _____ _____ _____ her!

Listen & Speak 2-A

1. W: Excuse me, are you _____ with your _____?

   M: Yes, it was really _____.

   W: Do you _____ _____ _____ the _____ home?

   M: Yes, _____.

   W: _____ _____ _____ _____ _____ the leftovers by tomorrow.

2. B: What's _____ _____ _____ this _____ _____?

   G: _____ _____ _____ visit Hong Kong _____ _____ _____.

   B: That _____ _____. What are you _____ _____ there?

   G: I'm _____ _____ _____ to an _____ park. I'm also going _____ _____ _____ of food.

   B: Good. _____ _____ _____ _____ some dim sum.

1. G: 네 휴대폰 소리를 키워줄 수 있겠니? 이 노래가 좋아.
   B: 소리를 더는 키울 수 없어. 음량이 이미 가장 높은데.
   G: 그냥 네 휴대폰을 유리잔 안에 넣게 해 줘. 유리잔이 스피커처럼 쓰인다고 들었어.
   B: 재미있는 생각이야! 지금 해 보자.

2. B: 우리 학교에 영화 배우가 온다고 들었어.
   G: 맞아. 내가 가장 좋아하는 여배우야.
   B: 오, 누군데?
   G: Miranda Kim이야. 영화 《주피터》에서 책임 과학자를 연기했어.
   B: 우와, 빨리 만나보고 싶은데!

1. W: 실례합니다, 식사를 마치셨나요?
   M: 네, 정말 좋았어요.
   W: 남은 음식을 집에 가져가시겠어요?
   M: 네, 부탁합니다.
   W: 내일까지는 남은 음식을 다 드시는 걸 잊지 마세요.

2. B: 이번 겨울 방학에는 뭘 할 거야?
   G: 부모님과 홍콩에 갈 거야.
   B: 신나겠는걸. 거기서 뭘 할 거니?
   G: 놀이공원에 갈 거야. 그리고 온갖 음식들을 먹어 볼 거야.
   B: 좋은데. 딤섬을 먹어 보는 걸 잊지 마.

Communicate A

Yuri: _____ _____, Jaden?

Jaden: My science homework is too _____.

Yuri: What do you _____ _____ do?

Jaden: I need to find _____ _____ _____ _____ trees.

Yuri: That's easy. _____ _____ _____ we _____ _____ trees _____ _____ _____ paper.

Jaden: Oh, I think _____ _____ _____, _____. Then, I can just _____ _____ _____ _____ _____.

Yuri: Yes! You _____ _____ _____ just one paper towel _____ _____ _____ your hands.

Jaden: That's _____. I need _____ _____ two or three paper towels.

Yuri: Just _____ your hands _____ you use a paper towel. Then, one will be _____ _____ _____.

Jaden: Oh, that's a good idea, Yuri! I'll _____ that _____ _____.

Yuri: Good! Just _____ _____ _____ _____ your hands _____ _____ 10 _____.

Communicate B

A: _____ _____ _____ that _____ _____ is the _____ _____ _____ _____ the Earth.

B: I've _____ _____, _____. What can we do to _____ _____?

A: _____ _____ we _____ _____ the light _____ we're not using it?

B: That's a good idea. _____ _____ to _____ _____ the light _____ you _____ your room.

Progress Check

1. **B:** _____ _____ _____ a famous baseball player _____ _____ to our school.

   G: That's right. He's _____ _____ _____.

   B: Oh, who is he?

   G: I'm _____ _____ _____ tell you. It's a _____!

2. **B:** What's your _____ _____ this _____ _____?

   G: I'm going _____ _____ Vietnam _____ my parents.

   B: That _____ _____. What are you _____ to do there?

   G: I'm going to _____ some time on the _____ and eat lots of _____.

   B: Good. _____ _____ _____ _____ the fruit there, too.

   G: O.K., I _____ _____.

유리: 무슨 일 있니, Jaden?
Jaden: 과학 숙제가 너무 어려워.
유리: 뭘 해야 하는데?
Jaden: 나무들을 살리는 방법을 찾아야 해.
유리: 그건 쉬워. 나는 종이를 덜 사용함으로써 나무들을 살릴 수 있다고 들었어.
Jaden: 아, 나도 들어 본 것 같아. 그럼, 종이컵 쓰는 걸 멈추면 되겠네.
유리: 맞아! 그리고 손을 말리는 데 종이 수건을 한 장만 쓸 수도 있지.
Jaden: 그건 불가능해. 나는 종이 수건이 적어도 두세 장은 필요해.
유리: 종이 수건을 쓰기 전에 손을 털어봐. 그럼, 한 장으로 충분하고도 남을 거야.
Jaden: 오, 좋은 생각이야, 유리야! 다음에 해 봐야겠어.
유리: 좋아! 손을 적어도 열 번은 털어야 한다는 걸 잊지 마.

A: 전기를 절약하는 게 지구를 살리는 데 가장 좋은 방법이라고 들었어.
B: 나도 들었어. 전기를 절약하기 위해 무엇을 할 수 있을까?
A: 사용하지 않을 때는 전기를 끄는 게 어때?
B: 좋은 생각이야. 방을 나갈 때 불 끄는 것을 잊지 마.

1. B: 유명한 야구 선수가 우리 학교로 온다고 들었어.
   G: 맞아. 그는 내가 가장 좋아하는 선수야.
   B: 오, 누군데?
   G: 말해주지 않을 거야. 놀라게 할 거야!

2. B: 이번 겨울 방학에 무슨 계획이 있니?
   G: 부모님과 함께 베트남에 갈 거야.
   B: 재미있겠다. 거기서 뭘 할 거야?
   G: 바닷가에서 시간을 좀 보내고 해산물을 많이 먹을 거야.
   B: 좋아. 거기 과일을 먹어 보는 것도 잊지 마.
   G: 알겠어, 잊지 않을게.

※ 다음 우리말에 맞도록 대화를 영어로 쓰시오.

Listen & Speak 1-A

1. G: _____

    B: _____

    G: _____

    B: _____

2. B: _____

    G: _____

    B: _____

    G: _____

    B: _____

1. G: 네 휴대폰 소리를 키워줄 수 있겠니? 이 노래가 좋아.
   B: 소리를 더는 키울 수 없어. 음량이 이미 가장 높은데.
   G: 그냥 네 휴대폰을 유리잔 안에 넣게 해 줘. 유리잔이 스피커처럼 쓰인다고 들었어.
   B: 재미있는 생각이야! 지금 해 보자.

2. B: 우리 학교에 영화 배우가 온다고 들었어.
   G: 맞아. 내가 가장 좋아하는 여배우야.
   B: 오, 누군데?
   G: Miranda Kim이야. 영화 《주피터》에서 책임 과학자를 연기했어.
   B: 우와, 빨리 만나보고 싶은데!

Listen & Speak 2-A

1. W: _____

    M: _____

    W: _____

    M: _____

    W: _____

2. B: _____

    G: _____

    B: _____

    G: _____

    B: _____

1. W: 실례합니다, 식사를 마치셨나요?
   M: 네, 정말 좋았어요.
   W: 남은 음식을 집에 가져가시겠어요?
   M: 네, 부탁합니다.
   W: 내일까지는 남은 음식을 다 드시는 걸 잊지 마세요.

2. B: 이번 겨울 방학에는 뭘 할 거야?
   G: 부모님과 홍콩에 갈 거야.
   B: 신나겠는걸. 거기서 뭘 할 거니?
   G: 놀이공원에 갈 거야. 그리고 온갖 음식들을 먹어 볼 거야.
   B: 좋은데. 딤섬을 먹어 보는 걸 잊지 마.

Communicate A

Yuri: _____

Jaden: _____

Yuri: _____

Jaden: _____

Yuri: _____

Jaden: _____

Yuri: _____

Jaden: _____

Yuri: _____

Jaden: _____

Yuri: _____

유리: 무슨 일 있니, Jaden?
Jaden: 과학 숙제가 너무 어려워.
유리: 뭘 해야 하는데?
Jaden: 나무들을 살리는 방법을 찾아야 해.
유리: 그건 쉬워. 나는 종이를 덜 사용함으로써 나무들을 살릴 수 있다고 들었어.
Jaden: 아, 나도 들어 본 것 같아. 그럼, 종이컵 쓰는 걸 멈추면 되겠네.
유리: 맞아! 그리고 손을 말리는 데 종이 수건을 한 장만 쓸 수도 있지.
Jaden: 그건 불가능해. 나는 종이 수건이 적어도 두세 장은 필요해.
유리: 종이 수건을 쓰기 전에 손을 털어 봐. 그럼, 한 장으로 충분하고도 남을 거야.
Jaden: 오, 좋은 생각이야, 유리야! 다음에 해 봐야겠어.
유리: 좋아! 손을 적어도 열 번은 털어야 한다는 걸 잊지 마.

Communicate B

A: _____

B: _____

A: _____

B: _____

A: 전기를 절약하는 게 지구를 살리는 데 가장 좋은 방법이라고 들었어.
B: 나도 들었어. 전기를 절약하기 위해 무엇을 할 수 있을까?
A: 사용하지 않을 때는 전기를 끄는 게 어때?
B: 좋은 생각이야. 방을 나갈 때 불 끄는 것을 잊지 마.

Progress Check

1. B: _____
   G: _____
   B: _____
   G: _____

2. B: _____
   G: _____
   B: _____
   G: _____
   B: _____
   G: _____

1. B: 유명한 야구 선수가 우리 학교로 온다고 들었어.
   G: 맞아. 그는 내가 가장 좋아하는 선수야.
   B: 오, 누군데?
   G: 말해주지 않을 거야. 놀라게 할 거야!

2. B: 이번 겨울 방학에 무슨 계획이 있니?
   G: 부모님과 함께 베트남에 갈 거야.
   B: 재미있겠다. 거기서 뭘 할 거야?
   G: 바닷가에서 시간을 좀 보내고 해산물을 많이 먹을 거야.
   B: 좋아. 거기 과일을 먹어 보는 것도 잊지 마.
   G: 알겠어, 잊지 않을게.

※ 다음 우리말과 일치하도록 빈칸에 알맞은 것을 골라 쓰시오.

1 _____ Magic _____
    A. Lamps   B. One-Dollar

2 "Wow, I can _____ a book in my room now!" _____ Marco, a boy in a _____ in the Philippines.
    A. shouted   B. village   C. read

3 His house has no _____ just _____ all the _____ houses in the _____.
    A. other   B. village   C. like   D. electricity

4 People in the village are _____ poor _____ _____ for electricity.
    A. pay   B. to   C. too

5 Even _____ the _____, they live in darkness _____ the houses are _____ close together.
    A. because   B. daytime   C. packed   D. during

6 Now _____ are changing _____ _____ a _____ plastic bottle.
    A. of   B. because   C. single   D. things

7 One plastic bottle in the ceiling can _____ _____ a whole room _____ _____ any electricity.
    A. without   B. light   C. using   D. up

8 This amazing plastic bottle is _____ a Moser lamp _____ it was _____ _____ Alfredo Moser.
    A. invented   B. called   C. by   D. because

9 In 2002, _____ _____ many _____ in his town in Brazil.
    A. blackouts   B. were   C. there

10 These blackouts made him _____ up _____ a new _____ to _____ his house.
    A. come   B. light   C. with   D. way

11 A Moser lamp can be _____ _____ about one dollar and _____ for _____ 10 years.
    A. for   B. made   C. about   D. lasts

12 It is _____ very _____.
    A. safe   B. also

1 1달러짜리 마법의 전구

2 "우와, 이젠 제 방에서 책을 읽을 수 있어요!" 필리핀의 한 마을에 사는 소년인 Marco가 외쳤다.

3 그의 집은 마을의 다른 모든 집들과 마찬가지로 전기가 없다.

4 마을 사람들은 너무나 가난해서 전기세를 낼 수가 없다.

5 심지어 낮 동안에도, 집들이 빽빽하게 들어차 있어서 그들은 어둠 속에 살아간다.

6 이제 플라스틱병 하나 때문에 상황이 바뀌고 있다.

7 천장에 있는 플라스틱병 하나는 전기를 쓰지 않고 방 전체를 밝힐 수 있다.

8 이 놀라운 플라스틱병은 Moser 램프라고 불리는데, 그것이 Alfredo Moser에 의해 발명되었기 때문이다.

9 2002년, 브라질에 있는 그의 마을에는 정전이 잦았다.

10 이 정전들은 그가 집을 밝히는 새로운 방법을 생각해 내도록 만들었다.

11 Moser 램프는 1달러 정도로 만들 수 있고 10년 정도 지속된다.

12 그것은 또한 매우 안전하다.

13 It can _____ _____ a house _____.

    A. fire   B. start   C. never

14 _____, it is very _____ to _____ this magic lamp.

    A. easy   B. surprisingly   C. make

15 _____ to _____ a Moser lamp _____ a bottle

    A. from   B. how   C. make

16 1. _____ a _____ plastic bottle _____ water.

    A. with   B. fill   C. clear

17 2. _____ some bleach _____ _____ the water _____.

    A. clear   B. keep   C. add   D. to

18 3. Make a hole in the _____, and _____ the bottle _____ the _____.

    A. hole   B. into   C. push   D. roof

19 4. _____ a _____ of the bottle _____ _____ the roof.

    A. remain   B. third   C. let   D. above

20 5. Sunlight _____ _____ by the water in the bottle and _____ _____ the room.

    A. spreads   B. bent   C. around   D. is

21 _____ the Philippines, Moser lamps are _____ _____ _____ the My Shelter Foundation.

    A. used   B. by   C. in   D. widely

22 The _____ also teaches _____ people _____ to make and _____ the lamps.

    A. install   B. charity   C. how   D. local

23 _____ _____ the charity, _____ _____ homes in the Philippines now have Moser lamps.

    A. of   B. thanks   C. thousands   D. to

24 It _____ also _____ Moser lamps popular in _____ countries, _____ as Argentina, India, and Fiji.

    A. has   B. other   C. made   D. such

25 Moser lamps will _____ _____ the lives of many people _____ many _____ to come.

    A. for   B. light   C. years   D. up

13 그것은 절대 집에 불을 낼 수 없다.

14 놀랍게도, 이 신기한 램프를 만드는 것은 매우 쉽다.

15 병으로 Moser 램프를 만드는 법

16 1. 투명한 플라스틱병에 물을 채운다.

17 2. 물을 깨끗이 유지하기 위해 표백제를 조금 넣는다.

18 3. 지붕에 구멍을 내고, 병을 구멍 안으로 넣는다.

19 4. 병의 3분의 1은 지붕 위에 남아 있도록 한다.

20 5. 햇빛이 병 속의 물에 의해 굴절되어 방에 퍼진다.

21 필리핀에서 Moser 램프는 My Shelter 재단에 의해 널리 사용된다.

22 또한 그 자선단체는 지역 사람들에게 램프를 만들고 설치하는 법을 가르친다.

23 이 자선단체 덕분에, 필리핀의 수천 가구가 이제 Moser 램프를 갖고 있다.

24 그 단체는 아르헨티나, 인도, 피지와 같은 다른 나라들에서도 Moser 램프가 유명해 지도록 만들었다.

25 Moser 램프는 앞으로 오랫동안 많은 사람들의 삶을 밝혀 줄 것이다.

※ 다음 우리말과 일치하도록 빈칸에 알맞은 말을 쓰시오.

1 _____ _____ Lamps

2 "Wow, I can read a book in my room now!" _____ Marco, a boy in a village _____ _____ _____.

3 His house _____ _____ _____ just like _____ _____ _____ _____ in the village.

4 People in the village are _____ poor _____ _____ _____ _____.

5 Even _____ the daytime, they live in darkness _____ the houses _____ _____ _____ _____ _____.

6 Now things _____ _____ _____ _____ a single plastic bottle.

7 One plastic bottle _____ _____ _____ can _____ a whole room _____ _____ any electricity.

8 This amazing plastic bottle _____ _____ a Moser lamp _____ it _____ _____ _____ Alfredo Moser.

9 In 2002, there _____ _____ _____ _____ in his town in Brazil.

10 These blackouts made him _____ _____ _____ a new _____ _____ _____ his house.

11 A Moser lamp can _____ _____ _____ about one dollar and _____ _____ _____ 10 years.

12 It is also _____ _____.

---

1 1달러짜리 마법의 전구

2 "우와, 이젠 제 방에서 책을 읽을 수 있어요!" 필리핀의 한 마을에 사는 소년인 Marco가 외쳤다.

3 그의 집은 마을의 다른 모든 집들과 마찬가지로 전기가 없다.

4 마을 사람들은 너무나 가난해서 전기세를 낼 수가 없다.

5 심지어 낮 동안에도, 집들이 빽빽하게 들어차 있어서 그들은 어둠 속에 살아간다.

6 이제 플라스틱병 하나 때문에 상황이 바뀌고 있다.

7 천장에 있는 플라스틱병 하나는 전기를 쓰지 않고 방 전체를 밝힐 수 있다.

8 이 놀라운 플라스틱병은 Moser 램프라고 불리는데, 그것이 Alfredo Moser에 의해 발명되었기 때문이다.

9 2002년, 브라질에 있는 그의 마을에는 정전이 잦았다.

10 이 정전들은 그가 집을 밝히는 새로운 방법을 생각해 내도록 만들었다.

11 Moser 램프는 1달러 정도로 만들 수 있고 10년 정도 지속된다.

12 그것은 또한 매우 안전하다.

13 It can _____ _____ a house fire.

14 Surprisingly, it is very easy _____ _____ this magic lamp.

15 _____ _____ _____ a Moser lamp from a bottle

16 1. _____ a clear plastic bottle _____ water.

17 2. _____ some _____ _____ _____ the water _____ .

18 3. Make a hole in the roof, and _____ the bottle _____ the hole.

19 4. Let _____ _____ of the bottle _____ _____ the roof.

20 5. Sunlight _____ _____ _____ the water in the bottle and _____ _____ the room.

21 In the Philippines, Moser lamps _____ _____ _____ by the My Shelter Foundation.

22 _____ _____ also teaches local people _____ _____ _____ and _____ the lamps.

23 _____ _____ the charity, _____ _____ homes in the Philippines now have Moser lamps.

24 It _____ also _____ Moser lamps popular in _____ _____, _____ _____ Argentina, India, and Fiji.

25 Moser lamps will _____ _____ the lives of many people _____ _____ _____ _____ _____ .

---

13 그것은 절대 집에 불을 낼 수 없다.

14 놀랍게도, 이 신기한 램프를 만드는 것은 매우 쉽다.

15 병으로 Moser 램프를 만드는 법

16 1. 투명한 플라스틱병에 물을 채운다.

17 2. 물을 깨끗이 유지하기 위해 표백제를 조금 넣는다.

18 3. 지붕에 구멍을 내고, 병을 구멍 안으로 넣는다.

19 4. 병의 3분의 1은 지붕 위에 남아 있도록 한다.

20 5. 햇빛이 병 속의 물에 의해 굴절되어 방에 퍼진다.

21 필리핀에서 Moser 램프는 My Shelter 재단에 의해 널리 사용된다.

22 또한 그 자선단체는 지역 사람들에게 램프를 만들고 설치하는 법을 가르친다.

23 이 자선단체 덕분에, 필리핀의 수천 가구가 이제 Moser 램프를 갖고 있다.

24 그 단체는 아르헨티나, 인도, 피지와 같은 다른 나라들에서도 Moser 램프가 유명해 지도록 만들었다.

25 Moser 램프는 앞으로 오랫동안 많은 사람들의 삶을 밝혀 줄 것이다.

※ 다음 문장을 우리말로 쓰시오.

1 One-Dollar Magic Lamps

➡ _____

2 "Wow, I can read a book in my room now!" shouted Marco, a boy in a village in the Philippines.

➡ _____

3 His house has no electricity just like all the other houses in the village.

➡ _____

4 People in the village are too poor to pay for electricity.

➡ _____

5 Even during the daytime, they live in darkness because the houses are packed close together.

➡ _____

6 Now things are changing because of a single plastic bottle.

➡ _____

7 One plastic bottle in the ceiling can light up a whole room without using any electricity.

➡ _____

8 This amazing plastic bottle is called a Moser lamp because it was invented by Alfredo Moser.

➡ _____

9 In 2002, there were many blackouts in his town in Brazil.

➡ _____

10 These blackouts made him come up with a new way to light his house.

➡ _____

11 A Moser lamp can be made for about one dollar and lasts for about 10 years.

➡ _____

12 It is also very safe.

➡ _____

13 ▸ It can never start a house fire.

➡ _____

14 ▸ Surprisingly, it is very easy to make this magic lamp.

➡ _____

15 ▸ How to make a Moser lamp from a bottle

➡ _____

16 ▸ 1. Fill a clear plastic bottle with water.

➡ _____

17 ▸ 2. Add some bleach to keep the water clear.

➡ _____

18 ▸ 3. Make a hole in the roof, and push the bottle into the hole.

➡ _____

19 ▸ 4. Let a third of the bottle remain above the roof.

➡ _____

20 ▸ 5. Sunlight is bent by the water in the bottle and spreads around the room.

➡ _____

21 ▸ In the Philippines, Moser lamps are widely used by the My Shelter Foundation.

➡ _____

22 ▸ The charity also teaches local people how to make and install the lamps.

➡ _____

23 ▸ Thanks to the charity, thousands of homes in the Philippines now have Moser lamps.

➡ _____

24 ▸ It has also made Moser lamps popular in other countries, such as Argentina, India, and Fiji.

➡ _____

25 ▸ Moser lamps will light up the lives of many people for many years to come.

➡ _____

※ 다음 괄호 안의 단어들을 우리말에 맞도록 바르게 배열하시오.

1 (Magic / One-Dollar / Lamps)
➡ _____

2 ("wow, / can / I / a / read / book / my / in / room / now!" / Marco, / shouted / boy / a / in / village / a / in / Philippines. / the)
➡ _____
_____

3 (house / his / no / has / just / electricity / like / the / all / other / in / houses / village. / the)
➡ _____

4 (in / people / the / village / too / are / poor / pay / to / electricity. / for)
➡ _____

5 (during / even / daytime, / the / live / they / darkness / in / because / houses / the / packed / are / together. / close)
➡ _____

6 (things / now / changing / are / of / because / a / plastic / single / bottle.)
➡ _____

7 (plastic / one / in / bottle / the / ceiling / light / can / up / a / room / whole / using / without / electricity. / any)
➡ _____

8 (amazing / this / bottle / plastic / called / is / Moser / a / lamp / it / because / invented / was / by / Moser. / Alfredo)
➡ _____
_____

9 (2002, / in / were / there / blcakouts / many / his / in / town / Brazil. / in)
➡ _____

10 (blackouts / these / him / made / come / with / up / a / way / new / light / to / house. / his)
➡ _____

11 (Moser / a / lamp / be / can / for / made / about / dollar / one / and / for / lasts / about / years. / 10)
➡ _____
_____

12 (is / it / also / safe. / very)
➡ _____

1 1달러짜리 마법의 전구

2 "우와, 이젠 제 방에서 책을 읽을 수 있어요!" 필리핀의 한 마을에 사는 소년인 Marco가 외쳤다.

3 그의 집은 마을의 다른 모든 집들과 마찬가지로 전기가 없다.

4 마을 사람들은 너무나 가난해서 전기세를 낼 수가 없다.

5 심지어 낮 동안에도, 집들이 빽빽하게 들어차 있어서 그들은 어둠 속에 살아간다.

6 이제 플라스틱병 하나 때문에 상황이 바뀌고 있다.

7 천장에 있는 플라스틱병 하나는 전기를 쓰지 않고 방 전체를 밝힐 수 있다.

8 이 놀라운 플라스틱병은 Moser 램프라고 불리는데, 그것이 Alfredo Moser에 의해 발명되었기 때문이다.

9 2002년, 브라질에 있는 그의 마을에는 정전이 잦았다.

10 이 정전들은 그가 집을 밝히는 새로운 방법을 생각해 내도록 만들었다.

11 Moser 램프는 1달러 정도로 만들 수 있고 10년 정도 지속된다.

12 그것은 또한 매우 안전하다.

13 (it / never / can / a / start / fire. / house)

➡ _____

14 (surprisingly, / is / it / easy / very / make / to / magic / this / lamp.)

➡ _____

15 (to / how / a / make / lamp / Moser / a / from / bottle)

➡ _____

16 (1. / a / fill / plastic / clear / with / bottle / water.)

➡ _____

17 (2. / some / add / to / bleach / the / keep / clear. / water)

➡ _____

18 (3. / a / make / hole / the / in / roof, / and / the / push / into / bottle / hole. / the)

➡ _____

19 (4. / a / let / of / third / the / remain / bottle / above / roof. / the)

➡ _____

20 (5. / is / sunlight / bent / by / water / the / in / bottle / and / spreads / the / around / room.)

➡ _____

21 (the / in / Philippines, / lamps / Moser / widely / are / by / used / the / Shelter / My / Foundation.)

➡ _____

_____

22 (charity / the / teaches / also / people / local / to / how / make / and / the / install / lamps.)

➡ _____

23 (to / thanks / charity, / the / of / thousands / homes / the / in / now / Philippines / have / lamps. / Moser)

➡ _____

_____

24 (has / it / made / also / lamps / Moser / in / popular / countries, / other / as / such / India, / Argentina, / Fiji. / and)

➡ _____

_____

25 (lamps / Moser / light / will / up / lives / the / many / of / for / people / years / many / come. / to)

➡ _____

_____

13 그것은 절대 집에 불을 낼 수 없다.

14 놀랍게도, 이 신기한 램프를 만드는 것은 매우 쉽다.

15 병으로 Moser 램프를 만드는 법

16 1. 투명한 플라스틱병에 물을 채운다.

17 2. 물을 깨끗이 유지하기 위해 표백제를 조금 넣는다.

18 3. 지붕에 구멍을 내고, 병을 구멍 안으로 넣는다.

19 4. 병의 3분의 1은 지붕 위에 남아 있도록 한다.

20 5. 햇빛이 병 속의 물에 의해 굴절되어 방에 퍼진다.

21 필리핀에서 Moser 램프는 My Shelter 재단에 의해 널리 사용된다.

22 또한 그 자선단체는 지역 사람들에게 램프를 만들고 설치하는 법을 가르친다.

23 이 자선단체 덕분에, 필리핀의 수천 가구가 이제 Moser 램프를 갖고 있다.

24 그 단체는 아르헨티나, 인도, 피지와 같은 다른 나라들에서도 Moser 램프가 유명해 지도록 만들었다.

25 Moser 램프는 앞으로 오랫동안 많은 사람들의 삶을 밝혀 줄 것이다.

※ 다음 우리말을 영어로 쓰시오.

1   1달러짜리 마법의 전구

➡ _____

2   "우와, 이젠 제 방에서 책을 읽을 수 있어요!" 필리핀의 한 마을에 사는 소년인 Marco가 외쳤다.

➡ _____

3   그의 집은 마을의 다른 모든 집들과 마찬가지로 전기가 없다.

➡ _____

4   마을 사람들은 너무나 가난해서 전기세를 낼 수가 없다.

➡ _____

5   심지어 낮 동안에도, 집들이 빽빽하게 들어차 있어서 그들은 어둠 속에 살아간다.

➡ _____

6   이제 플라스틱병 하나 때문에 상황이 바뀌고 있다.

➡ _____

7   천장에 있는 플라스틱병 하나는 전기를 쓰지 않고 방 전체를 밝힐 수 있다.

➡ _____

8   이 놀라운 플라스틱병은 Moser 램프라고 불리는데, 그것이 Alfredo Moser에 의해 발명되었기 때문이다.

➡ _____

9   2002년, 브라질에 있는 그의 마을에는 정전이 잦았다.

➡ _____

10   이 정전들은 그가 집을 밝히는 새로운 방법을 생각해 내도록 만들었다.

➡ _____

11   Moser 램프는 1달러 정도로 만들 수 있고 10년 정도 지속된다.

➡ _____

12   그것은 또한 매우 안전하다.

➡ _____

13 그것은 절대 집에 불을 낼 수 없다.

➡ _____

14 놀랍게도, 이 신기한 램프를 만드는 것은 매우 쉽다.

➡ _____

15 병으로 Moser 램프를 만드는 법

➡ _____

16 1. 투명한 플라스틱병에 물을 채운다.

➡ _____

17 2. 물을 깨끗이 유지하기 위해 표백제를 조금 넣는다.

➡ _____

18 3. 지붕에 구멍을 내고, 병을 구멍 안으로 넣는다.

➡ _____

19 4. 병의 3분의 1은 지붕 위에 남아 있도록 한다.

➡ _____

20 5. 햇빛이 병 속의 물에 의해 굴절되어 방에 퍼진다.

➡ _____

21 필리핀에서 Moser 램프는 My Shelter 재단에 의해 널리 사용된다.

➡ _____

22 또한 그 자선단체는 지역 사람들에게 램프를 만들고 설치하는 법을 가르친다.

➡ _____

23 이 자선단체 덕분에, 필리핀의 수천 가구가 이제 Moser 램프를 갖고 있다.

➡ _____

24 그 단체는 아르헨티나, 인도, 피지와 같은 다른 나라들에서도 Moser 램프가 유명해 지도록 만들었다.

➡ _____

25 Moser 램프는 앞으로 오랫동안 많은 사람들의 삶을 밝혀 줄 것이다.

➡ _____

※ 다음 우리말과 일치하도록 빈칸에 알맞은 말을 쓰시오.

Link-Share

1. We thought we could _____ _____ _____ _____ with a glass bottle.

2. We made one lamp _____ _____ a plastic bottle and _____ _____ out of a glass bottle.

3. _____ _____ _____ _____ were the same.

4. We _____ _____ the glass bottle lamp was _____ _____ the plastic bottle lamp.

1. 우리는 우리가 램프를 유리병으로 더 밝게 만들 수 있다고 생각했다.
2. 우리는 플라스틱병으로 램프를 하나 만들고 유리병으로 또 다른 하나를 만들었다.
3. 다른 모든 단계는 똑같았다.
4. 우리는 유리병 램프가 플라스틱병 램프보다 더 밝다는 것을 알았다.

Write

1. You can make _____ _____ _____ things _____ a CD case.

2. You _____ _____ _____ a grass container.

3. First, _____ _____ _____ the CD case with soil and water, and _____ grass seeds _____ the soil.

4. Second, _____ the case and tape _____ _____ _____ _____.

5. _____, leave _____ in the sun _____ _____ ten days.

6. Now, your grass container _____ _____.

7. It will _____ _____ _____ when the grass grows.

1. 당신은 CD 케이스로 많은 것들을 만들 수 있다.
2. 당신은 심지어 잔디를 기르는 용기를 만들 수도 있다.
3. 먼저 CD 케이스의 절반을 흙과 물로 채우고, 잔디 씨앗을 흙 안에 넣어라.
4. 두 번째, 케이스를 닫고 모든 옆면에 테이프를 붙여라.
5. 마지막으로, 햇빛이 비치는 곳에 약 10일 동안 놓아 두어라.
6. 이제, 당신의 잔디를 기르는 용기가 준비되었다.
7. 잔디가 자랄 때 그것은 당신을 행복하게 만들어 줄 것이다.

Culture Project-Share

1. We'd _____ _____ _____ about a pot-in-pot cooler.

2. It _____ _____ _____ without electricity.

3. _____'s very easy _____ _____ one.

4. First, _____ a pot _____ a larger pot.

5. Then, _____ sand and water _____ these pots.

6. Just _____ the water _____ _____, and it'll _____ the food.

1. 우리는 pot-in-pot cooler(항아리 냉장고)에 대해 이야기하고 싶다.
2. 그것은 전기 없이 식품을 신선하게 유지할 수 있다.
3. 그것을 만드는 것은 매우 쉽다.
4. 우선, 항아리 하나를 더 큰 항아리에 넣는다.
5. 그리고 항아리들 사이에 모래와 물을 넣는다.
6. 물이 그저 마르게 두면, 그것이 음식을 시원하게 할 것이다.

※ 다음 우리말을 영어로 쓰시오.

Link -Share

1. 우리는 우리가 램프를 유리병으로 더 밝게 만들 수 있다고 생각했다.
   ➡ _____

2. 우리는 플라스틱병으로 램프를 하나 만들고 유리병으로 또 다른 하나를 만들었다.
   ➡ _____

3. 다른 모든 단계는 똑같았다.
   ➡ _____

4. 우리는 유리병 램프가 플라스틱병 램프보다 더 밝다는 것을 알았다.
   ➡ _____

Write

1. 당신은 CD 케이스로 많은 것들을 만들 수 있다.
   ➡ _____

2. 당신은 심지어 잔디를 기르는 용기를 만들 수도 있다.
   ➡ _____

3. 먼저 CD 케이스의 절반을 흙과 물로 채우고, 잔디 씨앗을 흙 안에 넣어라.
   ➡ _____

4. 두 번째, 케이스를 닫고 모든 옆면에 테이프를 붙여라.
   ➡ _____

5. 마지막으로, 햇빛이 비치는 곳에 약 10일 동안 놓아 두어라.
   ➡ _____

6. 이제, 당신의 잔디를 기르는 용기가 준비되었다.
   ➡ _____

7. 잔디가 자랄 때 그것은 당신을 행복하게 만들어 줄 것이다.
   ➡ _____

Culture Project-Share

1. 우리는 pot-in-pot cooler(항아리 냉장고)에 대해 이야기하고 싶다.
   ➡ _____

2. 그것은 전기 없이 식품을 신선하게 유지할 수 있다.
   ➡ _____

3. 그것을 만드는 것은 매우 쉽다.
   ➡ _____

4. 우선, 항아리 하나를 더 큰 항아리에 넣는다.
   ➡ _____

5. 그리고 항아리들 사이에 모래와 물을 넣는다.
   ➡ _____

6. 물이 그저 마르게 두면, 그것이 음식을 시원하게 할 것이다.
   ➡ _____

MEMO

영어 기출 문제집

적중100

2학기

정답 및 해설

미래 | 최연희

중 2

적중100

영어 기출 문제집

적중100

2학기

정답 및 해설

미래 | 최연희

중 2

Lesson
5

Bravo! Brava!

시험대비 실력평가 p.08

01 brave   02 ①   03 ④   04 ⑤
05 ②   06 ⑤   07 (r)iddles
08 beautiful   09 (1) be late for   (2) take, off

01 둘은 반의어 관계이다. 알려지지 않은 : 유명한 = 겁 많은 : 용감한

02 새벽이다. 해가 떠오르고 있어.

03 배경 지식은 당신이 뮤지컬을 감상하는 데 도움이 될 것이다.

04 한 사람에 의해 불러지는 오페라의 음악

05 슬픔이나 공감의 강한 감정을 불러일으키는

06 nothing more than은 '~에 지나지 않은'의 뜻이다.

07 puzzle = riddle: 수수께끼

08 'of+추상명사'는 형용사와 뜻이 같다.

09 (1) be late for: ~에 늦다 (2) take off: (일을) 쉬다

서술형 시험대비 p.09

01 (1) right after   (2) correctly, agree to   (3) marry, riddles   02 (1) appreciate   (2) storyline
03 take   04 (1) most famous   (2) Like
(3) celebrated   (4) performance
05 (1) discount   (2) nothing more than   (3) fails
(4) until[till]

01 (1) right는 부사로 '바로'의 뜻이다. (2) correctly는 부사로 '맞게, 올바르게'의 뜻이고, '~에 동의하다'는 'agree to+동사원형'을 사용한다. (3) '~와 결혼하다'는 marry가 적절하다. 수수께끼는 three가 있으므로 복수형이 적절하다.

02 (1) 어떤 것이나 어떤 사람이 얼마나 좋은지 이해하다 (2) 책, 영화, 희곡 등에서 일어나는 일련의 사건

03 take off: 일을 쉬다, take+교통수단: ~을 타다

04 (1) of the whole opera(전체 오페라 중에서)와 호응이 되려면 'the+최상급' 형태가 적절하다. (2) like는 전치사로 '~와 같이'의 의미로 사용이 되었다. (3) celebrate: (특별한 날·경사 등을) 축하하다, 기념하다 / '그녀는 작년에 내 생일을 축하해 줬다.'는 의미로 과거시제가 적절하다. (4) 소유격 our 뒤에 명사형이 적절하므로 동사 perform의 명사형인 performance가 맞다.

05 (1) discount: 할인 (2) nothing more than: ~에 지나지 않은 (3) fail: 실패하다 (4) until[till]: ~할 때까지

교과서 Conversation

핵심 Check p.10~11

1 ③   2 ②   3 ③, ⑤
4 (W)hat about

교과서 대화문 익히기

Check(√) True or False p.12

1 F   2 T   3 T   4 T

교과서 확인학습 p.14~15

Listen & Speak 1-A
1 hurry up, already / be late for / Why don't we take / faster than
2 wrong / sure, well, Why don't we, celebrate / for / Of course

Listen & Speak 1-B
shall we / Why don't we / good idea

Listen & Speak 2-A
1 let's, parts, play / What time shall we meet / How about, right / Sounds
2 Where shall we / about, near / at

Listen & Speak 2-B
Let's / shall / How about / Let's meet

Communicate A
guess / Why not / anniversary / together / take, off / Why don't we, get, discount if / let's / shall we / How about / best

Communicate B
What shall we / Why don't we / time shall we / How / Let's

Progress Check
1 Why don't we take, faster, at this time of day
2 Let's go swimming / Where / How about

시험대비 기본평가 p.16

01 ④   02 ③   03 ①
04 (C) → (B) → (D) → (A)

2 정답 및 해설

01 B의 대답이 '지하철역에서 만나는 게 어때?'라고 했으므로 G는 어디서 만날지 묻는 말이 적절하다.

02 A의 답으로 보아 B는 몇 시에 만날지 묻고 있다는 것을 알 수 있다.

03 비교급 구문으로 faster than이 적절하다.

04 (C) '배드민턴 하지 않을래?'라는 제안 → (B) 승낙의 표현과 어디서 할 것인지 묻고 → (D) 장소 제안 → (A) 동의

01 ④   02 ②   03 ①
04 ①, ④, ⑤   05 ⑤   06 ④   07 station
08 ①   09 ③   10 anniversary
11 I guess I can take the afternoon off.   12 ②
13 (A) wrong   (B) celebrate

01 B가 '원더 우먼을 보러 가는 게 어때?'라고 답하는 걸로 보아 A는 오후에 무엇을 할 것인지 묻는 것을 알 수 있다.

02 B의 대답으로 보아 시간 약속을 정하는 표현이 적절하다.

03 '~이 어때?'라는 의미로 How about ~?을 사용한다.

04 '~하는 게 어때?', '~하자'는 표현으로 Let's+동사원형 ~, Shall we+동사원형 ~?, Why don't we+동사원형 ~?, What about+동사원형+-ing? 등을 사용할 수 있다.

05 ⑤ 'A: 서둘러. 벌써 10시야.' 'B: 먼저 무엇을 시도해 볼까?'라는 대답은 자연스럽지 못하다.

06 ⓐ '~하자'는 의미로 Let's가 적절하다. ⓑ 만날 장소를 묻는 말이 적절하다.

07 사람들이 타거나 내리기 위해 버스나 기차가 멈추는 건물이나 주변 지역

08 B의 물음은 어디서 배드민턴을 할지 장소를 묻고 있으므로 빈칸에는 장소를 제안하는 말이 적절하다.

09 아빠의 'What do you want to do?'라는 말 다음에 '뮤지컬을 보러 가는 게 어때요?'라는 말이 적절하다.

10 과거의 그 날에 일어난 일을 기억하거나 축하하는 날

11 '~일 것 같다'는 I guess로 문장을 시작한다. '휴무를 하다'는 표현으로 take the afternoon off를 사용한다.

12 Anna와 그녀의 아빠는 다음 주 수요일에 대한 계획에 대해 말하고 있다.

13 대화의 내용은 아들이 한국사 시험에서 한 문제만 틀려서 축하하기 위해 저녁에 외식을 간다는 내용이다.

01 are going to take the subway

02 The subway will be faster than the bus at this time of day.

---

03 (L)et's see a magic show.
(S)hall we see a magic show?
(W)hat about seeing a magic show?

04 What time shall we meet

05 A) take   (B) about

06 have a lunch → have lunch

07 a musical, Dad / next, 12 / Bravo Theater

01 지하철이 버스보다 빠르기 때문에 지하철을 탈 것이다.

02 '~보다 빠르다'는 의미로 비교급 than을 이용한다.

03 '~하는 게 어때?', '~하자'는 표현으로 Let's+동사원형 ~, Shall we+동사원형 ~?, Why don't we+동사원형 ~?, What about+동사원형+-ing ~? 등을 사용할 수 있다.

04 약속을 정하는 표현으로 '몇 시에 만날래?'의 의미다.

05 (A)는 '(일을) 쉬다'는 의미로 take off를 사용한다. (B)는 시간을 정하는 표현으로 How about을 사용하여 '12시 어때?'라는 의미이다.

06 식사 이름 앞에는 부정관사 a를 붙이지 않는다.

07 다음 주 수요일 12시에 Bravo 극장에서 아빠와 뮤지컬을 본다.

1 (1) will go   (2) miss   (3) are

2 (1) will exercise → exercise   (2) 틀린 곳 없음

3 (1) clever   (2) interesting   4 ②

01 (1) more expensive → expensive   (2) than → as   (3) will answer → answer   (4) won't → don't
02 ⑤   03 ④   04 ③

01 (1) 'as+원급+as' 구문으로 원급인 expensive를 써야 한다.
(2) 원급 비교는 'as+원급+as'를 사용하므로 than을 as로 고친다. (3), (4) 조건의 부사절을 이끄는 접속사 if절에는 미래시제 대신 현재시제를 사용해야 한다.

02 asked의 직접목적어 자리에 사용된 명사절 접속사 if와 조건을 나타내는 부사절 접속사 if가 적절하다.

03 두 대상의 정도가 같음을 나타낼 때 'as+원급(형용사/부사)+as'를 사용한다.

04 'as+원급(형용사/부사)+as'를 사용하고, 비교급(harder)은 than과 함께 사용된다. hardly는 부사로 '거의 ~ 않다'는 의미이다.

01 ①
02 faster
03 ⑤
04 (1) as (2) tall (3) yours
05 (1) If you have to use earphones, do not play your music loud.
  (2) If you miss the subway, you will be late for the meeting.
  (3) My voice is as loud as yours.
  (4) Nick can run as fast as Peter.
06 ②
07 ④, ⑤
08 ④
09 ①
10 (1) than → as (2) more beautiful → beautiful
  (3) highly → high (4) will miss → misses
11 (1) friend → friendly (2) faster → fast
12 ⑤
13 ④
14 (1) as (2) well
(3) mine
15 She is as light as a feather.
16 A tiger is not so big as an elephant.
17 so
18 ②, ③
19 ①, ⑤
20 go, will eat / meet, will

01 ① 두 대상을 비교할 때는 비교의 대상이 동일해야 한다. His riddle과 her riddle을 비교해야 하므로 her를 hers(= her riddle)로 고쳐야 한다.

02 대화의 흐름상 지하철이 버스보다 더 빠르다(faster)는 의미가 적절하다.

03 '~한다면'의 의미로 조건의 부사절 접속사 if가 적절하고, 조건의 부사절에는 미래시제 대신 현재시제를 사용해야 한다.

04 (1), (2) 'as+원급(형용사/부사)+as' 형태를 사용한다. (3) 두 대상을 비교할 때는 비교의 대상이 동일해야 한다. my room과 your room을 비교해야 하므로 소유대명사 yours가 적절하다.

05 (1), (2) if가 있는 부사절은 '접속사(If)+주어+동사 ~, 주어+동사 …'의 어순으로 쓴다. (3), (4) 'as+원급(형용사/부사)+as' 형태를 사용한다.

06 조건의 부사절에서는 미래시제 대신 현재시제를 사용해야 한다.

07 보기의 if는 조건의 부사절이다. ①, ②, ③은 동사의 목적어 자리에 사용된 명사절 접속사로 '~인지 아닌지'의 뜻이다.

08 두 대상의 동등함을 나타낼 때 'as+원급(형용사/부사)+as' 형태를 사용한다. ④번은 '민호는 원어민만큼 영어를 잘한다.'는 의미로 동사 speaks를 수식하는 부사 well이 적절하다.

09 조건의 부사절에서는 미래시제 대신 현재시제를 사용하지만, 주절에는 미래의 의미일 때 미래시제 will을 사용해야 한다.

10 (1) 두 대상의 동등함을 나타낼 때 'as+원급(형용사/부사)+as' 형태를 사용해야 한다. (2) 'as+원급(형용사/부사)+as' 형태가 적절하므로 비교급을 원급으로 바꾸어야 한다. (3) 'as+원급(형용사/부사)+as' 형태로 부사 highly는 '매우, 대단히'의 의미이므로, '높이, 높게'의 의미를 가진 high로 바꾸어야 한다. (4) 조건의 부사절에서는 미래시제 대신 현재시제를 사용한다. 주어가 she(3인칭 단수)이므로 misses가 적절하다.

11 (1) 'as+원급(형용사/부사)+as' 형태를 사용해야 하므로, 명사 friend를 형용사 friendly로 바꾸어야 한다. (2) 'as+원급(형용사/부사)+as' 형태로 비교급 faster를 fast로 바꾼다.

12 ⑤ 조건의 부사절에서는 미래시제 대신 현재시제를 사용하지만, 주절에는 미래의 의미일 때 미래시제 will을 사용해야 한다. you see the sunrise는 you will see ~.가 되어야 한다.

13 두 대상 간의 동등함을 나타낼 때 'as+원급(형용사/부사)+as' 형태를 사용한다. book은 셀 수 있는 명사이므로 much가 아니라 many로 수식한다.

14 (1), (2): 두 대상 간의 동등함을 나타내는 동등비교는 'as+원급(형용사/부사)+as' 형태를 사용해야 한다. (3) 두 대상을 비교할 때는 비교하는 대상이 동일해야 한다. Your house와 my house가 비교되어야 하므로 소유대명사 mine이 적절하다.

15 두 대상 간의 동등함을 나타내는 동등비교는 'as+원급(형용사/부사)+as' 형태를 사용해야 한다.

16 동등비교는 'as+원급+as' 형태를 취하지만 부정문에서는 'not so+원급+as'를 사용할 수 있다.

17 동등 비교인 'as+원급(형용사/부사)+as'는 부정문에서는 'not as[so]+원급+as'로 사용할 수 있다.

18 동등비교는 'as+원급(형용사/부사)+as'형태를 취한다.

19 동등비교인 'as+원급(형용사/부사)+as' 형태를 취하고, 부정문에서는 'not as[so]+원급+as'를 취한다.

20 조건이나 시간의 부사절에서는 미래시제 대신 현재시제를 사용하지만, 주절에는 미래의 의미일 때 미래시제 will을 사용해야 한다.

01 isn't as[so] big as
02 (1) I can finish the work if you help me.
  (2) If school finishes early tomorrow, I will go see a movie.
  (3) If my mom catches a cold, I will do the dishes for her.
03 (1) run as fast as (2) as, as
04 (1) me → mine[my car] (2) more popular → popular (3) won't → doesn't (4) won't → don't
05 (1) John is as tall as Susan.
  (2) This apple is as sweet as that pineapple.
  (3) My bike is not so[as] old as his[his bike].
  (4) I watch as many movies as Kate.
06 (1) as heavy as (2) as old as (3) as tall as
07 (1) If you eat too much chocolate, your teeth will go bad.
  (2) If Fred walks to school, it will take 40 minutes.

(3) If you follow the map, you'll get to my grandma's house.

08 than her → as hers / will find → finds

09 (1) as old as　(2) not so[as] tall as

(3) not so[as] fast as

10 (1) Her sister is as playful as a kitten.

(2) My home is as quiet as a grave.

(3) I'm not so[as] tall as my brother.

01 Mina가 Jenny보다 몸집이 더 크기 때문에 Jenny는 Mina만큼 크지 않다는 'not as[so]+원급+as'가 적절하다.

02 조건의 부사절에서는 미래시제 대신 현재시제를 사용하지만, 주절에는 미래의 의미일 때 미래시제 will을 사용해야 한다.

03 위의 그림은 두 대상 간의 동등한 성질을 나타내고 있으므로 'as+원급(형용사/부사)+as' 형태를 사용한다.

04 (1) 두 대상을 비교할 때는 비교하는 대상이 동일해야 한다. Your car와 my car가 비교되어야 하므로 소유대명사 mine이나 my car가 적절하다. (2) 'as+원급(형용사/부사)+as'를 사용하므로 원급 popular가 적절하다. (3) 조건 부사절에서는 미래시제 대신 현재시제를 사용하므로 won't를 3인칭 단수형 doesn't로 고친다. (4) 조건 부사절에서는 미래시제 대신 현재시제를 사용하므로 won't를 don't로 고친다.

05 두 대상 간의 동등한 성질을 나타내고 있으므로 'as+원급(형용사/부사)+as' 형태를 사용한다. 그리고 부정문은 'not as[so]+원급+as' 형태를 사용한다.

06 (1) Eric과 Amy가 동일한 것은 몸무게이므로 형용사 heavy를 이용한다. (2) Tom과 Amy가 동일한 것은 나이이므로 형용사 old를 이용한다. (3) Tom과 Eric이 동일한 것은 키이므로 형용사 tall을 이용하여 'as+원급+as' 형태를 사용한다.

07 부사절로 시작하는 문장의 형태는 '접속사(If)+주어+동사 ~, 주어+동사 …'이다. 조건의 부사절에는 미래시제 대신 현재시제를 사용한다.

08 첫 번째 틀린 부분은 as difficult 뒤에는 as가 적절하고, 두 대상을 비교할 때는 비교 대상이 같아야 하므로 his riddle과 her riddle을 비교해야 한다. 그러므로 소유대명사 hers가 적절하다. 두 번째 틀린 부분은 시간을 나타내는 부사절에는 미래시제 대신 현재시제를 사용해야 하므로 will find를 finds로 고친다.

09 (1) 수지와 민지는 나이가 같으므로 'as old as'를 사용한다. (2) 민지가 수지보다 키가 크지 않기 때문에 부정문 'not so[as] tall as'를 사용한다. (3) 수지가 민지보다 빠르지 않기 때문에 'not so[as] fast as'를 사용한다.

10 두 대상 간의 동등한 성질을 나타내고 있으므로 'as+원급(형용사/부사)+as' 형태를 사용한다. 그리고 부정문은 'not as[so]+원급+as' 형태를 사용한다.

Reading

확인문제　　　　　　　　　p.28

1 T　2 F　3 T　4 F　5 T　6 F　7 T　8 F

확인문제　　　　　　　　　p.29

1 F　2 T　3 T　4 F　5 T　6 F

교과서 확인학습 A　　　　　p.30~31

01 The Most Dangerous　02 Welcome

03 perform　04 Like, in Italian, in Italy

05 I'd like to tell　06 appreciate, if

07 of great beauty, as cold as ice

08 who, marry her　09 fails

10 has ever been　11 falls in love with

12 the first man　13 However, to marry

14 nothing more than　15 of his own

16 What　17 adds, to die, incorrectly

18 before dawn, as difficult as hers

19 until, finds out　20 the most famous aria

21 means　22 sleeps

23 not even you　24 safe

25 will know　26 At dawn

27 prince's　28 in time

29 Let's watch

교과서 확인학습 B　　　　　p.32~33

1 Turandot The Most Dangerous Love in the World

2 Welcome, everyone!

3 Tonight, we are going to perform Giacomo Puccini's opera *Turandot*.

4 Like many other famous operas, *Turandot* is in Italian because opera started in Italy in the 16th century.

5 Before we begin, I'd like to tell you the storyline of the opera *Turandot*.

6 You will appreciate it better if you know the story.

7 Turandot, a Chinese princess, is a woman of great beauty, but she is as cold as ice.

8 Any prince who wants to marry her must answer three riddles.

9 If he fails, he must die.

10 No one has ever been able to answer them.

11 One day, a brave prince falls in love with her at first sight.

12 He becomes the first man to answer all three riddles.

13 However, Turandot does not want to marry the prince.

14 He is nothing more than a stranger to her.

15 He then gives her a riddle of his own.

16 He asks her, "What is my name?"

17 He adds, "If you answer correctly, I will agree to die. If you answer incorrectly, you will have to marry me."

18 Turandot must find the answer before dawn, but his riddle is as difficult as hers.

19 She says to everyone, "No one will go to sleep until someone finds out his name."

20 The prince then sings the most famous aria of the whole opera, "Nessun Dorma."

21 It means no one sleeps.

22 No one sleeps.

23 No one sleeps, not even you, Princess.

24 My secret is safe.

25 No one will know my name.

26 At dawn, I will win! I will win!

27 The prince's name is Calaf.

28 Will the princess learn his name in time?

29 Let's watch the opera and find out.

시험대비 실력평가
p.34~37

01 (A) Italian (B) to tell (C) know   02 ④
03 ⑤   04 ①   05 ②   06 ③
07 ③   08 ②   09 ④   10 ③
11 ⑤   12 no one will know his name
13 learn   14 ④   15 ②   16 ⑤
17 Turandot, a Chinese princess, is a woman of great beauty, but she is as cold as ice.
18 three riddles   19 ②, ③, ⑤
20 ④   21 (A) to die (B) hers (C) finds
22 What is my name?   23 ①   24 ③
25 are looking for a good musical movie   26 ①, ③

01 (A) '이탈리아어로'라고 해야 하므로 Italian이 적절하다. in Italy: 이탈리아에서, in Italian: 이탈리아어로, (B) would like 다음에는 동명사가 아니라 to부정사를 써야 하므로 to tell 이 적절하다. (C) 조건 부사절에서는 현재시제가 미래시제를 대용하므로 know가 적절하다.

02 시작하기 전에 '오페라 《투란도트》의 줄거리를 알려 드리려고

한다'고 했으므로, ④번이 적절하다.

03 '줄거리'를 알면 이 오페라를 더 잘 감상하게 될 것이라고 했다.

04 앞에 나오는 내용과 상반되는 내용이 뒤에 이어지므로 However가 가장 적절하다. ② 그러므로, ③ 즉, 다시 말해, ④ 예를 들어, ⑤ 그 결과

05 주어진 문장의 a riddle of his own에 주목한다. ②번 다음 문장의 질문을 가리키므로 ②번이 적절하다.

06 ⓐ, ⓒ: Turandot, ⓑ, ⓓ, ⓔ: the prince

07 Turandot는 얼음처럼 차갑고 세 가지 수수께끼에 답하지 못한 왕자들은 죽어야 한다고 했기 때문에 성격이 '무정하고 비정하다'고 하는 것이 적절하다. heartless: 무정한, 비정한, ① 사려 깊은, ② 마음이 따뜻한, ⑤ 부주의한

08 ⓐ와 ②번: [보통 as ... as ~로 형용사·부사 앞에서] …와 같은 정도로, 마찬가지로 (앞의 as는 지시부사, 뒤의 as는 접속사), ① …한 대로(접속사), ③ [비례] …함에 따라, …할수록(접속사), ④ …이라고, …으로(전치사), ⑤ …이므로, …이기 때문에(접속사)

09 ④ Turandot가 물어보는 세 가지 수수께끼가 무엇인지는 대답할 수 없다. ① She is a Chinese princess. ② She is a woman of great beauty. ③ He must answer three riddles. ⑤ A brave prince who falls in love with her at first sight.

10 ⓐ Turandot는 동이 트기 '전에' 답을 찾아야 한다. ⓒ '동틀 녘에', 내가 이길 것이라고 하는 것이 적절하다.

11 글의 흐름상 현재시제로 써야 하고, no one의 경우 3인칭 단수 취급을 하므로 동사 sleep에 -s를 붙인 형태를 쓰는 것이 적절하다.

12 '누구도 그의 이름을 알지 못할 것이기' 때문이다.

13 공주는 그의 이름을 제때 '알아낼' 수 있을까요? 오페라를 보고 '알아봅시다.'라고 했으므로, learn으로 바꿀 수 있다. find out 알아내다, 발견하다

14 위 글은 '감상문'이다. review (책·연극·영화 등에 대한) 논평[비평], 감상문, ① 독후감, ② 수필, ③ (신문·잡지의) 글, 기사, ⑤ 전기

15 recommend: 추천[천거]하다, 권고[권장]하다, 민수는 미녀와 야수를 마음이 따뜻해지는 사랑 이야기를 좋아하는 사람들에게 '추천한다.' ① 요구하다, ③ 표현하다, ④ 보고하다, ⑤ 충고하다

16 ⑤ 민수가 누구와 그것을 보았는지는 알 수 없다. ① Beauty and the Beast. ② Last Saturday. ③ It is about a beautiful girl and a beast. ④ He enjoyed it a lot.

17 'of'를 보충하고, Turandot와 a Chinese princess는 동격이므로 a Chinese princess 앞뒤로 콤마를 찍는 것이 적절하다. of+추상명사 = 형용사

18 '세 가지 수수께끼'를 가리킨다.

19 ⓒ와 ①, ④는 형용사적 용법, ②, ⑤ 부사적 용법, ③ 명사적 용법

20 ④ Turandot는 그 왕자의 이름도 모르기 때문에, 그는 그녀에게 단지 '낯선 사람'일 뿐이라고 하는 것이 적절하다. ① 이웃, ⑤ 동료

21 (A) agree는 to부정사를 목적어로 취하므로 to die가 적절하다. (B) 그의 수수께끼는 '그녀의 것'만큼 어렵다고 해야 하므로 hers가 적절하다. (C) 시간을 나타내는 부사절에서는 현재시제가 미래시제를 대신하므로 finds가 적절하다.

22 왕자가 낸 수수께끼는 "제 이름이 무엇입니까?"이다.

23 Turandot는 동이 트기 전에 답을 찾아야 하지만 그의 수수께끼는 그녀의 것만큼 어렵다고 했기 때문에, Turandot의 심경은 절박하다고 하는 것이 적절하다. desperate: 필사적인, 절박한, ② 만족스러운, ③ 지루한, ④ 부끄러운, ⑤ 흥분한

24 ⓐ와 ③: 감동적인, ① 활기[생기] 넘치는, ② 발랄한, 쾌활한, ④ 정력[활동]적인, ⑤ 우울하게 만드는, 우울한

25 '좋은 뮤지컬 영화를 찾고 있는 사람들'에게 추천하고 있다.

26 ① not only A but also B: A뿐만 아니라 B도, ② not A but B: A가 아니라 B, ③ both A and B: A와 B 둘 다, ④ either A or B: A와 B 둘 중 하나, ⑤ neither A nor B: A와 B 둘 다 아닌

서술형 시험대비　　　　　　p.38~39

01 나는 여러분에게 오페라 〈투란도트〉의 줄거리를 알려 드리려고 합니다.　　**02** the opera *Turandot*

03 opera started in Italy in the 16th century

04 only

05 incorrectly → correctly, correctly → incorrectly

06 someone finds out his name

07 very beautiful　　**08** who 또는 that

09 a few → no　　**10** (A) is　(B) marry　(C) answer

11 at first sight　　**12** (A) three riddles　(B) must die

13 hers　　**14** before dawn

15 If you answer correctly, I will agree to die.

16 so → as

---

01 would like to+동사원형: ~하고 싶다

02 '오페라 《투란도트》'를 가리킨다.

03 《투란도트》가 이탈리아어로 되어 있는 이유는 '오페라가 16세기 이탈리아에서 시작되었기' 때문이다.

04 nothing more than: ~에 지나지 않는, ~에 불과한

05 "당신이 '맞게' 대답한다면 나는 죽는 것에 동의하겠습니다. 만약 답이 '틀리면' 당신은 저와 결혼해야 합니다."라고 고치는 것이 적절하다.

06 '누군가 그의 이름을 알아낼 때까지 그 누구도 잠들 수 없다'는 것은 '누군가 그의 이름을 알아낸' 후에야 사람들이 잠들 수 있다는 뜻이다.

07 of+추상명사 = 형용사, of great beauty = very beautiful

---

08 주격 관계대명사 who 또는 that이 적절하다.

09 그 누구도 수수께끼에 답할 수 없었고 어떤 용감한 왕자가 세 수수께끼를 모두 맞힌 첫 번째 사람이 된다고 했기 때문에, 'a few'를 'no'로 고치는 것이 적절하다.

10 (A) Turandot와 a Chinese princess는 동격으로 단수로 취급해야 하므로 is가 적절하다. (B) marry는 타동사이므로 전치사 없이 바로 목적어를 써야 하므로 marry가 적절하다. (C) answer는 타동사이므로 전치사 없이 바로 목적어를 써야 하므로 answer가 적절하다.

11 at first sight: 첫눈에, 언뜻 보기에

12 중국의 공주 Turandot는 자기와 결혼하기를 원하는 어떤 왕자에게도 '세 가지 수수께끼'를 낸다. 만약 그가 그것들에 올바르게 대답하지 못하면, 그는 '죽어야 한다.'

13 그의 수수께끼는 '그녀의 것'만큼 어렵다고 해야 하므로 'hers'가 적절하다.

14 '제때에'는 '동이 트기 전에'를 가리킨다.

15 'will'을 보충하면 된다.

16 'as+원급+as'를 사용하여 '그의 수수께끼가 그녀의 수수께끼만큼 어렵다'라고 하는 것이 적절하다. 부정문에서는 'not so+원급+as'도 가능하다.

영역별 핵심문제　　　　　　p.41~45

01 ⑤　　**02** ①　　**03** ③　　**04** ③

05 right　　**06** (A) Where　(B) How[What]

07 ④　　**08** ③　　**09** What time shall we meet?　　**10** (B) → (A) → (C) → (D)

11 (A) off　(B) if　(C) shall we

12 her school's 75th anniversary

13 If you do something special for the world, the world will change.

14 ③　　**15** He doesn't watch TV as[so] much as

16 ③　　**17** ⑤　　**18** ②

19 ④　　**20** ②　　**21** ④

22 (1) as[so] fast as　(2) as fast as　(3) as cheap as

23 ④　　**24** (1) as small as　(2) run as fast as　(3) as tall as　　**25** won't → doesn't

26 (1) will rain → rains　(2) comes → will come

27 ②　　**28** ④　　**29** ④　　**30** ①, ③

31 ④　　**32** (A) more　(B) agree　(C) difficult

33 ②, ⑤

---

01 ① 용감한 - 겁 많은, ② 안전한 - 위험한, ③ 어려운 - 쉬운, ④ 실패하다 - 성공하다 / 모두 반의어 관계이고 ⑤는 두 단어 모두 '감동적인'이라는 뜻의 유의어 관계이다.

02 surprising '놀라운' = amazing

03 ① brave: 용감한 / 어느 날, 어떤 용감한 왕자가 그녀에게 첫눈에 반합니다. ② century: 세기 / 오페라는 16세기에 이탈리아

에서 시작되었다. ③ '지하철을 타는 게 어때?'라는 의미로 동사 take가 자연스럽다. ④ dawn: 새벽 / 그녀는 동이 트기 전에 답을 찾아야 한다. ⑤ mean: 의미하다 / Nessun Dorma는 누구도 잠들지 못한다는 뜻이다.

04 celebrate: 축하하다

05 right는 부사로 '바로'의 의미로 사용된다.

06 (A) G의 말로 보아 B는 배드민턴을 칠 장소를 묻고 있다. (B) 상대방에게 제안할 때 사용하는 표현으로 How[What] about ~?을 사용한다.

07 위 대화는 오후에 친구와 무엇을 할 것인지에 대한 계획을 세우는 내용이다.

08 제안할 때 사용하는 표현으로 Why don't we+동사원형?, Let's+동사원형., Shall we+동사원형?, How[What] about+동사-ing?가 있다.

10 오늘 오후에 무엇을 할 건지 묻는 말에, (B) 미술관에 가는 게 어떠냐고 제안을 한다. (A) '좋아'라는 동의의 말을 하고 만날 시간을 물어본다. (C) 2시가 어떤지 시간을 제안하고 (D) 마지막으로 승낙의 표현과 함께 미술관 앞에서 만나자고 제안한다.

11 (A)는 take와 호응하여 '(일을) 쉬다'는 의미로 off를 사용하고, (B)는 의미상 '~한다면'의 의미를 가지는 조건의 부사절 접속사 if가 적절하다. (C)는 시간을 제안할 때 사용하는 표현으로 What time shall we ~?가 적절하다.

13 조건의 부사절에서는 미래시제 대신 현재시제를 사용하고, 주절에는 미래시제를 그대로 사용한다.

14 '~만큼 …한'의 의미로 'as+원급+as'를 사용한다. 부정문에서는 'not as[so]+원급+as'를 사용하지만, 긍정문에서는 as 대신 so를 사용하지 않는다.

15 TV를 보지 않는다는 일반동사 watch의 부정문을 사용해서 He doesn't watch TV를 쓰고, 그 다음 '~만큼 …하게'의 의미로 'as[so]+원급+as' 구문을 이용한다. 이때 watch를 수식하는 부사 much가 적절하다.

16 (1)은 check의 목적어 자리에 사용되는 접속사 if(~인지 아닌지), (2)는 조건의 부사절 접속사 if(만일 ~라면)가 적절하다.

17 ①~④는 동사의 목적어를 이끄는 명사절 접속사 if로 '~인지 아닌지'의 의미이고, ⑤는 조건의 부사절 접속사 if로 '만일 ~라면'의 의미다.

18 ②는 'as+원급+as' 구문으로 so를 as로 바꾸어야 한다.

19 ④ '~만큼 …하지 않다'의 의미로 'not as[so]+원급+as' 구문이 적절하다. 'so heavy so'를 'so[as] heavy as'로 바꾸어야 한다.

20 The subway is as faster as the train.은 as fast as가 되어야 하고, We will go swimming if the weather will be fine tomorrow.는 조건의 부사절에서 미래시제 대신 현재시제를 사용하므로 will be를 is로 고쳐야 한다.

21 조건의 부사절에서는 미래시제 대신 현재시제를 사용하므로 break가 적절하다. 복수 주어 my friends이므로 breaks는 적절하지 않다.

22 (1)은 지하철이 버스보다 빠르지 않기 때문에 'not as[so]+원급+as' 구문을 이용하고, (2)는 버스가 택시와 속도가 같으므로 'as+원급+as' 구문을 이용한다. (3)은 지하철이 버스와 요금이 같기 때문에 'as cheap as'가 자연스럽다.

23 ④는 '나는 너만큼 어리다.'라는 의미이고, 나머지는 모두 '네가 나보다 나이가 많다.'라는 의미이다.

24 '~만큼 …한[하게]'의 의미는 'as+원급+as' 구문을 이용한다.

25 조건을 나타내는 부사절에서는 미래시제 대신 현재시제를 사용해야 하므로, 미래시제 won't를 3인칭 단수 현재형인 doesn't로 바꾸어야 한다.

26 (1) 조건의 부사절에서는 미래시제 대신 현재시제를 사용하고, (2) be sure의 목적어 자리에 사용된 명사절 접속사 if는 미래시제를 사용할 수 있다.

27 시작하기 전에 오페라를 더 잘 '감상하도록' 《투란도트》의 줄거리를 알려 드리려고 한다고 말했기 때문에, 오페라 《투란도트》를 '공연할' 것이라고 하는 것이 적절하다. perform: 공연하다, ① 연습하다, ③ 잘되어 가다, 작동하다, ④ 이루다, 성취하다, ⑤ 완료하다, 끝마치다

28 ⑤와 ④번은 '~과 같이'라는 의미의 전치사로 사용되었다. 나머지는 다 '~을 좋아하다'라는 의미의 동사이다.

29 ④번 다음 문장의 He에 주목한다. 주어진 문장의 a brave prince를 받고 있으므로 ④번이 적절하다.

30 ⓐ와 ①, ③번은 경험 용법, ② 결과 용법, ④ 완료 용법, ⑤ 계속 용법

31 ④ 수수께끼에 답하지 못하면 죽어야 하는데, 그 누구도 수수께끼에 답할 수 없었다고 했기 때문에, 지금까지 수수께끼에 도전했던 왕자들은 다 죽었다.

32 (A) 그는 그녀에게 '단지 낯선 사람일 뿐'이라고 해야 하므로 more가 적절하다. nothing more than: ~에 지나지 않는, nothing less than: 다름 아닌 바로, (B) 당신이 맞게 대답한다면 나는 죽는 것에 '동의하겠다'고 해야 하므로 agree가 적절하다. refuse: 거절하다, (C) 그의 수수께끼는 그녀의 것만큼 '어렵다'고 해야 하므로 difficult가 적절하다. different: 다른

33 give, send, write는 3형식으로 고칠 때 'to'를 사용한다. ①, ③ buy, make는 for를 사용한다. ④ ask는 of를 사용한다. ⑤ thank-you note: 감사장

단원별 예상문제
p.46~49

01 answer **02** nothing more than

03 (1) beauty, cold (2) perform (3) incorrectly, marry (4) falls in love, sight

04 ② **05** ⑤

06 (1) Why don't we go on a picnic this weekend? (2) What about going on a picnic this weekend?

07 ④ **08** ⑤ **09** get, discount if

```
10 What time shall we meet?          11 ③
12 ③          13 ④          14 ②          15 ⑤
16 (1) finish   (2) give   (3) changes          17 ②
18 ③          19 ⑤          20 (1) not as[so] tall as
(2) well   (3) as heavy as          21 ③          22 ①
23 knowing the story          24 as sweet as honey →
as cold as ice          25 riddles          26 ⑤
```

01 둘은 유의어 관계이다. 제안 : 대답하다

02 nothing more than ~: ~에 지나지 않는

03 (1) of+추상명사 = 형용사. of beauty = beautiful(아름다운) (2) perform: 공연하다 (3) incorrectly: 올바르지 않게, 틀리게, marry: 결혼하다 (4) fall in love: 사랑에 빠지다. at first sight: 첫눈에

04 예상된 시간보다 더 이르게

05 ⑤번 뒤의 문장에 나오는 See you there.에서 there가 the subway station을 가리키므로 ⑤가 적절하다.

06 상대에게 제안을 할 때 사용하는 표현으로 Let's+동사원형, Why don't we+동사원형?, What about+동명사/명사? 등이 있다.

07 시간이나 장소를 정할 때 How about이나 What about을 이용한다.

08 흥미롭거나 놀라운 일을 말하기 전에 사용되는 표현

09 get a discount: 할인받다, if: ~한다면

10 제안할 때 사용하는 표현으로 shall we ~를 이용하고 시간을 묻는 표현인 What time으로 문장을 시작한다.

12 '~하자'는 제안이나 권유의 의미로 사용할 수 없는 표현은 ③번이다.

13 대화의 흐름상 한국사 시험에서 한 문제 틀린 것에 대해 오늘 밤 축하하러 나가자는 의미로 celebrate가 적절하다. appreciate는 '감상하다'라는 뜻이다.

14 '만일 ~한다면'의 의미로 조건을 나타내는 접속사 if가 적절하다.

15 ⑤ Jane은 Mike보다 성적이 높기 때문에 Mike isn't as smart as Jane.으로 쓰는 것이 적절하다.

16 조건의 부사절에서는 의미가 미래라 할지라도 현재시제를 사용한다.

17 ② 시간을 나타내는 부사절에서는 미래시제 대신 현재시제를 사용한다. will find를 finds로 고쳐야 한다.

18 ③ as ~ as 사이에는 형용사나 부사의 원급을 사용해야 한다. bigger를 big으로 고쳐야 한다.

19 ⑤번은 tell의 직접목적어 자리에 사용된 명사절 접속사 if다. '~인지 아닌지'로 해석한다.

20 두 대상 간의 동등함을 나타낼 때 'as+원급+as'를 사용한다. 부정문은 '~만큼 …하지 않은'의 의미로 'not as[so]+원급+as'를 사용한다.

21 in Italian: 이탈리아어로, in Italy: 이탈리아에서, in the 16th century: 16세기에

22 ④와 ①번은 감상하다, architecture: 건축학[술], 건축 양식, ②와 ④ 고마워하다, ③과 ⑤ (제대로) 인식하다

23 여러분이 '줄거리를 알면' 이 오페라를 더 잘 감상하게 될 것이다. 전치사 By 다음에 동명사로 쓰는 것이 적절하다.

24 수수께끼에 답하는 데 실패하면 죽어야 한다고 했기 때문에, 그녀는 '얼음처럼 차갑다'고 하는 것이 적절하다.

25 riddle: 수수께끼, 터무니없는 것 같지만 영리하거나 재미있는 대답을 지닌 질문을 하는 수수께끼나 농담

26 ⑤ 절차를 통과하지 못한 왕자들이 몇 명인지는 대답할 수 없다. ① 중국의 공주, ② 굉장히 아름답다. ③ 반드시 세 가지 수수께끼에 답해야 한다. ④ 만약 세 가지 수수께끼에 답하지 못하면 죽어야 한다.

서술형 실전문제

p.50~51

01 (A) What time shall we meet?
(B) Where shall we meet?
02 Why don't we take the subway
03 (A) What shall we do this afternoon?
(B) Why don't we go see *Wonder Woman*?
(C) How about 4 o'clock?
04 (1) as expensive as mine[my ring]
(2) not so kind as   (3) comes, take, to
05 (1) will rain → rains   (2) will need → need
06 (1) as old as, not as[so] old as
(2) as tall as, Mike[Minho] is not as[so] tall as
(3) as heavy as, is not as[so] heavy as
07 won't pay → don't pay   08 as cold as ice
09 (A) Any   (B) ever   (C) sight   10 failed
11 He is nothing more than a stranger to her.
12 her riddles   13 (A) marry him   (B) to die
```

01 약속을 정할 때 사용하는 표현으로, (A)는 만날 시간을 (B)는 만날 장소를 물어보는 표현이 적절하다.

02 제안을 할 때 'Why don't we+동사원형?'을 이용한다.

03 (A)에는 무엇을 할 것인지 묻는 말로 대화를 시작하는 것이 적절하다. (B)는 구체적으로 무엇을 할 것인지 제안하는 표현이 적절하다. (C)는 '몇 시에 만날래?'라는 물음에 시간을 정하는 표현이 적절하다.

04 (1) 두 대상 간의 동일한 것을 나타낼 때 'as+원급+as'를 사용하고, 비교하는 대상은 같아야 하므로 her ring과 my ring을 비교해야 한다. (2) '~만큼 …하지 않다'는 의미로 'not so[as]+원급+as' 구문을 사용한다. (3) 조건의 부사절에서는 미래시제 대신 현재시제를 사용한다. take A to B는 A를 B로 데려오다라는 의미다.

05 조건 부사절에서는 미래시제 대신 현재시제를 사용한다.

06 두 대상 간의 동일한 것을 나타낼 때 'as+원급+as'를 사용한다. '~만큼 …하지 않다'는 의미로 'not so[as]+원급+as' 구문을
```

사용한다.

07 조건 부사절에서는 미래시제 대신 현재시제를 사용한다.

08 as cold as ice = very cold

09 (A) 그녀와 결혼하길 원하는 왕자는 '누구든지'라고 해야 하므로 Any가 적절하다. 긍정문의 any: '어떤 ~이라도', some+셀 수 있는 명사 복수: '약간의', some+셀 수 있는 명사 단수: '어떤(a certain)', (B) 부정의 의미인 No one이 주어이므로 ever가 적절하다. (C) 그녀에게 '첫눈에' 반한다고 해야 하므로 sight가 적절하다. at first sight: 첫눈에

10 목숨을 걸고 세 가지 수수께끼에 답하려고 시도했던 모든 왕자들이 한 왕자를 제외하고는 다 '실패했다.' at the risk of one's life: 목숨을 걸고, except: ~을 제외하고는

11 nothing more than: ~에 지나지 않는, ~에 불과한

12 '그녀의 수수께끼들'을 가리킨다.

13 만약 Turandot가 왕자의 수수께끼에 틀리게 대답한다면 그녀는 '그와 결혼해야 한다.' 만약 Turandot가 맞게 대답한다면 그는 '죽는 것에' 동의할 것이다.

창의사고력 서술형 문제 p.52

|모범답안|

01 (1) A: What shall we do at the park?
　　　B: Why don't we ride the roller coaster?
　　　A: That's a good idea.
　　(2) A: What shall we do at the park?
　　　B: Why don't we visit the flower garden?
　　　A: That's a good idea.

02 (1) The subway fare is as expensive as the bus fare.
　　(2) The subway is not so[as] fast as the bus.

03 (A) Review　(B) the dreams and love
　　(C) beautiful and moving　(D) story

단원별 모의고사 p.53~56

01 ⑤　　　02 (1) take, off　(2) practice, play
(3) don't, celebrate　　03 ③　　04 moving
05 late　　06 ③　　07 ②　　08 ④
09 ④　　10 ③
11 What do you want to do?　　12 ③
13 (1) Anna is as beautiful as Julie.
　　(2) I will let you go out if you do finish your job.
14 ③　　15 (1) as not larger → not as large as
(2) as bigger as → as big as　16 not as[so] tall as
17 ④　　18 ⑤　　19 Italian　　20 ③
21 ③　　22 ask → answer　　23 ②
24 ④

01 ⑤의 appreciate는 'to understand how good something or someone is' (어떤 것이나 어떤 사람이 얼마나 좋은지 이해하다)라는 설명이 적절하다. to do something enjoyable on a special occasion은 celebrate에 대한 설명이다.

02 (1) take off: (일을) 쉬다 (2) practice: 연습하다, play: 연극 (3) Why don't we ~?: ~하는 게 어때?, celebrate: 축하하다

03 빈칸에는 be동사 뒤에 형용사가 보어로 와야 하므로 ①은 적절하지 못하다. as와 as 사이에는 형용사 원급 형태 good이 적절하다. ⑤의 the best는 셋 이상에서 '가장 ~한'의 의미인 최상급이다.

04 moving: 감동적인

05 '계획되고, 예상되고, 일상적인 또는 필요한 시간 후에 발생하거나 도착하는', 즉 '늦은'의 의미이다.

06 콘서트가 언제 시작되는지는 대화에 언급되어 있지 않다.

07 한국사 시험에서 한 문제만 틀렸다고 했으므로, 시험을 못 본 것이 아니라 잘 봤다는 것을 알 수 있다. poorly를 well로 바꾸어야 한다.

08 ④ 시험을 잘 본 사람은 Joe다.

09 '몇 시에 만날래?'라는 물음에 장소를 말하는 것은 어색하다.

10 다음 주 수요일에 학교를 가지 않는다는 말에 이유를 물어보는 것이 자연스럽다.

11 의문사 what으로 문장을 시작하고, '~하고 싶다'는 'want to+동사원형'을 이용한다.

12 ③ Ann과 아빠는 뮤지컬을 보러 갈 것이다.

13 (1) 'as+원급+as' 구문으로 형용사 beautiful은 as와 as 사이에 넣는다. (2) 접속사 if 뒤에는 '주어+동사'가 나와야 한다.

14 ③ 두 대상인 Her hair와 my hair를 비교하는 문장이므로 I를 mine이나 my hair로 바꾸어야 한다.

15 'as+원급+as' 구문으로, 원급은 형용사와 부사를 사용해야 한다.

16 Ann이 Tom보다 키가 작으므로 'not so[as]+원급+as' 구문을 사용한다.

17 조건의 부사절에서는 미래시제 대신 현재시제를 사용하지만 주절에는 미래시제를 그대로 사용한다.

18 ⑤번은 '테니스는 축구만큼 인기가 없다'는 의미로 is not as[so] popular as가 되어야 한다.

19 'Italy'의 언어를 나타내는 'Italian'을 쓰는 것이 적절하다. in Italian: 이탈리아어로

20 storyline: (소설·연극·영화 등의) 줄거리, ③ plot: (소설, 극, 영화 등의) 구성[플롯/줄거리], ① 주제, 테마, ② 배경, ④ 개념, ⑤ (논의 등의) 주제[대상/화제]

21 ⓐ of+추상명사 = 형용사, of great beauty = very beautiful, ⓒ fall in love with: ~와 사랑에 빠지다

22 그녀와 결혼하길 원하는 왕자는 누구든지 반드시 세 가지 수수께끼에 '답해야' 한다고 해야 하므로 ask를 answer로 고치는 것이 적절하다.

23 ⓐ와 ②, ⑤는 명사적 용법, ①, ③은 부사적 용법, ④는 형용사적 용법

24 ④ 만약 Turandot의 답이 틀리면 '그녀는 왕자와 결혼해야 한다.'

Lesson 6

Food in History

시험대비 실력평가 p.60

01 different　02 ③　03 ⑤　04 ②

05 ④　06 ④　07 disappointed

08 by himself

01 둘은 반의어 관계이다. 실내의 : 실외의 = 같은 : 다른

02 탕평채와 신선로, 송편에 대해 말하고 있으므로 전통 음식이 적절하다.

03 나는 음식에 특별한 재료를 더했다.

04 지방이나 국가 정부에서의 지위를 얻기 위해 선거에서 경쟁하는 특정한 정치적 신념을 가진 사람들의 조직은 '정당'이다.

05 다른 것보다 어떤 하나를 좋아하거나 선택하거나 원하다

06 'recommend'는 '추천하다'는 뜻이다.

07 누군가나 무언가가 당신이 희망하거나 기대했던 것만큼 좋지 않았기 때문에 행복하지 않은

08 'alone'은 '혼자'의 뜻으로 'by oneself'와 같다. 신선은 일반적으로 남자를 가리키므로 himself를 쓰는 것이 적절하다.

서술형 시험대비 p.61

01 (1) policy, 정책　(2) recommend, 추천하다

　(3) symbolize, 상징하다

02 (1) fortune teller　(2) pot　(3) worried　(4) mainly

03 (1) (r)ecently　(2) (s)cholar

04 (1) Honesty, policy　(2) party

05 (1) half moon　(2) parties, harmony　(3) official

01 (1) 특정한 상황에서 무엇을 해야 하는지에 대한 집단이나 정부, 또는 정당이 공식적으로 동의한 일련의 생각이나 계획 (2) 어떤 사람이나 어떤 것이 특정 직업이나 목적에 좋거나 적합할 것이라고 제안하다 (3) 어떤 것을 나타내다

02 (1) 왕은 왕국의 미래를 알기 위해 점쟁이가 필요하다. (2) 우유 약간과 닭고기를 냄비에 넣어라. (3) 왕은 그의 왕국이 걱정이 되었다. '~에 관해 걱정하다'는 'be worried about'이다. 동사 worry를 become 동사 뒤에 사용하기 위해 형용사 worried로 바꾸어 준다. (4) 그가 혼자 그곳에 사는 동안, 그는 주로 채소를 먹었다.

03 (1) 얼마 전, 혹은 얼마 전에 시작된 때에: 최근에 (2) 특히 대학에서 특정한 과목을 매우 세부적으로 공부하는 사람: 학자

04 (1) 정직, 정직함: honesty, 정책: policy (2) 정당: party

05 (1) half moon: 반달 (2) party: 정당, four와 함께 쓰여서 복수 명사로 parties가 적절하다. in harmony: 조화롭게 (3) official: 관리

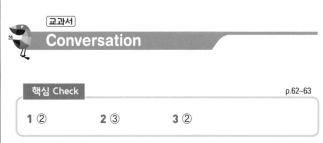

교과서 Conversation

핵심 Check p.62~63

1 ②　　2 ③　　3 ②

교과서 대화문 익히기

Check(√) True or False p.64

1 T　2 F　3 T　4 T

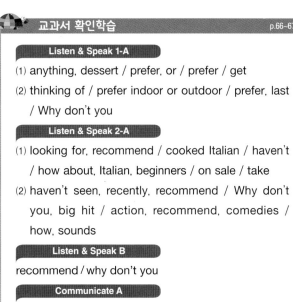

교과서 확인학습 p.66~67

Listen & Speak 1-A

(1) anything, dessert / prefer, or / prefer / get

(2) thinking of / prefer indoor or outdoor / prefer, last / Why don't you

Listen & Speak 2-A

(1) looking for, recommend / cooked Italian / haven't / how about, Italian, beginners / on sale / take

(2) haven't seen, recently, recommend / Why don't you, big hit / action, recommend, comedies / how, sounds

Listen & Speak B

recommend / why don't you

Communicate A

Have, been to / talking about / the one, ago / so, went, last / How was / ordered, different dishes, fried / recommend, for, tonight / prefer, or / prefer seafood / should try, fried fish

Communicate B

Could you recommend / Do, prefer, or / prefer / try

Progress Check

(1) I'm thinking of / prefer, or / prefer / one

(2) looking for, recommend / color / favorite / how about, on sale / take

11

01 recommend, for　　02 ③　　03 ①
04 ④

01 '(제게) ~을 추천해 주시겠어요?'라는 뜻으로 상대방에게 추천을 부탁할 때 'Could you recommend ~ (for me)?' 표현을 쓴다.

02 B의 답으로 보아 빈칸에는 어떤 것을 좋아하는지 묻는 말이 적절하다.

03 B의 마지막 말에서 일곱 마리의 고양이 중 한 마리를 주겠다는 말로 보아 G는 고양이를 좋아한다는 것을 알 수 있다.

04 Do you prefer A or B?는 상대방의 선호를 묻는 표현이다.

01 ④　　　　02 ⑤　　　　03 ②
04 Do you prefer pie or cake?　　05 ③
06 beginner　　　　07 ①　　　08 ⑤
09 ③　　　　　　10 ④
11 Have you been to the new Chinese restaurant

01 빈칸 다음의 G의 말과 실내 스포츠를 좋아한다는 B의 대답으로 보아 '스포츠 동아리에 가입할 생각 중이다.'라는 말이 가장 적절하다.

02 ⑤는 '탁구 동아리에 어떻게 가입하니?'라는 뜻이고, 나머지는 모두 '~하는 게 어때?'라고 제안하는 표현이다.

03 ② 'A: 치킨을 좋아하니 소고기를 좋아하니?'라는 물음에 'B: 나는 돼지고기를 좋아하지 않아.'라는 대답은 자연스럽지 못하다.

04 둘 중 더 좋아하는 것에 대해 물을 때는 'Do you prefer A or B?' 표현을 쓴다.

05 ⓐ '추천해 주실 수 있으세요?'라는 뜻으로 recommend가 적절하다. ⓑ 제안하는 말로 '~은 어때?'라는 how about이 적절하다.

06 '어떤 것을 하기 시작하거나 처음으로 어떤 것을 배우는 사람'은 '초보자'를 의미한다.

07 G가 액션 영화는 좋아하지 않는다는 말에 B가 '*Funny Families*는 어때?'라고 말하는 것으로 보아 빈칸에는 추천을 부탁하는 말이 적절하다.

08 '~하는 게 어때?'라는 표현으로 'Why don't you+동사원형 ~?', 'What about+동사원형+-ing' 등을 사용할 수 있다.

09 '음식은 어땠나요?'라고 묻는 Jaden의 말 다음에 오는 Ms. Park의 답변에 들어가는 것이 적절하다.

10 빈칸 (a) 다음에 Ms. Park이 '해산물을 더 좋아하니, 육류를 더 좋아하니?'라고 묻고 있기 때문에 빈칸에는 음식을 추천해 달라는 말이 적절하다.

11 현재완료 의문문(Have+주어+과거분사 ~?)을 이용하여 문장을 쓴다.

01 He is going to eat naengmyeon.
02 Do you prefer hot or cold food?
03 (1) Do you prefer rainy days or sunny days?
　(2) prefer sunny days.
04 Could you recommend a book for me?
05 Could you recommend a dish for me?
06 Do you prefer[Which do you prefer,] seafood or meat?

01 남자는 어떤 음식을 먹을 예정인가?

02 둘 중 더 좋아하는 것에 대해 물을 때는 Do you prefer A or B? 표현을 쓴다.

03 둘 중 더 좋아하는 것에 대해 물을 때는 Do you prefer A or B? 표현을 쓴다. 선호하는 것을 답할 때는 'I prefer ~'을 사용한다.

04 '제게 ~을 추천해 주시겠어요?'라는 뜻으로 상대방에게 추천을 부탁할 때 'Could you recommend ~ for me?' 표현을 쓴다.

핵심 Check　　　　　　p.72~73

1 (1) was painted　(2) to　(3) with
2 (1) anything long　(2) Something terrible
　(3) anyone nice to talk with

01 ⑤　　　　02 ②
03 (1) was built　(2) was written　(3) someone funny
　(4) somebody important
04 (1) cleans → is cleaned
　(2) to read interesting → interesting to read

01 동사를 시제에 맞게 'be+pp'로 바꾸고 수동태 문장의 주어 자리에는 능동태 문장의 목적어가 오고, by 다음에는 능동태 문장의 주어를 목적격으로 쓴다.

02 '-thing'으로 끝나는 대명사는 형용사가 뒤에서 수식한다. 동사 다음에 '-thing+형용사'를 쓴다.

03 (1) 수동태는 'be+pp'의 형태이다. (2) 책 이름은 단수로 취급하며 과거에 쓰여진 것이므로 과거로 쓴다. (3), (4) '-one, -body'로 끝나는 대명사는 형용사가 뒤에서 수식한다.

04 (1) 방이 청소되는 것이므로 수동태가 적절하다. (2) '-thing'으로 끝나는 대명사를 형용사와 to부정사가 동시에 수식하는 경우 '대명사+형용사+to부정사'의 어순임에 유의한다.

시험대비 실력평가
p.75~77

01 ④	02 ⑤	03 ③	04 ①
05 ②	06 ⑤	07 ①	

08 (1) to (2) for (3) of   09 anything funny

10 ③

11 (1) In 1964, China's first nuclear test took place.
  (2) *Two Sisters* was painted by Auguste Renoir in 1881.
  (3) Give me something cold to drink.
  (4) They will see her as someone respectable.

12 ④

13 (1) A nice cap was bought for me by him.
  (2) French is spoken in France (by them).
  (3) By whom was the picture *The Sunflowers* drawn?
  (4) Delicious spaghetti was made for Sam by Marianne last night.
  (5) Emily was heard talking to her friend in class by me.

14 ④   15 ⑤

16 be told / are made / was surprised at / was interested in / was covered with / was filled with

01 This toy가 만들어지는 것이므로 수동태가 적절하다.

02 '-one, -body'로 끝나는 대명사는 형용사가 뒤에서 수식한다. I don't have anyone reliable.

03 ③ 목적격보어가 원형부정사인 경우 수동태 문장에서는 to부정사로 바뀐다.

04 ② How did tangpyeongchae and sinseollo get their names? ③ The Mona Lisa was painted by Leonardo da Vinci. ④ There was something wrong with my bill. ⑤ The dress will be bought for her by Mary.

05 목적어 only 33를 수동태의 주어로 한 구문이다.

06 be satisfied with: ~에 만족하다 be filled with: ~로 가득 차다

07 Dave에 의해 개최되는 것이므로 수동태가 적절하고 '-one'으로 끝나는 대명사는 형용사가 뒤에서 수식한다.

08 직접목적어를 주어로 한 수동태에서 간접목적어 앞에 (1) send는 전치사 to를, (2) make는 전치사 for를, (3) ask는 전치사 of를 쓴다.

09 의문문이므로 anything을 쓰고 '-thing'으로 끝나는 대명사이므로 funny가 뒤에서 수식하도록 한다.

10 ③ give는 간접목적어 앞에 전치사 to를 붙인다.

11 (1) take place는 자동사이므로 수동태로 쓰이지 않는다. (2) *Two Sisters*(두 자매)가 그려지는 것이므로 수동태가 적절하다. (3) '-thing'으로 끝나는 대명사를 형용사와 to부정사가 동시에 수식하는 경우 '대명사+형용사+to부정사'의 어순이다. (4) '-one'으로 끝나는 대명사는 형용사가 뒤에서 수식한다.

12 '-thing'으로 끝나는 대명사는 형용사가 뒤에서 수식하며 happen은 자동사이므로 수동태로 쓰이지 않는다.

13 (1), (2) 동사를 'be+pp'로 바꾸고 수동태 문장의 주어 자리에는 능동태 문장의 목적어가 오고, by 다음에는 능동태 문장의 주어를 목적격으로 쓴다. 일반 주어인 by them은 생략할 수 있다. (3) 수동태를 의문문 형태로 만들 때는 주어와 be동사의 위치를 바꾼다. by whom은 의문사로 취급하여 문장의 맨 앞에 써야 한다. (4) 직접목적어를 주어로 한 수동태에서 made는 간접목적어 앞에 전치사 for를 쓴다. 또한 간접목적어를 주어로 수동태를 만들지 않는다. (5) 시제가 heard로 과거형이므로 was heard으로 쓰고, 목적격보어 talking은 그대로 써준다.

14 '-thing'으로 끝나는 대명사를 수식하는 형용사는 대명사 뒤에 위치한다.

15 give up은 구동사로 하나의 단어처럼 취급하여 be given up으로 나타낸다. up이나 by를 빠뜨리지 않도록 주의한다.

16 줄거리가 말해지고, 자동차가 만들어지는 것이므로 수동태가 적절하다. be surprised at: ~에 놀라다 be interested in: ~에 흥미가 있다 be covered with: ~로 덮여 있다 be filled with: ~로 가득 차다

서술형 시험대비
p.78~79

01 (1) A different political party was symbolized by each ingredient.
  (2) He was never listened to by the king.
  (3) A small sandcastle was made for his son by Dan.
  (4) Many computers are thrown away every year in the United States.
  (5) By whom was the novel, *Christmas Carol*, written?

02 (1) I want to show something wonderful to you.
  (2) I want to work with somebody honest for our business.
  (3) There was nobody important at the meeting.

03 (1) The bench was painted by the man. 또는 The man painted the bench.
  (2) Spicy food is loved by all of my family members.

13

(3) The bookshelf was made of wood.

(4) Amy was heard to sing in front of all the classmates by us.

(5) A long letter was written (to) her by him. 또는 He wrote her a long letter.

(6) A wedding ring with a small ruby will be bought for her.

04 nothing interesting

05 (1) Something was written on its back.

(2) Rome was not built in a day.

(3) I called him, but his phone was turned off.

(4) My homework must be finished by me by Sunday.

(5) I heard something interesting from Tom.

(6) There will be nobody happy in that house.

06 (1) funny someone → someone funny

(2) new something → something new

(3) cold to drink something → something cold to drink

(4) new nobody → nobody new

07 (1) The light bulb was invented by Thomas

(2) Many people respect Mahatma Gandhi.

(3) All the flights were canceled due to the bad weather (by them).

08 was painted, was titled, was completed

01 (1) 수동태는 'be+pp'의 형태이다. (2) 전치사 to의 목적어를 주어로 수동태로 바꾼다. (3) make는 직접목적어를 주어로 하는 수동태만 가능하며 간접목적어 앞에 for를 써야 한다. (4) throw away는 구동사로 하나의 단어처럼 취급하여 be thrown away로 나타낸다. away나 by를 빠뜨리지 않도록 주의한다. (5) 의문사 who가 by whom으로 바뀌어 문두에 쓰이는 것에 주의한다.

02 '-thing, -one, -body'로 끝나는 부정대명사는 형용사가 뒤에서 수식한다.

03 (1) The bench를 주어로 하면 수동태가, the man을 주어로 하면 능동태가 적절하다. (2) Spicy food가 무엇을 사랑하는 것이 아니므로 진행형이 아닌 수동태가 적절하다. (3) be made of: ~로 만들어지다(물리적 변화), be made from: ~로 만들어지다(화학적 변화) (4) 목적격보어가 원형부정사인 경우, 수동태 문장에서는 to부정사로 바뀐다. (5) write는 직접목적어를 주어로 하는 수동태만 가능하다. (6) buy는 직접목적어를 주어로 한 수동태에서는 간접목적어 앞에 for를 쓰고 미래 시제의 수동태는 'will be+과거분사'이다.

04 '-thing'으로 끝나는 부정대명사는 형용사가 뒤에서 수식한다.

05 (1) 수동태는 '주어+be동사+동사의 과거분사+by+행위자'의 형식이다. 누가 그 동작을 했는지 중요하지 않거나 잘 모를

때 'by+행위자'를 생략한다. (2) 수동태의 부정은 'be+not+과거분사'이다. (3) turn off를 하나의 단위처럼 생각해서 'be turned off'로 써야 한다. (4) 조동사가 있는 문장의 수동태는 '조동사+be+p.p.' 형식을 갖는다. (5), (6) '-thing, -body'로 끝나는 대명사는 형용사가 뒤에서 수식한다.

06 '-thing, -one, -body'로 끝나는 대명사는 형용사가 뒤에서 수식한다. 형용사와 to부정사가 동시에 수식하는 경우 '대명사+형용사 +to부정사'의 어순에 유의한다.

07 능동태를 수동태로 바꿀 때 동사를 'be+p.p.'로 바꾸고 수동태 문장의 주어 자리에는 능동태 문장의 목적어가 오고, by 다음 에는 능동태 문장의 주어를 목적격으로 쓴다. 일반 주어인 by them은 생략할 수 있다.

08 이 그림은 Vincent Van Gogh에 의해 그려졌다. 이것은 '별이 빛나는 밤(The Starry Night)'이라는 제목이 붙여졌고 1889 년에 완성되었다.

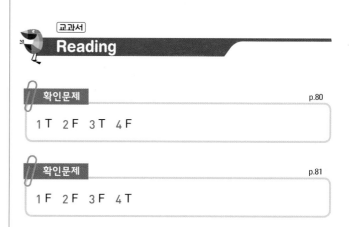

Reading

확인문제	p.80

1 T 2 F 3 T 4 F

확인문제	p.81

1 F 2 F 3 F 4 T

교과서 확인학습 A p.82~83

01 Bite
02 How, get their names
03 Why, look like
04 traditional food
05 dive into
06 was having dinner, something special
07 four colorful ingredients
08 a different political party
09 in harmony
10 was called
11 came from
12 was famous for
13 something wrong, afraid of telling
14 However
15 so, that
16 by himself
17 a special pot
18 called, the food in it
19 because, like, imaginary
20 the last king
21 a strange turtle
22 was written
23 is like, is like
24 What, mean
25 smaller

26 On the other hand, grow bigger

27 worried

28 However, in the shape of

29 Since then, have enjoyed

26 On the other hand, a half moon will grow bigger and become a full moon."

27 The king became worried about his kingdom.

28 However, people of Silla were very happy to learn this and made rice cakes in the shape of a half moon.

29 Since then, people have enjoyed these half-moon shaped rice cakes, songpyeon.

1 A Bite of Korean History

2 How did tangpyeongchae and sinseollo get their names?

3 Why does songpyeon look like a half moon?

4 There are many interesting stories about our traditional food.

5 Let's dive into the fun history of our food.

6 One day, King Yeongjo was having dinner with his officials and offered them something special.

7 It was a dish with four colorful ingredients.

8 Each ingredient symbolized a different political party.

9 Yeongjo wanted to say that the four parties should work in harmony like this dish.

10 This dish was called tangpyeongchae.

11 The name came from Yeongjo's policy tangpyeongchaek.

12 In the time of King Yeonsan, there was a scholar who was famous for his honesty.

13 When the king did something wrong, the scholar was never afraid of telling him so.

14 However, the king never listened to him.

15 The scholar was so disappointed that he went to live on a mountain.

16 While he lived there by himself, he mainly ate vegetables.

17 He made a special pot to cook many different vegetables together.

18 People called this pot and the food in it sinseollo.

19 That is because the scholar lived like a sinseon, an imaginary person who lives alone in nature.

20 It was the time of the last king of Baekje.

21 One day, the king and his servants found a strange turtle.

22 Something was written on its back.

23 It said, "Baekje is like a full moon, but Silla is like a half moon."

24 The king asked a fortune teller, "What does this mean?"

25 The fortune teller answered, "A full moon will soon become smaller.

01 ②

02 (A) How   (B) look like   (C) interesting   03 ④

04 ③   05 ④   06 ②

07 offered them something special   08 ③

09 (A) special   (B) ingredient   (C) a different

10 ②   11 ④   12 ①   13 ⑤

14 ①, ④, ⑤   15 full moon, full moon, smaller

16 ⑤   17 ②   18 ③   19 ⑤

20 ③   21 a strange turtle

22 ⑤   23 ③

24 They are rice, vegetables, and fish skin.

01 ② 탕평채, 신선로, 송편은 우리의 전통 '음식'이다. ① 의식, ③ 문화, ④ 명절, ⑤ 풍습

02 (A) '어떻게 해서'라고 해야 하므로 How가 적절하다. (B) 뒤에 명사가 있으므로 look like가 적절하다. look+형용사, look like+명사: ~처럼 보이다, (C) '재미있는' 역사라고 해야 하므로 interesting이 적절하다.

03 Let's 동사원형 ~. = How about ~ing ~? = What about ~ing ~? = Why don't we 동사원형 ~? = Shall we 동사원형 ~?: ~하는 게 어때?

04 본문 끝에서 '우리 음식의 재미있는 역사 속으로 들어가 보자.'라고 하고 있다.

05 ④ '탕평책'은 영조의 정책이다. policy: 정책, ① 조리[요리]법, ② 정의, ③ 풍습, ⑤ 후식

06 ⓐ와 ②번: 정당, ①, ③ 파티, ④ 관계자, 당사자, a third party: (이해관계가 없는) 제삼자, ⑤ (여행방문 등을 함께 하는) 단체

07 something과 같이 -thing으로 끝나는 대명사를 수식할 때는 형용사가 뒤에 온다.

08 (A) in harmony: (~와) 조화되어, 협조하여 (B) come from: ~에서 생겨나다

09 (A) '특별한' 무언가를 권했다고 해야 하므로 special이 적절하다. ordinary: 보통의, 일상적인, (B) each 뒤에 단수 명사를 써야 하므로 ingredient가 적절하다. (C) '서로 다른' 당파를 상

15

징했다고 해야 하므로 different가 적절하다.

10 영조가 권한 것은 '네 가지 종류의 음식'이 아니라 '네 가지의 다채로운 재료로 만든 음식'이었다.

11 so+형용사/부사+that+주어+동사: 너무 ~해서 …하다

12 ①의 him은 King Yeonsan을, 나머지는 다 the scholar를 가리킨다.

13 이 글은 신선로라는 이름이 생기게 된 유래에 관한 글이므로, 주제로는 '신선로라는 음식의 뒷이야기'가 적절하다.

14 ⓐ와 ②, ③번: 계속 용법, ① 결과 용법, ④ 완료 용법, ⑤ 경험 용법

15 거북의 등에 "백제는 '보름달'과 같다."라는 글자가 써져 있었는데, 점술가가 "'보름달'은 곧 '작아질' 것입니다."라고 말했기 때문이다.

16 ⑤ 신라 사람들이 송편의 소로 무엇을 사용했는지는 대답할 수 없다. filling: (음식의) 소, 속, ① The last king of Baekje and his servants did. ② They meant that a full moon will soon become smaller, on the other hand, a half moon will grow bigger and become a full moon. ③ No. ④ In the shape of a half moon.

17 앞에 나오는 내용과 상반되는 내용이 뒤에 이어지므로 However가 가장 적절하다. ① 그러므로, ④, ⑤: 게다가, 더욱이

18 ③번 다음 문장의 this pot에 주목한다. 주어진 문장의 a special pot을 받고 있으므로 ③번이 적절하다..

19 학자가 신선이 된 것이 아니라, 사람들이 솥과 그 안의 음식을 신선로라고 불렀던 이유가 그 학자가 마치 자연 속에 홀로 사는 상상의 인물인 신선처럼 살았기 때문이라고 했다.

20 점술가가 "보름달은 곧 작아질 것입니다."라고 답했기 때문에, 왕은 자신의 왕국이 '걱정되었다'고 하는 것이 적절하다.

21 '이상한 거북'을 가리킨다.

22 이 글은 송편을 반달 모양으로 만들게 된 기원에 관한 글이므로, 제목으로는 '송편은 왜 반달 모양일까?'가 적절하다.

23 ③번 다음 문장의 She가 주어진 문장의 my grandma를 가리키므로 ③번이 적절하다.

24 재료는 쌀, 채소, 그리고 생선 껍질이다.

서술형 시험대비   p.90~91

01 his officials   02 harmoniously
03 (A) four   (B) political party
04 the king did something wrong
05 The scholar was so disappointed that he went to live on a mountain.
06 alone   07 like   08 smaller → bigger
09 백제는 세력이 약해질 것이다. / 신라는 세력이 커질 것이다.

---

10 Each ingredient symbolized a different political party.
11 People[They] called this dish tangpyeongchae.
12 Baekje is like a full moon, but Silla is like a half moon.
13 half, half, bigger, full

01 '그의 신하들'을 가리킨다.
02 in+추상명사 = 부사, in harmony = harmoniously: 조화되어
03 탕평채는 '네 가지의' 다채로운 재료로 만든 음식이었고, 각 재료는 서로 다른 '당파'를 상징했다.
04 '왕이 무언가를 잘못한 것'을 가리킨다.
05 'so'를 보충하면 된다.
06 by himself = alone: 혼자서, 홀로
07 be like: ~와 같다
08 반달은 점점 '커져서' 보름달이 될 것이라고 하는 것이 적절하다.
09 보름달은 약해지는 백제의 세력을, 반달은 강해지는 신라의 세력을 상징한다.
10 each 뒤에 단수 명사를 쓰는 것이 적절하다.
11 People[They]을 주어로 하여 고치는 것이 적절하다.
12 "백제는 보름달과 같지만 신라는 반달과 같다."는 거북의 등에 쓰여 있는 말을 가리킨다.
13 거북의 등에 "신라는 '반달'과 같다."라는 글자가 써져 있었는데, 점술가가 "'반달'은 점점 '커져서' 보름달이 될 것입니다."라고 말했기 때문이다.

영역별 핵심문제   p.93~97

01 outdoor   02 (d)ive into   03 ③   04 ⑤
05 look like   06 ④   07 It's on sale now.
08 ⑤   09 ②   10 ⑤
11 She recommends the fried fish.
12 ④   13 looking for someone special
14 (1) was chosen for his son by him
   (2) was asked of me by a lady
15 ④   16 ③   17 ②
18 ③   19 ①
20 was seen to walk on the street by Jack yesterday
21 saw something strange   22 ②
23 four parties   24 ⑤
25 Baekje is like a full moon, but Silla is like a half moon.
26 ②   27 ②, ⑤
28 People called this pot and the food in it sinseollo.
29 ④   30 ③   31 ①, ③, ④

01 반의어 관계다. 실내의 : 실외의

02 dive into: …로 뛰어들다, …에 몰두하다

03 '각 재료는 서로 다른 당파를 상징했다.'는 뜻으로 'symbolized'가 알맞다.

04 ① prefer: 선호하다 / 실내 스포츠가 더 좋아, 야외 스포츠가 더 좋아? ② servant: 신하 / 어느 날, 왕과 신하는 이상한 거북을 한 마리 발견했다. ③ afraid: 두려워하는 / 왕이 무언가를 잘못하면, 그 학자는 왕에게 그렇게 말하는 것을 절대 두려워하지 않았다 ④ policy: 정책 / 그 이름은 영조의 정책인 탕평책에서 왔다. ⑤ imaginary: 상상의 / 이 이야기는 상상의 동물에 근거한다.

05 look like+명사: ~처럼 보이다

06 치마를 찾고 있다고 했기 때문에 추천해 달라는 말이 적절하다.

07 '세일 중'은 'on sale'을 쓴다.

08 대화의 내용상 '애완동물을 기를까 생각 중이야.'가 적절하다.

09 they가 cats를 가리키므로 (②)에 들어가는 것이 적절하다.

10 근처의 식당을 추천해 달라는 말에 '좋아. 시도해 볼게. 고마워.'라고 말하는 것은 자연스럽지 않다.

12 Ms. Park은 야채볶음을 좋아했다.

13 '-one'으로 끝나는 대명사는 형용사가 뒤에서 수식한다.

14 능동태의 목적어가 주어 자리에 있으므로 수동태로 쓴다. (1) choose는 직접목적어를 주어로 수동태로 만들 때 간접목적어 앞에 전치사 for를, (2) ask는 of를 쓴다.

15 ① The National Museum of Korea was built in 1945. ② My wallet was stolen (by someone) on the crowded subway. ③ She was made to leave her family by him. ⑤ Is there anybody available this weekend?

16 첫 문장은 '-thing'으로 끝나는 대명사는 형용사가 뒤에서 수식하므로 something red, 두 번째 문장은 by로 보아 수동태로 쓰인 were given이 적절하다.

17 상태나 소유를 나타내는 동사(have, smell, become, resemble 등)는 수동태로 쓸 수 없다. The soup smells good.으로 써야 한다.

18 '-thing, -body, -one'으로 끝나는 대명사는 형용사가 뒤에서 수식하는데 빈칸에 알맞은 것이 사람은 아니므로 ①과 ②는 답이 아니고, 두 번째 문장에서 의미상 '무언가 잘못되었다'는 말이 자연스러우므로 something이 적절하다.

19 be satisfied with: ~에 만족하다. 나머지는 전치사 by를 쓴다.

20 목적격보어가 원형부정사인 경우, 수동태 문장에서는 to부정사로 바뀐다.

21 '-thing'으로 끝나는 대명사는 형용사가 뒤에서 수식한다.

22 ⓐ having, ② have는 '가지다'는 뜻일 때는 진행형으로 쓸 수 없다. ① (시간 등을) 보내다, 지내다, ③, ④, ⑤ [보통 동작·행위를 나타내는 부정관사가 달린 명사를 목적어로 하여] (~을)하다, ④ 경험하다

23 영조는 '네 당파'가 탕평채의 네 가지 재료처럼 화합을 이루어 일

24 보름달은 곧 작아질 것이지만, 반면에 반달은 점점 커져서 보름달이 될 것이라고 해야 하므로 'On the other hand'가 적절하다. on the other hand: 다른 한편으로는, 반면에 ① 똑같이, ② 이와 같이, ③ 즉, 다시 말해, ④ 그러므로

25 is like: ~와 같다

26 이 글은 송편을 반달 모양으로 만들게 된 기원에 관한 글이다.

27 ⓐ와 ②, ⑤번: 동명사, ①, ③, ④: 현재분사

28 앞 문장의 내용을 가리킨다.

29 학자는 산속에서 '혼자' 살았고, 여러 다양한 채소들을 함께 요리하기 위해 특별한 솥을 만들었다.

30 ⓐ be made of: ~으로 만들어지다(물리적 변화), be made from: 화학적 변화 ⓑ be from: ~ 출신이다

31 ⓒ와 ②, ⑤: 형용사적 용법, ①, ③: 부사적 용법, ④ 명사적 용법

단원별 예상문제   p.98~101

01 imaginary   02 (A) fortune teller   (B) offered

03 ③   04 ②   05 ②

06 recommend, prefers, to, comedy

07 ④   08 ③

09 Could you recommend a dish for me?

10 ⑤   11 ④   12 ③

13 (1) I resemble my father.
　　(2) I want something hot to eat.

14 (1) Something strange was written on the card.
　　(2) Korean history and culture can be found in its traditional food.
　　(3) It is made of rice, vegetables, and fish skin.

15 offered something special to them

16 ①, ⑤   17 ③, ⑤   18 ②

19 (A) different vegetables   (B) alone   20 ②

21 ③   22 (A) last   (B) worried   (C) shaped

23 to make

24 My family eats something special on Chuseok.

25 ④

01 둘은 유의어 관계이다. 최근에, 허구의

02 (A) fortune teller: 점술가 (B) offer: 제안하다

03 누군가나 또는 무언가가 당신이 희망하거나 기대했던 것만큼 좋지 않았기 때문에 행복하지 않은: 실망한

04 식사가 끝났을 때 먹는 단 음식: 디저트

05 ②번의 'Why don't you'는 뒤에 동사원형이 나온다.

06 소녀는 최근에 영화를 보지 않았기 때문에 소년에게 영화를 추천해 달라고 요청한다. 소녀는 액션 영화보다 코미디를 더 좋아한다. 그래서 소년은 코미디 영화인 *Funny Families*를 추천한다.

07 냉면을 먹어 보라고 말하므로 차가운 음식을 좋아한다.

08 주어진 문장 '약 2주 전에 문을 열었어요, 그렇죠?'라는 말에 'I thinks so.'라는 동의의 말이 오는 (③)이 적절하다.

09 추천을 부탁할 때 'Could you recommend ~ (for me)?' 표현을 쓴다.

10 요리를 해 본 적이 없다고 한 말에 대해 초보자를 위한 요리책을 제안하는 표현이 적절하다.

11 The baby will be looked after by my mom while I'm away. look after가 하나의 단위처럼 쓰여서 'will be looked after by'의 형태로 써야 한다.

12 '-thing, -one, -body'로 끝나는 대명사는 형용사가 뒤에서 수식한다.

13 (1) 상태나 소유를 나타내는 동사(have, become, resemble 등)는 수동태로 쓸 수 없다. (2) '-thing'으로 끝나는 대명사를 형용사와 to부정사가 동시에 수식하는 경우 '대명사+형용사+to부정사'의 어순이다.

14 (1) '-thing'으로 끝나는 대명사는 형용사가 뒤에서 수식하며 '적혀 있는' 것이므로 수동태가 적절하다. (2) 조동사가 있는 문장의 수동태는 '조동사+be+p.p.' 형식을 갖는다. (3) be made of: ~로 만들어지다(물리적 변화), be made from: ~로 만들어지다(화학적 변화)

15 offer는 'to'를 사용하여 3형식으로 고친다.

16 symbolize = represent = stand for: 상징하다, ② (기꺼이) 받아들이다, ③ 상의[의논/논의]하다, ④ 언급하다

17 ⓐ와 ③, ⑤: 부사적 용법, ① 형용사적 용법, ②, ④ 명사적 용법

18 이 글은 신선로라는 이름이 생기게 된 유래에 관한 글이므로, 제목으로는 '신선로는 어떻게 해서 그런 이름을 얻게 되었을까?'가 적절하다. ① cruelty: 잔인함

19 그것은 산속에서 '혼자' 살던 학자에 의해 여러 '다양한 채소들을' 함께 요리하기 위해 만들어진 특별한 솥이다.

20 앞에 나오는 내용과 상반되는 내용이 뒤에 이어지므로 However가 적절하다. ③ 게다가, ④ 즉, ⑤ 한편으로는

21 주어진 문장의 Something에 주목한다. ③번 다음 문장의 내용이므로 ③번이 적절하다.

22 (A) 백제의 '마지막' 왕 때였다고 해야 하므로 last가 적절하다. last: 마지막의, latest: 최근의, (B) 감정을 나타내는 동사는 수식받는 명사가 감정을 느끼게 되는 경우에 과거분사를 써야 하므로 worried가 적절하다. (C) 반달 '모양으로 만들어진' 떡이라는 뜻이므로 과거분사 shaped가 적절하다.

23 decide는 to부정사를 목적어로 취한다.

24 something과 같이 -thing으로 끝나는 대명사를 수식할 때는 형용사가 뒤에 온다.

25 '송편소로 준비했던 견과의 종류'는 알 수 없다. ① 초콜릿 송편, ② 쌀가루, 초콜릿, 그리고 견과, ③ 남동생, ⑤ 3년 전, 남동생이 송편의 모든 소를 먹었기 때문이다.

---

01 (1) It is on Main Street.

(2) He will go there with his family.

02 Why don't you see *Iron Woman 2*?

03 Do you prefer indoor or outdoor sports?

04 (1) BTS appeared on TV last night.

(2) It was made to run on city streets and highways.

(3) This pot and the food in it were called sinseollo by people.

(4) There was nothing new in this magazine.

05 (A) disappointed   (B) because   (C) imaginary

06 could[might] cook

07 This pot and the food in it were called sinseollo (by people).

08 a half moon will grow bigger and become a full moon

09 bigger, bigger   **10** people of Silla

---

01 (1) 새로 생긴 중국 식당은 어디에 있는가? (2) Jaden은 누구와 식당에 갈 것인가?

02 제안을 할 때 'Why don't you+동사원형 ~?'을 이용한다.

03 선호하는 것을 물을 때 'Do you prefer A or B?' 구문을 이용한다.

04 (1) appear는 자동사이므로 수동태로 쓰이지 않는다. (2) 목적격보어가 원형부정사인 경우, 수동태 문장에서는 to부정사로 바뀐다. (3) 목적어와 목적격 보어 자리에 모두 명사가 오더라도 목적어만 수동태의 주어 자리에 올 수 있다. (4) '-thing'으로 끝나는 대명사는 형용사가 뒤에서 수식한다.

05 (A) 감정을 나타내는 동사는 수식받는 명사가 감정을 느끼게 되는 경우에 과거분사를 써야 하므로 disappointed가 적절하다. (B) 그 학자가 신선처럼 살았기 '때문'이라고 해야 하므로 because가 적절하다. because+이유, why+결과, (C) '상상의' 인물인 신선이라고 해야 하므로 imaginary가 적절하다. imaginary: 상상의, imaginative: 상상력이 풍부한

06 그는 여러 다양한 채소들을 함께 '요리하기 위해' 특별한 솥을 만들었다. in order that 주어 can[may] 동사원형 ~: ~하기 위하여

07 this pot and the food in it을 주어로 하여 고치는 것이 적절하다.

08 '반달은 점점 커져서 보름달이 될 것'이라는 내용을 가리킨다.

09 그들은 점점 '커져서' 보름달이 되는 반달처럼 신라의 힘이 '커질' 것이라고 믿었기 때문이다.

10 반달 모양의 떡이 '신라 사람들'에 의해 만들어진 이래로 사람들은 반달 모양의 떡인 송편을 즐겨 먹고 있다.

|모범답안|

01 (1) A: Could you recommend a main dish for me?
　　　B: Do you prefer seafood spaghetti or
　　　　bibimbap?
　　　A: I prefer bibimbap.
　　(2) A: Could you recommend a dessert for me?
　　　B: Do you prefer chocolate ice cream or
　　　　patbingsu?
　　　A: I prefer patbingsu.

02 (1) These pictures were painted by my sister.
　　(2) These dresses were made by a famous
　　　designer.
　　(3) Hangeul was invented by King Sejong.
　　(4) *Harry Potter* was written by J. K. Rowling.

03 (A) Chuseok　(B) fish skin　(C) North Korea
　　(D) my grandma's home

01 ⑤　　　　02 (1) dove　(2) (i)nteresting
03 ③　　　04 pot　　05 ⑤　　06 ④
07 ②　　　08 ④　　　09 ⑤　　10 ③
11 liked the fried vegetables　　　12 ④
13 (1) People of Silla made songpyeon in the shape
　　　of a half moon.
　　(2) Was the picture painted by John?
　　(3) Her daughter was told a funny story by Mariel.
　　　A funny story told to her daughter by Mariel.
　　(4) People[They] speak English in many countries.
14 ②　　　　15 ④
16 (1) I can learn something new at the class
　　(2) Have you heard anything interesting today
17 ②　　　18 colorful　19 ③　　　20 ①, ④
21 People called this pot and the food in it sinseollo.
22 ②　　　　23 ⑤

01 ⑤번은 'ingredient'에 관한 설명이다.
02 (1) dive into: ~에 몰두하다, ~에 빠져들다 (2) interesting:
흥미로운
03 왕이나 여왕이 통치하는 나라
04 일반적으로 둥글고, 특히 음식을 요리하기 위해 사용되는 다　양한 형태의 용기
05 파이와 케이크 중에서 선호하는 것을 물을 때 사용하는 것은
'prefer'이다.
06 A가 옷을 추천해 달라고 하자 (C) 좋아하는 색을 묻고 (B) 이에
답하고 (A) 세일 중인 선호하는 색 제품을 권하자 (D) 이에 응하

는 순서가 자연스럽다
07 command는 '명령하다'는 뜻이고, 문맥상 '추천하다'는
'recommend'가 적절하다.
08 스포츠 클럽에 가입할 생각 중이라는 말에 액션영화를 좋아한다
는 대답은 자연스럽지 않다.
09 '추천하다'는 recommend가 적절하다.
10 Jaden이 해산물을 더 좋아한다고 했기 때문에 Ms. Park은 해
산물을 추천해 줄 것이다.
11 Ms. Park은 식당에서 어떤 음식을 좋아했나?
12 Jaden의 가족들이 식당에서 얼마나 많은 요리를 주문할지는 언
급되어 있지 않다.
13 (1) 동사를 'be+pp'로 바꾸고 수동태 문장의 주어 자리에는 능동
태 문장의 목적어가 오고, by 다음에는 능동태 문장의 주어를 목
적격으로 쓴다. (2) 의문문의 수동태는 능동태의 의문문을 평서
문으로 바꾼 후 이것을 수동태로 고치고, 다시 의문문으로 바꾸면
쉽다. (3) 4형식 문장의 수동태는 간접목적어와 직접목적어 각각
을 주어로 하는 수동태가 가능하며 직접목적어를 주어로 한 수동
태에서 tell 동사는 간접목적어 앞에 전치사 to를 쓴다. (4) 일반
인이 주어인 능동태 문장의 수동태에서는 흔히 'by+목적격'이 생
략된다. 특히 누가 그 동작을 했는지 중요하지 않거나 잘 모를 때,
수동태 문장으로 표현한다.
14 '-one'으로 끝나는 대명사는 형용사가 뒤에서 수식한다. We
are waiting for someone special.
15 일반 사람이 주어인 능동태를 수동태로 바꿀 때 'by+일반 사람'
은 생략 가능하다.
16 '-thing'으로 끝나는 대명사는 형용사가 뒤에서 수식한다.
17 ① The food is made of rice flour, chocolate, and
nuts. ③ This song was written by a famous musician.
④ I want to drink something cold. ⑤ I want to do
something special for my brother's birthday party.
18 color의 형용사형은 colorful이다.
19 ⓐ와 ③번: ~와 (똑)같이[마찬가지로], ~처럼(전치사), ① [외
관·형태·성질 등이] 같은(형용사), ②, ⑤: 좋아하다(동사), ④
비슷한 것(명사), and the like: 기타 같은 종류의 것(etc.보다
형식적인 표현)
20 주격 관계대명사 who나 that이 적절하다.
21 5형식 문장으로 쓰는 것이 적절하다.
22 ② 반면에, 다른 한 편으로 (두 가지 사실을 비교·대조할 때 씀),
① (만약) 그렇지 않으면, ③ 게다가, ④ 그렇기는 하지만, 그럼
에도 불구하고, ⑤ 게다가
23 '신라 사람들'이 반달 모양의 떡을 만들었다.

Think Big, Start Small

Conversation

시험대비 실력평가　p.112

01 whole　　02 ④　　03 ⑤　　04 ①
05 ③　　06 ④　　07 come up with
08 a[one] third of

01 둘은 반의어 관계이다. 어려운 : 쉬운 = 일부분의 : 전체의
02 방에서 책을 읽을 수 없다고 소리치고 있으므로 그의 집에 전기가 없다는 것이 적절하다.
03 Alfredo Moser에 의해 발명되었다가 적절하다.
04 '특히 덮개가 있는 빛을 제공하는 장치'의 의미로 'lamp(등, 램프)'가 적절하다.
05 '여러 가지 방법으로 생산될 수 있고 빛, 열 등을 만드는 장치에 동력을 제공하는 에너지의 형태'라는 의미로 '전기'가 적절하다.
06 ④의 'chief'는 명사로 사용되었다. '장, 우두머리'의 의미이다.
07 'come up with'는 '~을 생각해 내다'라는 뜻이다.
08 '~의 1/3'은 'a[one] third of'를 사용한다.

서술형 시험대비　p.113

01 (1) daytime, 낮　(2) ceiling, 천장　(3) blackout, 정전
02 (1) light up　(2) bent, spreads
03 (1) leftover　(2) Foundation
04 (1) chief　(2) bleach　(3) widely
05 (1) hole, hole　(2) magic

01 (1) 해가 뜨는 시간과 지는 시간 사이의 기간이나 저녁도 밤도 아닌 하루의 부분 (2) 위쪽을 바라볼 때 볼 수 있는 방의 안쪽 표면 (3) 전기 시스템의 고장으로 빛이나 전력이 없는 때
02 (1) light up: ~을 밝히다 (2) bend가 수동태로 과거분사 bent가 적절하고, '퍼지다'는 'spread'를 사용하고 주어가 3인칭 단수 'sunlight'이므로 'spreads'로 쓴다.
03 (1) 남은 음식: leftover (2) 재단: foundation
04 (1) 그녀는 영화 '주피터'에서 책임 과학자를 연기했어. (2) 물을 깨끗이 유지하기 위해 표백제를 조금 넣어라. (3) 오늘날 가스는 요리할 때 널리 쓰인다. / 형용사 'wide'는 동사 'is used'를 수식할 때 부사 'widely'가 되어야 한다.
05 (1) 물체의 표면에 개구부가 있거나 물체를 완전히 관통하는 개구부가 있는 물체의 빈 공간 (2) 특별한 힘을 가진 또는 비정상적이거나 예상치 못한 방식으로 또는 쉽게 또는 빠르게 발생하는

핵심 Check　p.114~115

1 ②　2 ③

교과서 대화문 익히기

Check(√) True or False　p.116

1 T　2 F　3 T　4 F

교과서 확인학습　p.118~119

Listen & Speak 1-A
(1) turn up, turn it up anymore, highest / Let, put, I've heard, works like / What an interesting idea, Let's
(2) I've heard, is coming / favorite actress / played, chief / can't wait to

Listen & Speak 2-A
(1) finished, good, want to take, leftovers / Don't forget to eat
(2) your plan for, winter break / I'm going to / exciting, going to do / going to go, amusement, all kinds / Don't forget to try

Communicate A
wrong / difficult / have to / to save / I've heard that, by using less / I've heard that, too, stop using / to dry off / impossible, at least / shake, before, more than enough / try, next time / don't forget to shake, at least, times

Communicate B
I've heard, saving electricity, to save / heard that, too, save / turn off, when / Don't forget, turn off, when, leave

Progress Check
(1) I've heard that, is coming / favorite / surprise
(2) plan for / to visit / sounds exciting / spend, beach, seafood / Don't forget to try / won't forget

시험대비 기본평가　p.120

01 ③　　02 are you finished with your meal?　　03 ⑤

01 빈칸에는 어떤 사실을 들어서 알고 있음을 말하는 표현이 온다. B의 마지막 말에 'who is he?'라고 그가 누군지 모르고 있기 때문에 ⑤는 자연스럽지 않다.
02 be동사 의문문으로 'be finished with'는 '~을 마치다'는 의미다.
03 (B)에는 'Don't forget to부정사'를 이용하여 '~할 것을 잊지 마라'는 당부의 말이 적절하다. remember / forget + 동명사는 '~한 것을 기억하다[잊다]'의 뜻으로 과거의 일을 나타낸다.

01 ②	02 ④	03 ③	04 ⑤
05 dim sum	06 ④	07 ④	08 ①
09 ③			

01 'A: 무슨 일 있어?'라는 물음에 'B: '내일 내 과학 숙제 가져올 것을 잊지 마.'라는 대답은 자연스럽지 못하다.

02 B의 첫 번째 말에서 더 이상 볼륨을 올릴 수 없다고 했으므로 빈칸 (A)는 볼륨을 올려달라는 부탁의 말이 적절하다.

03 B의 마지막 말에 '정말 재미있는 생각이야!'라고 말하는 것으로 보아 빈칸에는 '유리잔이 스피커처럼 작동한다.'는 말이 적절하다.

04 (A) 미래의 계획을 말할 때 'I'm going to부정사'를 사용하고, (B) '~할 것을 잊지 마'라는 상기시켜 주는 표현으로 'Don't forget to부정사'나 'Remember to부정사'를 사용한다.

05 튀기거나 증기로 익힌 여러 음식을 포함하는 중국식 식사 또는 간단한 간식 요리

06 Yuri의 '손을 말리는 데 종이 수건을 한 장만 쓸 수도 있지.'라는 말에 대한 Jaden의 반응으로 (④)가 적절하다.

07 종이컵을 사용하는 것을 멈추는 것은 Jaden이 한 말이다.

08 대화의 내용상 '전기를 절약하는 것'이 적절하다.

09 '~하는 게 어때?', '~하자'는 표현으로 'Why don't we+동사원형 ~?'을 사용할 수 있다.

01 she try the fruit there   02 I won't forget.

03 I've heard that we can save trees by using less paper.

04 don't forget to shake your hands at least 10 times.

05 Don't forget to

06 I've heard that a movie star is coming to our school.

01 소년은 여행에서 과일을 먹어 보라고 제안하고 있다.

02 '~하지 않을 거야'는 will not의 축약형 won't를 사용하여 3단어로 만든다.

03 'I've heard (that) ~.' 표현을 이용하고, '~함으로써'는 'by -ing'를 사용한다. '덜' 사용한다는 것은 little을 비교급 less로 바꾸어 준다.

05 소녀는 날씨가 나쁠까봐 걱정을 하고 있으므로 '우산을 가져갈 것을 잊지 마.'라는 충고가 적절하다. '~하는 것을 잊지 마'라는 뜻으로 상대방에게 해야 할 일을 상기시켜 줄 때 'Don't forget to부정사'를 사용한다.

06 어떤 사실을 들어서 알고 있음을 말할 때 'I've heard (that) ~.' 표현을 쓴다. 현재진행형 'is coming'이 미래의 일을 나타낼 때 사용될 수 있다.

Grammar

1 (1) famous   (2) happy
2 (1) wash   (2) painted   (3) to do   (4) to sign

01 (1) to laugh → laugh   (2) finishing → finish
    (3) sadly → sad   (4) tiring → tired
02 (1) throw   (2) thrown   (3) to meet
    (4) do(또는 to do)
03 ②   04 Let me know her name.

01 (1), (2) 사역동사의 목적어와 목적격보어의 관계가 능동일 경우 목적격보어로 원형부정사를 쓰는 것이 적절하다. (3) 동사 make의 보어로 부사가 아닌 형용사가 적절하다. (4) 내가 지치게 되는 것이므로 tired가 적절하다.

02 (1) 사역동사의 목적격보어는 목적어와의 관계가 능동일 경우 원형부정사가 쓰인다. (2) 사역동사의 목적격보어는 목적어와의 관계가 수동일 경우 과거분사가 쓰인다. (3) get이 '~하게 하다'라는 사역동사의 뜻으로 쓰일 때에는 목적격보어로 to부정사를 쓴다. (4) help는 목적격보어로 동사원형이나 to부정사가 나오며 뜻의 차이는 없다.

03 동사 make의 보어로 부사가 아닌 형용사가 적절하며 소설이 그녀를 유명하게 만든 것이므로 The novel이 주어가 되어야 한다.

04 사역동사 let의 목적격보어로 목적어와의 관계가 능동일 경우 원형부정사를 쓴다.

01 ⑤   02 ①, ⑤   03 ①
04 The pot can keep the fruit cold.   05 ③
06 (1) learn   (2) see   (3) cleaned   (4) help
    (5) to read   (6) interesting   (7) regularly, healthy
07 ③   08 ②   09 steal → stolen
10 ③, ④   11 ④   12 ⑤   13 ④
14 ②, ③   15 ⑤
16 (1) the test was   (2) he is silly
17 (1) to wear → wear   (2) write → to write
    (3) steal → stolen
18 (1) My father keeps his car clean.
    (2) Rainy days make me sad.
    (3) Her new book made her famous.

(4) I will not let my children watch TV.

(5) The funny story made me laugh.

(6) I had the man fix my computer.

19 ①   **20** ④

---

01 목적어와의 관계가 능동이므로 사역동사 let의 목적격보어로 원형부정사가 적절하고, 동사 found의 보어로 부사가 아닌 형용사가 적절하다.

02 help는 준사역동사로 목적어와 목적격보어의 관계가 능동일 경우 목적격보어로 원형부정사 또는 to부정사를 취한다.

03 5형식을 만들 수 있는 동사로 형용사를 목적격보어로 받을 수 있는 동사가 나와야 한다. call은 call A B(명사) 형태로 쓰이며, ask, order, beg 등은 목적격보어로 to부정사가 나온다.

04 '주어+동사+목적어+목적격보어'의 어순으로 쓰는데 동사 keep의 목적격보어로 형용사를 써야 하는 것에 주의한다.

05 이름이 불리는 것으로 목적어와의 관계가 수동이므로 사역동사 have의 목적격보어로 과거분사가 적절하다. Her wish was to have her son's name mentioned at graduation.

06 (1), (2) 사역동사 have와 let의 목적격보어로 동사원형이 적절하다. (3) 방이 청소되는 것이므로 목적격보어로 수동의 의미를 갖는 과거분사가 적절하다. (4) help는 준사역동사로 목적격보어로 원형부정사 또는 to부정사를 받는다. (5) get이 '~하게 하다'라는 사역동사의 뜻으로 쓰일 때에는 목적격보어로 to부정사를 쓴다. (6) 동사 find의 목적격보어로 형용사가 적절하다. (7) 첫 번째 괄호에는 동사를 수식하는 부사가 알맞으므로 regularly, 두 번째 괄호에는 keep의 목적격보어로 형용사를 쓴다.

07 목적격보어로 부사가 아닌 형용사가 사용된다는 것에 주의한다. ④ well은 부사이므로 형용사 good이 적절하다. Reading a lot of books will make me good at English.

08 소고기가 무엇을 요리하는 것이 아니라 요리되도록 하는 것이므로 사역동사 have의 목적격보어로 과거분사 cooked를 쓰는 것이 적절하다.

09 지갑이 무엇을 훔치는 것이 아니라 훔쳐진[도난당한] 것이므로 수동의 의미를 갖는 과거분사가 적절하다.

10 Marie가 의자에 앉는 것으로 목적어와의 관계가 능동이므로 사역동사 help의 목적격보어로 원형부정사 혹은 to부정사가 적절하다.

11 '주어(I)+동사(keep)+목적어(the baby)+목적격보어(safe)'의 어순으로 쓰는데 동사 keep의 목적격보어로 형용사를 써야 하는 것에 주의한다.

12 get은 사역동사의 뜻으로 쓰일 때 목적어와 목적격보어의 관계가 능동일 경우 목적격보어로 to부정사를 쓴다.

13 ④번은 4형식으로 쓰였고 나머지는 5형식이다.

14 ② Elizabeth had the meat roasted in the garden. ③ Morris got the girl to stand up in front of students.

15 (A) 사역동사 make의 목적어와 목적격보어의 관계가 능동이

므로 원형부정사가 적절하다. (B) 동사 get의 목적어와 목적격보어의 관계가 능동이므로 to부정사가 적절하다. (C) 사역동사의 목적어와 목적격보어의 관계가 수동이므로 과거분사가 적절하다.

16 목적어와 목적격보어를 that절의 주어와 동사로 써서 문장을 바꿔 쓴다.

17 (1) 목적어와 목적격보어의 관계가 능동이므로 목적격보어로 원형부정사가 적절하다. (2) 목적어와 목적격보어의 관계가 능동이므로 get의 목적격보어로 to부정사가 적절하다. (3) 목적어와 목적격보어의 관계가 수동이므로 목적격보어로 과거분사가 적절하다. handcuffs: 수갑

18 (1)~(3) '주어+동사+목적어+목적격보어'의 어순으로 쓰는데 동사의 목적격보어로 형용사를 써야 하는 것에 주의한다. (4), (5), (6) 목적어와 목적격보어의 관계가 능동이므로 사역동사의 목적격보어로 원형부정사를 이용한다.

19 형용사를 목적격보어로 받을 수 있는 동사가 나와야 한다.

20 get은 사역동사의 뜻으로 쓰일 때 목적어와 목적격보어의 관계가 능동일 경우 목적격 보어로 to부정사를 쓴다.

서술형 시험대비   p.130~131

01 (1) She made him finish his work by the next day.

  (2) She doesn't let her children play online games.

  (3) I must go to the dry cleaner's to have my suit cleaned.

  (4) Mom got me to help my sister with her homework.

  (5) I helped him calm[to calm] down before playing the guitar on the stage.

02 (1) me sad   (2) made him healthy

03 Eric had his camera repaired by a repairman.

04 (1) A strange man broke into my house, but he stole nothing and left it clean.

  (2) They made Stacy happy by saying white lies.

  (3) He found his new smartphone broken.

  (4) At first, Samanda thought William honest.

  (5) This thick blanket will keep you warm.

05 turn

06 (1) clean   (2) carried   (3) to be   (4) find[to find]

  (5) watch

07 Having lots of holidays next year makes her excited.

08 (1) Eve let Adam use her pen.

  (2) She made Dan follow her advice.

09 (1) He had his car washed yesterday.

  (2) We could make the lamp brighter.

01 (1), (2) 목적어와 목적격보어의 관계가 능동이므로 목적격보어로 원형부정사가 적절하다. (3) 목적어와 목적격보어의 관계가 수동이므로 목적격보어로 과거분사가 적절하다. (4) get이 사역동사의 뜻으로 쓰일 때 목적격보어로 to부정사를 쓴다. (5) help는 목적격보어로 동사원형이나 to부정사가 나온다.

02 (1) 책을 읽으며 슬펐다는 내용을 목적어와 형용사를 목적격보어로 하는 5형식으로 나타낸다. (2) 운동해서 건강하게 되었다는 내용을 목적어와 형용사를 목적격보어로 하는 5형식으로 나타낸다.

03 사역동사의 목적어와 목적격보어의 관계가 수동일 경우 목적격보어로 과거분사를 쓴다.

04 (1) 동사 leave의 목적격보어로 부사가 아닌 형용사가 적절하다. (2) 동사 make의 목적격보어로 명사가 아닌 형용사가 적절하다. (3) 목적어와 목적격보어의 관계가 수동이므로 목적격보어로 과거분사가 적절하다. (4), (5) 동사 think, keep의 목적격보어로 부사가 아닌 형용사가 적절하다. break into: 침입하다 blanket: 담요

05 사역동사 make의 목적어와 목적격보어의 관계가 능동이므로 목적격보어로 원형부정사가 적절하다.

06 (1) 사역동사의 목적어와 목적격보어의 관계가 능동이므로 목적격보어로 원형부정사가 적절하다. (2) 목적어와 목적격보어의 관계가 수동이므로 목적격보어로 과거분사가 적절하다. (3) get은 사역동사의 의미로 쓰일 수 있지만 목적격보어로 to부정사가 나온다. (4) help는 준사역동사로 목적격보어로 원형부정사 또는 to부정사가 나온다. (5) 사역동사의 목적어와 목적격보어의 관계가 능동이므로 목적격보어로 원형부정사가 적절하다.

07 '주어+동사+목적어+목적격보어'의 어순으로 쓰며 동사의 목적격보어로 형용사를 써야 하는 것에 주의한다.

08 get은 have, allow는 let, force는 make와 같은 의미로 쓰인다.

09 (1) 목적어와 목적격보어의 관계가 수동이므로 목적격보어로 과거분사로 쓴다. (2) '주어+동사+목적어+목적격보어'의 어순으로 쓰며 동사의 목적격보어로 형용사를 쓴다. 또한 '더 밝게'이므로 비교급으로 써야 한다.

교과서
Reading

확인문제 　　　　　　　　　　　p.132

1 T 2 F 3 T 4 F

확인문제 　　　　　　　　　　　p.133

1 T 2 F 3 F 4 T 5 T 6 T

01 One-Dollar　　　　02 in the Philippines
03 has no electricity, all the other houses
04 too, to　　　　05 are packed close together
06 because of　　　　07 light up, without using
08 is called, because, was invented by
09 many blackouts　　　10 come up with
11 be made for, lasts for
12 very safe　　　　13 never start
14 to make　　　　15 How to make
16 Fill, with　　　　17 Add, to keep, clear
18 push, into　　　　19 a third, remain
20 is bent, spreads　　　21 are widely used
22 The charity, how to make, install
23 Thanks to, thousands of
24 has, made, such as 25 for many years to come

1 One-Dollar Magic Lamps

2 "Wow, I can read a book in my room now!" shouted Marco, a boy in a village in the Philippines.

3 His house has no electricity just like all the other houses in the village.

4 People in the village are too poor to pay for electricity.

5 Even during the daytime, they live in darkness because the houses are packed close together.

6 Now things are changing because of a single plastic bottle.

7 One plastic bottle in the ceiling can light up a whole room without using any electricity.

8 This amazing plastic bottle is called a Moser lamp because it was invented by Alfredo Moser.

9 In 2002, there were many blackouts in his town in Brazil.

10 These blackouts made him come up with a new way to light his house.

11 A Moser lamp can be made for about one dollar and lasts for about 10 years.

12 It is also very safe.

13 It can never start a house fire.

14 Surprisingly, it is very easy to make this magic lamp.

15 How to make a Moser lamp from a bottle

16 1. Fill a clear plastic bottle with water.

17 2. Add some bleach to keep the water clear.

18 3. Make a hole in the roof, and push the bottle into the hole.

19 4. Let a third of the bottle remain above the roof.

20 5. Sunlight is bent by the water in the bottle and spreads around the room.

21 In the Philippines, Moser lamps are widely used by the My Shelter Foundation.

22 The charity also teaches local people how to make and install the lamps.

23 Thanks to the charity, thousands of homes in the Philippines now have Moser lamps.

24 It has also made Moser lamps popular in other countries, such as Argentina, India, and Fiji.

25 Moser lamps will light up the lives of many people for many years to come.

시험대비 실력평가
p.138~141

01 ④ 02 ② 03 ④ 04 ③
05 ③ 06 two-thirds
07 The water in the bottle bends sunlight
08 lasts 09 ①, ③, ④ 10 ③ 11 ④
12 thousands of homes in the Philippines
13 like 14 ① 15 ⑤ 16 ②
17 to remain → remain 18 ① 19 how to
20 ④ 21 ③ 22 ②
23 A Moser lamp 24 ⑤
25 (A) for (B) happy (C) grows 26 ⑤
27 (1) CD 케이스의 절반을 흙과 물로 채우고, 잔디 씨앗을 흙 안에 넣는다.
(2) 케이스를 닫고 모든 옆면에 테이프를 붙인다.
(3) 햇빛이 비치는 곳에 약 10일 동안 놓아둔다.

01 ⓐ pay for: ~의 대금을 지불하다, ⓑ in darkness: 어둠 속에

02 '전기'를 쓰지 않고 방 전체를 밝힐 수 있다고 하는 것이 적절하다. ① (사물의) 원천, 근원, ③ 화학 약품, ⑤ 자원

03 ④번 다음 문장의 One plastic bottle에 주목한다. 주어진 문장의 a single plastic bottle을 가리키므로 ④번이 적절하다.

04 낮 동안에도, 집들이 빽빽하게 들어차 있어서 그들은 어둠 속에 살아간다.

05 ⓒ에는 keep을 쓰는 것이 적절하다. ⓐ Fill, ⓑ Add, ⓓ Make, ⓔ push

06 two-thirds: 3분의 2, 병의 3분의 1은 지붕 위에 남아 있도록 한다. = 병의 '3분의 2'는 지붕 아래에 남아 있도록 한다.

07 'The water in the bottle'을 주어로 해서 고치는 것이 적절하다.

08 last: (기능이) 지속되다, 특정한 시간 동안 계속해서 사용될 수 있다.

09 ⓐ와 ②, ⑤: 형용사적 용법, ① 명사적 용법, ③, ④ 부사적 용법

10 ③ 이 글은 값싸고 매우 안전한 Moser 램프에 관한 글이므로, 제목으로는 '값싸고 안전한 신기한 램프'가 적절하다.

11 이 자선단체 '덕분에', ①, ③: ⋯ 대신에, ② ⋯ 없이, ⋯이 없다면, ⑤ ⋯와는 달리

12 thousands of+명사: 수천의 ~

13 such as = like: 예를 들어, ⋯와 같은

14 light up: ~을 환하게 밝히다

15 ⓐ fill A with B: A를 B로 채우다, ⓒ push A into B: A를 B에 넣다

16 ⓑ와 ②, ③, ⑤는 부사적 용법, ① 형용사적 용법, ④ 명사적 용법

17 사역동사 let+목적어+목적격보어(동사원형): ~이 ⋯하게 하다

18 투명한 플라스틱병에 물을 채워 넣어야 하므로, 올바르게 이해하지 못한 사람은 성민이다.

19 install은 teaches와 병렬 구문이 아니라, how to make and how to install에서 중복되는 'how to'를 생략한 것이다.

20 ⓑ와 ⑤: 형용사적 용법, ①, ④: 명사적 용법, ②, ③: 부사적 용법

21 이 글은 My Shelter 재단의 여러 활약에 관한 글이므로, 주제로는 'My Shelter 재단의 놀랄 만한 활약들'이 가장 적절하다. remarkable: 놀랄 만한, 놀라운, 주목할 만한, long-lasting: 오래 지속되는

22 ⓐ와 ②번: 약, ~쯤(부사), ①, ③ ⋯에 대한(전치사), ④ 주위에, 근처에, 가까이에(부사 = around), ⑤ ⋯에 종사하여, ⋯에 착수하여(전치사)

23 'Moser 램프'를 가리킨다.

24 Moser lamp를 만드는 데 얼마나 오래 걸리는지는 대답할 수 없다. ① A Moser lamp. ② Because in 2002, there were many blackouts in his town in Brazil. ③ No. ④ For about 10 years.

25 (A) 약 '10일' 동안이라고 해야 하므로 for가 적절하다. during+기간을 나타내는 명사, for+숫자, (B) 'make+목적어+목적격보어'의 형태로 쓰인 5형식 구문으로, 목적격보어의 자리에 형용사 happy를 쓰는 것이 적절하다. (C) 때를 나타내는 부사절에서는 현재시제가 미래시제를 대신하므로, grows가 적절하다.

26 뒤에 복수 명사가 나오므로 much로는 바꿔 쓸 수 없다.

27 First, Second, Finally 다음의 내용을 쓰는 것이 적절하다.

01 so, that, can't

02 because the houses are packed close together.

03 with using some electricity → without using any electricity

04 two thousand (and) two   05 A Moser lamp

06 (1) to make   (2) making   (3) this magic lamp

07 the My Shelter Foundation widely uses Moser lamps / the My Shelter Foundation uses Moser lamps widely

08 popularly → popular   09 Because of

10 A Moser lamp can be made for about one dollar and lasts for about 10 years.

11 (1) 1달러 정도로 만들 수 있다.   (2) 10년 정도 지속된다.
    (3) 매우 안전하다.   (4) 만드는 것이 매우 쉽다.

12 (A) widely   (B) how   (C) light up

13 to have Moser lamps

01 too+형용사+to부정사 = so+형용사+that+주어+cannot ...: 너무 ~하여 …할 수 없다

02 'are'를 보충하면 된다. be packed: 들어차다

03 천장에 플라스틱병 하나를 설치함으로써 '전기를 쓰지 않고' 방 전체를 밝힐 수 있다고 하는 것이 적절하다.

04 연도는 보통 두 자리씩 끊어서 읽지만, 2000년부터는 보통 'two thousand ~(미국식)', 'two thousand and ~(영국식)'로 읽는다.

05 'Moser 램프'를 가리킨다.

06 to부정사나 동명사를 주어로 해서 고치거나, make의 목적어인 this magic lamp를 주어로 해서 고치는 것이 적절하다.

07 부사 widely는 타동사 앞이나 목적어 뒤에 쓰는 것이 적절하다.

08 make+목적어+목적격보어'의 형태로 쓰인 5형식 구문으로, 목적격보어의 자리에 형용사를 쓰는 것이 적절하다.

09 이 정전들은 그가 집을 밝히는 새로운 방법을 생각해 내도록 만들었다. = 이 정전들 '때문에', 그는 집을 밝히는 새로운 방법을 생각해 냈다. Because of, Due to 등 이유를 나타내는 말을 쓰는 것이 적절하다.

10 'for'를 보충하면 된다.

11 두 번째 단락의 내용을 쓰는 것이 적절하다.

12 (A) 동사를 꾸며주므로 부사 widely가 적절하다. (B) '어떻게' 램프를 만드는지를 가르치는 것이므로 how가 적절하다. (C) 많은 사람들의 삶을 '밝혀 줄' 것이라고 해야 하므로 light up이 적절하다. light up: ~ 를 환하게 밝히다, lighten up: 기운 내다, lighten: (일·부채·걱정 등을) 가볍게 해주다, 밝아[환해]지다

13 가목적어, 진목적어 구문으로 고치는 것이 적절하다.

01 (i)nstall   02 hanger   03 ②   04 ⑤

05 (t)hings   06 ④   07 leftovers : 남은 음식

08 ③   09 ③   10 ③

11 Shake your hands before you use a paper towel.

12 ⑤   13 ⑤   14 plant

15 She thinks television is a waste of time, so she doesn't let her children watch TV.

16 (1) me happy   (2) her nervous   17 ③

18 ⑤   19 ④   20 ①   21 ①

22 ②   23 using   24 ①, ⑤

25 Many blackouts   26 ②, ④   27 ⑤

28 bleach   29 (A) clear   (B) a third   (C) is bent

30 ④   31 ①, ④   32 your book holder

01 유의어 관계다. 외치다 : 설치하다

02 'hang'은 동사로 '걸다'는 뜻이고, 'hanger'는 명사로 '옷걸이'이다..

03 ① volume: 음량 / 음량을 줄여 주시겠어요? ② spread: 퍼뜨리다 / 다른 사람들에 대한 소문을 퍼뜨리지 마라. ③ leftovers: 남은 음식 / 낭비를 막기 위해 남은 음식을 집으로 가져가는 것이 좋다. ④ lamp: 램프, 등 / 어두울 때 등을 켜라. ⑤ forward: 앞으로 / 더 자세히 보기 위해 앞으로 가자.

04 마을 사람들은 너무나 가난해서 전기세를 낼 수가 없다. pay for: ~을 지불하다

05 'thing'은 '상황'이란 의미가 있다. 복수 동사 'are'가 사용이 되었으므로 복수형 'things'를 쓴다.

06 '~할 것을 잊지 마'라는 의미로 'forget to부정사'를 사용한다. 'forget -ing'는 '~한 것을 잊다'는 의미가 된다. ⓔ는 '내일까지'라는 시간의 부사구다.

07 영어 설명: 식사 후에 남은 음식

08 무엇을 할 것인지에 관한 물음에 '놀이동산에 갈 거야'라고 말하고 있으므로 (③)이 적절하다.

09 G의 '온갖 음식을 먹어 볼 거야.'라는 말에 '딤섬을 먹어 보는 걸 잊지 마.'라고 상기시켜 주는 말이 적절하다.

10 A가 '캔과 병을 재활용할 것을 잊지 마.'라고 말할 때 B가 '물론 이야. 잊을게'라고 말하는 것은 어색하다. 'I won't.'가 적절하다.

11 질문: 유리는 Jaden에게 무엇을 제안했나요? 종이 수건을 사용하기 전에 손을 털라고 제안하고 있다.

12 유리가 하루에 얼마나 많은 종이 수건을 사용하는지는 대화에 언급되어 있지 않다.

13 목적어와 목적격보어의 관계가 수동이므로 과거분사를 써야 한다. He got his car washed yesterday.

14 사역동사의 목적격보어로 '나무를 심는' 능동의 의미가 필요하므로 원형부정사가 적절하다.

15 사역동사 let의 목적격보어로 목적어와의 관계가 능동일 경우 원형부정사를 쓴다.

16 (1), (2) 딸이 태어나서 행복했고, 사고에 대해 듣고 초조하게 되었으므로 동사 make를 이용하여 행복하게 만들고 초조하게 만들었다고 '주어+동사+목적어+목적격보어'의 형식으로 쓴다. 목적격보어로 형용사를 쓰는 것에 유의한다.

17 문맥에 맞게 형용사를 목적격보어로 받는 동사는 keep이다.

18 ⓒ My parents won't let me go out late at night. ⓓ It will help me (to) improve my English. ⑧ Eating an apple a day can make us healthy.

19 make는 5형식 문장에서 목적격보어로 명사, 형용사, 동사원형을 쓸 수 있다.

20 keep의 목적격보어로 형용사가 적절하다. clean은 동사로도 쓰이지만 형용사로도 쓰인다.

21 사역동사 have의 목적격보어로 목적어와의 관계가 능동이므로 원형부정사가 적절하다.

22 주어진 문장과 ②번의 make는 사역동사로 그 쓰임이 같다.

23 전치사 뒤에 동명사를 쓰는 것이 적절하다.

24 ⓐ와 ①, ⑤번: …와 (똑)같이[마찬가지로], …처럼(전치사), ② 비슷한(형용사), ③, ④: 좋아하다(동사)

25 2002년, 브라질에 있는 그의 마을의 '많은 정전들'이 그가 집을 밝히는 새로운 방법을 생각해 내도록 만들었다.

26 ⓑ와 ①, ③, ⑤: 명사적 용법, ② 형용사적 용법, ④ 부사적 용법

27 이 신기한 램프를 만드는 것은 매우 쉽다.

28 bleach: 표백제, 천을 하얗게 만들기 위해 사용되는 화학 물질

29 (A) keep+목적어+목적격보어(5형식): 목적격보어의 자리에 형용사를 써야 하므로 clear가 적절하다. (B) 분자가 2이상일 때부터 분모에 s를 붙이므로 a third가 적절하다. (C) 뒤에 by가 있고, 햇빛이 병 속의 물에 의해 '굴절된다'고 해야 하므로 수동태 is bent가 적절하다. bend: 구부러지다, 구부리다

30 위 글은 '병으로 Moser 램프를 만드는 법'에 관한 글이다.

31 ① 마지막으로, 끝으로(무엇을 열거하면서 마지막 요소 앞에 붙이는 말), ④ Finally: 마지막으로, 마침내, ②, ③: 마침내, ⑤: 결과적으로

32 '당신의 독서대'를 가리킨다.

단원별 예상문제　　　　　　　　　　p.150~153

01 safe　　　　02 (A) packed　　(B) Thanks to
03 ③　　　　04 ⑤　　　　05 ②
06 put my phone in a glass　　　　07 ①
08 Don't forget to turn off the light when you leave your room.
09 ⑤　　　　10 ④　　　　11 ①, ⑤　　　12 ③, ④, ⑤

---

13 (1) This movie made the actors famous.
　　(2) My parents made me study hard.
14 wash → to wash
15 People in the village are too poor to pay for electricity.
16 (A) during　(B) packed　(C) any
17 ④, for　　　18 ①, ③, ④　　　　19 ⑤
20 to keep the water clear[clean]
21 ④　　　　22 ②
23 The charity also teaches local people how to make and install the lamps.
24 ④

01 둘은 반의어 관계이다. 인기 있는 : 인기 없는 = 위험한 : 안전한

02 (A) packed: 꽉 들어찬 (B) thanks to: ~ 덕분에

03 물건을 청소하거나 사물에서 색을 제거하는 데 사용되는 강한 화학물질

04 '더 넓은 또는 증가하는 영역을 덮거나, 도달하거나, 영향을 미치다'라는 의미로 'spread(퍼지다)'가 적절하다.

05 ②번의 'turn up'은 '동사+부사'로 이루어진 이어동사로 인칭대명사가 목적어일 때는 '동사+대명사+부사'의 어순으로 써야 한다. 'turn up it'을 'turn it up'으로 고쳐야 한다.

06 '지금 해 보자'라는 말은 '휴대폰을 유리 속에 넣어 보자'는 것을 의미한다.

07 유명 여배우가 학교로 온다는 소식에 빨리 만나보고 싶다는 말이 자연스럽다.

08 '~하는 것을 잊지 마'는 'Don't forget to부정사'를 사용한다.

09 위의 대화에서 Yuri는 종이 수건을 한 장만 사용하는 방법에 대해 이야기하고 있다. 종이 수건을 사용하기 전에 손을 털면 '종이 수건 한 장이면 충분할 거야'라는 말이 자연스럽다.

10 손을 말리기 위해 종이 수건 한 장만 사용할 수 있다는 말에 적어도 두세 장의 종이 수건이 필요하다고 했기 때문에 ⓓ는 'impossible'이 적절하다.

11 ② Let him join your club. ③ He made me introduce myself. ④ She had Mike call me.

12 ① We found the window broken. ② I saw him sing[singing] in front of students.

13 (1) '주어+동사+목적어+목적격보어(형용사)'의 어순으로 쓴다.
　(2) 사역동사의 목적격보어로 동사원형을 쓴다.

14 get은 목적격보어로 to부정사가 적절하다.

15 too+형용사+to부정사: 너무 ~하여 …할 수 없다

16 (A) during+기간을 나타내는 명사, while+주어+동사, (B) pack은 '(사람, 물건으로) 빽빽히 채우다'는 뜻이므로, 수동태로 써서 '빽빽하게 들어차 있다'고 하는 것이 적절하다. be packed: 들어차다, (C) '전기를 쓰지 않고'라는 부정의 뜻이 되어야 하는데, 빈칸 앞에 without이 있으므로 부정을 나타내는

'no'를 또 쓰는 것은 적절하지 않다.

17 about one dollar는 행위자가 아니라 '1달러 정도'라는 뜻이므로, for로 고치는 것이 적절하다.

18 ⓐ와 ②, ⑤번: 가주어, ① 목적어, ③ 가목적어, ④ 비인칭 주어

19 '제작 방법'은 알 수 없다. ① Moser lamp, ② Alfredo Moser, ③ 2002년, 브라질에 있는 Alfredo Moser의 마을에는 정전이 잦았기 때문에, 그가 집을 밝히는 새로운 방법을 생각해 내게 되었다. ④ 1달러 정도

20 keep+목적어+목적격보어(5형식): 목적격보어의 자리에 형용사를 쓰는 것이 적절하다.

21 Moser lamp를 설치하는 데 얼마나 오래 걸리는지는 대답할 수 없다. ① We need a clear plastic bottle, water, and some bleach. ② To keep the water clear. ③ In the roof. ⑤ Sunlight is bent by the water in the bottle and spreads around the room. operate: 작동되다

22 'ⓐ와 ②번: 재단, ①, ④: (일의 바탕이 되는) 토대[기반/근거], ③, ⑤: 설립, 창립, National Foundation Day: 건국기념일

23 'how'를 보충하면 된다. also는 일반동사 앞에 쓰는 것이 적절하다.

24 필리핀의 '수천' 가구가 이제 Moser 램프를 갖게 해주었다.

서술형 실전문제   p.154~155

01 I've heard that we can save trees by using less paper.

02 Just shake your hands before you use a paper towel.

03 Don't forget to try the fruit there

04 (1) I didn't want to go to my cousin's birthday party, but my mom made me go.
   (2) They had their house painted.
   (3) The present made the children happy all day long.

05 (1) The noise kept me awake.
   (2) He found the exam difficult.
   (3) These blackouts made him come up with a new way to light his house.
   (4) He had his computer repaired yesterday.
   (5) Help me (to) take some pictures of them.

06 People call this amazing plastic bottle a Moser lamp

07 blackouts   08 very safe

09 the My Shelter Foundation

10 thousand → thousands

02 just로 동사 shake를 수식하여 just shake로 문장을 시작한다(명령문). '~ 전에'라는 접속사 before 뒤에 '주어+동사' 어순으로 'you use a paper towel'을 쓴다.

03 '~할 것을 잊지 마라'는 뜻으로 상대방에게 해야 할 일을 상기시켜 줄 때 'Don't forget to부정사'를 사용한다.

04 (1) make의 목적격보어로 목적어와의 관계가 능동이므로 원형부정사를 쓴다. (2) had의 목적격보어는 목적어와의 관계가 수동이므로 과거분사를 쓴다. (3) '주어+동사+목적어+목적격보어(형용사)'의 어순으로 쓴다.

05 (1) 동사 keep의 목적격보어로 동사원형이 아닌 형용사가 적절하다. (2) 동사 find의 목적격보어로 부사가 아닌 형용사가 적절하다. (3) 사역동사 make의 목적격보어로 목적어와의 관계가 능동이므로 원형부정사를 써야 한다. (4) 사역동사 have의 목적격보어로 목적어와의 관계가 수동이므로 과거분사를 써야 한다. (5) help는 목적격보어로 동사원형이나 to부정사가 나오며 뜻의 차이는 없다.

06 People을 주어로 해서 고치는 것이 적절하다.

07 blackout: 정전, 어떤 지역에 대한 전기 공급이 일시적으로 끊기는 기간

08 Moser 램프는 절대 집에 불을 낼 수 없기 때문에, '매우 안전하다'고 말할 수 있다.

09 'My Shelter 재단'을 가리킨다.

10 thousands of+명사: 수천의 ~, cf. hundred, thousand, million 등의 단어가 숫자 뒤에서 단위로 사용될 때는 단수형으로만 사용한다. e.g. two hundred, three million

창의사고력 서술형 문제   p.156

|모범답안|

01 (1) A: I'm going to go to Gyeongju.
      B: Don't forget to visit the National Museum.
      A: O.K., I won't forget.
   (2) A: I'm going to go on a field trip.
      B: Don't forget to take something to eat.
      A: O.K., I won't forget.

02 (1) Mom made me do the dishes this morning.
   (2) The doctor made him stop smoking.
   (3) Miranda made her husband buy some fruit.

03 (A) wire hanger   (B) bend
   (C) both ends   (D) top part   (E) free

단원별 모의고사   p.157~160

01 ⑤	02 (1) hole (2) wire	03 ②
04 (a)mazing	05 ④	06 ④
07 ⑤	08 ④	

09 her parents, winter break, amusement park, food, dim sum

10 heard, movie star, favorite actress, played, chief

11 ③

12 shake our hands before we use a paper towel

13 me happy　　　　　14 ①

15 (1) tidily → tidy　(2) plant → planted

16 ③　　　　　17 to have → have　　　18 ②

19 (A) the Philippines　(B) because　(C) because of

20 No, it doesn't.

21 because Alfredo Moser invented it

22 to come → come

23 The My Shelter Foundation does.　　　24 ⑤

---

01 ⑤번은 'widely'에 관한 설명이다. 'surprisingly'에 대한 영어 설명은 'unexpectedly or in a way that is unusual(예상치 못하거나 특이한 방식으로)'이다.

02 (1) hole: 구멍 (2) wire: 전선

03 병들거나 가난하거나 집이 없기 때문에 어려움에 처한 사람들에게 무료로 돈, 음식 또는 도움을 주는 시스템, 또는 이런 식으로 돈과 도움을 제공할 목적을 가지고 있는 단체

04 '매우 놀라운'의 의미를 가진 'amazing'이 적절하다.

05 그가 누군지 묻는 B의 말에 '말해주지 않을 거야.'라고 말하고 있으므로 빈칸에는 '놀라게 할 거야!'라는 'It's a surprise!'가 적절하다.

06 식사를 마쳤는지 묻는 말에 (C) 정말 맛있었다고 답하고, (B) 남은 음식을 집으로 가져가고 싶은지 묻고 (A) 부탁한다고 말하고 나서 마지막으로 (D) 내일까지 남은 음식 먹으라고 상기시켜주는 말을 하는 것이 자연스럽다.

07 전기를 절약하는 방법에 관한 대화로, 방을 떠날 때 불을 끄는 것을 잊지 마라는 의미가 적절하다. 'enter'를 'leave'로 바꾸어야 한다.

08 다음 달에 체육관이 개장한다는 말에 '그렇게 할게. 고마워.'라고 답하는 것은 어색하다.

11 Jaden이 종이 컵 사용을 줄일 수 있다고 말하고 있으므로 종이를 덜 사용하는 것에 대한 내용이 오는 것이 적절하다.

12 손을 말리기 위해서 어떻게 종이 수건 한 장만 사용할 수 있는가? → 종이 수건을 사용하기 전에 손을 털라고 말하고 있다.

13 make 동사로 '주어+동사+목적어+목적격보어(형용사)'의 형식을 이용한다.

14 사역동사의 목적어와 목적격보어가 수동의 관계에 있을 경우 목적격보어로 과거분사를 쓴다..

15 (1) 동사 keep의 목적격보어로 부사가 아닌 형용사가 적절하다. (2) 사역동사의 목적어와 목적격보어가 수동의 관계에 있을 경우 목적격보어로 과거분사를 쓴다.

16 ③은 4형식으로 쓰였고 주어진 문장과 나머지는 모두 목적어와

17 사역동사의 목적격보어로 동사원형이 적절하다.

18 too+형용사+to부정사: 너무 ~하여 …할 수 없다

19 (A) 나라 이름이 복수형일 때는 the를 붙여야 하므로 the Philippines가 적절하다. (B)와 (C) 'because+주어+동사', 'because of+명사'이므로 (B)는 because가, (C)는 because of가 적절하다.

20 천장에 있는 플라스틱병 하나는 '전기를 쓰지 않고' 방 전체를 밝힐 수 있다.

21 Alfredo Moser를 주어로 해서 고치는 것이 적절하다.

22 사역동사 make+목적어+목적격보어(동사원형)

23 'My Shelter 재단' 덕분에, 필리핀의 수천 가구가 이제 Moser 램프를 갖고 있다. enable+목적어+to부정사: (사람에게) ~할 수 있게 하다

24 '그 단체(My Shelter 재단)'가 아르헨티나, 인도, 피지와 같은 다른 나라들에서도 Moser 램프가 인기가 있도록 만들었다.

교과서 파헤치기

단어 TEST Step 1   p.40

01 연습하다	02 지하철
03 진가를 알아보다, 감상하다, 감사하다	04 용감한
05 세기	06 실은, 사실은, 실제로
07 ~와 결혼하다	08 새벽 09 공연하다, 수행하다
10 실패하다	11 줄거리 12 수수께끼
13 공주	14 기념하다 15 이미, 벌써
16 공연	17 비밀 18 정확하게, 바르게
19 제안	20 유명한 21 추측하다
22 정확하지 않게, 틀리게	23 낯선 사람, 이방인
24 할인	25 어려운 26 의미하다
27 놀라운	28 타조
29 (말을) 덧붙이다, 더하다	30 기념일
31 즉시, 곧바로	32 안전한 33 극장
34 전체, 모든, 전부의	35 서두르다 36 ~에 늦다, 지각하다
37 ~하는 게 어때?	38 ~하고 싶다 39 …만큼 ~한
40 ~와 사랑에 빠지다	41 ~에 지나지 않는
42 제시간에, 늦지 않게	43 알아내다, 발견하다

단어 TEST Step 2   p.41

01 secret	02 guess	03 century
04 incorrectly	05 actually	06 princess
07 brave	08 ostrich	09 discount
10 appreciate	11 stranger	12 correctly
13 agree	14 play	15 storyline
16 already	17 anniversary	18 marry
19 perform	20 fail	21 whole
22 subway	23 add	24 celebrate
25 famous	26 safe	27 performance
28 suggestion	29 practice	30 moving
31 difficult	32 amazing	33 riddle
34 beauty	35 be late for ~	36 in time
37 find out	38 hurry up	39 fall in love with ~
40 take off	41 one day	42 at first sight
43 would like to+동사원형		

단어 TEST Step 3   p.42

1 century, 세기 2 already, 이미
3 perform, 수행하다, 공연하다 4 amazing, 놀라운
5 storyline, 줄거리 6 aria, 아리아, 영창 7 brave, 용감한
8 discount, 할인 9 appreciate, 진가를 알아보다

10 celebrate, 축하하다, 기념하다   11 moving, 감동적인
12 guess, 추측하다   13 secret, 비밀   14 marry, 결혼하다
15 anniversary, 기념일   16 riddle, 수수께끼

대화문 TEST Step 1   p.43~44

Listen & Speak 1-A
1 hurry up, already / going to be late for / Why don't we take, faster than / good idea
2 got only, wrong / sure, well, Why don't we go out to celebrate / have pizza for / Of course

Listen & Speak 1-B
What shall we do / Why don't we see / a good idea

Listen & Speak 2-A
1 let's practice, parts, school play / What time shall we meet / How about, right after school / Sounds
2 play badminton / Where shall we / How about, near / See you there at

Listen & Speak 2-B
Let's go on a picnic / What time shall we meet / How about, on / Let's meet

Communicate A
guess what, have no school / Why not / anniversary / together / take, off, What, want to / Why don't we go see, near your work, get, discount if, go on a Wednesday / let's just meet / shall we / How about, have lunch / best

Communicate B
What shall we / Why don't we / time shall we meet / How about / Let's meet

Progress Check
1 hurry up, already / be late for / Why don't we take, faster than, at this time of day / good idea
2 hot today, Let's go swimming / Where shall, meet / How about / See, tere

대화문 TEST Step 2   p.45~46

Listen & Speak 1-A
1 M: Liz, hurry up. It's already 6 o'clock.
  W: Oh, we're going to be late for the concert.
  M: Why don't we take the subway? The subway will be faster than the bus at this time of day.
  W: That's a good idea.
2 B: Mom, I got only one question wrong on the Korean history exam!
  W: Great! I was sure you would do well. Why don't

29

we go out to celebrate tonight?

B: Yes! Can we have pizza for dinner?

W: Of course, Joe. I'll call your dad.

Listen & Speak 1-B

A: What shall we do at the park?

B: Why don't we see a magic show?

A: That's a good idea.

Listen & Speak 2-A

1 B: Karen, let's practice our parts for the school play today.

G: O.K. What time shall we meet?

B: How about 4 o'clock, right after school?

G: Sounds good.

2 G: Do you want to play badminton together this afternoon, Mark?

B: Sure. Where shall we play?

G: How about at the park near your place?

B: O.K. See you there at 3 o'clock.

Listen & Speak 2-B

A: Let's go on a picnic this weekend.

B: Good idea. What time shall we meet?

A: How about 10 o'clock on Saturday?

B: O.K. Let's meet at the subway station. See you there.

Communicate A

Anna: Dad, guess what! I have no school next Wednesday.

Dad: Really? Why not?

Anna: It's our school's 75th anniversary.

Dad: Oh, I see.

Anna: Can we do something together that day?

Dad: I guess I can take the afternoon off. What do you want to do?

Anna: Why don't we go see a musical at Bravo Theater near your work? We can get a discount if we go on a Wednesday.

Dad: Good idea, Anna! Then, let's just meet at the theater.

Anna: O.K. What time shall we meet?

Dad: How about 12? Then, we can have lunch together, too.

Anna: You're the best, Dad!

Communicate B

A: What shall we do this afternoon?

B: Why don't we go see *Wonder Woman*?

A: Good idea! What time shall we meet?

B: How about 4 o'clock?

A: O.K. Let's meet at Moon Theater.

Progress Check

1 G: Jim, hurry up. It's already 10 o'clock.

B: Oh, we're going to be late for the movie.

G: Why don't we take the bus? The bus will be faster than the subway at this time of day.

B: That's a good idea.

2 B: It's very hot today. Let's go swimming, Julie.

G: Good idea! Where shall we meet?

B: How about at the subway station near my place?

G: O.K. See you there at 11 o'clock.

본문 TEST Step 1   p.47~48

01 Most Dangerous, World

02 Welcome, everyone

03 going, perform, opera

04 Like, other, Italian because

05 Before, like, storyline

06 appreciate, better if

07 of, beauty, cold as

08 who, marry, must

09 fails, die   10 has, been able

11 One, falls, at, sight

12 becomes, answer, riddles

13 However, marry, prince

14 nothing more than   15 then, of, own

16 asks, What

17 adds, correctly, die, incorrectly

18 before dawn, as, hers

19 to, until, finds out

20 most famous aria, whole   21 means, sleeps

22 No, sleeps   23 one, not even 24 secret, safe

25 No, will know 26 At dawn, will 27 prince's, is

28 learn, in time   29 watch, find out

본문 TEST Step 2   p.49~50

01 The Most Dangerous, World

02 Welcome, everyone

03 are going to, perform

04 Like, other famous operas, in Italian because, in Italy, 16th century

05 I'd like to tell, storyline of the opera

06 appreciate, better if

07 of great beauty, as cold as ice

08 who, marry her, three riddles

09 fails, must die 10 has ever been able to

11 falls in love with, at first sight

12 the first man to answer

13 However, to marry

14 nothing more than

15 her a riddle of his own

16 asks her, What

17 adds, correctly, agree to die, incorrectly, have to marry

18 before dawn, as difficult as hers

19 go to sleep until, finds out

20 the most famous aria, whole opera

21 means, sleeps

22 No, sleeps   23 not even you

24 My secret, safe

25 No one will know

26 At dawn, will win   27 prince's name

28 Will, learn, in time

29 Let's watch, find out

---

1 투란도트, 세상에서 가장 위험한 사랑

2 여러분, 환영합니다!

3 오늘 밤, 우리는 지아코모 푸치니의 오페라 《투란도트》를 공연할 것입니다.

4 다른 많은 유명한 오페라들처럼 《투란도트》는 이탈리아어로 되어 있는데, 오페라가 16세기 이탈리아에서 시작되었기 때문입니다.

5 시작하기 전에 오페라 《투란도트》의 줄거리를 알려 드리려고 합니다.

6 여러분이 줄거리를 알면 이 오페라를 더 잘 감상하게 될 것입니다.

7 중국의 공주 Turandot는 굉장히 아름다운 여인이지만, 그녀는 얼음처럼 차갑습니다.

8 그녀와 결혼하길 원하는 왕자는 누구든지 반드시 세 가지 수수께끼에 답해야 합니다.

9 만약 실패하면 그는 죽어야 합니다.

10 그 누구도 수수께끼에 답할 수 없었습니다.

11 어느 날, 어떤 용감한 왕자가 그녀에게 첫눈에 반합니다.

12 그는 세 수수께끼를 모두 맞힌 첫 번째 사람이 됩니다.

13 그러나 Turandot는 그 왕자와 결혼하길 원하지 않습니다.

14 그는 그녀에게 단지 낯선 사람일 뿐입니다.

15 그러자 그는 그녀에게 자신의 수수께끼를 냅니다.

16 그는 그녀에게 "제 이름이 무엇입니까?"라고 묻습니다.

17 그는 "당신이 맞게 대답한다면 나는 죽는 것에 동의하겠습니다. 만약 답이 틀리면 당신은 저와 결혼해야 할 것입니다."라고 덧붙입니다.

---

18 Turandot는 동이 트기 전에 답을 찾아야 하지만 그의 수수께끼는 그녀의 것만큼 어렵습니다.

19 그녀는 모두에게 "누군가 그의 이름을 알아낼 때까지 그 누구도 잠들 수 없다."라고 말합니다.

20 그리고 왕자는 이 오페라 전체에서 가장 유명한 아리아, Nessun Dorma를 부릅니다.

21 그것은 누구도 잠들지 못한다는 뜻입니다.

22 누구도 잠들지 못하네.

23 누구도 잠들지 못하네, 당신조차도, 공주여.

24 나의 비밀은 안전하다네.

25 누구도 나의 이름을 알지 못할 것이네.

26 동틀 녘에, 내가 이길 것이라네! 내가 승리할 것이라네!

27 왕자의 이름은 Calaf입니다.

28 공주는 그의 이름을 제때 알아낼 수 있을까요?

29 오페라를 보고 알아봅시다.

---

1 Turandot The Most Dangerous Love in the World

2 Welcome, everyone!

3 Tonight, we are going to perform Giacomo Puccini's opera *Turandot.*

4 Like many other famous operas, *Turandot* is in Italian because opera started in Italy in the 16th century.

5 Before we begin, I'd like to tell you the storyline of the opera *Turandot.*

6 You will appreciate it better if you know the story.

7 Turandot, a Chinese princess, is a woman of great beauty, but she is as cold as ice.

8 Any prince who wants to marry her must answer three riddles.

9 If he fails, he must die.

10 No one has ever been able to answer them.

11 One day, a brave prince falls in love with her at first sight.

12 He becomes the first man to answer all three riddles.

13 However, Turandot does not want to marry the prince.

14 He is nothing more than a stranger to her.

15 He then gives her a riddle of his own.

16 He asks her, "What is my name?"

17 He adds, "If you answer correctly, I will agree to die. If you answer incorrectly, you will have to marry me."

18 Turandot must find the answer before dawn, but his riddle is as difficult as hers.

19 She says to everyone, "No one will go to sleep until someone finds out his name."

20 The prince then sings the most famous aria of the whole opera, "Nessun Dorma."

21 It means no one sleeps.

22 No one sleeps.

23 No one sleeps, not even you, Princess.

24 My secret is safe.

25 No one will know my name.

26 At dawn, I will win! I will win!

27 The prince's name is Calaf.

28 Will the princess learn his name in time?

29 Let's watch the opera and find out.

4. I enjoyed its beautiful and moving songs.

5. The story was also as good as the songs.

6. If you are looking for a good musical movie, you should see this movie.

7. by Kim Jisu on Aug. 11

Write

1. Review of *Beauty and the Beast*

2. I saw *Beauty and the Beast* last Saturday.

3. It is about a beautiful girl and a beast.

4. I enjoyed it a lot.

5. The songs were great, and the love story was as beautiful as a gem.

6. If you like heart-warming stories about love, you will like it, too.

7. by Lee Minsu on Aug. 12

구석구석지문 TEST Step 1   p.57

Link

1. How, our performance

2. amazing, seen, as great as, musical's

Write

1. Review of

2. saw, last Friday

3. is about, dreams, love

4. its beautiful, moving songs

5. was also as good as

6. are looking for, should see

7. by, on

Write

1. Review of

2. saw, last Saturday

3. beautiful girl, beast

4. it a lot

5. as beautiful as a gem

6. like heart-warming stories, will like, too

7. by, on Aug

구석구석지문 TEST Step 2   p.58

Link

1. A: How was our performance?

2. B: It was amazing! Actually, I've seen the musical *Cats* before, and your song was as great as the musical's.

Write

1. Review of *La La Land*

2. I saw *La La Land* last Friday.

3. It is about the dreams and love of Mia and Sebastian.

Lesson 6

단어 TEST Step 1   p.21

01 초보자	02 해산물	03 실망한
04 점쟁이	05 혼자, 홀로	06 등
07 선호하다	08 반달	09 정책
10 문화	11 웃긴, 재미있는	12 육류, 고기
13 학자	14 정직함	15 전통의, 전통적인
16 상상의, 가상의	17 제안하다, 권하다	18 실내의
19 최근에	20 재료	21 추천하다
22 상징하다	23 신하, 하인	24 음식, 요리
25 화합, 조화	26 특별한	27 왕국
28 주문하다	29 모양	30 주로
31 신하, 관리, 공직자	32 다른	33 실외의
34 정치의, 정당의	35 세일 중	36 반면에
37 ~을 두려워하다	38 ~처럼 보이다	39 혼자서, 홀로
40 ~으로 뛰어들다	41 ~에 대해 걱정하다	
42 ~에 가 본 적이 있다		
43 ~의 이름을 따서 지어지다		

단어 TEST Step 2   p.22

01 traditional	02 culture	03 seafood
04 mainly	05 offer	06 official
07 different	08 servant	09 indoor
10 special	11 ingredient	12 alone
13 back	14 prefer	15 beginner
16 funny	17 political	18 fortune teller
19 half	20 disappointed	21 recommend
22 symbolize	23 harmony	24 policy
25 order	26 hit	27 honesty
28 half-moon	29 imaginary	30 scholar
31 kingdom	32 outdoor	33 party
34 recently	35 on sale	36 look like+명사
37 be afraid of	38 dive into	
39 on the other hand		40 by oneself
41 be named after		
42 be thinking of -ing		
43 become worried about		

단어 TEST Step 3   p.23

1 dessert, 후식 2 kingdom, 왕국

3 symbolize, 상징하다 4 imaginary, 상상의, 가상의

5 beginner, 초보자 6 prefer, 선호하다

7 ingredient, 재료 8 official, 관리, 신하

9 scholar, 학자 10 recommend, 추천하다

11 servant, 하인, 신하 12 culture, 문화

13 disappointed, 실망한 14 party, 정당

15 order, 주문하다 16 policy, 정책

대화문 TEST Step 1   p.24~25

Listen & Speak 1-A

1. anything, dessert / prefer, or / prefer / get, some

2. thinking of joining / prefer indoor or outdoor / prefer, last / Why don't you join / good idea

Listen & Speak 2-A

1. Excuse, looking for, recommend / have, cooked Italian / haven't, to try / how about, Italian, beginners, on sale / take

2. haven't seen, recently, recommend / Why don't you, big hit / action, recommend, comedies / how about / sounds

Listen & Speak B

recommend, for me / why don't you read

Communicate A

Have, been to / talking about / the one, about, ago, right / so, went, last / How was / ordered, different dishes, fried / recommend, for, tonight with / prefer, or / prefer seafood / should try, fried fish

Communicate B

Could you recommend, near / Do, prefer, or / prefer / try, at the end of

Progress Check

1. I'm thinking of getting / prefer, or / prefer, cute / give you one

2. looking for, recommend / What color, like / favorite colors / how about, on sale / take

대화문 TEST Step 2   p.26~27

Listen & Speak 1-A

1. B: Do you have anything for dessert, *Aunt May*?

   W: Yes, Johnny. Do you prefer pie or cake?

    B: I prefer cake.

   W: O.K. I have some chocolate cake. I'll get you some.

2. B: I'm thinking of joining a sports club.

   G: Do you prefer indoor or outdoor sports?

   B: I prefer indoor sports. I was in the badminton club last year.

G: Why don't you join the table tennis club, then?

B: That's a good idea. Thank you.

1. W: Excuse me. I'm looking for an Italian cookbook. Could you recommend one?

M: Well, have you ever cooked Italian food?

W: No, I haven't, but I want to try. I really like spaghetti.

M: Then, how about this Italian cookbook for beginners? It's on sale now.

W: Good! Thank you. I'll take it.

2. G: I haven't seen a movie recently. Could you recommend a good one?

B: Why don't you see *Iron Woman 2*? It's a big hit.

G: Well, I don't like action movies. Can you recommend any good comedies?

B: Then, how about *Funny Families*?

G: That sounds good.

A: Could you recommend a book for me?

B: Well, why don't you read *The Flying Pan*?

A: Great idea. Thanks.

Jaden: Have you been to the new Chinese restaurant, Ms. Park?

Ms. Park: Are you talking about the one on Main Street, Jaden?

Jaden: Yes, that's the one. They opened about two weeks ago, right?

Ms. Park: I think so. I went there last Friday with my friends.

Jaden: How was the food?

Ms. Park: It was great. We ordered many different dishes. I really liked the fried vegetables.

Jaden: Could you recommend a dish for me? I'm going there for dinner tonight with my family.

Ms. Park: Do you prefer seafood or meat?

Jaden: I prefer seafood.

Ms. Park: Then, you should try their fried fish. You'll love it!

M: Could you recommend a Korean restaurant near here?

W: Do you prefer hot or cold food?

M: I prefer cold food.

W: Then, you should try the naengmyeon place at the end of this block.

M: Thank you.

1. G: I'm thinking of getting a pet.

B: Do you prefer dogs or cats?

G: I prefer cats. They're so cute.

B: Great! I can give you one. I have seven cats at home.

G: Thank you.

2. W: Excuse me. I'm looking for a skirt. Could you recommend one?

M: What color do you like?

W: Blue and pink are my favorite colors.

M: Then, how about this blue one? It's on sale now.

W: Good! Thank you. I'll take it.

본문 TEST Step 1   p.28~29

01 Bite, Korean History   02 How, get, names

03 look like, half

04 There are, traditional food

05 Let's dive into

06 having, officials, something special

07 dish, colorful ingredients

08 Each, symbolized, political

09 that, in harmony like   10 was called

11 came from, policy

12 time, was, famous for

13 something wrong, afraid, telling

14 However, listened to   15 so, that, on

16 While, by himself, mainly 17 special pot, different

18 called, pot, in

19 because, like, imaginary, alone

20 time, last king

21 One, servants, strange

22 Something, written, back 23 like, full, half

24 fortune teller, What, mean

25 fortune, full, become smaller

26 On, other, grow bigger

27 became worried about

28 However, to, in, shape

29 Since then, have, shaped

본문 TEST Step 2   p.30~31

01 Bite, Korean History   02 How, get their names

03 Why, look like, half moon

04 There are, traditional food

05 dive into

06 was having dinner, officials, offered, something special

07 with four colorful ingredients

08 a different political party   09 in harmony like

10 was called   11 came from

12 was a scholar, was famous for

13 something wrong, was never afraid of telling

14 However, listened to   15 so, that

16 While, by himself   17 a special pot, together

18 called, the food in it

19 because, like, imaginary, lives alone

20 the last king

21 servants, a strange turtle

22 was written on its back

23 is like, full moon, is like, half moon

24 What, mean

25 fortune teller, become smaller

26 On the other hand, grow bigger, become, full moon

27 became worried about

28 However, in the shape of

29 Since then, have enjoyed, shaped rice cakes

---

20 백제의 마지막 왕 때였다.

21 어느 날, 왕과 신하들은 이상한 거북을 한 마리 발견했다.

22 그 거북의 등에 무언가가 쓰여 있었다.

23 그것은 "백제는 보름달과 같지만 신라는 반달과 같다."였다.

24 왕은 점술가에게 "이게 무슨 뜻인가?"라고 물었다.

25 점술가는 "보름달은 곧 작아질 것입니다.

26 반면에, 반달은 점점 커져서 보름달이 될 것입니다."라고 답했다.

27 왕은 자신의 왕국이 걱정되었다.

28 그러나 신라 사람들은 이것을 알고 매우 기뻐하며 반달 모양의 떡을 만들었다.

29 그 후로 사람들은 이 반달 모양의 떡인 송편을 즐겨 먹고 있다.

1 A Bite of Korean History

2 How did tangpyeongchae and sinseollo get their names?

3 Why does songpyeon look like a half moon?

4 There are many interesting stories about our traditional food.

5 Let's dive into the fun history of our food.

6 One day, King Yeongjo was having dinner with his officials and offered them something special.

7 It was a dish with four colorful ingredients.

8 Each ingredient symbolized a different political party.

9 Yeongjo wanted to say that the four parties should work in harmony like this dish.

10 This dish was called tangpyeongchae.

11 The name came from Yeongjo's policy tangpyeongchaek.

12 In the time of King Yeonsan, there was a scholar who was famous for his honesty.

13 When the king did something wrong, the scholar was never afraid of telling him so.

14 However, the king never listened to him.

15 The scholar was so disappointed that he went to live on a mountain.

16 While he lived there by himself, he mainly ate vegetables.

17 He made a special pot to cook many different vegetables together.

18 People called this pot and the food in it sinseollo.

19 That is because the scholar lived like a sinseon, an imaginary person who lives alone in nature.

20 It was the time of the last king of Baekje.

21 One day, the king and his servants found a strange turtle.

1 한국 역사 한 입

2 탕평채와 신선로는 어떻게 해서 그런 이름을 얻게 되었을까?

3 송편은 왜 반달 모양일까?

4 우리의 전통 음식에 대한 재미있는 이야기들이 많이 있다.

5 우리 음식의 재미있는 역사 속으로 들어가 보자.

6 어느 날, 영조가 그의 신하들과 저녁을 먹다가 그들에게 특별한 무언가를 권했다.

7 그것은 네 가지의 다채로운 재료로 만든 음식이었다.

8 각 재료는 서로 다른 당파를 상징했다.

9 영조는 이 음식처럼 네 당파가 화합을 이루어 일해야 한다는 것을 말하고 싶었다.

10 이 음식은 탕평채라고 불렸다.

11 그 이름은 영조의 정책인 탕평책에서 왔다.

12 연산군 시대에 정직하기로 유명한 한 학자가 있었다.

13 왕이 무언가를 잘못하면, 그 학자는 왕에게 그렇게 말하는 것을 절대 두려워하지 않았다.

14 그러나 왕은 그의 말에 전혀 귀 기울이지 않았다.

15 학자는 너무 실망하여 산속으로 살러 들어갔다.

16 그곳에서 혼자 사는 동안, 그는 주로 채소를 먹었다.

17 그는 여러 다양한 채소들을 함께 요리하기 위해 특별한 솥을 만들었다.

18 사람들은 이 솥과 그 안의 음식을 신선로라고 불렀다.

19 그것은 그 학자가 마치 자연 속에 홀로 사는 상상의 인물인 신선처럼 살았기 때문이다.

35

22 Something was written on its back.

23 It said, "Baekje is like a full moon, but Silla is like a half moon."

24 The king asked a fortune teller, "What does this mean?"

25 The fortune teller answered, "A full moon will soon become smaller.

26 On the other hand, a half moon will grow bigger and become a full moon."

27 The king became worried about his kingdom.

28 However, people of Silla were very happy to learn this and made rice cakes in the shape of a half moon.

29 Since then, people have enjoyed these half-moon shaped rice cakes, songpyeon.

구석구석지문 TEST Step 1   p.38

Work Together

1. Could you recommend

2. Do you prefer, or

3. prefer

4. Here you are

5. Thank

Write

1. Chocolate

2. something special

3. is made of, flour, nuts

4. a kind of

5. When, always think of

6. ago, fillings, decided to make

7. chance to remember

Culture Project

1. comes from, famous Chinese poet

2. During, to keep, for a long time

3. sweet and salty

4. Afterwards, or, became popular across

구석구석지문 TEST Step 2   p.39

Work Together

1. A: Could you recommend a salad for me?

2. B: We have two salads today. Do you prefer chicken salad or green salad?

3. A: I prefer green salad.

4. B: O.K. Here you are .

5. A: Thank you.

Write

1. Chocolate Songpyeon

2. My family eats something special on Chuseok.

3. It is made of rice flour, chocolate, and nuts.

4. It is a kind of tteok.

5. When I eat this food, I always think of my little brother.

6. Three years ago, he ate all the fillings for songpyeon, so we decided to make chocolate songpyeon.

7. This food gives us a chance to remember that funny day.

Culture Project

1. The word *dongporou* comes from the name of the famous Chinese poet Su Dongpo.

2. During his time in Hangzhou, he invented a way to keep pork fresh for a long time.

3. He made the pork sweet and salty.

4. Afterwards, dongporou or dongpo pork became popular across China.

14 daytime, 낮   15 electricity, 전기
16 charity, 자선, 자선단체

단어 TEST Step 1
p.40

01 단 하나의	02 주요한; 우두머리, 부장	
03 어둠, 암흑	04 퍼지다	05 전기
06 재단	07 놀이공원	08 대규모 정전 사태
09 주거지, 쉼터	10 불가능한	11 천장
12 널리, 폭넓게	13 구부리다, 휘다	14 자선단체
15 설치하다	16 외치다	17 발명하다
18 흔들다, 털다	19 마법의, 신기한	20 남은 음식
21 전체의	22 표백제	23 충분한
24 꽉 들어찬	25 인기 있는	26 놀랍게도
27 남아 있다	28 지붕	29 안전한
30 마을	31 작동하다	32 구하다
33 더 적은	34 놀라운	35 지불하다
36 최소한, 적어도	37 ~을 환하게 밝히다	
38 더 이상 ~ 않다	39 ~할 것을 잊다	40 (소리 등을) 높이다
41 ~ 덕분에	42 ~을 생각해 내다, ~을 만들어 내다	
43 ~와 꼭 마찬가지로		

단어 TEST Step 2
p.41

01 bend	02 ceiling	03 shake
04 charity	05 darkness	06 difficult
07 whole	08 blackout	09 widely
10 leftover	11 chief	12 less
13 impossible	14 shout	15 electricity
16 single	17 work	18 save
19 amusement park		20 foundation
21 roof	22 magic	23 shelter
24 village	25 popular	26 install
27 remain	28 safe	29 last
30 surprisingly	31 bleach	32 packed
33 enough	34 invent	35 light up
36 thanks to	37 not ~ anymore	
38 dry off	39 pay for	40 forget to부정사
41 come up with	42 turn up	43 fill A with B

단어 TEST Step 3
p.42

1 last, 지속되다   2 village, 마을   3 roof, 지붕
4 leftover, 남은 음식   5 blackout, 정전   6 save, 구하다
7 ceiling, 천장   8 popular, 인기 있는   9 lamp, 램프, 등
10 spread, 퍼지다   11 invent, 발명하다
12 bleach, 표백제   13 install, 설치하다

대화문 TEST Step 1
p.43~44

Listen & Speak 1-A

1. turn up / turn it up anymore, highest / Let, put, I've heard, works like / What an interesting idea, Let's

2. I've heard, is coming / right, favorite actress / played, chief scientist / can't wait to see

Listen & Speak 2-A

1. finished, meal / good / want to take, leftovers / please / Don't forget to eat

2. your plan for, winter break / I'm going to, with my parents / sounds exciting, going to do / going to go, amusement / to try all kinds / Don't forget to try

Communicate A

What's wrong / difficult / have to / a way to save / I've heard that, can save, by using less / I've heard that, too, stop using paper cups / can also use, to dry off / impossible, at least / shake, before, more than enough / try, next time / don't forget to shake, at least, times

Communicate B

I've heard, saving electricity, best way to save / heard that, too, save electricity / Why don't, turn off, when / Don't forget, turn off, when, leave

Progress Check

1. I've heard that, is coming / my favorite player / not going to, surprise

2. plan for, winter break / to visit, with / sounds exciting, going / spend, beach, seafood / Don't forget to try / won't forget

대화문 TEST Step 2
p.45~46

Listen & Speak 1-A

1. G: Can you turn up the volume on your phone? I like this song.
   B: I can't turn it up anymore. It's the highest volume.
   G: Let me just put your phone in a glass. I've heard a glass works like a speaker.
   B: What an interesting idea! Let's try it now.

2. B: I've heard that a movie star is coming to our school.

G: That's right. She's my favorite actress.

B: Oh, who is she?

G: Miranda Kim. She played the chief scientist in the movie *Jupiter*.

B: Wow, I can't wait to see her!

Listen & Speak 2-A

1. W: Excuse me, are you finished with your meal?

M: Yes, it was really good.

W: Do you want to take the leftovers home?

M: Yes, please.

W: Don't forget to eat the leftovers by tomorrow.

2. B: What's your plan for this winter break?

G: I'm going to visit Hong Kong with my parents.

B: That sounds exciting. What are you going to do there?

G: I'm going to go to an amusement park. I'm also going to try all kinds of food.

B: Good. Don't forget to try some dim sum.

Communicate A

Yuri: What's wrong, Jaden?

Jaden: My science homework is too difficult.

Yuri: What do you have to do?

Jaden: I need to find a way to save trees.

Yuri: That's easy. I've heard that we can save trees by using less paper.

Jaden: Oh, I think I've heard that, too. Then, I can just stop using paper cups.

Yuri: Yes! You can also use just one paper towel to dry off your hands.

Jaden: That's impossible. I need at least two or three paper towels.

Yuri: Just shake your hands before you use a paper towel. Then, one will be more than enough.

Jaden: Oh, that's a good idea, Yuri! I'll try that next time.

Yuri: Good! Just don't forget to shake your hands at least 10 times.

Communicate B

A: I've heard that saving electricity is the best way to save the Earth.

B: I've heard that, too. What can we do to save electricity?

A: Why don't we turn off the light when we're not using it?

B: That's a good idea. Don't forget to turn off the light when you leave your room.

Progress Check

1. B: I've heard that a famous baseball player is coming to our school.

G: That's right. He's my favorite player.

B: Oh, who is he?

G: I'm not going to tell you. It's a surprise!

2. B: What's your plan for this winter break?

G: I'm going to visit Vietnam with my parents.

B: That sounds exciting. What are you going to do there?

G: I'm going to spend some time on the beach and eat lots of seafood.

B: Good. Don't forget to try the fruit there, too.

G: O.K., I won't forget.

본문 TEST Step 1   p.47~48

01 One-Dollar, Lamps   02 read, shouted, village

03 electricity, like, other, village

04 too, to pay

05 during, daytime, because, packed

06 things, because of, single

07 light up, without using

08 called, because, invented by

09 there were, blackouts

10 come, with, way, light

11 made for, lasts, about

12 also, safe   13 never start, fire

14 Surprisingly, easy, make

15 How, make, from   16 Fill, clear, with

17 Add, to keep, clear

18 roof, push, into, hole 19 Let, third, remain above

20 is bent, spreads around

21 in, widely used by   22 charity, local, how, install

23 Thanks to, thousands of

24 has, made, other, such

25 light up, for, years

본문 TEST Step 2   p.49~50

01 One-Dollar Magic

02 shouted, in the Philippines

03 has no electricity, all the other houses

04 too, to pay for electricity

05 during, because, are packed close together

06 are changing because of

07 in the ceiling, light up, without using

08 is called, because, was invented by

09 were many blackouts

10 come up with, way to light

11 be made for, lasts for about

12 very safe   13 never start

14 to make   15 How to make

16 Fill, with

17 Add, bleach to keep, clear

18 push, into   19 a third, remain above

20 is bent by, spreads around

21 are widely used

22 The charity, how to make, install

23 Thanks to, thousands of

24 has, made, other countries, such as

25 light up, for many years to come

1 1달러짜리 마법의 전구

2 "우와, 이젠 제 방에서 책을 읽을 수 있어요!" 필리핀의 한 마을에 사는 소년인 Marco가 외쳤다.

3 그의 집은 마을의 다른 모든 집들과 마찬가지로 전기가 없다.

4 마을 사람들은 너무나 가난해서 전기세를 낼 수가 없다.

5 심지어 낮 동안에도, 집들이 빽빽하게 들어차 있어서 그들은 어둠 속에 살아간다.

6 이제 플라스틱병 하나 때문에 상황이 바뀌고 있다.

7 천장에 있는 플라스틱병 하나는 전기를 쓰지 않고 방 전체를 밝힐 수 있다.

8 이 놀라운 플라스틱병은 Moser 램프라고 불리는데, 그것이 Alfredo Moser에 의해 발명되었기 때문이다.

9 2002년, 브라질에 있는 그의 마을에는 정전이 잦았다.

10 이 정전들은 그가 집을 밝히는 새로운 방법을 생각해 내도록 만들었다.

11 Moser 램프는 1달러 정도로 만들 수 있고 10년 정도 지속된다.

12 그것은 또한 매우 안전하다.

13 그것은 절대 집에 불을 낼 수 없다.

14 놀랍게도, 이 신기한 램프를 만드는 것은 매우 쉽다.

15 병으로 Moser 램프를 만드는 법

16 1. 투명한 플라스틱병에 물을 채운다.

17 2. 물을 깨끗이 유지하기 위해 표백제를 조금 넣는다.

18 3. 지붕에 구멍을 내고, 병을 구멍 안으로 넣는다.

19 4. 병의 3분의 1은 지붕 위에 남아 있도록 한다.

20 5. 햇빛이 병 속의 물에 의해 굴절되어 방에 퍼진다.

21 필리핀에서 Moser 램프는 My Shelter 재단에 의해 널리 사용된다.

22 또한 그 자선단체는 지역 사람들에게 램프를 만들고 설치하는 법을 가르친다.

23 이 자선단체 덕분에, 필리핀의 수천 가구가 이제 Moser 램프를 갖고 있다.

24 그 단체는 아르헨티나, 인도, 피지와 같은 다른 나라들에서도 Moser 램프가 유명해 지도록 만들었다.

25 Moser 램프는 앞으로 오랫동안 많은 사람들의 삶을 밝혀 줄 것이다.

1 One-Dollar Magic Lamps

2 "Wow, I can read a book in my room now!" shouted Marco, a boy in a village in the Philippines.

3 His house has no electricity just like all the other houses in the village.

4 People in the village are too poor to pay for electricity.

5 Even during the daytime, they live in darkness because the houses are packed close together.

6 Now things are changing because of a single plastic bottle.

7 One plastic bottle in the ceiling can light up a whole room without using any electricity.

8 This amazing plastic bottle is called a Moser lamp because it was invented by Alfredo Moser.

9 In 2002, there were many blackouts in his town in Brazil.

10 These blackouts made him come up with a new way to light his house.

11 A Moser lamp can be made for about one dollar and lasts for about 10 years.

12 It is also very safe.

13 It can never start a house fire.

14 Surprisingly, it is very easy to make this magic lamp.

15 How to make a Moser lamp from a bottle

16 1. Fill a clear plastic bottle with water.

17 2. Add some bleach to keep the water clear.

18 3. Make a hole in the roof, and push the bottle into the hole.

19 4. Let a third of the bottle remain above the roof.

20 5. Sunlight is bent by the water in the bottle and spreads around the room.

21 In the Philippines, Moser lamps are widely used by the My Shelter Foundation.

22 The charity also teaches local people how to make and install the lamps.

23 Thanks to the charity, thousands of homes in the Philippines now have Moser lamps.

24 It has also made Moser lamps popular in other countries, such as Argentina, India, and Fiji.

25 Moser lamps will light up the lives of many people for many years to come.

구석구석지문 TEST Step 1 p.57

Link-Share

1. make the lamp brighter
2. out of, another lamp
3. All the other steps
4. learned that, brighter than

Write

1. a lot of, with
2. can even make
3. fill half of, put, into
4. close, all of the sides
5. Finally, it, for about
6. is ready
7. make you happ

Culture Project-Share

1. like to talk
2. keeps food fresh
3. It, to make
4. put, inside
5. pour, between
6. let, dry off, cool

구석구석지문 TEST Step 2 p.58

Link-Share

1. We thought we could make the lamp brighter with a glass bottle.
2. We made one lamp out of a plastic bottle and another lamp out of a glass bottle.
3. All the other steps were the same.
4. We learned that the glass bottle lamp was brighter than the plastic bottle lamp.

Write

1. You can make a lot of things with a CD case.
2. You can even make a grass container.
3. First, fill half of the CD case with soil and water, and put grass seeds into the soil.
4. Second, close the case and tape all of the sides.
5. Finally, leave it in the sun for about ten days.
6. Now, your grass container is ready.
7. It will make you happy when the grass grows.

Culture Project-Share

1. We'd like to talk about a pot-in-pot cooler.
2. It keeps food fresh without electricity.
3. It's very easy to make one.
4. First, put a pot inside a larger pot.
5. Then, pour sand and water between these pots.
6. Just let the water dry off, and it'll cool the food.

적중100

영어 기출 문제집

정답 및 해설

미래 | 최연희